# What's That Number A

Numbers continually occur in dreams, in d.
magick, in astral traveling—what do they mean?

*You already know.* You may not be aware of i
collective unconscious is well aware of the arch
numbers as revealed in the ancient tradition of *gem*            .....ala.

Originally conceived as a method of encoding es_ ...nc meaning into
holy writings, gematria has applications to everyday life that are startling
and far-reaching.

Here is a valuable source book for students of the cabala, ceremonial
magicians, and numerologists which *you can use* to bring to consciousness
the significance of numbers and archetypal images occurring in whatever
endeavor in which you are engaged, whether conversing with supernor-
mal entities, working out the numerological significance of a name, analyzing a dream, working a divination, channeling, spirit scrying, working
the Enochian keys, designing a talisman, creating or analyzing a magickal
or pagan ritual—any area of activity where numbers are likely to occur!

Gematria was used by medieval cabalists primarily for Biblical
exegesis and as a means of encoding secret lore. The Bible contains internal
evidence that the system was used by the authors of the scriptures. After
thousands of years of tradition, the numerical correspondences and correla-
tions of gematria have entered the collective unconscious. The names of
extramundane entities are commonly in accordance with this system, and to
know the name of something is to have power over it. The dreaming mind
is aware of these correspondences and their significance. You may have to
labor to add up all those letters consciously, but the subconscious mind
can do it with no apparent effort and use the number to express an idea in a
dream. As for divination, this book serves as well as the Tarot, the *I Ching*,
or a horoscope as a tool for the intuition of the diviner.

This is not popular numerology, wherein everything is reduced to a
single digit. The universe contains more than nine numbers, more than
nine phenomena, and more than nine hidden meanings! If the number is
418, don't reduce it to 4—look up the number in this book to see the
significance for the New Age.

This book is a complete guide to cabalistic magick and gematria in
which every demon, angel, power, and name of God; every Sephiroth,
Path, and Plane of the Tree of Life; and each attribute and association is
fully described and cross-indexed by the Hebrew, English, and numerical forms.

This encyclopedia brings gematria and the cabala into practical
understanding and usage by everyone. It is at once a working tool for the
student, diviner, scryer, ritualist, mage, and witch not only in arriving at an
understanding of gematria but in its general application in spiritual development and psychological growth.

## About David Godwin

David Godwin, born in 1939 in Dallas, Texas, is a long-time student of esoteric lore. He has successfully tried most of the techniques described in this book and has been continually surprised by the way in which gematriatic correspondences keep cropping up unbidden in everyday life—as warnings and guides.

A practicing astrologer until other activities claimed his interest, Godwin has lectured to the Houston Astrology Club. His articles have appeared in *Gnostica* (the forerunner of *The Llewellyn New Times*) and, in the largely (but not entirely) unrelated field of fantasy role-playing games, in *Dragon Magazine*.

Godwin has worked as a manual laborer, a newspaper reporter, an editor for a petrochemical magazine, a technical editor for two NASA contractors during the Apollo missions, a typesetter, and a free-lance writer.

He has never been to a writers' workshop, owns no cats, and is entirely ignorant of the martial arts.

A subscriber to both *The Skeptical Inquirer* and *The American Theosophist*, *Science News* and *Eldritch Tales*, Godwin believes in maintaining the open-minded, balanced attitude advocated by the middle path of cabalism.

## To Write to the Author

We cannot guarantee that every letter written to the author can be answered, but all will be forwarded. Both the author and the publisher appreciate hearing from readers, learning of your enjoyment and benefit from this book. Llewellyn also publishes a bi-monthly news magazine with news and reviews of practical esoteric studies and articles helpful to the student, and some readers' questions and comments to the author may be answered through this magazine's columns if permission to do is included in the original letter. The author sometimes participates in seminars and workshops, and dates and places are announced in *The Llewellyn New Times*. To write to the author, or to ask a question, write to:

David Godwin
c/o THE LLEWELLYN NEW TIMES
P.O. Box 64383-292, St. Paul, MN 55164-0383, U.S.A.

Please enclose a self-addressed, stamped envelope for reply, or $1.00 to cover costs.

# Llewellyn's Sourcebook Series

Llewellyn's "Sourcebooks" are designed to be *resource files for esoteric technicians.*

For some readers, it may at first seem strange to apply the word "technology" to the concept of esotericism. Technology is basically how-to-knowledge, and esotericism (by whatever name) is *True Sacred Living.* We publish many practical books that teach the reader "how to" in many areas of the esoteric sciences. These are the techniques, the practical programming, the procedures to follow in working toward a particular accomplishment, the *modus operandi.*

But, the *technician of the Sacred* needs more than the knowledge of the method of operation. He or she also has to have basic information about the materials that will be utilized, or about the beings that will be invoked, or the tools to be used. And this information must be organized and presented from a sound, esoteric foundation.

Sourcebooks may be presented in the form of dictionaries, encyclopedias, anthologies, or new editions of classical works. Always, we produce these to actually meet the needs of the esoteric practitioner and student. They bring to the reader *what* he or she needs to know in order to apply the *how-to* knowledge gained from text and guide books.

A sourcebook is the distillation of factual knowledge from dozens of books and sources (sometimes veritable libraries) compounded with the practical experience of the author. No one can do an adequate job of gathering such factual knowledge unless they are themselves expert in the field represented.

As publishers, we seek to provide the student with three out of the four vital elements essential to the sacred life: theoretical knowledge, practical knowledge, and factual knowledge. The fourth element can only come as the student brings these together, and gains experiential knowledge. These four kinds of knowledge then become the *pillars of wisdom.*

LLEWELLYN'S SOURCEBOOK SERIES

# G O D W I N ' S

# CABALISTIC ENCYCLOPEDIA

## A Complete Guide to Cabalistic Magick

## DAVID GODWIN

1989
Llewellyn Publications
St. Paul, Minnesota, 55164-0383

International Standard Book Number: 0-87542-292-6
Library of Congress Catalog Number: 88-32562

First Edition, 1979
Second Edition, Revised and Enlarged, 1989
First Printing, 1989

**Library of Congress Cataloging-in-Publication Data**

Godwin, David.
    Godwin's cabalistic encyclopedia.

    (Llewellyn's sourcebook series)
    Bibliography: p.
        1. Cabala—Dictionaries—Hebrew.  2. Gematria.
    3. Hebrew language—Dictionaries—English.  I. Title.
    II. Series.
    [BM526.G53 1988]    135'.4    88-32562
    ISBN 0-87542-292-6

**Cover Design: Brooke Luteyn**

Produced by Llewellyn Publications
Typography and Art property of Chester-Kent, Inc.

Published by
**LLEWELLYN PUBLICATIONS**
**A Division of Chester-Kent, Inc.**
P.O. Box 64383
St. Paul, MN 55164-0383, U.S.A.

Printed in the United States of America

# Dedication and
# Acknowledgements

This book is dedicated to the legions of people who have inspired, helped, and encouraged me during the long history of the writing, editing, publication, and re-publication of this book.

First and foremost, my thanks must go to Carl Weschcke for his unending patience, understanding, and tolerance. To Richard L. Tierney, the "mensch" who had the monumental task of editing the first manuscript. To Phyllis Galde, whose helpfulness, patience, and attention to detail have made this edition a reality. To Bijou, who insisted I finish the manuscript and submit it to begin with. To Burney Kent, who was patient and/or crazy enough to listen to me expound. To my parents, for being proud even though my work lay beyond their areas of interest and concern. To Shelby, for the same reason. To Brenda, for discovering the book's possibilities for divination. To Donald Michael Kraig, for thinking well enough of the book to mention it favorably in his own and for providing inspiration through his own work when my outlook was going through a sour period. To James Randi, Martin Gardner, and H. P. Lovecraft for teaching me (all unbeknownst to themselves) the value *and* the limitations of a hard-headed skeptical attitude.

To all the dozens of people, living and dead, who have helped, contributed, supported, encouraged, intrigued, inspired, and/or tolerated me through the whole process, intentionally or without ever having heard of me—including Aleister Crowley, Israel Regardie, W. A. Mozart, Ursula K. LeGuin, Tanith Lee, Samuel Taylor Coleridge, Attar, Ibn 'Arabi, and many, many others. To my Holy Guardian Angel, to the Goddess, and to God. Thanks.

# Contents

    From *The Equinox*
by Aleister Crowley
Vol. 1, No. 8

# PREFACE

**N**ow that the paperback edition of *Godwin's Cabalistic Encyclopedia* is being published, it seems a good and appropriate opportunity to point out the general usefulness of a book of this kind—a usefulness perhaps not immediately apparent. Superficially, any cabalistic compendium of this kind would appear to be an abstruse work, of interest only to scholars or, at best, ceremonial magicians. Not so. The cabalistic system is universally applicable in a surprising variety of fields not normally associated with anything of the kind. There is a certain amount of evidence that the cabala and the Tree of Life (see Introduction) is present in the collective unconscious mind of every person, even if he/she has never heard of it. (For example, before I had become even slightly acquainted with the cabala and knew nothing of the Tree of Life or the sephiroth, I did a painting that I later discovered to be an excellent representation of the 24th path along with the adjoining sephiroth of Tiphareth and Netzach, entirely accurate as to symbolism, relative placement, and even color.) If the cabala is present as a system of archetypes in the unconscious of every individual, then it is not difficult to see how it can apply to virtually every area of occult and mental endeavor; not only magick (including witchcraft) but also, for example, divination, character reading, dream interpretation, and meditation.

One of the more important aspects of the cabala is the system of *gematria*, which can be loosely defined as "Hebrew numerology." *Webster's New International Dictionary* (1927 Edition) defines gematria as follows: "A cryptograph in the form of a word the letters of which have the numerical values of the word taken as the hidden meaning; also, the cabalistic method of explaining the Hebrew Scriptures by means of the cryptographic significance of the words. Thus, the first word of Genesis in Hebrew, meaning 'in the beginning,' has the numerical value 913, which is the same as that of the Hebrew phase meaning 'in the law it was made.' Hence, the cabalists declare the law to have existed from the beginning, and that the creation was effected by it."

Gematria, as in the above example, was used by medieval cabalists primarily for Biblical exegesis and as a means of encoding secret lore, but it has a much wider application than that, particularly now that it seems to have entered (along with the cabala as a whole) the collective unconscious (or, if you prefer, the akashic record). The names of extramundane entities are commonly in accordance with its system, and to know the name of something is to have power over it. The dreaming mind is apparently aware of the numerical correspondences and their significance, especially in the case of those who have become acquainted with the cabala. You may have to labor to add up all those letters consciously, but the subconscious mind can do it with no apparent effort and use the number to express an idea in a dream. As for divination, this encyclopedia serves just as well as a tool for the intuition of the diviner as the Tarot, the *I Ching*, a horoscope, or any other method.

Let us examine some of these applications:

**Dream interpretation.** Numbers very commonly occur in dreams as street addresses, telephone numbers, automobile license plates, room numbers, and so on; as a number of persons or things; or simply as abstract numbers. It is a very straightforward matter to consult this book for the number in question and note the correspondences. For example, if you dream that you went to 175 Laurel Street and were set upon by seven dobermans, the dream could mean that you unconsciously love a certain person or that you have creative urges of which you are not aware. The numbers 175 and 7 are connected with the planet Venus and the sephira Netzach. If you had been aware of this attraction or urge, it would not have been thus veiled in a dream.

The question of dream interpretation can become more sophisticated than the simple analysis of numbers that occur in dreams. For example, if you dream of seeing a tank full of colorful tropical fish, the natural (Jungian, at least) psychological assumption would be that the fish represent interesting and attractive thoughts submerged in the unconscious mind (represented by water). But if you happen to know that the Hebrew for fish is Dagim, or can find out that such is the case by the use of an inexpensive English-Hebrew dictionary, you can immediately arrive at the number 617 (or 57). Looking up the correspondences in this book, perhaps both in Section IV and in the appended *Sepher Sephiroth*, you find that these unconscious thoughts may very well present a terrible danger (AYWM, terrible; ABRN, ruin; AWN, strength and wealth but also sorrow).* There may be some connection between these thoughts and the "liberal sciences" (astrology, alchemy, etc.), since the number corresponds with both Alloces and Avnas, two demons who offer instruction in this area. Note also a connection with the Tarot's 5 of Cups (disappointment). The dreamer would probably be well advised to become acquainted with these unconscious contents before they "break loose" and result in his obsession and ruination.

**Divination** is similar in method to the interpretation of numbers occurring in dreams. It is only necessary to arrive at a random number. The ideal way to do so, in my opinion, would be to obtain three or four 10-sided dice to arrive at units, tens, hundreds, and thousands. (Of course, you have to decide which is which beforehand.) If, for example, you roll 0, 4, 1, and 8, the resulting number is 418, not the simple addition, 13. Such dice are commonly used in fantasy role-playing games and are available at most game stores

---

* Here, as throughout this book, English letters are used to designate Hebrew letters. The exact method of and the reasons for doing so are explained in the Introduction.

and some toy stores. A home computer can also be used to generate random numbers. Of course, if the explanation of accurate divination is that the diviner discovers the requested information by telepathy or clairvoyance and then causes the dice (or coins or yarrow stalks or cards) to produce the appropriate result by unconscious manipulation or by psychokinesis, then the use of a computer is not too good. If, on the other hand, the explanation is that all events in the universe at any given time are related and in tune with one another, and hence any divination reflects those current conditions, then a computer (being, after all, a part of the universe) is as good as any other method.

One example of divination that came to my attention not long ago involved a young lady who was expecting a male visitor and inquired as to the results of going out with him. She used a "double handful of [normal, six-sided] dice" to generate a random number and then consulted this book. The resulting number was 88—and 88 = PCh = *Pach* = "Danger." In light of this result, the inquirer did not go out with the young man. It was later discovered that the fellow had been under the false impression that the girl had "ratted" on him to the "narcs" for dealing in marijuana and was consequently not a safe person for her to be around.

**Character reading.** In order to do a character analysis in the style of astrology or palm reading, it is necessary to arrive at a cabalistic number for the name of the querent and then look up the correspondences. You can arrive at such a number by several methods, and almost all of them are legitimate. Which one to use? It is essentially a matter of personal preference and intuition, but it may be helpful to try out *all* the possibilities.

You will probably not arrive at a complete, well-rounded character analysis (as in astrology) by this method—unless you are conversant with the cabala and, even more importantly, with Hebrew. But the information you do obtain will be highly significant and will tend to indicate not only the more important features of the individual's character but also directions and warnings concerned with personal conduct and with the inner mental or spiritual life. The one feature of the cabala and of gematria that you should not forget is that *everything can be understood on many levels.*

The simplest method is the use of standard popular numerology whereby everything is reduced to one digit (for example, 418 = 4 + 1 + 8 = 13 and 1 + 3 = 4). In my opinion, this method is a bit oversimplified and the results too general to be of much use. In any case, it is not cabalism nor gematria. Another method is to number the letters of the English alphabet and then add the letters of the name in question. This has a certain validity, particularly if you wish to generate a dictionary of English words enumerated by one of these methods, but it is only marginally related to the cabala. (However, note that "God" = 7 + 15 + 4 = 26, the same as the Hebrew *YHWH.*) So we are left with altering the letters of the name to Hebrew.

The method that I prefer, perhaps unjustifiably, for this transliteration is to spell the name as if it were Hebrew, substituting the appropriate phonetic values. In this way, the *sounds* of the letters are preserved. For example, "Smith" would be SMTh, or possibly ShMTh. (The Hebrew letter *Shin* can be pronounced either as S or Sh.) Of course, Hebrew has no vowels, only diacritial marks that indicate vowels. These marks have no numerical values. Nevertheless, as early as Biblical times, the practice arose of substituting a consonant for a vowel when it was thought necessary to clarify a word: *Aleph* for A, *Waw* for U or O, and *Yod* for I. This was usually done only in the case of a long vowel or sometimes in the case of a short vowel if it occurred in an accented syllable. Therefore, the spellings SMYTh or ShMYTh are also acceptable. "Godwin" could be GDWN, GWDWN, GWDWYN, or even GDWYN. Also note that the final N can be legitimately counted as either 50 or 700.

The only difficulty with the phonetic method is that some sounds in English have no Hebrew equivalent, and vice-versa. We have no *Aleph* or *Ayin* sound, and do not differentiate between hard and soft consonants (*Teth* and *Taw*, *Samekh* and *Shin*, etc.). If you are trying to transliterate a name such as "Charles" do you represent the "Ch" by *Cheth*, commonly transliterated Ch, but which has little resemblance to the English phonetic value, or do you try to approximate the actual sound more accurately by *Shin*, or still more accurately by *Teth-Shin* or *Taw-Shin*?

Such difficulties are avoided by another method—the one usually preferred by Aleister Crowley—that uses the Hebrew letter from which the English letter evolved through Phoenician, Greek, and Latin. In this case, there may not be much relationship between the way the name is pronounced and the way it is spelled, but the visible *forms* of the letters are preserved; that is to say, their archetypal, pre-Creation essence devoid of such mundane attributes and associations as phonetic values. In this system, "Smith" becomes ShMYTh or even ShMYThH, while "Godwin" becomes GOD-WYN (where O represents the Hebrew letter *Ayin*). Cabalists are not always overly precise with regard to this method, and sometimes the Hebrew letter with the correct phonetic value may be used instead of the letter from which, strictly speaking, the English letter was derived. Hence, for "Smith," SMYTh or possibly SMYTH would be acceptable, using *Samekh* instead of *Shin* for the S.

For the sake of convenience and reference, here is a table showing the various enumerations that may be given to each English letter. Note that only the first two methods ("Hebrew Phonetic" and "Hebrew Origin") have much value in cabalistic interpretations, although the other three methods may be useful in a strictly English numerology.

| English Letter | Hebrew Phonetic | Hebrew Origin | Popular Numerology | English Numerology A | English Numerology B |
|---|---|---|---|---|---|
| A | 1 | 1 | 1 | 1 | 1 |
| B | 2 | 2 | 2 | 2 | 2 |
| C | As K or S | 3 (or as K or S) | 3 | 3 | 3 |
| D | 4 | 4 | 4 | 4 | 4 |
| E | (No Value) | 5 | 5 | 5 | 5 |
| F | 80 or (final) 800 | 6 (or as P=Ph) | 6 | 6 | 6 |
| G | 3 | 3 | 7 | 7 | 7 |
| H | 5 | 8 | 8 | 8 | 8 |
| I | 10 | 10 | 9 | 9 | 9 |
| J | 10 or 3 | 10 | 9 | 9 | 9 |
| K | 20 or (final) 500 | 20 or (final) 500 | 2 | 11 | 20 |
| L | 30 | 30 | 3 | 12 | 30 |
| M | 40 or (final) 600 | 40 or (final) 600 | 4 | 13 | 40 |
| N | 50 or (final) 700 | 50 or (final) 700 | 5 | 14 | 50 |
| O | 6 | 70 | 6 | 15 | 60 |
| P | 80 or (final) 800 | 80 or (final) 800 | 7 | 16 | 70 |
| Q | 100 | 100 | 8 | 17 | 80 |
| R | 200 | 200 | 9 | 18 | 90 |
| S | 60 or 300 | 60 or 300 | 1 | 19 | 100 |
| T | 9 or 400 | 9 or 400 | 2 | 20 | 200 |
| U | 6 | 6 | 3 | 21 | 300 |
| V | 6 | 6 | 4 | 22 | 400 |
| W | 6 | 6 | 5 | 23 | 500 |
| X | As Z, 7; or as KS | 60 | 6 | 24 | 600 |
| Y | 10 | 6 | 7 | 25 | 700 |
| Z | 7 | 7 | 8 | 26 | 800 |
| CH | 8, 300, 309, or 700 | 11 | 2 | 11 | 11 |
| SH | 300 | 300 or 305 | 9 | 27 | 108 |
| TH | 400 | 400 or 405 | 1 | 28 | 208 |
| TS | 90 or (final) 900 | 90 or (final) 900 or 69, 309, 460, or 700 | 3 | 39 | 300 |
| TZ | 90 or (final) 900 | 90 or (final) 900 or 16 or 407 | 1 | 46 | 1000 |

Applying cabalistic numerology to the dream mentioned above, when the dreamer was attacked by 7 dobermans, further clarification of the dream might be obtained by spelling "doberman" in Hebrew as DWBRMAN, yielding an enumeration of 303, thus indicating that the unknown beloved reminds the dreamer of the Queen of Sheba.

As for enumerating English names by spelling them in Hebrew, another possibility is to *translate* the name directly, if possible. Thus, "Smith" becomes *Charash* (ChRSh, 508) and "Godwin," Anglo-Saxon for "friend of God," becomes *Reuel* (ROWAL, 307).

It is apparent why Crowley preferred the "origin" method, inasmuch as it was by this enumeration that he evaluated his own name (with the seldom-used middle initial E) as 666, the Beast: ALHISTHR H KROWLHY.

As an example of character reading, let us take the name of Howard Phillips Lovecraft, the author of a number of weird tales. By the phonetic method, this becomes HWWRD PYLPS LWW-KRPTh (1223).

But "Phillips" could just as well be spelled PYLPSh (since *Shin* can be either S or Sh), and the final letter of "Lovecraft" could just as easily be *Taw* as *Teth*. It would likewise be legitimate to count the "C" in "Lovecraft" as *Qoph*. By using all the combinations of these variables, we can come up with a dozen enumerations.

But we must also consider the fact that all of Lovecraft's stories are always attributed to "H. P. Lovecraft," so we need to get values for "H. P." with the four possible spellings of "Lovecraft"—436, 516, 827, and 907. Out of these four, I would pick 827 as the most likely to be significant (H. P. LWWKRPTh).

By the "origin" method, we get ChOWARD PChYLLYPSh LOWHGRAWTh (1558). As mentioned before, it is legitimate to make some phonetic substitutions in this method, as Crowley did in his own name, particularly in view of the fact that no fewer than five letters of our alphabet (F, U, V, W, and Y) came from the single

Hebrew letter *Waw* (W) through the Greek *upsilon* and *digamma*. To me, the spelling HOWARD PHYLLYPSh LOWHKRAPTh (1643) seems generally preferable, if only for aethestic reasons.

In any event, there are at least two ways to spell "Howard," six ways to spell "Phillips," and six ways to spell "Lovecraft" by this method, depending on how letters are transliterated, and thus no fewer than 84 enumerations! I would choose 897 (H. P. LOWH-KRAPTh) as the most likely and the most important of the lot.

Note that, in Hebrew, a doubled consonant is indicated by a diacritical mark, not by writing the letter twice, and it is only counted once. But in the letter-by-letter method, L occurs twice in Phillips and therefore *Lamed* may be used twice—but it is also acceptable to use it only once, if you care to multiply the enumerations even further. And, if the subject has a name ending with one of the letters that can have either of two values as a final consonant, the number of enumerations is doubled. Such is not the case with our example, however.

And, of course, there are also nicknames—"Ed," "Bill," etc. In the present case, Lovecraft did not have any nicknames as such, but he often signed his letters Grandpa, Theobald, Theobaldus, or Grandpa Theobald. This might almost be regarded as his "magickal name." Phonetically, we have GRANDPA ThWBLD (781), and, by the "origin" method, GRANDPA ThChHOBALD (859) (or ThHHO-BALD or ThHOBALD).

Not only that, but it might be advisable to translate "Grandpa" into Hebrew—*sab, sab'*, or *ab gaqen*; that is, SB, SBA, or AB GQN. Numerically, that is 62, 63, 156, or (counting *Nun* as final) 806. (Note that 806 is also the enumeration of H. P. LOWHGRAWTh, and 63 = DGWN, "Dagon," the title of the first story of Lovecraft's to be published in *Weird Tales*.) It might be possible to mix the Hebrew words with the letter-origins method, but it does not seem appropriate to do so—either the name is taken as Hebrew or it isn't.

Lovecraft often signed his letters simply "HPL" (115; or, by letter-origins, ChPL, 118), and frequently spelled this out phonetically so that it resembled the name of an ancient wizard—"Ech Pi El." This can be represented phonetically as ATSh PY AL (431 = LWWQRPT), AThSh PY AL (822 = LWWQRPTh), or ACh PY AL (130), and, by the letter-origin method as HGCh PY HL (141).

Thus, by the phonetic method, we arrive at 21 enumerations, after eliminating duplicates. We get 87 different enumerations by the "origins" method, and a further eight when we resort to translation. Not only that, but we can translate "Lovecraft" (love + craft) as *ahbah 'Umanuth* (AHBH AWMNWTh, 516, which happens to be the same as H. P. LWWQRPT) and start combining *that* with H. P. and the various phonetic spellings of "Howard Phillips."

Why this wholesale, scattergun approach? Surely, some of these numbers must be better than others! They are, of course; I have indicated a couple of choices above. But this is a character reading, not a determination of the most significant number. The idea is to get a panoply of enumerations for the diviner to work with so as to form general impressions and then work down to specifics. Why wouldn't random numbers do just as well? Indeed, with proper concentration by the proper scryer, they would—but at least the numbers generated by this method are sure to be actually related to the subject at hand in some way to begin with.

If we take 827 as the most important and probable enumeration (that is, H. P. LWWKRPTh), we find only one correspondence— GN ODN—the Garden of Eden!

What are we to make of this? Paradise before the Fall seems a strange result for a writer of terrifying tales of eldritch horrors! But, remember, we are doing a character reading, not a literary analysis.

All his life, Lovecraft longed for the Providence of his childhood, and his fiction describes it in glowing terms in several stories, perhaps most notably the novel-length *Dream-Quest of Unknown Kadath*. The house of his boyhood in an unspoiled Providence, Rhode Island—that is is HPL's Eden, from which home the child and his mother had to move after the death of his grandfather and from which he was "driven" even as the Perizzites (PRZM, 897 = H. P. LOWHKRAPTh) and Hittites (ChThYM, 1018 = ChOWARD PChYLLYPS LOWHKRAPT) were driven from Palestine.

Thus begins a typical analysis. It can and should be carried much further, of course, by considering all the numbers involved, looking up their correspondences in Section IV, in Appendices C and E, and in Crowley's 777. Write down the correspondences and then let them all churn around in your subconscious for a while, and see what you get!

This is the procedure to follow with any name with which you may choose to deal, and it goes without saying that, the better you are at divination by other methods, the better results you will get with this one. I am a rank amateur, but, as indicated here, even I can get a good start toward significant results.

It is helpful at times to remember that there is a certain amount of legitimate "fudging" that may be done in all these analyses, whether dream interpretation, divination, or character analysis. For example, the value of any Hebrew noun can be increased by 5 simply by adding the definite article "the" in front of it; that is, the letter *Heh*. Hence, *Bath*, BTh, 402, daughter, but *Ha-Bath*, HBTh, 407, *the* daughter.

From this sketch, it is hoped that the reader will have gained some idea as to the mechanics of character analysis via gematria.

**Talismans:** This encyclopedia is simply invaluable in the construction of talismans for any purpose. It is only necessary to relate the purpose of the talisman to one of the sephiroth, usually and most easily through the associated planet. Thus, Binah would be used for limitation; Chesed for growth and expansion (including riches); Geburah for aggressiveness and justice; Tiphareth for enlightenment and individuation; Netzach for love, creativity, and right-brain functions; Hod for skill, speed, or intellectual reasoning and left-brain functions; Yesod for scrying, divination, ESP, and so on; and Malkuth for matters to do with the earth, such as farming, gardening, or weather. Looking up the appropriate planet or sephira in this encyclopedia, you are presented with a wealth of material that may be used on the talisman. It should in any case include the appropriate God name, the name of the archangel, the name of the choir of angels, and the name of the planetary sphere. It would also be helpful to include the name of the spirit and the intelligence of that sphere. All of these should be engraved in well-made Hebrew characters, ideally on the appropriate metal (copper for Venus, gold for the Sun, tin for Jupiter, etc.).

It would also be extremely helpful to include on the talisman the name (in Hebrew) of the individual involved, whether yourself or another, if at all possible in a form that enumerates to an appropriate number—but in any case not to a disharmonious number. Besides the numbers involved with the names of the planetary spheres, sephiroth, angels, and so on, certain numbers are associated with each planet because of the so-called magic squares of those planets, as follows:

| Saturn | 3 | 9 | 15 | 45 |
| Jupiter | 4 | 16 | 34 | 136 |
| Mars | 5 | 25 | 65 | 325 |
| Sun | 6 | 36 | 111 | 666 |
| Venus | 7 | 49 | 175 | 1225 |
| Mercury | 8 | 64 | 260 | 2080 |
| Moon | 9 | 81 | 369 | 3321 |

For a complete description of magic squares and for a detailed recipe for the consecration of talismans, you can do no better than to consult Israel Regardie's *The Golden Dawn*, published by Llewellyn.

**Magick:** Now we come to the crux of the cabala. Gematria is integral to the use of the cabala in ceremonial magick, whether for theurgic (God-seeking) or thaumaturgic (pragmatic) ends. Once you have passed beyond the stage of the novice and are engaged in such practices as traveling or scrying in the spirit vision, astral travel, or active imagination—different names for real or imaginary out-of-the-body experiences—gematria is invaluable. The method once taught by the Hermetic Order of the Golden Dawn has the advantage (if not the necessity) of involving controls and protections and also encourages the understanding and verification of the experiences undergone in that state. It is here that gematria comes into its own.

Gematria is the one effective method used to test the validity of the experience and the authenticity of the beings encountered, as well as to understand the natures of these beings. I cannot do better than to quote an example given in a letter by Aleister Crowley (*Magick Without Tears*, Llewellyn, 1973). While traveling astrally, a formidable giant is encountered. The traveler determines his environment to be of a Saturnian nature and assumes an appropriate god-form.

> *The Chimaera, recognizing your divine authority, becomes less formidable and menacing in appearance. He may, in some way, indicate his willingness to serve you. Very good, so far; but it is of course, the first essential to make sure of his integrity. Accordingly you begin by asking his name. This is vital; because if he tells you the truth, it gives you power over him . . .*
> *Ottilia . . . we start with OTYLIAH . . . It adds up to 135. I daresay you don't remember what the* Sepher Sephiroth *tells you about that number; but as luck will have it, there is no need to inquire; for 135 = 3 x 45. Three is the first number of Saturn and 45 is the last. That corresponds beautifully with everything you have got so far . . .*

Concerning Crowley, any perusal of his writings makes it clear that he relied heavily on gematria during his astral scrying as well as in many other matters. In fact, his acceptance of *The Book of the Law* (dictated to him in Cairo in 1904 by an entity known as *Aiwass*) was primarily based on the large number of gematriatic correspondences; for example, Heru-Ra-Ha, Boleskine (his retreat in Scotland), Abrahadabra, *Cheth* (spelled out), *To Me*, Parzival, and Pallas Athene all add up to 418.

A related use of Gematria in ceremonial magick is to test the integrity of beings who manifest themselves during evocation, both as to their names and natures and as to the validity of their replies. This testing applies as well to the beings summoned in the rites of Wicca as to the entities evoked in high ceremony. (For a warning as to the inadvisability of a novice's evoking anything, see Appendix D on Pronunciation.) According to the basic tenets of magick, knowing the correct name of an entity gives you power over it. Gematria is essential for establishing the authenticity of such names and is practically indispensable for the effectiveness of the ceremony and ceremonial objects used to evoke them in the first place! Any talisman, seal, or "pentacle" used in the ceremony (or rite) should be appropriately inscribed with names and words that are not cabalistically disharmonious. It would be detrimental if not dangerous for a magician named, for example, Milton Harris, to inscribe his initials, *Mem Heh* (45), on a device meant to control a spirit associated with Chesed and Jupiter. (This also applies to names and words written in English.)

As an example, suppose we ask some such being, as a test, to give us a number associated with the King David of the Bible. If he says "fourteen," we will be disappointed; that is simply the enumeration of *David* in Hebrew. But suppose he gives us "twenty-eight." That is twice fourteen, which is some indication, but it is also *yadid*, meaning "one beloved." Inasmuch as the name *David* means "beloved," the number serves to verify that the being is giving correct information. (Twenty-eight is also *koch*, "strength," and *yichudh*, "union with God," both of which could be said to pertain to King David. It is also the number of the seventh path of the Tree of Life—that is, of Netzach—and is further identified with love through the association of that sephira with Venus.)

If, on the other hand, the being were to give us "thirty-five" in answer to our question, we might well be at a loss to make any connection with *David*. If no such connection can be found even after diligent investigation, the being can be assumed to be deceitful or evasive and obedience must be enforced.

To conclude, the cabalistic ceremonial magician who disdains the use of gematria is like a carpenter who tries to build a house without a hammer. It's very difficult to get the nails in with the butt end of a screwdriver.

**Mental training:** It is well known that the primary requisites for success in a magician are will and imagination. These faculties may be developed through what might be termed "gematriatic contemplation." The mere act of adding and comparing words and phrases develops the intellectual faculty (left brain functions), while consideration of the significance of correspondences develops the intuition (right brain functions).

A useful practice is the contemplation of numeric correspondences. Not only does this constitute a good mental exercise, but it expands your understanding of magick and the magickal universe. Such contemplation exercises could be worked into a ceremonial act that would be useful to an aspiring magician in several ways. For example, begin the practice with the Lesser Ritual of the Pentagram (see Regardie's *The Golden Dawn*) or Star Ruby ritual (Crowley, *Magick in Theory and Practice* and elsewhere) in order to assure purity of thought, free from negative influences. Then sit down in a comfortable position or in a practiced asana and free the mind from all other thoughts but the matter at hand. Then consider—not too intellectually—the chosen correspondence and, by leaving the mind open to impressions, try to understand the relationship involved. It might be well to begin with fairly straightforward correspondences, such as *gadhol* ("great), *yedidiah* ("beloved of God," used in reference to Solomon), and *mag* ("magus"), all 43, and work up to more abstruse matters such as correspondences that *seem* contradictory and disharmonious, such as *tohu* ("desolation, without form") and *Hekel Ratzon* ("Palace of Delight," one of the seven heavens), both 411. Finally, consider the nature of numbers that seem to have more than their share of correspondences, such as 52. Following such a contemplative exercise (which, by the way, is *not* meditation and should not be substituted for it), close with the same ritual as was used to begin. Fifteen or twenty minutes should do as a start.

It will be noted that such an exercise, aside from developing both halves of the brain, provides practice in ceremonial procedure and in concentration and visualization (*dharana*).

Skeptics may object that anyone engaging in such a practice is fooling himself/herself, inasmuch as he/she may be trying to see relationships where none exist aside from an artificial numerical correspondence. But the ability to see relationships where none *seem* to exist is the basis of all creative thought. Even if gematria were indeed delusion and nonsense (and it *can* be if it is taken too seriously and used carelessly, arbitrarily, and liberally; or if it becomes obsessional), the aim of the exercise remains the same— mental development, an expansion of consciousness, perhaps an indirect perception of the unity of all things.

★ ★ ★

In this paperback edition of the *Encyclopedia*, several changes, corrections, improvements, and additions have been made to the original edition. Perhaps one of the more noteworthy changes is in the listing of the Seven Hells of cabalism. The original edition contained a list from *The Magus* by Francis Barrett, the early 19th-century occultist. Unfortunately, the Hebrew in *The Magus*, probably because of the inaccuracy of 19th-century proofreading and printing, is not what it should be. The present edition contains a revised listing taken from Crowley's 777, which is more in accordance with the traditional material and at least has the advantage of being intelligible Hebrew.

Inasmuch as most of the organized cabala was transmitted to (and altered by?) Jewish sources in Moorish Spain from Arabic originals, a few key Arabic words have been included in this edition. Arabic "gematria" is a field that deserves its own separate study. That the Hebrew system is derivative, although perhaps at a date far earlier than the Middle Ages, may be indicated by the fact that the Arabic alphabet contains 28 characters—exactly enough to indicate numbers up to 1,999 without the somewhat awkward device of using secondary forms of letters such as the "finals" of Hebrew.

The student researching a number is advised to consult the appended *Sepher Sephiroth* of Aleister Crowley as well as Section IV of the *Encyclopedia* proper and the Appendices. And in particular, the new Appendix E (Notes to the 2nd Edition) contains a good many additions to the *Encyclopedia*, listed both by subject and numerically. As for *Sepher Sephiroth*, Crowley had access to sources no longer available, most notably Knorr von Rosenroth's *Kabbala Denudata*. But beware of errors and double-check Crowley's addition, for his work is not always 100% accurate. While on the subject, I feel I must disavow the cheap anti-Semitic sentiments expressed by Crowley in his preface to *Sepher Sephiroth*. In part, this defamation refers to an unfortunate essay ("The Jew") by the English explorer Sir Richard Burton, who should have known better.

In conclusion, it is hoped that this edition, more affordable and widely available than the original, will be of great value to the student and practitioner of magick in all its forms, and that this little preface will help to point out some of the more practical uses that may not have occurred to many readers.

David F. Godwin

# INTRODUCTION

THIS DICTIONARY was originally compiled for my own use, primarily for the study of *gematria* (Hebrew numerology). It has occurred to me, however, that many students might find it of some use. Perhaps it should be said at once that this book is *not* a comprehensive dictionary of the Hebrew language. Nor is it a complete dictionary of the cabala as understood by true cabalists, who are Jewish scholars and mystics of vast learning in the Talmud and the Torah. Rather, it is a dictionary of cabalism as understood and interpreted by the Christian (or Christian-biased) mystery schools and hermetic societies of the West, in particular the Hermetic Order of the Golden Dawn as it existed in the waning years of the 19th century.

This book is intended for those who wish a relatively complete dictionary, arranged alphabetically both in English and in Hebrew as well as numerically, of cabalism as thus understood. It is no longer necessary to have access to a large number of books on mysticism, magic, and the occult in order to trace down the basic meanings, Hebrew spellings, and enumerations of the hundreds of terms, words, and names included in this dictionary. This book contains a great many Hebrew words important for religious, philosophical, mystical, numerical, and other reasons, as well as all the two-letter words to be found in biblical Hebrew. It contains the many names of God, the planets and astrological signs, and a large number of angels and demons, including those of the Shem Hamphorash and the Goetia. Also included are most of the correspondences of the 32 Paths of Wisdom, that is, the ten Sephiroth and the twenty-two letters of the Hebrew alphabet.

In this dictionary, little or no knowledge is assumed on the part of the student. Aleister Crowley published a numerological dictionary of the names and terms of cabalism in *The Equinox*, included here as an appendix. Crowley's dictionary, however, assumed that the reader had an extensive knowledge of cabalism already and would use the dictionary merely to discover numerological connections. It was arranged numerically only, not alphabetically, and no transliteration of the Hebrew was provided. In the present volume, however, very little is assumed. This introduction provides a basic outline of the Tree of Life and the Sephiroth, the Hebrew alphabet, the 32 Paths of Wisdom, the four "worlds" of cabalism, etc. If there is any other term used in a definition which the student does not understand, he need only look it up for a brief but informative clarification. For example, he may find *Nachashiron* defined as the Qlippoth of Sagittarius and wonder what *Qlippoth* means. Looking it up, he finds that Qlippoth are shells or demons, so that the Nachashiron are the demonic order associated with Sagittarius. If he has only the vaguest idea—or no idea at all—as to what all the business is about *Shem Hamphorash*, he need only look up that term to find a full explanation.

Why, one may well ask, should a western, primarily Christian mystery school or occult society concern itself with the cabala, which is, after all, a form of Jewish mysticism? This point needs to be elucidated. Some of my friends are under the impression that I have compiled a dictionary of Judaism, which is certainly far from the truth. The Golden Dawn has been accused by anti-Semites of being a Zionist front organization because of its use of the cabala and the Hebrew language. This accusation is obviously absurd.

First of all, it must be remembered that the basic religious text and holy book of Christianity is the Bible, and that the Old Testament was originally written in Hebrew. Therefore, the use of Hebrew names and terms is inevitable in any western organization that concerns itself with mysticism, even if it involves only a passing reference to "Jehovah." "Amen" is a Hebrew word; so are "hallelujah" and "sabaoth."

Secondly, the western occult societies were, and are, much concerned with ceremonial magic for the purpose of integrating the personality and achieving union with God (or cosmic consciousness, in modern parlance). Any study or pursuit of ceremonial magic inevitably involves the cabala.

Thirdly, cabalism includes the only really complete and comprehensive method of classifying the universe, both macrocosm and microcosm, the various levels of existence, and the extensive hierarchies of angels and demons. I suppose that the unpublished literature of Sufism may contain something similar, and that this dictionary could just as well have been in Arabic. However, that literature is not available, and those interested in the subject are far more familiar with the Hebrew system.

At this point, it should be stated that I have no connection with or membership in any mystery school or occult society of any kind. The information included in this dictionary is widely available in published material and is not part of any teaching that has ever been passed to me. All I have done is to make a collection of these names and terms, determine their numerical values by adding the values of the letters, arrange them alphabetically and by numerical value, make a few corrections that I felt to be necessary in some of the spellings and transliterations, and put the result together in this dictionary.

**C**ABALISM, at least in the western occult tradition, is built around a diagram called the Tree of Life (see figure on facing page). This diagram contains ten circles representing the *Sephiroth* (singular: *Sephira*), that is, the "spheres," "numbers," or "emanations." The Sephiroth are the numbers 1 through 10 considered in their archetypal sense. Each Sephira is an archetypal idea. Also, the Sephiroth represent emanations from God and describe the process of creation. In the material world, they represent the heavenly spheres according to the classical conception.

Beyond the first Sephira, *Kether* ("Crown"), are the "three veils of negative existence": Nothing, Infinity, and the Limitless Light (or *Ain, Ain-Soph,* and *Ain-Soph Or*). These describe the process of manifestation from nothingness prior to the existence of unity (represented by Kether). They are without number, although Crowley designated them as 0, 00, and 000.

The user of this dictionary will constantly encounter references to these Sephiroth, so it is well to keep them in mind. The following table gives their numbers, Hebrew names, English names, and correspondences in the physical universe.

| 1. | Kether | Crown | Primum Mobile |
|---|---|---|---|
| 2. | Chokmah | Wisdom | Sphere of the Zodiac or Fixed Stars |
| 3. | Binah | Understanding | Sphere of Saturn |
| 4. | Chesed | Mercy | Sphere of Jupiter |
| 5. | Geburah | Severity | Sphere of Mars |
| 6. | Tiphareth | Beauty | Sphere of the Sun |
| 7. | Netzach | Victory | Sphere of Venus |
| 8. | Hod | Splendor | Sphere of Mercury |

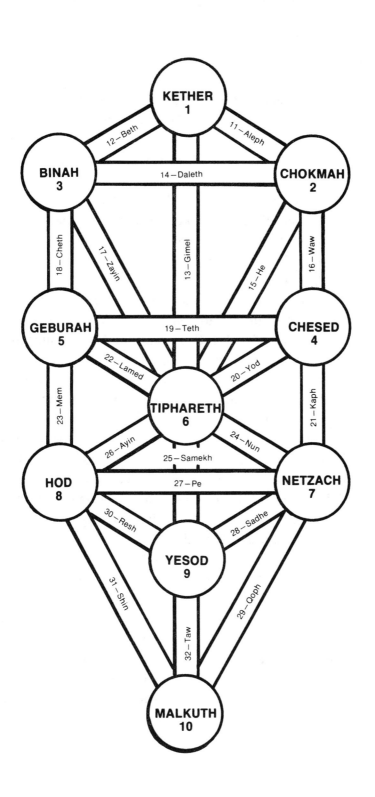

| 9. | **Yesod** | Foundation | Sphere of the Moon |
| 10. | **Malkuth** | Kingdom | Sphere of the Elements: the Earth and the four elements, Fire, Water, Air, and Earth |

But these correspondences in the physical universe are in the lowest stage of manifestation, that is, material existence. As such, they are referred to the lowest, grossest, and most material of the four "worlds" of cabalism, namely, the World of Action (*Olam ha-Assiah*). The Tree of Life also exists in three higher stages or planes. The highest and least material of these is the World of Nobility (*Olam Atziluth*), Plato's world of archetypes. In Atziluth, each Sephira is associated with a name of God peculiar to its nature. For example, Geburah is associated with the name *Elohim Gibor*, "God Almighty," God in His role as a stern judge and dispenser of justice untempered by mercy. In Roman mythology, the corresponding god-name is, of course, Mars.

Next comes the World of Creation, *Olam ha-Briah,* wherein the Sephiroth are associated with various archangels. Here one encounters the familiar names of Raphael, Michael, and Gabriel. Below Briah is the World of Formation, *Olam ha-Yetzirah*; here, the Sephira are associated with various angelic choirs or orders of angels. Finally comes Assiah, the physical world.

The ten Sephiroth are connected by twenty-two lines or "paths." These twenty-two paths correspond to the twenty-two letters of the Hebrew alphabet. Each path is associated with an element, a planet, or an astrological sign. The three "mother letters" of Hebrew, Aleph, Mem, and Shin, are associated with the three original elements: Air, Water, and Fire, respectively. The seven "double letters" are associated with the seven traditional planets, and the twelve "single letters" with the signs of the Zodiac.

In addition to the correspondences and associations described above, the Sephiroth and the twenty-two paths, collectively referred to as the 32 Paths of Wisdom, are associated with any number of other systems and conceptions. For example, the seven heavens, seven hells, and seven earths are associated with the Sephiroth in a very orderly manner, as are the Dukes and Kings of Edom listed in Genesis. The forty-two-letter name of God is broken into groups of letters and assigned to the Sephiroth. The trumps of the Tarot cards are assigned to the twenty-two letters, and the small cards are associated with the decanates of the Zodiac, which are in turn associated with the twelve single letters. (A decanate is a span of ten degrees. Each sign of the Zodiac therefore contains three decanates. A quinance is a span of five degrees, or half a decanate. Thus, the entire Zodiac of 360 degrees contains 36 decanates or 72 quinances.) In fact, nothing whatever exists that cannot somehow be attributed to the parts of the Tree of Life. In some cases, such attributions may seem arbitrary or forced. In most instances, however, they work out surprisingly well. A friend of mine, Burney Kent, has even suggested that the system can be applied to the thirty-one flavors of Baskin-Robbins ice cream! (In this case, Kether would represent milk, the essence of ice cream, and the other thirty-one paths would follow naturally.)

Also central to cabalism is Tetragrammaton, the four-letter name of God, *YHWH* (Yod-He-Waw-He), *Yahweh*, sometimes rendered as "Jehovah" and usually translated as "the Lord." The four consonants of the Name correspond to the four elements (Fire, Water, Air, and Earth, respectively) and to the four "worlds" described above. The four consonants are often described as a family: Yod is the Father, the masculine aspect of God, or Yang in Chinese thought; it is associated with the Sephira Chokmah, which is also called *Abba*, "the Supernal Father." (The Supernal Sephiroth, by the way, are Kether, Chokmah, and Binah—the first triad. These are said to be separated from the other Sephiroth by the Abyss.) The first He is the Mother, the feminine aspect of God, Yin, *Aima* or "the Supernal Mother," associated with Binah. Binah is thus the archetype of the Great Mother. Waw is the Son and includes the Sephiroth 4 through 9, although it is particularly associated with Tiphareth. Tiphareth is therefore associated with Christ. The final He is the Daughter, associated with Malkuth and variously called *Malkah,* "the Queen," or *Kalah,* "the Bride." This Daughter is the beautiful Maya of Hinduism and represents material existence. She is redeemed by the mystical marriage to the Son, Tiphareth.

This basic explanation of the Tree of Life has been necessarily brief and superficial. A fuller understanding of the concepts involved may be obtained by a study of some of the texts listed in the bibliography at the end of this dictionary.

N o ATTEMPT has been made in this dictionary to reproduce the characters of the Hebrew alphabet. One may consult the "alphabet" entry or endleaf of any standard dictionary of English to see what these letters look like. I have avoided their use because of the difficulties involved in typing and printing, and because misprints are easy to make and difficult to spot in proofreading due to the similarities of some of the characters. At least, this seems to be the case in almost every book I have encountered that attempts the extensive use of both English and Hebrew characters, the only exceptions being Hebrew-English dictionaries or Hebrew language textbooks. Therefore, following the example of S. L. Mathers, I have used English letters to indicate Hebrew letters. In most cases, the English characters I have used are the phonetic equivalent of the Hebrew letters. However, inasmuch as English contains no equivalent for the consonants Aleph and Ayin, I have designated these by *A* and *O*, respectively. One should not be misled by this usage into the misconception that Aleph and Ayin are vowels or that they have any similarity with *A* and *O*. The only connection is one of origin: the character A in the Latin alphabet comes from the Greek Alpha, which was adopted from the Semitic Aleph, a glottal stop, and used for the vowel sound. The situation is similar with Ayin, a voiced spirant. These consonants exist only in Semitic alphabets such as Hebrew and Arabic. Also, the Hebrew Cheth has no exact English equivalent, but is similar to the German *ch,* or the *ch* in the Scottish *loch.* It has been rendered here as *Ch.* Crowley, in my opinion, was in error in transliterating English names into Hebrew inasmuch as he commonly transliterated *A* as Aleph and *O* as Ayin. The letter *O* is much more accurately rendered as Waw, which, with certain added marks, is used to designate *U* or *O.* The important point is that Hebrew has no vowels in its alphabet; these are designated, if at all, by certain dots and dashes under or within the letters.

The table on the following page gives the names of the Hebrew letters, the English letters I have used to designate them throughout this dictionary, and the associated elements, planets, or zodiacal signs. Also given are the numerical values of the letters. Arabic numbers are (or were) not used in Hebrew; instead, numbers were indicated by the consonants. Hence, each letter has a numerical value. This leads very naturally into the concept of gematria, numerology, wherein every word or name has a numerical value. Words, names, and phrases with the same numerical value are assumed to be somehow related. This concept is basic to cabalism.

Some letters have two numerical values. The second, larger value is used (usually) when the letter falls at the end of the word. The letter then takes on a different shape and is, in fact, a different character. These characters are called the "finals."

| | | | |
|---|---|---|---|
| **Aleph** | A | 1 | Air |
| **Beth** | B | 2 | Mercury |
| **Gimel** | G | 3 | Moon |
| **Daleth** | D | 4 | Venus |
| **He** | H | 5 | Aries (or Aquarius) |
| **Waw** | W | 6 | Taurus |
| **Zayin** | Z | 7 | Gemini |
| **Cheth** | Ch | 8 | Cancer |
| **Teth** | T | 9 | Leo |
| **Yod** | Y | 10 | Virgo |
| **Kaph** | K | 20 | Jupiter |
| | | 500 | |
| **Lamed** | L | 30 | Libra |
| **Mem** | M | 40 | Water |
| | | 600 | |
| **Nun** | N | 50 | Scorpio |
| | | 700 | |
| **Samekh** | S | 60 | Sagittarius |
| **Ayin** | O | 70 | Capricorn |
| **Pe** | P | 80 | Mars |
| | | 800 | |
| **Sadhe** | Tz | 90 | Aquarius (or Aries) |
| | | 900 | |
| **Qoph** | Q | 100 | Pisces |
| **Resh** | R | 200 | Sun |
| **Shin** | Sh | 300 | Fire |
| **Taw** | Th | 400 | Saturn |

THIS DICTIONARY is divided into four sections. The first and most comprehensive is the "Transliterated Hebrew" section. In this section, the words and names are given in their transliterated form, with vowels, arranged alphabetically according to the English alphabet. Section I contains the most nearly complete definitions and the various subsidiary data and correspondences of the more important concepts. For example, each entry for a sign of the Zodiac gives the hierarchy of angels and demons associated with that sign, the color, the scent (from Crowley's 777), the Tarot Trump and Tarot cards of the decanates, the direction, the tribe of Israel, the apostle of Christ, the geomantic figure, the mystic number of the associated path, the ruling planet, the planet exalted in that sign, the planet in detriment, and the planet in fall. The entries for the demons of the Goetia (see *Goetic Demons* in Section II) include complete descriptions: the rank of the demon and the number of legions of infernal spirits he commands, the form in which he appears, and his powers or offices.

Section I is arranged in four columns. The first column gives the transliterated word or name, the second column, the Hebrew consonants (designated by English letters, as explained previously), the third column, the definition or explanation, and the fourth column, the numerical value. In many cases, more than one numerical value is given. In these cases, a "final" letter is involved, and finals may be counted at either their higher or lower value.

Section II is the section containing English words and a few names whose Hebrew equivalents are very dissimilar to the English forms of the names. It is intended primarily as a key or guide to Section I. For example, if one wishes to find some information about the sign Aries, he may consult Section II to find the Hebrew word meaning Aries, namely, *Taleh*. He then looks up *Taleh* in

Section I to find the information he needs. Such information has been included in Section I rather than in Section II for the sake of consistency, inasmuch as many of the expanded entries have no English equivalent.

Section III, "Hebrew," is arranged alphabetically according to the Hebrew spellings and order of the Hebrew alphabet. It is essentially the same as Section I, except that the first two columns are reversed and the definitions are not as extensive. This section is intended to be used when the Hebrew spelling is known but not the transliterated form. It is quite common in the literature to come upon a word or name that is given only in the form of Hebrew consonants and is accompanied by minimal explanation. Such words or names may easily be sought in Section III.

Finally, Section IV, "Numerology," is arranged according to the numerical values of the words and names. Here, one may see at once all the numerical identities between various names and words. In other words, Section IV is the section on gematria. All the entries under any one particular number are, according to the doctrine, somehow related. In many cases, the connection is far from obvious. These cases may form the subjects of intellectual "meditations," wherein one tries to see just how two apparently unrelated words may be related. Such meditations are useful in a number of ways. An orthodox cabalist would say it helps one to understand the nature of the universe and of God. In any event, it does sharpen the mind and helps one to see the innate unity of all things.

In looking through this section, one is continually amazed at the number of entries that relate the sublimest concepts to the lowest. For example, the numerical value is the same (1190) for both the Seraphim, an angelic choir, and *Seirim*, meaning hairy ones or demons. *Tath Zal*, the Profuse Giver, a "title" (name) of Kether, has the same numerical value as Paimon, the demon king of Fire. The solution to such problems, if they are problems, may lie in the cabalistic doctrine, "As above, so below." This statement is merely the cabalistic way of stating the doctrine of the macrocosm and the microcosm, but it is also true that all the divine and angelic hierarchies have their equivalents in hell. In fact, Kether itself has the same numerical value as the lowest hell.

Those who argue for the validity of gematria seldom advance such examples. Far more popular are such numerical identities as "love" (*Ahbah*) and "unity" (*Echad*), which both equal 13. In any event, the correspondences are always interesting. For example, one learns from the number 260 that Tiriel, the intelligence of Mercury, is ill-humored.

It should be pointed out that numerology of this kind works equally well with any alphabet and any language. If one assigns numbers to the letters of the English alphabet, from 1 to 26 consecutively, one may arrive with a little experimentation at any number of astounding numerical correspondences. For example, "Jesus" and "Messiah" both add to 74. ("Jesus" is 10 plus 5 plus 19 plus 21 plus 19, or 74; "Messiah" is 13 plus 5 plus 19 plus 19 plus 9 plus 1 plus 8, or 74.) (Incidentally, the English word "God" in this system adds to 26, the same as YHWH in Hebrew.)

One may therefore argue that gematria, and in fact all numerology, is the purest nonsense. On the other hand, one may take such phenomena as proof that it *does* have validity. In any case, it is doubtless a mistake to take it too seriously or carry it too far. As Crowley's "autohagiography" attests, doing so can result in the grossest delusions. Nevertheless, numerology does form an interesting exercise that enhances the thinking process, or at least one aspect of the thinking process (the ability to see relationships, vital to the artist or scientist), and that inevitably leads to the final conclusion, fundamental to mysticism, that all things are related and are, in fact, one. The final realization of the student of gematria is that, as stated in *The Book of the Law* (the

Word as revealed to Crowley, not to be confused with the Torah), "Every number is infinite; there is no difference."

Gematria is not to be confused with popular numerology wherein any number is reduced to a single digit by adding the digits of that number. In gematria—and in all valid numerology—every number has its own meaning. Reducing everything in creation to nine digits is a gross and misleading oversimplification, only three-quarters as good as the popular newspaper horoscopes, which lump the entire population of the world into *twelve* categories. If one believes such "horoscopes," then it follows that approximately 300 million people (one-and-a-half times the population of the United States) should, on any given day, "receive unexpected news," "make new business contacts," or whatever. Astrology is an individual affair; no two people have the same horoscope. In numerology, no two numbers—of however many digits—have the same meaning.

Another cautionary note must be added: it is a mistake to think of the Tree of Life, the Sephiroth, the Paths, the planetary spheres, and so on as having some sort of physical or objective existence. All these things are only ordered concepts to aid one in thinking about abstract matters, primarily divine or supernatural matters. We know now, of course, that the classical conception of the universe embodied in the cabala has no relation to physical reality. The earth is not the center of nine heavenly spheres inhabited by choirs of angels; there are more than seven planets, and the sun and moon are not planets at all, properly speaking; all matter is not made up of only four elements. It is important to realize that these things, in cabalism as now understood, are concepts, labels for classification, archetypal ideas, etc., and *not* physical realities. The astronauts did not encounter Chashmodai in Mare Tranquillitatis.

As for the innumerable angels, demons, spirits, and so on to be encountered in cabalism and magic, it is simply a matter of opinion and belief as to whether they have any objective reality. At one time, Crowley thought they represented unconscious forces in the psyche. This view seems as good as any. In one case, a man evokes a spirit in order to control it. In another case, he tries to come to an understanding of some aspect of his unconscious mind that is affecting his behavior for the worse or that could affect it for the better. The first instance is magic, condemned as nonsense and delusion. The second is psychology, usually recognized as valid. But the difference is mainly one of terminology. The methods of magic are the methods of psychology, and they work about as well.

THE SYSTEM of correspondences followed in this dictionary is that taught by the Hermetic Order of the Golden Dawn, with some additions by Aleister Crowley, a onetime member of that order. The bulk of this system is to be found in *The Golden Dawn* by Israel Regardie (Llewellyn Publications) and in *777* by Aleister Crowley (Samuel Weiser, Inc.), although these two books were far from my only sources in compiling this dictionary. Unfortunately, both these texts contain a number of misprints, especially in the names rendered in Hebrew letters. It has been possible to verify the Hebrew spellings of the seventy-two angels of the Shem Hamphorash from other sources, ultimately from the Hebrew text of Exodus. However, these two books are the only sources I know for the Hebrew spellings of the thirty-six angels of the decanates and of various other angels, and they do not always agree. In cases of conflict, I have arbitrarily chosen Crowley's spelling and made a note in the definition of Regardie's. The only reason for this choice is that Crowley had access to earlier documents of the order which are less likely to have been altered by repeated copying. In cases where only one source is available, I have corrected what I took to be obvious misprints.

I have found it necessary to supply my own English transliterations of the names of many of these zodiacal angels, inasmuch as English versions are given neither by Crowley nor Regardie. I have also taken the liberty of improving the transliterations of Mathers and of Francis Barrett in many cases. In a few instances, such as with the names of the Olympic Planetary Spirits, I have supplied my own version of likely Hebrew spellings where none are otherwise available. The Hebrew spellings of the Goetic demons are Crowley's. The names of the angels of the twelve astrological houses are to be found in various sources as the angels of the twelve signs of the Zodiac, and the English spellings of these names indicate in some instances that the Hebrew spellings given both by Crowley and Regardie contain misprints. In these cases, I have ignored the older English version and taken the Hebrew spelling of Crowley and Regardie as a correct "restoration."

In conclusion, it is my firm hope that those interested in these matters will find this dictionary an invaluable and helpful text.

—*David Godwin*
*Houston, Texas*

# SECTION I

| | | | |
|---|---|---|---|
| A'abiriron | | See *Abiriron.* | |
| A'amamiah | | See *Amamiah.* | |
| A'aneval | | See *Anevel.* | |
| A'arab Zaraq | | See *Oreb Zaraq.* | |
| A'ariel | | See *Ariel* (ORYAL). | |
| Aaron | AHRN | Brother of Moses. | 906 |
| | | | 256 |
| A'asliah | | See *Asaliah.* | |
| A'athiel | | See *Athiel.* | |
| Ab | AB | Father (a title of Chokmah); the first two letters of the 42-letter name of God, associated with Kether. | 3 |
| Ab | OB | The secret name of the World of Atziluth; density; thicket; darkness; cloud. | 72 |
| Abaddon | ABDWN | "Destruction." (Job XVI:6); the angel of the bottomless pit (Rev. IX:11), called in Greek Apollyon; the 6th hell, corresponding to Chesed and to the Islamic *Jahim*, reserved for pagans and idolators. | 713 63 |
| Abar | ABR | Lead, the metal of Saturn. | 203 |
| Abba | ABBA | The Supernal Father, a title of Chokmah. | 6 |
| Abdaron | ABDRWN | Angel of 2nd decanate of Aquarius. | 913 263 |
| Abel (Hebel) | HBL | Vapor, breath, vanity; the son of Adam, slain by Cain. | 37 |
| Ab-gi-thetz-qerashamen-kegadikesh-bamratztag-haqamamna-yaglepzeq-sheqi-ayeth | ABGYThTz-QROShMN-KGDYKSh-BMRTzThG-HQMMNO-YGLPZQ-ShQYOYTh | The name of God of 42 letters. | 3783 |
| Abib | ABYB | Spring. | 15 |

| Abimelech | ABYMLK | A King of the Philistines. | 583 |
| | | | 103 |
| Abir | ABYR | The Almighty. | 213 |
| Abiriron | OBYRYRWN | The Clayish Ones, Qlippoth of Libra. | 1198 |
| | | | 548 |
| Aboha | ABWHA | Angel of 3rd decanate of Sagittarius. | 15 |
| Aboz | ABWZ | Francis Barret's misprint for ABDWN, Abaddon, q.v. | |
| Abracadabra | | Magic word used to cure fevers and to ward off the plague; original Hebrew form, Abrakala (ABRAKALA); see also *Abrahadabra*. | |
| Abrahadabra | ABRAHA-DABRA | Crowley's spelling of Abracadabra. | 418 |
| Abraham | ABRHM | Son of Terah, father of Isaac and Ishmael. | 808 |
| | | | 248 |
| Abrakala | ABRAKALA | Original form of Abracadabra. | 526 |
| Abram | ABRM | Abraham's original name. | 803 |
| | | | 243 |
| Accad | AKD | Akkad, dynasty of ancient Mesopotamia. | 25 |
| Ach | ACh | Brother. | 9 |
| Achad | | See *Echad*. | |
| Achad-Asar | AChD-OShR | Eleven. | 583 |
| Achbor | OKBWR | Father of Baal-Hanan, a King of Edom. | 298 |
| Achodraon | AChW-DRAWN | Lord of Triplicity by Night for Libra. | 926 |
| | | | 276 |
| Achoth | AChWTh | Sister. | 415 |
| Ad | OD | Eternity, duration; during; booty. | 74 |
| Adah | ODH | Wife of Lamech of the line of Cain; mother of Jabal and Jubal. | 79 |
| Adam | ADM | The first man; literally, "man"; a title of Tiphareth. | 605 |
| | | | 45 |
| Adamah | ADMH | Earth; one of the seven earths, corresponding to Chesed. | 50 |
| Adam Belial | ADM BLYAL | "Man Without God"; an arch-demon corresponding (according to A. E. Waite) to Chokmah. | 678 |
| | | | 118 |
| Adam Qadmon | ADM QDMWN | The archetypal man. | 1455 |
| | | | 895 |
| | | | 245 |

| | | | |
|---|---|---|---|
| **Adar** | ADR | The sixth Hebrew month, February-March, corresponding roughly to the period when the Sun is in Pisces. | 205 |
| **Adhom** | ADM | Red. | 605<br>45 |
| **Adimiron** | ADY-<br>MYRWN | The Bloody Ones, Qlippoth of Taurus. | 971<br>321 |
| **Adonai** | ADNY | A name of God originally used as a euphemism for YHWH. In the Lesser Ritual of the Pentagram, this name is vibrated to the South and is associated with Fire; in the Greater Ritual of the Pentagram, it is vibrated to the North and is associated with Earth. | 65 |
| **Adonai ha-<br>Eretz** | ADNY<br>HARTz | Lord of the Earth; divine name associated with Malkuth, with Earth, and with the North. | 1171<br>361 |
| **Adramelek** | | Arch-demon corresponding to Hod; no Hebrew spelling; also Adrammelech. | |
| **Advakiel** | ADWKYAL | Archangel of Sagittarius; also spelled Advachiel. | 72 |
| **Agares** | AGAR | Goetic demon by day of 2nd decanate of Aries; also spelled Agreas.<br>Duke commanding 31 legions.<br>Under the power of the East.<br>Appears as an old, fair man riding on a crocodile and carrying a goshawk on his fist, "yet mild in appearance."<br>Powers: makes those run who stand still; brings back runaways; teaches languages; destroys dignities; causes earthquakes.<br>Formerly of the Order of Virtues. | 205 |
| **Aggerath** | | See *Agrath*. | |
| **Agiel** | AGYAL | Intelligence of Saturn. | 45 |
| **Agla** | AGLA | A name of God; acronym for Ateh Gibor le-Olam Adonai (AThH GBWR LOWLM ADNY), "Thou art mighty forever, O Lord."<br>In the Lesser Ritual of the Pentagram, this name is vibrated to the North and is associated with Earth. In the Greater | 35 |

Ritual of the Pentagram, it is vibrated with the Passive Pentagrams of Spirit (the passive elements bring Water and Earth) to the West and North and is thus associated with the passive elements.

| | | | |
|---|---|---|---|
| **Agrath** | AGRTh | A Queen of Demons; see *Agrath bath Mahalath.* | 604 |
| **Agrath bath Mahalath** | AGRTh BTh MChLTh | Agrath, daughter of Mahalath; a Queen of Demons, one of the three wives of Samael; variously spelled Agrath, Aggerath, Igrath, Agrat, etc. | 1484 |
| **Agshekeloh** | | See Gasheklah. | |
| **Ahab** | AHB | Love. | 8 |
| **Ahbah** | AHBH | Love; beloved. | 13 |
| **Aholibamah** | AHLYBMH | A Duke of Edom, associated with Chesed. | 93 |
| **Ahoz** | AHWZ | Lord of Triplicity by Day for Sagittarius. | 19 |
| **Aiel** | | See *Ayel.* | |
| **Aim** | AYM | Goetic demon by day of 2nd decanate of Scorpio. | 611 51 |

Duke commanding 26 legions.

Appears as a very handsome man with three heads: that of a serpent, that of a man with two stars on his forehead, and that of a calf; riding on a viper and carrying a firebrand with which he ignites cities, castles, and great places.

Powers: makes one witty in a variety of ways; answers truly about private matters.

| | | | |
|---|---|---|---|
| **Aima** | AYMA | The Supernal Mother, a title of Binah. | 52 |
| **Ain** | AYN | Nothing; the highest state of negative existence above Kether. | 711 61 |
| **Ain-Soph** | AYN-SWP | Infinity (without limit); the middle state of negative existence above Kether. | 1577 927 207 |
| **Ain-Soph Or** | AYN-SWP AWR | The Limitless Light; the first state of negative existence above Kether. | 1784 1134 414 |
| **Aiq Bekar** | AYQ BKR | The cabala of nine chambers, a division of Temurah, viz.: | 333 |

| A | 1 | B | 2 | G | 3 |
|---|---|---|---|---|---|
| Y | 10 | K | 20 | L | 30 |
| Q | 100 | R | 200 | Sh | 300 |
| D | 4 | H | 5 | W | 6 |
| M | 40 | N | 50 | S | 60 |
| Th | 400 | K* | 500 | M* | 600 |
| Z | 7 | Ch | 8 | T | 9 |
| O | 70 | P | 80 | Tz | 90 |
| N* | 700 | P* | 800 | Tz* | 900 |

*Finals

| | | | |
|---|---|---|---|
| **Aiwass** | AYWAS | The supposed author of *The Book of the Law.* | 78 |
| **Ak** | AK | But, only; surely, indeed. | 501 |
| | | | 21 |
| **Aka** | AKA | 7th name of Shem Hamphorash; associated with 1st quinance of Virgo. | 22 |
| **Akaiah** | AKAYH | Angel of 1st quinance of Virgo; angel by day of the 8 of Pentacles; also spelled Akhaiah. | 37 |
| **Akel** | OKAL | Lord of Triplicity by Night for Cancer. | 121 |
| **Akhaiah** | | See *Akaiah.* | |
| **Akkad** | AKD | Dynasty of ancient Mesopotamia. | 25 |
| **Akrab** | OQRB | Scorpion, Scorpio. | 372 |
| | | Corresponds to Nun and the 24th Path. | |
| | | Archangel: Barkiel. | 263 |
| | | Angel: Saitzel | 202 |
| | | Lord of Triplicity by Day: Bethchon. | 1126 |
| | | | 476 |
| | | Lord of Triplicity by Night: Sahaqnab. | 217 |
| | | Angel Ruling 8th House: Sosul. | 162 |
| | | Angel of 1st Decanate: Kamotz. | 966 |
| | | | 156 |
| | | Angel of 1st Quinance: Luviah. | 57 |
| | | Angel of 2nd Quinance: Pahaliah. | 130 |
| | | Angel of 2nd Decanate: Nundohar. | 325 |
| | | Angel of 3rd Quinance: Nelakiel. | 131 |
| | | Angel of 4th Quinance: Yeyayel. | 61 |
| | | Angel of 3rd Decanate: Uthrodiel. | 657 |
| | | Angel of 5th Quinance: Melahel. | 106 |
| | | Angel of 6th Quinance: Chahaviah. | 34 |
| | | Qlippoth: Necheshthiron (The Brazen | 1674 |

Ones); (from *Necheshthi,* "coppery,   1024
brassy").

Goetic Demons by Day:

    1st Decanate: Ipos.   396

    2nd Decanate: Aim.   611

      51

    3rd Decanate: Naberius.   252

Goetic Demons by Night:

    1st Decanate: Avnas (Amy).   707

      57

    2nd Decanate: Oriax (Orias).   1117

      307

    3rd Decanate: Naphula (Vapula).   166

Color: Turquoise (Blue-Green).

Scent: Siamese Benzoin, Opoponax.

Tarot Trump: XIII. Death.

Tarot Cards associated with Decanates:

    1st Decanate: 5 of Cups.

    2nd Decanate: 6 of Cups.

    3rd Decanate: 7 of Cups.

Direction: Southwest.

Tribe of Israel: Dan.

Apostle: Philip.

Geomantic Figure: Rubeus.

Mystic Number of 24th Path: 300.

Ruling Planet: Mars.

Planet Exalted in: Pluto.

Planet in Detriment in: Venus.

Planet in Fall in: Moon.

| | | | |
|---|---|---|---|
| **Al** | OL | Upper part; on, above, over, to, toward, after, because. | 100 |
| **Aldiah** | ALDYH | Angel of 4th quinance of Virgo; angel by night of the 9 of Pentacles; also spelled Aladiah. | 50 |
| **Allah** | ALLH | *(Arabic)* Contraction of El Elah, "the god." | 66 |
| **Alem** | OLM | 4th name of Shem Hamphorash; associated with 4th quinance of Leo. | 700 |
| | | | 140 |
| **Aleph** | A | 1st letter of Hebrew alphabet; a glottal stop, transliterated as '. | 1 |

Spelled out, ALP, Ox (831 or 111).

Corresponds to the element Air, the 11th
Path (between Kether and Chokmah),

|  |  | and the Tarot Trump 0. The Fool; for additional correspondences, see *Ruach*. |  |
|---|---|---|---|
| **Alinkir** | ALYNKYR | Angel of 3rd decanate of Cancer. | 321 |
| **Alloces** | ALWK | Goetic demon by night of 1st decanate of Virgo; also spelled Alocas. Duke commanding 36 legions. Appears as a soldier riding a horse; very red face, like a lion's, flaming eyes; speaks hoarsely and "very big." Powers: teaches astronomy and liberal sciences; gives good familiars. | 537 57 |
| **Aloyar** | ALWYR | Lord of Triplicity by Night for Capricorn. | 247 |
| **Alup** | ALWP | Chief, duke (see *Edom*). | 837 117 |
| **Alvah** | OLWH | A Duke of Edom; with Timnah and Jetheth, associated with Daath. | 111 |
| **Am** | OM | Nation, populace. | 670 110 |
| **Ama** | AMA | Mother; a title of Binah. | 42 |
| **Amaimon** | AMAYMWN | Demon King of Earth and the North; according to the Goetia, Demon King of the East. | 798 148 |
| **Amam** | OMM | To darken, to dim. | 710 150 |
| **Amamiah** | OMMYH | Angel of 4th quinance of Aries; angel by night of the 3 of Wands; also spelled A'amamiah or Imamiah. | 165 |
| **Abriel** | AMBRYAL | Archangel of Gemini. | 284 |
| **Amdukias** | AMDWK | Goetic demon by night of 1st decanate of Aquarius; also spelled Amdusias. Duke commanding 29 legions. Appears as a unicorn; assumes human form upon request, eventually causing trumpets and "all manner of Musical Instruments" to be heard, but not immediately. Powers: bends trees; gives good familiars. | 551 71 |
| **Amem** | OMM | 52nd name of Shem Hamphorash; associated with 4th quinance of Aries. | 710 150 |
| **Amen** | AMN | Firm, faithful; so be it!; a title of Kether. | 741 91 |

| | | | |
|---|---|---|---|
| **Amnitziel** | AMNYTz-YAL | Amnitziel. | 232 |
| **Amon** | AMWN | Goetic demon by day of 1st decanate of Gemini; chief god of Egypt. Marquis commanding 40 legions. Appears as a wolf with the tail of a serpent, vomiting flames; upon command, he assumes the form of a man with a raven's head with or without dog's teeth. Powers: tells fortunes; causes feuds; reconciles controversies between friends. | 747 97 |
| **An** | AN | Where? | 701 51 |
| **Anael** | ANAL | Angel ruling Venus and Friday. | 82 |
| **Anak** | ONQ | A giant. | 220 |
| **Ananaurah** | ANNAWRH | Angel of 1st decanate of Virgo. | 313 |
| **Anath** | ONTh | Semitic goddess similar to Astarte. | 520 |
| **Anaw** | ONW | Humble, afflicted. | 126 |
| **Andras** | ANDR | Goetic demon by night of 3rd decanate of Sagittarius. Marquis commanding 30 legions. Appears as an angel with a black night raven, riding a strong black wolf and flourishing aloft a sharp, bright sword. Powers: sows discord. "If the Exorcist have not a care, he will slay both him and his fellows." | 255 |
| **Andrealphus** | ANDRALP | Goetic demon by night of 2nd decanate of Capricorn. Marquis commanding 30 legions. Appears as a peacock accompanied by loud noises; assumes human form after a while. Powers: teaches geometry, mensuration, and astronomy; transforms men into birds. | 1086 366 |
| **Andromalius** | ANDRW-MAL | Goetic demon by night of 3rd decanate of Pisces. Earl commanding 36 legions. Appears as a man holding a large serpent. Powers: retrieves stolen goods; brings back and punishes thieves and other mis- | 332 |

| | | creants; finds out all wickedness and underhanded dealing; finds hidden treasures. | |
|---|---|---|---|
| **Anevel** | ONWAL | Angel of 3rd quinance of Gemini; angel by day of the 9 of Swords; also spelled A'aneval or Annauel. | 157 |
| **Ani** | ANY | I; fleet (of ships); 37th name of Shem Hamphorash, associated with 1st quinance of Aquarius. | 61 |
| **Aniel** | ANYAL | Angel of 1st quinance of Aquarius; angel by day of the 5 of Swords. | 92 |
| **Annauel** | | See *Anevel.* | |
| **Ansuel** | ANSWAL | Angel of 11th astrological house. | 148 |
| **Anu** | ONW | 63rd name of Shem Hamphorash, associated with 3rd quinance of Gemini. | 126 |
| **Aph** | AP | Also. | 801 81 |
| **Apollyon** | | See *Abaddon.* | |
| **Ar** | OR | Enemy. | 270 |
| **Arab** | ORB | To exchange; to pawn; to grow dark; poplar or willow; Arabia. | 272 |
| **Arabhoth** | ORBWTh | Plains; the 7th Heaven, corresponding to the three Supernal Sephiroth. | 678 |
| **Aral** | ARAL | Angel of Fire. | |
| **Aralim** | ARALYM | The Mighty Ones; Angelic Choir associated with Binah and with the Sphere of Saturn. | 842 282 |
| **Arar** | ARR | To curse. | 401 |
| **Ararita** | ARARYThA | A name of God; acronym for Echad Rosh Achdotho Rosh Ichudo Temurahzo Echad (AChD RASh AChDWThW RASh YChWDW ThMWRHZW AChD), "One is his beginning, one is his individuality, his permutation is one." Used in the Lesser and Greater Rituals of the Hexagram. | 813 |
| **Arathron** | ARAThRWN | Olympic Planetary Spirit of Saturn; also spelled Aratron or Arathor. | 1508 858 |
| **Araziel** | ARZYAL | Angel of Taurus. | 249 |
| **Arbaah** | ARBOH | Four. | 278 |
| **Arbaah-Asar** | ARBOH-OShR | Fourteen. | 848 |
| **Arbaim** | ARBOYM | Forty. | 883 323 |

| | | | |
|---|---|---|---|
| **Arbeh** | ARBH | Locusts; the 8th of the 10 plagues of Egypt. | 208 |
| **Areb** | ORB | Sweet, pleasant. | 272 |
| **Aretz** | | See *Eretz*. | |
| **Ari** | ARY | Lion. | 211 |
| **Ari** | ARYH | Lion; Leo. | 216 |

Corresponds to Teth and the 19th Path.

| | |
|---|---|
| Archangel: Verkiel. | 267 |
| Angel: Sharatiel. | 550 |
| Lord of Triplicity by Day: Sanahem. | 715 |
| | 155 |
| Lord of Triplicity by Night: Zalbarhith. | 654 |
| Angel Ruling 5th House: Oel | 107 |
| Angel of 1st Decanate: Losanahar. | 351 |
| Angel of 1st Quinance: Vahaviah. | 32 |
| Angel of 2nd Quinance: Yelayel. | 81 |
| Angel of 2nd Decanate: Zachi. | 95 |
| Angel of 3rd Quinance: Sitael. | 110 |
| Angel of 4th Quinance: Elemiah. | 155 |
| Angel of 3rd Decanate: Sahiber. | 277 |
| Angel of 5th Quinance: Mahashiah. | 360 |
| Angel of 6th Quinance: Lelahel. | 96 |
| Qlippoth: Shalhebiron (The Flaming Ones) (from *Shalhebeth*, "flame"). | 1253 603 |

Goetic Demons by Day:

| | |
|---|---|
| 1st Decanate: Beleth (Bileth, Bilet). | 433 |
| 2nd Decanate: Leraje (Leraikha, Leraie). | 741 261 |
| 3rd Decanate: Eligos. | 350 |

Goetic Demons by Night:

| | |
|---|---|
| 1st Decanate: Crocell (Crokel). | 276 |
| 2nd Decanate: Furcas. | 586 106 |
| 3rd Decanate: Balam (Balaam). | 702 142 |

Color: Yellow.
Scent: Frankincense.
Tarot Trump: XI. Strength.
Tarot Cards associated with Decanates:
  1st Decanate: 5 of Wands.
  2nd Decanate: 6 of Wands.

3rd Decanate: 7 of Wands.
Direction: North, above.
Tribe of Israel: Judah.
Apostle: Peter.
Geomantic Figures: Fortuna Major and Fortuna Minor.
Mystic Number of 19th Path: 190.
Ruling Planet: Sun.
Planet Exalted in: Uranus.
Planet in Detriment in: Saturn.
Planet in Fall in: Neptune.

| | | | |
|---|---|---|---|
| **Ariel** | ARYAL | Ruler of Air. | 242 |
| **Ariel** | ORYAL | Angel of 4th quinance of Pisces; angel by night of the 9 of Cups; also spelled A'ariel. | 311 |
| **Arik Anpin** | ARYK ANPYN | The Vast Countenance, the Greater Countenance, Macroprosopus; literally, "long of nose"; a title of Kether. | 1551 1072 422 |
| **Arik Apim** | ARYK APYM | Long of Face; a title of Kether. | 1402 922 362 |
| **Ariton** | ARYTWN | Demon King of Water and the West. | 926 276 |
| **Arlah** | ORLH | Foreskin. | 305 |
| **Aron** | ARN | Ark (of the Covenant). | 901 251 |
| **Aron ha-Edeth** | ARN HODTh | Ark of the Testimony. | 1386 736 |
| **Arov** | ORWB | Wild beasts; the 4th of the 10 plagues of Egypt. | 278 |
| **Arphaxad** | ARPKShD | Son of Shem and father of Salah; lived 438 years (1658-2096 after Creation); spelled Arpachshad in R.S.V. | 605 |
| **Arqa** | ARQA | Earth; one of the seven earths, corresponding to Hod; contains the seven hells. | 302 |
| **Arur** | ARWR | Cursed. | 407 |
| **Asaliah** | OShLYH | Angel of 5th quinance of Pisces; angel by day of the 10 of Cups; also spelled A'asliah. | 415 |
| **Asarah** | OShRH | Ten. | 575 |
| **Asch** | | See *Esh*. | |
| **Ashel** | OShL | 47th name of Shem Hamphorash, associated with 5th quinance of Pisces. | 400 |

| Asher | AShR | A tribe of Israel, associated with Libra. | 501 |
| Asherah | AShRH | Phoenician goddess of prosperity. | 506 |
| Ashim | | See *Eshim*. | |
| Ashtaroth | ASh-ThRWTh | Arch-demon corresponding to Chesed (Mathers, Waite) or to Geburah (777); also Goetic demon by day of 2nd decanate of Capricorn. Duke commanding 40 legions. Appears as a "hurtful" angel riding an infernal, dragon-like beast and carrying a viper in his right hand. Powers: tells fortunes; teaches liberal sciences. | 1307 |
| Ashtoreth | OShThRTh | Astarte, a Phoenician goddess. | 1370 |
| Ashur | AShWR | Assyria. | 507 |
| Asimon | ASYMWN | Old coin; telephone token; an infernal being associated with the northwest. | 817 167 |
| Asmodai | ASMWDAY | Arch-demon corresponding to Geburah (Mathers, Waite) or to Netzach (777); also spelled Asmoday or Asmodeus; Goetic demon by day of 2nd decanate of Aquarius. (Crowley gives AshMDAY, 356, in his list of Princes to the Qlippoth and the above spelling elsewhere) King commanding 72 legions. Appears as a being with three heads: that of a bull, that of a man, and that of a ram; with a serpent's tail and webbed feet like a goose, shooting flames from his mouth, riding an infernal dragon, and carrying a lance with a banner. Powers: gives the Ring of Virtues; teaches arithmetic, astronomy, geometry, and handicrafts; answers demands truly and fully; makes one invincible; finds and guards hidden treasures. | 122 |
| Asmodel | ASMWDAL | Archangel of Taurus. | 142 |
| Asmodeus | | See *Asmodai*. | |
| Assiah | OShYH | The Material World, the fourth and most manifest of the four cabalistic worlds; associated with the final *He* of Tetragram- | 385 |

maton. The names of the heavenly spheres associated with the Sephiroth are also associated with Assiah, also called Olam ha-Assiah. Also spelled Asia, whence that continent derives its name. The secret name of Assiah is Ben.

The Heavenly Spheres of Assiah:

**Kether**      Rashith ha-Gilgalim (Primum Mobile)

**Chokmah**     Mazloth (Sphere of the Zodiac)

**Binah**       Shabbathai (Sphere of Saturn)

**Chesed**      Tzedek (Sphere of Jupiter)

**Geburah**     Madim (Sphere of Mars)

**Tiphareth**   Shemesh (Sphere of the Sun)

**Netzach**     Nogah (Sphere of Venus)

**Hod**         Kokab (Sphere of Mercury)

**Yesod**       Levanah (Sphere of the Moon)

**Malkuth**     Cholam Yesodoth or Olam Yesodoth (Sphere of the Elements).

| | | | |
|---|---|---|---|
| **Astaroth** | | See *Ashtaroth.* | |
| **Astarte** | | See *Ashtareth.* | |
| **At** | AT | Whisper (*n.*). | 10 |
| **Ateh Gibor** | AThH GBWR | "Thou art mighty forever, O Lord"; usu- | 1418 |
| **le-Olam** | LOWLM | ally abbreviated AGLA and used as a | 858 |
| **Adonai** | ADNY | name of God; see *Agla.* | |
| **Athiel** | OThYAL | "Uncertainty"; Qlippoth of Ain Soph Or. | 511 |
| **Athor** | OThWR | Lord of Triplicity by Day for Aquarius. | 676 |
| **Atik Yomin** | OThYK YWMYN | The Ancient of Days, a title of Kether. | 1746 1266 616 |
| **Atiqa** | OThYQA | The Ancient One, a title of Kether. | 581 |
| **Atiqa de- Atiqin** | OThYQA D- OThYQYN | The Ancient of the Ancient Ones, a title of Kether. | 1875 1225 |
| **Atiqa Qadisha** | OThYQA QDYShA | The Most Holy Ancient One, a title of Kether. | 996 |

**Atziluth**    ATzYLWTh   The Divine or Archetypal World, the first      537
and highest of the four cabalistic worlds;
associated with *Yod* of Tetragrammaton.
The divine names associated with the
Sephiroth are also associated with the
world of Atziluth. Also called Olam Atziluth. The secret name of Atziluth is Ab.
The Divine Names of Atziluth:

| | |
|---|---|
| **Kether** | Ehyeh |
| **Chokmah** | Yah |
| **Binah** | Yahweh Elohim |
| **Chesed** | El |
| **Geburah** | Elohim Gibor |
| **Tiphareth** | Yahweh Eloah wa-Daath |
| **Netzach** | Yahweh Tzabaoth |
| **Hod** | Elohim Tzabaoth |
| **Yesod** | Shaddai El Chai |
| **Malkuth** | Adonai ha-Eretz |

**Aub**                        See *Ab*.
**Aum**         AWM            30th name of Shem Hamphorash, asso-      607
ciated with 6th quinance of Sagittarius.      47
**Auphanim**                   See *Ophanim*.
**Auriel**                     See *Uriel*.
**Ausiul**                     See *Ansuel*.
**Av**          AB             The 11th Hebrew month, July-August,        3
corresponding roughly to the period
when the Sun is in Leo.
**Avamel**      AWMAL          Angel of 6th quinance of Sagittarius;     78
angel by night of the 10 of Wands; also
spelled Omael.
**Avith**       OWYTh          A city of Edom; the city of King Hadad.   486
**Avnas**       AWN            Goetic demon by night of 1st decanate of  707
Scorpio; also spelled Amy.                    57
President commanding 36 legions.
Appears as a flaming fire; later, a man.
Powers: teaches astrology and liberal sci-
ences; gives good familiars; bewrays
treasure kept by spirits.
**Avron**       AWRWN          Angel of 2nd decanate of Pisces.          913
                                                                          263

| Ay | AY | Where?; island. | 11 |
|----|----|-----------------|----|
| Ay | OY | A town near Bethel. | 80 |
| Aya | AYO | 67th name of Shem Hamphorash, associated with 1st quinance of Cancer. | 81 |
| Ayel | AYAL | Angel of 1st astrological house. | 42 |
| Ayeth | OYTh | The last three letters of the 42-letter name of God, associated with Malkuth. | 480 |
| Ayin | O | 16th letter of Hebrew alphabet; a voiced laryngal spirant, a guttural consonant pronounced with a slight movement of the uvula; transliterated as ' (in older writings, often transliterated as *a'a* or *gh*).<br>Spelled out, OYN, Eye (780 or 130).<br>Corresponds to Capricorn, the 26th Path (between Tiphareth and Hod), and the Tarot Trump XV. The Devil; for additional correspondences, see *Gedi*. | 70 |
| Ayish | OYSh | Ursa Major. | 380 |
| Ayoel | AYOAL | Angel of 1st quinance of Cancer; angel by day of the 2 of Cups; also spelled Eiael. | 112 |
| Az | AZ | Then. | 8 |
| Azael | OZAL | Demon Prince of Water. | 108 |
| Azazel | OZAZL | Demon Prince of Air. | 115 |

| Baal | BOL | Lord, owner; arch-demon corresponding to Netzach (Mathers). | 102 |
|------|-----|-------------------------------------------------------------|-----|
| Baal Chanan | | See *Baal-Hanan*. | |
| Baal-Hanan | | A King of Edom, associated with Yesod; son of Achbor; arch-demon corresponding to Netzach (Waite). | 860<br>210 |
| Baal-Hanan<br>　ben Achbor | BOL ChNN<br>BN OKBWR | Baal-Hanan, son of Achbor. | 1860<br>1210<br>560 |
| Ba'airiron | | See *Beiriron*. | |
| Babel | BBL | Babel. | 34 |

| | | | |
|---|---|---|---|
| **Bad** | BD | White linen. | 6 |
| **Badshechath** | BADShChTh | Francis Barrett's misprint for BARShChTh, Bar Shachath, q.v. | |
| **Bael** | BAL | Goetic demon by day of 1st decanate of Aries. | 33 |
| | | King commanding 66 legions; rules in the East. | |
| | | Appears sometimes as a cat, sometimes as a toad, sometimes as a man, sometimes in all these forms at once; speaks hoarsely. | |
| | | Powers: invisibility. | |
| **Bag** | BG | Food. | 5 |
| **Bahimiron** | BHY-MYRWN | The Bestial Ones, Qlippoth of Aquarius. | 973 323 |
| **Bal** | BL | Not. | 32 |
| **Balaam** | BLOM | See Numbers XXII. | 702 142 |
| **Balam** | BOLM | Goetic demon by night of 3rd decanate of Leo; also spelled Balaam. | 702 142 |
| | | King commanding 40 legions. | |
| | | Appears as a creature with three heads: that of a bull, that of a man, and that of a ram; with a serpent's tail and flaming eyes, riding a furious bear and carrying a goshawk on his fist; speaks hoarsely. | |
| | | Powers: fortunetelling; invisibility; making men witty. | |
| **Bamratztag** | BMRTzThG | The 19th through 24th letters of the 42-letter name of God, associated with Tiphareth. | 735 |
| **Bar** | BR | Corn, grain; son; chosen, pure, empty. | 202 |
| **Bar Shachath** | BARShChTh | Pit of Ruin; the fifth hell, corresponding to Geburah and to the Islamic *Sakar*, reserved for Gabars. | 911 |
| **Bara** | BRA | Created (the second word of Genesis). | 203 |
| **Barad** | BRD | Hail; the 7th of the 10 plagues of Egypt. | 206 |
| **Barak** | BRK | To kneel, bless. | 702 222 |
| **Barbatos** | BRBTWSh | Goetic demon by day of 2nd decanate of Gemini. | 519 |
| | | Duke commanding 30 legions. | |
| | | Appears when Sun is in Sagittarius with four noble kings and their companies of | |

great troops.

Powers: enables one to understand the speech of animals; breaks enchantment on hidden treasures; knows past and future; reconciles friends and those in power. Formerly of the Order of Virtues.

| | | | |
|---|---|---|---|
| **Barkiel** | BRKYAL | Archangel of Scorpio; also spelled Barchiel. | 263 |
| **Bartzabel** | BRTzBAL | Spirit of Mars. | 325 |
| **Baruk** | BRWK | Blessed. | 708 |
| | | | 228 |
| **Barzel** | BRZL | Iron, the metal of Mars. | 239 |
| **Bath** | BTh | Daughter. | 402 |
| **Bathin** | BAThYN | Goetic demon by day of 3rd decanate of Virgo. | 1113 |
| | | | 463 |

Duke commanding 30 legions.

Appears as a strong man with a serpent's tail, riding a pale horse.

Powers: knows virtues of herbs and precious stones; associated with teleportation.

| | | | |
|---|---|---|---|
| **Baz** | BZ | Booty; prey. | 9 |
| **Bedad** | BDD | Father of Hadad, a King of Edom. | 10 |
| **Bedil** | BDYL | Tin, the metal of Jupiter. | 46 |
| **Beelzebub** | BOLZBWB | Lord of the Flies; arch-demon corresponding to Chokmah. | 119 |
| **Behahemi** | BHHMY | Angel of 2nd decanate of Aries. | 62 |
| **Behemoth** | BHMWTh | The great land-monster of Hebrew mythology. | 453 |
| **Beir** | BOYR | Beast, cattle. | 282 |
| **Beiriron** | BOYRY-RWN | The Herd; Qlippoth of Aries. | 1198 |
| | | | 548 |
| **Beker** | BKR | Young male camel. | 222 |
| **Bel** | BL | Chief god of the Babylonians. | 32 |
| **Bela** | BLO | A King of Edom, associated with Daath; son of Beor; his city was Dinhabah. | 102 |
| **Bela ben Beor** | BLO BN BOWR | Bela, son of Beor. | 1082 |
| | | | 432 |
| **Beleth** | BLATh | Goetic demon by day of 1st decanate of Leo; also spelled Bileth or Bilet. | 433 |

King commanding 85 legions.

Appears as a mighty, terrible king riding a

| | | | |
|---|---|---|---|
| | | pale horse, trumpets and other instruments playing before him; furious upon first appearance.<br>Powers: procures love.<br>Formerly of the Order of Powers. | |
| **Belial** | BLYAL | "Without God"; an arch-demon, corresponding to Hod (777); Qlippoth of Ain Soph; Goetic demon by night of 2nd decanate of Aquarius; see also *Adam Belial*; also spelled Belia'al.<br>King commanding 50 legions.<br>Appears as two beautiful angels sitting in a chariot of fire; speaks with a comely voice.<br>Powers: distributes presentations and senatorships etc.; causes favor of friends and foes; gives excellent familiars.<br>Created next after Lucifer; a notorious liar. | 73 |
| **Belphegor** | BLPGWR | Arch-demon corresponding to Tiphareth. | 321 |
| **Ben** | BN | Son; a title of Tiphareth; the secret name of the World of Atziluth. | 702<br>52 |
| **Ben Ayish** | BN OYSh | Son of Ayish; i.e., Ursa Minor. | 1082<br>432 |
| **Beni Elohim** | BNY<br>ALHYM | Sons of God; Angelic Choir associated with Hod and with the Sphere of Mercury. | 708<br>148 |
| **Benjamin** | BNYMN | A tribe of Israel, associated with Sagittarius. | 802<br>152 |
| **Beor** | BOWR | Father of Bela, a King of Edom. | 278 |
| **Berakah** | BRKH | Blessing. | 227 |
| **Berek** | BRK | Knee, lap. | 702<br>222 |
| **Bereshith** | BRAShYTh | In the beginning; the first word of Genesis; the Beth is counted as 2000. | 2911 |
| **Berith** | BRYTh | Goetic demon by day of 1st decanate of Capricorn, also spelled Beale, Beal, Bofry, or Bolfry; covenant.<br>Duke commanding 26 legions.<br>Appears as a soldier with red clothing riding a red horse and wearing a gold crown; speaks clearly and subtly. | 612 |

|  |  | Powers: tells fortunes; transmutes any metal into gold; gives and confirms dignities. | |
|---|---|---|---|
| **Beth** | B | 2nd letter of Hebrew alphabet; transliterated as *b* or *v*. | 2 |
|  |  | Spelled out, BYTh, "house" (412). | |
|  |  | Corresponds to Mercury, the 12th Path (between Kether and Binah), and the Tarot Trump I. The Magician; for additional correspondences, see *Kokab*. | |
| **Bethchon** | BYThChWN | Lord of Triplicity by Day for Scorpio. | 1126 |
|  |  |  | 476 |
| **Bethel** | BYTh-AL | House of God. | 443 |
| **Bethon** | BYThWN | Angel of 3rd decanate of Gemini (Regardie gives BYThWR, 618). | 918 |
|  |  |  | 468 |
| **Bethor** | BYThWR | Olympic Planetary Spirit of Jupiter. | 618 |
| **Betulah** | BThWLH | Virgin; Virgo; The Virgin, a title of Malkuth. | 443 |
|  |  | Virgo corresponds to Yod and the 20th Path. | |
|  |  | Archangel: Hamaliel. | 116 |
|  |  | Angel: Shelathiel. | 771 |
|  |  | Lord of Triplicity by Day: Laslara. | 321 |
|  |  | Lord of Triplicity by Night: Sasia. | 131 |
|  |  | Angel Ruling 6th House: Veyel. | 47 |
|  |  | Angel of 1st Decanate: Ananaurah. | 313 |
|  |  | Angel of 1st Quinance: Akaiah. | 37 |
|  |  | Angel of 2nd Quinance: Kehethel. | 456 |
|  |  | Angel of 2nd Decanate: Rayadyah. | 230 |
|  |  | Angel of 3rd Quinance: Haziel. | 53 |
|  |  | Angel of 4th Quinance: Aldiah. | 50 |
|  |  | Angel of 3rd Decanate: Mishpar. | 620 |
|  |  | Angel of 5th Quinance: Laviah. | 52 |
|  |  | Angel of 6th Quinance: Hihayah. | 95 |
|  |  | Qlippoth: Tzaphiriron (The Scratchers). | |
|  |  | Goetic Demons by Day: | |
|  |  |    1st Decanate: Zepar. | 288 |
|  |  |    2nd Decanate: Botis. | 327 |
|  |  |    3rd Decanate: Bathin. | 1113 |
|  |  |  | 463 |
|  |  | Goetic Demons by Night: | |

|  |  |  |
|---|---|---|
| | 1st Decanate: Alloces (Alocas). | 537 |
| | | 57 |
| | 2nd Decanate: Camio (Caim). | 731 |
| | | 81 |
| | 3rd Decanate: Murmus (Murmur, Murmux). | 846 |
| | | 286 |

Color: Yellow-Green.

Scent: Narcissus.

Tarot Trump: IX. The Hermit.

Tarot Cards associated with Decanates:
  1st Decanate: 8 of Pentacles.
  2nd Decanate: 9 of Pentacles.
  3rd Decanate: 10 of Pentacles.

Direction: North, below.

Tribe of Israel: Naphtali.

Apostle: Andrew.

Geomantic Figure: Conjunctio.

Mystic Number of 20th Path: 210.

Ruling Planet: Mercury.

Planet Exalted in: Mercury.

Planet in Detriment in: Jupiter.

Planet in Fall in: Venus.

| | | | |
|---|---|---|---|
| **Bi** | BY | Please, pray. | 12 |
| **Bifrons** | BYPRW | Goetic demon by night of 1st decanate of Cancer; also spelled Bifröus, Bifrovs. Earl commanding 6 legions. Appears as a monster; assumes human form upon command. Powers: teaches astrology, geometry, and other arts and sciences; teaches the virtues of precious stones and woods; changes dead bodies from one place to another; lights seeming candles on graves. | 298 |
| **Bihelami** | BHLMY | Angel of 1st decanate of Pisces. | 87 |
| **Bilhah** | BLHH | Rachel's handmaiden; mother of Dan and Naphtali. | 42 |
| **Bimé** | BYM | Goetic demon by day of 2nd decanate of Sagittarius; also spelled Buné or Bim. Duke commanding 30 legions. Appears as a dragon with three heads; that of a dog, that of a griffin, and that of | 612 |
| | | | 52 |

a man; speaks with a high and comely voice.

Powers: changes the place of the dead; causes the spirits under him "to gather together upon your Sepulchres"; brings wealth, wisdom, and eloquence; gives true answers to demands.

| | | | |
|---|---|---|---|
| **Binah** | BYNH | Understanding; the 3rd Sephira. | 67 |

Divine Name: Yahweh Elohim.

Archangel: Tzaphqiel.

Choir of Angels: Aralim; Thrones.

Material World: Shabbathai, the Sphere of Saturn.

Associated with the first He of Tetragrammaton.

Additional titles are Ama, The Mother; Aima, The Supernal Mother; and Korsia, The Throne.

| | | | |
|---|---|---|---|
| **Boaz** | BOZ | One of the pillars in the Temple of Solomon, the other being Jachin; Boaz is the black pillar, on the right, corresponding to the female or Yin principle. | 79 |
| **Bohu** | BHW | Waste ("void"—Gen. I:2). | 13 |
| **Boqer** | BQR | Morning. | 302 |
| **Bor** | BR | Purity, innocence. | 202 |
| **Botis** | BWTYSh | Goetic demon by day of 2nd decanate of Virgo. | 327 |

President and Earl commanding 60 legions. Appears as an ugly viper; upon command, assumes human form, but with great teeth and two horns, carrying a bright, sharp sword.

Powers: tells fortunes; reconciles.

| | | | |
|---|---|---|---|
| **Botz** | BTz | Mud. | 902 |
| | | | 92 |
| **Bozrah** | BTzRH | A city of Edom; the city of King Jobab. | 297 |
| **Briah** | BRYAH | Creation; the Archangelic or Creative World, the second of four cabalistic worlds; associated with the first He of Tetragrammaton. The archangelic names associated with the Sephiroth are also as- | 218 |

sociated with the world of Briah, also called Olam ha-Briah. The secret name of Briah is Seg.

**The Archangels of Briah:**

| | |
|---|---|
| **Kether** | Metatron |
| **Chokmah** | Raziel |
| **Binah** | Tzaphqiel |
| **Chesed** | Tzadqiel |
| **Geburah** | Kamael |
| **Tiphareth** | Raphael |
| **Netzach** | Haniel |
| **Hod** | Michael |
| **Yesod** | Gabriel |
| **Malkuth** | Sandalphon |

**Buer**   BWAR   Goetic demon by day of 1st decanate of   209
Cancer.
President commanding 50 legions.
Appears as a centaur, when the Sun is in Sagittarius.
Powers: teaches moral and natural philosophy, the art of logic, and the virtues of all herbs and plants; heals all human distempers; gives good familiars.
(For an account of the evocation of this demon, see *The Eye in the Triangle* by Israel Regardie, Llewellyn Publications, 1970, pp. 199-200.)

# C

**Cabala**   QBLH   Tradition.   137
Cabala is spelled any number of ways: beginning with c, k, or q; with and without the b doubled; with and without the l doubled; and with and without a final h.

Crowley used *Qabalah*, the correct transliteration of the Hebrew. Mathers and
Waite used *Kabbalah*. C. C. Zain used
*Kabala*. I have used the Merriam-Webster
spelling.

| | | | |
|---|---|---|---|
| **Cael** | | See *Kael.* | |
| **Cahethel** | | See *Kehethel.* | |
| **Cain (Qayin)** | QYN | Son of Adam, slayer of Abel; by some ac- | 810 |
| | | counts, the son of Eve and the Serpent. | 160 |
| **Cainan** | QYNN | Son of Enos and father of Mahalaleel; | 860 |
| | | great-grandson of Adam; lived 910 years | 210 |
| | | (325-1235 after Creation); spelled Kenan | |
| | | in R.S.V. | |
| **Caliel** | | See *Kaliel.* | |
| **Camael** | | See *Kamael.* | |
| **Cambriel** | | See *Kambriel.* | |
| **Camio** | KAYN | Goetic demon by night of 2nd decanate | 731 |
| | | of Virgo; also spelled Caim. | 81 |
| | | President commanding 30 legions. | |
| | | Appears at first as a thrush, later as a man | |
| | | carrying a sharp sword; seems to answer | |
| | | in burning ashes or coals. | |
| | | Powers: debates; gives understanding of | |
| | | the speech of birds, bulls, dogs, and other | |
| | | animals and of the voice of the waters; | |
| | | foretells the future. | |
| | | Formerly of the Order of Angels. | |
| **Canaan** | KNON | Canaan. | 840 |
| | | | 190 |
| **Cassiel** | KSYAL | Angel ruling Saturn and Saturday. | 121 |
| **Casujoiah** | | See *Kashenyayah.* | |
| **Cha'amiah** | | See *Chamiah.* | |
| **Chabuyah** | ChBWYH | Angel of 2nd quinance of Cancer; angel | 31 |
| | | by night of the 2 of Cups; also spelled | |
| | | Chabooyah or Habuiah. | |
| **Chach** | ChCh | Hook, brooch, ring. | 16 |
| **Chad** | ChD | Sharp. | 12 |
| **Chag** | ChG | Feast. | 11 |
| **Chahaviah** | ChHWYH | Angel of 6th quinance of Scorpio; angel | 34 |
| | | by night of the 7 of Cups; also spelled | |
| | | Hahuiah. | |

| | | | |
|---|---|---|---|
| **Chaho** | ChHW | 24th name of Shem Hamphorash, associated with 6th quinance of Scorpio. | 19 |
| **Chai** | ChY | Living. | 18 |
| **Chaigidel** | | See *Ogiel.* | |
| **Chaigidiel** | | See *Ogiel.* | |
| **Chalav** | ChLB | Milk. | 40 |
| **Cham** | ChM | Father-in-law; warm, hot; warmth, heat. | 608 |
| | | | 48 |
| **Cham** | ChOM | 38th name of Shem Hamphorash; associated with 2nd quinance of Aquarius. | 678 |
| | | | 118 |
| **Chamiah** | ChOMYH | Angel of 2nd quinance of Aquarius; angel by night of the 5 of Swords; also spelled Cha'amiah or Haamiah. | 133 |
| **Chamishah** | ChMShH | Five. | 353 |
| **Chamishah-Asar** | ChMShH-OShR | Fifteen. | 923 |
| **Chamishim** | ChMShYM | Fifty. | 958 |
| | | | 398 |
| **Chapap** | ChPP | To cover, protect. | 888 |
| | | | 168 |
| **Chaph** | ChP | Pure, innocent. | 808 |
| | | | 88 |
| **Charabhah** | ChRBH | Parched land; one of the seven earths, corresponding to Geburah. | 215 |
| **Charavoth** | ChRBWTh | Swords. | 616 |
| **Chartom** | ChRTM | Magician. | 817 |
| | | | 257 |
| **Chashmalim** | ChShMLYM | Brilliant Ones (Ez. IV:4); Angelic Choir associated with Chesed and with the Sphere of Jupiter. | 988 |
| | | | 428 |
| **Chashmodai** | ChShMW-DAY | Spirit of the Moon. | 369 |
| **Chassan** | ChShN | Angel of Air. | 1008 |
| | | | 358 |
| **Chath** | ChTh | Broken; terrified. | 408 |
| **Chavakiah** | | See *Keveqiah.* | |
| **Chavvah** | ChWH | Eve (King James spelling); also spelled Havvah. | 19 |
| **Chayim** | ChYYM | Life. | 628 |
| | | | 68 |

| | | | |
|---|---|---|---|
| **Chayoth** | ChYWTh | Living Creatures (Ez. I). | 424 |
| **Chayoth ha-Qadesh** | ChYWTh HQDSh | Holy Living Creatures (Ez. I); Angelic Choir associated with Kether and with the Primum Mobile. | 833 |
| **Chebo** | ChBW | 68th name of Shem Hamphorash, associated with 2nd quinance of Cancer. | 16 |
| **Chedeqiel** | ChDQYAL | Angel of Libra. | 153 |
| **Chek** | ChK | Palate. | 508 |
| | | | 28 |
| **Chel** | ChL | Bulwark, wall, rampart. | 38 |
| **Cheled** | ChLD | World; one of the seven earths; with Tebhel, corresponds to Yesod and Malkuth; our own Earth. | 42 |
| **Chen** | ChN | Grace, charm; often cited as an acronym of Chokmah Nisetar, Secret Wisdom. | 708 |
| | | | 58 |
| **Cherev** | ChRB | Sword. | 210 |
| **Cherubim** | | See *Kerubim.* | |
| **Chesed** | ChSD | Mercy, love; the 4th Sephira. Divine Name: El. Archangel: Tzadqiel. Choir of Angels: Chashmalim; Dominations. Material World: Tzedek, the Sphere of Jupiter. An additional title is *Gedulah*, "greatness" or "magnificence." | 72 |
| **Cheshvan** | ChShWN | The 2nd Hebrew month, October-November, corresponding roughly to the period when the Sun is in Scorpio. | 1014 |
| | | | 364 |
| **Cheth** | Ch | 8th letter of Hebrew alphabet, transliterated as Ch or Ḥ; sometimes spelled Heth. Spelled out, ChYTh, "fence" or "enclosure" (418). Corresponds to Cancer, the 18th Path (between Binah and Geburah), and the Tarot Trump VII. The Chariot; for additional correspondences, see *Sarton.* | 8 |
| **Chetz** | ChTz | Arrow; lightning; punishment; wound. | 908 |
| | | | 98 |
| **Chevrah** | ChBRH | Society, association. | 215 |

| | | | |
|---|---|---|---|
| **Chevrah** | ChRBH | Society of the Shining Light of Dawn; the | 939 |
| **Zerach** | ZRCh | official Hebrew name of the Hermetic Or- | |
| **Boqer Or** | BQR AWR | der of the Golden Dawn. | |

Regardie quotes Mathers' transliteration as "Chabrath Zereh Bokher Aour"; however, ChBRTh means "junction" or "joining," whereas ChRBH is the proper word for "society"; similarly, ZRH means "to scatter."

Francis King quotes a somewhat butchered version: "Chalbrath or Cheurah Lereh sour bokher."

| | | | |
|---|---|---|---|
| **Chiah** | ChYH | Part of the soul referred to Chokmah. | 23 |
| **Chioa** | ChYWA | The Beast, the union or offspring of Samael, Prince of Demons, and Isheth Zenunim, Demon of Prostitution; the arch-demon corresponding to Tiphareth (777). | 25 |
| **Chob** | ChB | Bosom. | 10 |
| **Chodesh** | ChDSh | Month. | 312 |

The months of the Hebrew calendar are:

| | | |
|---|---|---|
| **1. Tishri** | Sept.-Oct. | Libra |
| **2. Cheshvan** | Oct.-Nov. | Scorpio |
| **3. Kislev** | Nov.-Dec. | Sagittarius |
| **4. Tevet** | Dec.-Jan. | Capricorn |
| **5. Shevet** | Jan.-Feb. | Aquarius |
| **6. Adar** | Feb.-Mar. | Pisces |
| **— Veadar** | Mar. | Intercalary month |
| **7. Nisan** | Mar.-Apr. | Aries |
| **8. Iyar** | Apr.-May | Taurus |
| **9. Sivan** | May-June | Gemini |
| **10. Tammuz** | June-July | Cancer |
| **11. Av** | July-Aug. | Leo |
| **12. Elul** | Aug.-Sept. | Virgo |

| | | | |
|---|---|---|---|
| **Chokmah** | ChKMH | Wisdom; the 2nd Sephira. | 73 |

Divine Name: Yah.
Archangel: Raziel.
Choir of Angels: Ophanim; Cherubim.
Material World: Mazloth, the Sphere of

the Zodiac.
Associated with the Yod of Tetragrammaton.
Additional titles are Ab, The Father; Abba, The Supernal Father; and Kochmah, Power of Yetzirah.

| | | | |
|---|---|---|---|
| **Chokmah** | ChKMH | Secret Wisdom. | 788 |
| **Nisetarah** | NSThRH | | |
| **Chol** | ChL | Profane, unholy. | 38 |
| **Cholam** | ChLM | The Breaker of Foundations; The Sphere | 1124 |
| **Yesodoth** | YSWDWTh | of the Elements; the part of the material | 564 |
| | | world corresponding to Malkuth; the "restored" spelling is Olam Yesodoth, the World of Foundations (Regardie). | |
| **Choq** | ChQ | Statute; share; task; boundary. | 108 |
| **Chor** | ChR | Hole. | 208 |
| **Choreph** | ChRP | Winter. | 1008 |
| | | | 288 |
| **Choshek** | ChShK | Darkness; the 9th of the 10 plagues of | 808 |
| | | Egypt. | 328 |
| **Choshen** | ChShN | Breastplate of the High Priest. | 1008 |
| | | | 358 |
| **Corson** | | See *Korson.* | |
| **Crocell** | KRWKL | Goetic demon by night of 1st decanate of | 276 |
| | | Leo; also spelled Crokel. | |
| | | Duke commanding 48 legions. | |
| | | Appears as an angel. | |
| | | Powers: teaches geometry and liberal sciences; makes noises like rushing water; warms water; finds baths. | |
| | | Formerly of the Order of Potestates or Powers. | |
| **Cush** | KWSh | A Biblical land. | 326 |

| | | | |
|---|---|---|---|
| **Daath** | DOTh | Knowledge; a non-Sephira located in the | 474 |
| | | Abyss below Chokmah and Binah but | |

|            |              | above Chesed and Geburah.                                         |      |
|------------|--------------|------------------------------------------------------------------|------|
| **Dadh**   | DD           | Breast.                                                          | 8    |
| **Dag**    | DG           | Fish.                                                            | 7    |
| **Dagdagiron** | DGDG-YRWN | The Fishy Ones; Qlippoth of Capricorn.                           | 930  |
|            |              |                                                                  | 280  |
| **Dagim**  | DGYM         | Fishes; Pisces.                                                  | 617  |

Corresponds to Qoph and the 29th Path. 57
Archangel: Amnitziel. 232
Angel: Vakabiel. 69
Lord of Triplicity by Day: Ramara. 441
Lord of Triplicity by Night: Nathdorinel. 751
Angel Ruling 12th House: Pasiel. 421
Angel of 1st Decanate: Bihelami. 87
Angel of 1st Quinance: Vavaliah. 73
Angel of 2nd Quinance: Yelahiah. 60
Angel of 2nd Decanate: Avron. 913
263

Angel of 3rd Quinance: Saliah. 106
Angel of 4th Quinance: Ariel. 311
Angel of 3rd Decanate: Satrip. 1079
359

Angel of 5th Quinance: Asaliah. 415
Angel of 6th Quinance: Mihael. 86
Qlippoth: Nashimiron (Malignant Wom- 1316
  en) (from *Nashim*, "women," "wives"). 666
Goetic Demons by Day:
  1st Decanate: Furfur. 572
  2nd Decanate: Marchosias. 554
  3rd Decanate: Stolas (Stolos). 651
Goetic Demons by Night:
  1st Decanate: Seere (Sear, Seir). 501
  2nd Decanate: Dantalian. 94
  3rd Decanate: Andromalius. 332
Color: Crimson (Red-Violet).
Scent: Ambergris.
Tarot Trump: XVIII. The Moon.
Tarot Cards associated with Decanates:
  1st Decanate: 8 of Cups.
  2nd Decanate: 9 of Cups.
  3rd Decanate: 10 of Cups.
Direction: South, below.

Tribe of Israel: Simeon.
Apostle: James, son of Alphaeus.
Geomantic Figure: Laetitia.
Mystic Number of 29th Path: 435.
Ruling Planet: Jupiter.
Planet Exalted in: Venus.
Planet in Detriment in: Mercury.
Planet in Fall in: Mercury.

| | | | |
|---|---|---|---|
| **Dagon** | DGWN | Philistine fish god. | 713 |
| | | | 63 |
| **Dak** | DK | Oppressed. | 504 |
| | | | 24 |
| **Dal** | DL | Wretched. | 34 |
| **Daleth** | D | 4th letter of Hebrew alphabet; transliterated as *d* or *dh*. | 4 |

Spelled out, DLTh, "door," 434.
Corresponds to Venus, the 14th Path (between Chokmah and Binah), and the Tarot Trump III. The Empress; for additional correspondences, see *Nogah*.

| | | | |
|---|---|---|---|
| **Dam** | DM | Blood; the 1st of the 10 plagues of Egypt. | 604 |
| | | | 44 |
| **Damabiah** | DMBYH | Angel of 5th quinance of Gemini; angel by day of the 10 of Swords; also spelled Dambayah. | 61 |
| **Dameb** | DMB | 65th name of Shem Hamphorash, associated with 5th quinance of Gemini. | 46 |
| **Damesq** | DMShQ | Damascus. | 444 |
| **Dan** | DN | A tribe of Israel, associated with Scorpio. | 704 |
| | | | 54 |
| **Daniel** | DNYAL | Angel of 2nd quinance of Aries; angel by night of the 2 of Wands; also spelled Deneyal. | 95 |
| **Dani** | DNY | 50th name of Shem Hamphorash, associated with 2nd quinance of Aries. | 64 |
| **Dantalion** | DNTAL | Goetic demon by night of 2nd decanate of Pisces. | 94 |

Duke commanding 36 legions.
Appears as a man with many faces, both men's and women's, with a book in his right hand.

Powers: teaches arts and sciences; reads and controls minds; procures love; shows images of anyone by vision regardless of their whereabouts.

| | | | |
|---|---|---|---|
| **Daq** | DQ | Crushed, fine, thin. | 104 |
| **Dar** | DR | Pearl. | 204 |
| **Darom** | DRWM | South; see also *Esh*. | 810 |
| | | | 250 |
| **Dath** | DTh | Royal command, law. | 404 |
| **Davar** | DBR | Word, thing. | 206 |
| **David** | DWD | King of Israel. | 14 |
| **Day** | DY | Sufficiency, plenty. | 14 |
| **Dea** | DO | Knowledge, wisdom. | 74 |
| **Decarabia** | DKAWRAB | Goetic demon by night of 3rd decanate | 234 |

of Aquarius.

Marquis commanding 30 legions.

Appears as a star in a pentacle; assumes the form of a man upon command.

Powers: discovers the virtues of birds and precious stones; brings visions of various birds, singing and drinking as do natural birds.

| | | | |
|---|---|---|---|
| **Deli** | DLY | Bucket; Aquarius. | 44 |

Corresponds to Sadhe (or He) and the 28th (or 15th) Path.

| | |
|---|---|
| Archangel: Kambriel. | 304 |
| Angel: Tzakmiqiel. | 291 |
| Lord of Triplicity by Day: Athor. | 676 |
| Lord of Triplicity by Night: Polayan. | 821 |
| | 171 |
| Angel Ruling 11th House: Ansuel. | 148 |
| Angel of 1st Decanate: Saspam. | 800 |
| | 240 |
| Angel of 1st Quinance: Aniel. | 92 |
| Angel of 2nd Quinance: Chamiah. | 133 |
| Angel of 2nd Decanate: Abdaron. | 913 |
| | 263 |
| Angel of 3rd Quinance: Rehael. | 306 |
| Angel of 4th Quinance: Yeyazel. | 58 |
| Angel of 3rd Decanate: Gerodiel. | 254 |
| Angel of 5th Quinance: Hahahel. | 46 |

Angel of 6th Quinance: Michael.                             101
Qlippoth: Bahimiron (The Bestial Ones).          973
                                                                           323
Goetic Demons by Day:
    1st Decanate: Foras.                            587
    2nd Decanate: Asmoday (Asmodai).    122
    3rd Decanate: Gäap.                              873
                                                                           153
Goetic Demons by Night:
    1st Decanate: Amdukias (Amdusias).  551
                                                                            71
    2nd Decanate: Belial.                             73
    3rd Decanate: Decarabia.                       234
Color: Violet.
Scent: Galbanum.
Tarot Trump: XVII. The Star.
Tarot Cards associated with Decanates:
    1st Decanate: 5 of Swords.
    2nd Decanate: 6 of Swords.
    3rd Decanate: 7 of Swords.
Direction: South, above.
Tribe of Israel: Reuben.
Apostle: Matthew.
Geomantic Figure: Tristitia.
Mystic Number of 28th Path: 406.
Ruling Planet: Saturn.
Planet Exalted in: Neptune.
Planet in Detriment in: Sun.
Planet in Fall in: Uranus.

| | | | |
|---|---|---|---|
| **Demamiah** | DMMH | Silence, whisper. | 89 |
| **Deneyal** | | See *Daniel.* | |
| **Detzak Adh-** | DTzK ODSh | The 10 plagues of Egypt (taking the first | 981 |
| **ash Beachav** | BAChB | letter of each); see also *Negep.* | 501 |
| **Dever** | DBR | Murrain; the 5th of the 10 plagues of | 206 |
| | | Egypt. | |
| **Din** | DYN | Justice; a title of Geburah. | 714 |
| | | | 64 |
| **Dinhabah** | DNHBH | A city of Edom; city of King Bela. | 66 |
| **Dob** | DB | Bear. | 7 |
| **Domem** | DWMM | Silent. | 650 |
| | | | 90 |

| Dumiah | DWMYH | Silence, quietness. | 65 |

| Eber | OBR | Son of Salah and father of Peleg; great-grandson of Shem; lived 464 years (1723-2187 after Creation). | 272 |
| Echad | AChD | One, unity; also spelled Achad. | 13 |
| Echad Rosh Achdotho Rosh Ichudo Temurahzo Echad | AChD RASh AChDW-ThW RASh YChWDW ThMWRH-ZW AChD | One is his beginning, one is his individuality, his permutation is one; usually abbreviated ARARITA and used as a name of God. | 2151 |
| Ed | OD | Witness, proof; ruler. | 74 |
| Eden | ODN | Eden. | 774 124 |
| Edeth | ODTh | Testimony. | 474 |
| Edh | AD | Vapor, mist. | 5 |
| Edom | ADWM | The Kings and Dukes of Edom (Gen. XXXVI:31-43), of the line of Esau, who sold his birthright, "symbolize unlawful and chaotic forces" and are associated with the Sephira as follows: | 611 51 |

| Sephira | King | Duke |
| --- | --- | --- |
| Daath | Bela | ⎧ Timnah<br>⎨ Alvah<br>⎩ Jetheth |
| Chesed | Jobab | Aholibamah |
| Geburah | Husham | Elah |
| Tiphareth | Hadad | Pinon |
| Netzach | Samlah | Kenaz |
| Hod | Saul | Teman |
| Yesod | Baal-hanan | Mibzar and Magdiel |
| Malkuth | Hadar | Eram |

Cities are given for most of the kings, and some of their fathers are named:

| King | Father | City |
|------|--------|------|
| **Bela** | Beor | Dinhabah |
| **Jobab** | Zerah | Bozrah |
| **Husham** | — | Temani |
| **Hadad** | Bedad | Avith |
| **Samlah** | — | Masrekah |
| **Saul** | — | Rehoboth |
| **Baal-Hanan** | Achbor | — |
| **Hadar** | — | Pau |

Hadar's wife was Mehetabel, daughter of Matred, daughter of Mezahab.

| | | | |
|---|---|---|---|
| **Ehyeh** | AHYH | "I AM" (Ex. XIII:14); divine name associated with Kether; often spelled Eheieh (the middle *e* is a schwa). | 21 |

In the Lesser Ritual of the Pentagram, this name is vibrated to the West and is associated with Water. In the Greater Ritual of the Pentagram, it is vibrated with the Active Pentagram of Spirit (the active elements being Fire and Air) to the East and South and is thus associated with the active elements.

| | | | |
|---|---|---|---|
| **Ehyeh Asher Ehyeh** | AHYH AShR AHYH | Existence of Existences; "I AM WHAT AM" (Ex. XIII:14); a title of Kether. | 543 |
| **Eiael** | | See *Ayoel.* | |
| **El** | AL | Divine name associated with Chesed. | 31 |

In the Greater Ritual of the Pentagram, this name is vibrated to the West and is thus associated with Water.

| | | | |
|---|---|---|---|
| **Elad** | ALD | 10th name of Shem Hamphorash, associated with 4th quinance of Virgo. | 35 |
| **Elah** | ALH | Goddess; a Duke of Edom, associated with Geburah. | 36 |
| **Elemiah** | OLMYH | Angel of 4th quinance of Leo: angel by night of the 6 of Wands; also spelled Olmiah. | 155 |

| | | | |
|---|---|---|---|
| **Elep** | ALP | Thousand. | 831 |
| | | | 111 |
| **Eligos** | ALYGWSh | Goetic demon by day of 3rd decanate of Leo. | 350 |
| | | Duke commanding 60 legions. | |
| | | Appears as a goodly knight carrying a lance, an ensign, and a serpent. | |
| | | Powers: discovers hidden things; foretells the future, especially as regards war; causes the love of lords and great persons. | |
| **Elil** | ALYL | God. | 71 |
| **Elilah** | ALYLH | Goddess. | 76 |
| **Eloah** | ALH | God. | 36 |
| **Eloah** | ALWH | God. | 42 |
| **Elohi** | ALHY | The God of Abraham. | 854 |
| **Abraham** | ABRHM | | 294 |
| **Elohi** | ALHY | The God of Abraham, the God of Isaac, | 1342 |
| **Abraham** | ABRHM | and the God of Jacob. | 782 |
| **Elohi Itz-** | ALHY | | |
| **chaq we-** | YTzChQ | | |
| **Elohi Yaaqob** | WALHY | | |
| | YOQB | | |
| **Elohi ha-** | ALHY | God of the Hebrews. | 933 |
| **Ibrim** | HOBRYM | | 373 |
| **Elohi Itzchaq** | ALHY | The God of Isaac. | 254 |
| | YTzChQ | | |
| **Elohim** | ALHYM | A name of God; a masculine plural of a feminine noun, signifying the androgynous character of God; used in combination in such names as Yahweh Elohim, Elohim Gibor, and Elohim Tzabaoth. Usually enumerated with the final M as 40 (i.e., as 86); the Angelic Choir associated with Netzach and the Sphere of Venus. | 646 |
| | | | 86 |
| | | In the Greater Ritual of the Pentagram, this name is vibrated to the South and is thus associated with Fire. | |
| **Elohim Gibor** | ALHYM | Almighty God; divine name associated | 857 |
| | GBWR | with Geburah. | 297 |
| **Elohim** | ALHYM | God of Hosts; divine name associated | 1145 |
| **Tzabaoth** | TzBAWTh | with Hod, with Water, and with the West. | 585 |

| | | | |
|---|---|---|---|
| **Elohi Yaaqob** | ALHY YOQB | The God of Jacob. | 228 |
| **El Shaddai** | AL ShDY | God Almighty. | 345 |
| **Elul** | ALWL | The 12th Hebrew month, August-September, corresponding roughly to the period when the Sun is in Virgo. | 67 |
| **Elyon** | OLYWN | The Most High; a title of Kether. | 816 166 |
| **Em** | AM | Mother. | 601 41 |
| **Enoch (Chanok)** | ChNWK | 1. Son of Cain and father of Irad; 2. Son of Jared and father of Methuselah; great-grandfather of Noah; "And Enoch walked with God: and he was not, for God took him." (Gen. V:24); lived 365 years (622-987 after Creation). | 564 84 |
| **Enos (Enosh)** | ANWSh | Son of Seth and father of Cainan (Kenan); lived 905 years (235-1140 after Creation). | 357 |
| **Ephod** | APWD | Part of the paraphernalia of the high priest (Ex. XXVIII). | 91 |
| **Ephraim** | APRAYM | A tribe of Israel, associated with Taurus. | 892 332 |
| **Eram** | OYRM | A Duke of Edom, associated with Malkuth. | 880 320 |
| **Ereb** | ORB | Evening. | 272 |
| **Erech** | ARK | Uruk, a city of ancient Mesopotamia (now Warka). | 701 221 |
| **Eretz** | ARTz | Earth, one of the four elements; one of the seven earths, corresponding to the three Supernal Sephiroth. | 1101 291 |

Cardinal Point: North (Tzaphon).

Tetramorph: Ox.

Evangelist: Luke.

Color: Black; Green; or Citrine, Olive, Russet, and Black.

Properties: Cold and Dry.

Elementals: Gnomes.

Letter of Tetragrammaton: He final.

Cabalistic World: Assiah.

Archangel: Uriel.

Angel: Phorlakh.

Ruler: Kerub.

King: Ghob.

Supreme Elemental King (Enochian): THAHAAOTAHE.

Demon Prince: Mahazael.

Demon King: Amaimon.

Demon King (Goetia): Zimimay.

River of Eden: Phrath (Euphrates).

Infernal River: Acheron.

Tarot Suit: Pentacles (also called Coins, Money, or Disks).

Tarot Court Cards: Pages (also called Knaves or Princesses).

Enochian Word: NANTA.

Enochian Divine Names: MOR DIAL HCTGA.

Tattwa: Prithivi (Yellow Square).

Scent: Storax.

Humor: Melancholy.

Jungian Function: Sensation.

Chinese System: Center, Yellow, Man.

In cabalism, there are seven earths, just as there are seven heavens and seven hells. Different sources give them differently:

| Sephira | Midrash Konen | Crowley (777) |
|---|---|---|
| Supernals | Eretz (Earth) | Eretz (Earth) |
| Chesed | Adamah (Earth) | Adamah (Earth) |
| Geburah | Charabhah (Parched Land) | Gaye (Valley) |
| Tiphareth | Tziah (Dryness) | Neshiah (Oblivion) |
| Netzach | Yabbashah (Dry Land) | Tziah (Dryness) |
| Hod | Arqa (Earth) | Arqa (Earth) |
| Yesod and Malkuth | Tebhel (World) and Cheled (World) | Tebhel (World) Cheled (World) |

Crowley (777) calls these the "Ten Earths in Seven Palaces." His source may be the *Zohar Hadash*.

Cheled is our own earth. Arqa contains the seven hells. The other five (or six) are inhabited by men or beings who do not have Adam as their ancestor.

**Eri**      ORY      46th name of Shem Hemphorash, associ-    280
ated with 4th quinance of Pisces.

**Esau**      OShW      The son of Isaac who sold his birthright    376
to his brother Jacob; see also *Edom*.

**Esh**      ASh      Fire, one of the four elements, associ-    301
ated with Shin and the 31st Path.

Cardinal Point: South (Darom).

Tetramorph: Lion.

Evangelist: Mark.

Color: Red.

Properties: Hot and Dry.

Elementals: Salamanders.

Letter of Tetragrammaton: Yod.

Cabalistic World: Atziluth.

Archangel: Michael.

Angel: Aral.

Ruler: Seraph.

King: Djin.

Supreme Elemental King (Enochian): OHOOOHATAN.

Demon Prince: Samael.

Demon King: Paimon.

Demon King (Goetia): Göap.

River of Eden: Pison.

Infernal River: Phlegethon.

Tarot Trump: XX. Judgment.

Tarot Suit: Wands.

Tarot Court Cards: Knights.

Enochian Word: BITOM.

Enochian Divine Names: OIP TEAA PDOCE.

Tattwa: Tejas (Red Triangle).

Scent: Frankincense.

Humor: Choler.

|  |  | Jungian Function: Feeling. |  |
| --- | --- | --- | --- |
|  |  | Chinese System: South, Red, Bird. |  |
| **Eshim** | AShYM | Flames; Angelic Choir associated with Malkuth. | 911 |
| **Esrim** | OShRYM | Twenty. | 1180 |
|  |  |  | 620 |
| **Esrim we-** | OShRYM | Twenty-one. | 1199 |
| **Echad** | WAChD |  | 639 |
| **Esrim u-** | OShRYM | Twenty-two. | 2146 |
| **Shenaim** | WShNYM |  | 1586 |
|  |  |  | 1026 |
| **Et** | OT | Writing instrument. | 79 |
| **Eth** | ATh | Word used in Hebrew to indicate a direct object; no English equivalent; used by the Golden Dawn adepts to mean "essence" and to designate the fifth element, Spirit; attributions for the element Spirit include the center of the four cardinal points, the color white, and the Tattwa symbol Akasa (black egg). | 401 |
| **Eth** | OTh | Time, season. | 470 |
| **Etz** | OTz | Tree. | 970 |
|  |  |  | 160 |
| **Etz ha-** | OTz | Tree of Life. | 1603 |
| **Chayim** | HChYYM |  | 793 |
|  |  |  | 233 |
| **Etz ha-** | OTz | Tree of Knowledge. | 1449 |
| **Daath** | HDOTh |  | 639 |
| **Etz ha-** | OTz | Tree of the Knowledge of Good and Evil. | 1742 |
| **Daath Tob** | HDOTh |  | 932 |
| **wa-Ra** | TWB WRO |  |  |
| **Etzem** | OTzM | Bone, substance, essence, body. | 760 |
|  |  |  | 200 |
| **Euphrates** |  | See *Phrath*. |  |
| **Eve** |  | See *Chavvah*. |  |
| **Ey** | AY | Where. | 11 |
| **Ez** | OZ | Goat. | 77 |
| **Ezah** | OZA | A giant. | 78 |
| **Ezal** | OZAL | A giant. | 108 |

| | | | |
|---|---|---|---|
| **Focalor** | PWKLWR | Goetic demon by night of 2nd decanate of Taurus; also spelled Forcalor or Furcalor. | 342 |

Duke commanding 30 legions.

Appears as a man with griffin's wings.

Powers: kills and drowns men; overthrows warships; has power over wind and seas; restrains himself if commanded by exorcist.

Hopes to return to the 7th throne after 1000 years.

**Foras**  PWRASh  Goetic demon by day of 1st decanate of Aquarius.  587

President commanding 29 legions.

Appears as a strong man.

Powers: teaches virtues of herbs and precious stones, logic, and ethics; makes men invisible, long-lived, and eloquent; discovers treasures; recovers lost objects.

**Forneus**  PWRNASh  Goetic demon by day of 3rd decanate of Capricorn.  637

Marquis commanding 29 legions.

Appears as a great sea-monster.

Powers: teaches rhetoric; causes men to have a good name; understands languages; makes one beloved by foes and friends.

**Furcas**  PWRK  Goetic demon by night of 2nd decanate of Leo.  786 / 306

Knight commanding 20 legions.

Appears as a cruel old man with a long beard and a hoary head, riding a pale horse and carrying a sharp weapon.

Powers: teaches philosophy, astrology, rhetoric, logic, cheiro- and pyromancy.

(Crowley, 777, gives the Hebrew spelling as PWK, but this is no doubt either a misprint or a joke. In *Sephir Sephiroth*, he unaccountably gives PWD, 90.)

**Furfur**      PWRPWR      Goetic demon by day of 1st decanate of      572
Pisces.
Earl commanding 26 legions.
Appears as a hart with a fiery tail; assumes the form of an angel once compelled within a triangle; speaks hoarsely.
Powers: procures love; raises storms; answers truly concerning divine and secret matters.
A recalcitrant fellow, Furfur will not speak at all unless asked to do so; when he does, he tends to lie consistently "unless compelled or brought up within a triangle."

**Gäap**      GOP      Goetic demon by day of 3rd decanate of      873
Aquarius.      153
President and Prince commanding 66 legions.
Appears as a human being guiding four mighty kings.
Powers: makes men insensible or stupid; teaches philosophy and liberal sciences; causes love or hatred; teaches how to consecrate things belonging to the dominion of Amaymon, his king; steals familiars from other magicians; tells fortunes; teleports the exorcist at his will and pleasure. Formerly of the Order of Potentates.

**Gab**      GB      Elevation, top.      5
**Gabriel**   GBRYAL   Archangel associated with Yesod, with      246

|  |  | the Moon, with the West, and with Water. |  |
|---|---|---|---|
| **Gad** | GD | A tribe of Israel, associated with Aries; good luck, fortune; Babylonian god of fortune. | 7 |
| **Gadhol** | GDWL | Great. | 43 |
| **Gag** | GG | Flat roof; cover of an altar. | 6 |
| **Gal** | GL | Ruins; well; fountain; wave. | 33 |
| **Galab** |  | See *Golachab.* |  |
| **Galash** | GLSh | To lie down. | 333 |
| **Gam** | GM | Together; also. | 603 |
|  |  |  | 43 |
| **Gamaliel** | GMLYAL | The Obscene Ones; Qlippoth of Yesod. | 114 |
| **Gamchicoth** |  | See *Gasheklah.* |  |
| **Gamigin** | GMYGYN | Goetic demon by day of 1st decanate of Decanate of Taurus; also spelled Samigina. | 766 |
|  |  | | 116 |
|  |  | Marquis commanding 30 legions. |  |
|  |  | Appears as a small horse or ass; changes to human form upon request; speaks hoarsely. |  |
|  |  | Powers: teaches liberal sciences; gives account of the souls of those who died in sin. |  |
| **Gamori** | GMWR | Goetic demon by night of 2nd decanate of Libra; also spelled Gremory. | 249 |
|  |  | Duke commanding 26 legions. |  |
|  |  | Appears as a beautiful woman with a duchess' crown tied about her waist and riding a large camel. |  |
|  |  | Powers: tells fortunes; finds treasures; procures love. |  |
| **Gan** | GN | Garden. | 703 |
|  |  |  | 53 |
| **Gan Eden** | GN ODN | Garden of Eden. | 1477 |
|  |  |  | 827 |
|  |  |  | 177 |
| **Gaph** | GP | Back, top; body, person. | 803 |
|  |  |  | 83 |
| **Gar** | GR | Dwelling. | 203 |
| **Gash** | GOSh | Quaking. | 373 |
| **Gasheklah** | GOShKLH | The Smiters, the Disturbers of All Things, | 428 |

the Breakers in Pieces; Qlippoth of
Chesed; variously given as Gha'ahsheblah
(Crowley), Gamchicoth (Mathers), Ag-
shekeloh (Regardie), Gog Sheklah (Waite);
probably related to *Gash* (GOSh), "quaking."

| | | | |
|---|---|---|---:|
| **Gath** | GTh | Wine press. | 403 |
| **Gav** | GW | Back (n.). | 9 |
| **Gay** | GY | Valley. | 13 |
| **Gaye** | GYA | Valley; one of the seven earths, corre-<br>sponding to Geburah. | 14 |
| **Ge** | GA | Proud. | 4 |
| **Geb** | GB | Pit, water hole. | 5 |
| **Geburah** | GBWRH | Severity; the 5th Sephira. | 216 |

Divine Name: Elohim Gibor.

Archangel: Kamael.

Choir of Angels: Seraphim; Powers;
Potentates.

Material World: Madim, the Sphere of
Mars.

Additional titles are *Din*, "justice," and
*Pachad*, "fear."

| | | | |
|---|---|---|---:|
| **Gedi** | GDY | Kid, young goat; Capricorn. | 17 |

Corresponds to Ayin and the 26th Path.

| | | |
|---|---|---:|
| Archangel: Hanael. | | 86 |
| Angel: Sameqiel (Regardie has Saritiel,<br>reversing Capricorn and Sagittarius). | | 241 |
| Lord of Triplicity by Day: Sandali. | | 224 |
| Lord of Triplicity by Night: Aloyar. | | 247 |
| Angel Ruling 10th House: Kashenyayah. | | 465 |
| Angel of 1st Decanate: Misnin. | | 860 |
| Angel of 1st Quinance: Lekabel. | | 83 |
| Angel of 2nd Quinance: Veshriah. | | 521 |
| Angel of 2nd Decanate: Yasyasyah. | | 155 |
| Angel of 3rd Quinance: Yechaviah. | | 39 |
| Angel of 4th Quinance: Lehachiah. | | 58 |
| Angel of 3rd Decanate: Yasgedibarodiel. | | 340 |
| Angel of 5th Quinance: Keveqiah. | | 141 |
| Angel of 6th Quinance: Mendel. | | 125 |
| Qlippoth: Dagdagiron (The Fishy Ones) | | 930 |
| (from *Dag*, "fish"). | | 280 |

Goetic Demons by Day:

    1st Decanate: Berith (Beale, Beal,   612
Bafry, Balfry).

    2nd Decanate: Astaroth.   1307

    3rd Decanate: Forneus.   637

Goetic Demons by Night:

    1st Decanate: Haures (Hauras, Havres,   212
Flauros).

    2nd Decanate: Andrealphus.   1086

    366

    3rd Decanate: Kimaris (Cimejes,   277
Cimeies).

Color: Indigo (Blue-Violet).

Scent: Musk, Civet.

Tarot Trump: XV. The Devil.

Tarot Cards associated with Decanates:

    1st Decanate: 2 of Pentacles.

    2nd Decanate: 3 of Pentacles.

    3rd Decanate: 4 of Pentacles.

Direction: West, below.

Tribe of Israel: Zebulun.

Apostle: Thomas.

Geomantic Figure: Carcer.

Mystic Number of 26th Path: 351.

Ruling Planet: Saturn.

Planet Exalted in: Mars.

Planet in Detriment in: Moon.

Planet in Fall in: Jupiter.

**Gedulah**   GDWLH   Greatness, magnificence; a title of Chesed.   48

**Gehenna**   GYHNWM   Ge-Hinnom, the valley of Hinnom, ancient   48
Jerusalem's garbage dump and crematorium   674
for criminals and the poor. Hence, by   114
extension or analogy, Hell. Specifically, the
1st hell, corresponding to Yesod and
Malkuth and to the Islamic *Jehannam*,
reserved for damned Moslems. In cabalism,
there are seven hells, just as there are seven
heavens:

| | | |
|---|---|---|
| **7th** | Supernals | Sheol (Abyss) |
| | | (the lowest) |
| **6th** | Chesed | Abaddon |
| | | (Destruction) |

| | | | |
|---|---|---|---|
| **5th** | Geburah | Bar Shachath (Pit of Ruin) | |
| **4th** | Tiphareth | Tit-ha-yawen (Mire of Mud) | |
| **3rd** | Netzach | Shaare-Maweth (Gates of Death) | |
| **2nd** | Hod | Tzal-Maweth (Shadow of Death) | |
| **1st** | Yesod and Malkuth | Ge-Hinnom (Valley of Hinnom | |

| | | | |
|---|---|---|---|
| **Gel** | GL | Dung. | 33 |
| **Gematria** | GMTRYA | Hebrew numerology; the cabalistic theory that words or phrases adding to the same number are somehow related. | 263 |
| **Gerodiel** | GRWDYAL | Angel of 3rd decanate of Aquarius. | 254 |
| **Gey-Tzal-maweth** | GYA-TzL-MWTh | Valley of the Shadow of Death. | 580 |
| **Gez** | GZ | Fleece. | 10 |
| **Gha'ag-sheblah** | | See *Gasheklah.* | |
| **Ghagiel** | | See *Ogiel.* | |
| **Gharab Tzerek** | | See *Oreb Zaraq.* | |
| **Ghogiel** | | See *Ogiel.* | |
| **Gi** | GY | The second two letters of the 42-letter name of God, associated with Chokmah. | 13 |
| **Giel** | GYAL | Angel of 3rd astrological house. | 44 |
| **Gihebem** | | Francis Barrett's misprint for GYHNWM, Gehenna, q.v. | |
| **Gihon** | GYHWN | A river of Eden, associated with Water. | 724 74 |
| **Gilead** | GLOD | A Biblical land. | 107 |
| **Gimel** | G | 3rd letter of Hebrew alphabet; transliterated as G or Gh. Spelled out, GML, "camel" (73). Corresponds to the Moon, the 13th Path (between Kether and Tiphareth), and the Tarot Trump II. The High Priestess; for additional correspondences, see *Lebanah.* | 3 |
| **Glasya-Labolas** | GLASLBWL | Goetic demon by day of 1st decanate of Sagittarius. President and Earl commanding 36 legions. Appears as a dog with griffin's wings. | 162 |

Powers: teaches arts and sciences instantly; authors bloodshed and manslaughter; teaches past and future; causes the love of friends and foes; allows one to become invisible.

| | | | |
|---|---|---|---|
| **Göap** | GWAP | Goetic Demon King of the South. | 810 |
| | | | 90 |
| **Gog** | GWG | Prince of Magog. | 12 |
| **Gog we-** | GWG | Gog and Magog (Rev. XX:8). | 70 |
| **Magog** | WMGWG | | |
| **Gog Sheklah** | | See *Gasheklah.* | |
| **Gol** | GL | Oil vessel. | 33 |
| **Golab** | | See *Golachab.* | |
| **Golachab** | GWLChB | The Arsonists; Qlippoth of Geburah; variously given as Galab (Mathers), Golohab (Regardie), Golab (Waite). | 49 |
| **Golgoltha** | GLGLTh | Skull, head; correct transliteration is Gelgoleth. | 466 |
| **Golohab** | | See *Golachab.* | |
| **Gomorah** | OMRH | The wicked city of the Bible; the correct transliteration is Amorah. | 315 |
| **Gonah** | GWNH | Serenity. | 64 |
| **Graphiel** | GRAPYAL | Intelligence of Mars. | 325 |
| **Gremory** | | See *Gamori.* | |
| **Gusion** | GWSYWN | Goetic demon by day of 2nd decanate of Cancer. | 785 |
| | | | 135 |
| | | Duke commanding 40 legions. | |
| | | Appears as "a Xenopilus." | |
| | | Powers: tells fortunes; shows meaning and resolution of all questions asked; reconciles friends; bestows honor and dignity to anyone. | |

| | | | |
|---|---|---|---|
| **Haa** | HAA | 26th name of Shem Hamphorash, associated with 2nd quinance of Sagittarius. | 7 |
| **Haagenti** | HOGNTh | Goetic demon by night of 3rd decanate of Cancer. | 528 |

President commanding 33 legions.

Appears as a mighty bull with griffin's wings; assumes human form upon command.

Powers: makes men wise and instructs them in various matters; transmutes all metals into gold; changes water into wine and vice versa.

| | | | |
|---|---|---|---|
| Haaiah | | See *Haayah.* | |
| Haamiah | | See *Chamiah.* | |
| Haayah | HAAYH | Angel of 2nd quinance of Sagittarius; angel by night of the 8 of Wands; also spelled Haäyah or Haaiah. | 22 |
| Habuiah | | See *Chabuyah.* | |
| Hachash | HChSh | 51st name of Shem Hamphorash, associated with 3rd quinance of Aries. | 313 |
| Hadad | HDD | A King of Edom, associated with Tiphareth; son of Bedad. His city was Avith. It is written that Hadad smote Midian in the field of Moab. | 13 |
| Hadad ben Bedad | HDD BN BDD | Hadad, son of Bedad. | 725 75 |
| Hadar | HDR | A King of Edom, associated with Malkuth. His city was Pau. | 209 |
| Hagar | HGR | Sarai's maid, mother of Ishmael. | 208 |
| Haggith | ChGYTh | A wife of David, mother of Adonijah. | 421 |
| Hagiel | HGYAL | Intelligence of Venus. | 49 |
| Hagith | ChGYTh | Olympic Planetary Spirit of Venus. | 421 |
| Hah | HH | Alas! | 10 |
| Hahahel | HHHAL | Angel of 5th quinance of Aquarius; angel by day of the 7 of Swords; also spelled Hahihel. | 46 |
| Hahaziah | | See *Hechashiah.* | |
| Hahiah | | See *Hihayah.* | |
| Hahihel | | See *Hahahel.* | |
| Hahuiah | | See *Chahaviah.* | |
| Haiaiel | | See *Hayayel.* | |
| Hakamiah | | See *Haqmiah.* | |
| Hallelujah | HLLWYH | Praise the Lord (i.e., Yah). | 86 |
| Halphas | HALP | Goetic demon by night of 2nd decanate of Aries; also spelled Malthas, Malthus, or | 836 116 |

Malthous.
Earl commanding 26 legions.
Appears as a stock-dove; speaks hoarsely.
Powers: builds towers and supplies them
with armaments; sends warriors.

| | | | |
|---|---|---|---|
| **Ham (Cham)** | ChM | Son of Noah. | 608 |
| | | | 48 |
| **Hamaliel** | HMLYAL | Archangel of Virgo. | 116 |
| **Hanael** | HNAL | Archangel of Capricorn; sometimes given as the archangel or angel of Venus, which are, however, Haniel and Anael, respectively. | 86 |
| **Haniel** | HANYAL | Archangel associated with Netzach and with Venus. | 97 |
| **Haqabah** | HQBH | A name of God; acronym for Ha-qadosh Baruk Hu, "The Holy One, blessed be he." | 112 |
| **Ha-qadosh Baruk Hu** | HQDWSh BRWK HWA | The Holy One, blessed be he. | 1135 655 |
| **Haqamamna** | HQMMNO | The 25th through 30th letters of the 42-letter name of God, associated with Netzach. | 305 |
| **Haqem** | HQM | 16th name of Shem Hamphorash; associated with 4th quinance of Libra. | 705 145 |
| **Haqmiah** | HQMYH | Angel of 4th quinance of Libra; angel by night of the 3 of Swords; also spelled Hoqmiah or Hakamiah. | 160 |
| **Har** | HR | Mountain. | 205 |
| **Harab Serap** | | See *Oreb Zaraq.* | |
| **Harab-Serapel** | | See *Oreb Zaraq.* | |
| **Harach** | HRCh | 59th name of Shem Hamphorash, associated with 5th quinance of Taurus. | 213 |
| **Harahel** | | See *Herachiel.* | |
| **Haran** | HRN | 1. Son of Terah, father of Lot, and brother of Abraham; 2. Father of Milcah and Iscah, Milcah being the wife of Nahor, son of Terah; 3. The land where Abraham and his family went after leaving Ur of the Chaldees. | 905 255 |
| **Harayel** | | See *Hariel.* | |
| **Hari** | HRY | Aspect, characteristic; 15th name of Shem Hamphorash, associated with 3rd | 215 |

quinance of Libra.

| | | | |
|---|---|---|---|
| **Hariel** | HRYAL | Angel of 3rd quinance of Libra; angel by day of the 3 of Swords; also spelled Harayel. | 246 |
| **Har Sinai** | HR SYNY | Mount Sinai. | 335 |
| **Has** | HS | Silence! | 65 |
| **Ha-Shem** | HShM | The Name; Tetragrammaton. | 905 |
| | | | 345 |
| **Hasmodai** | | See *Chashmodai.* | |
| **Hattaah** | HTAH | Sin. | 20 |
| **Haures** | HAWR | Goetic demon by night of 1st decanate of Capricorn; also spelled Hauras, Havres, or Flauros; name probably derived from the Egyptian god Horus.<br>Duke commanding 36 legions.<br>Appears as a mighty, terrible, and strong leopard; assumes human form upon command, but with flaming eyes and a terrible countenance.<br>Powers: tell fortunes; talks about the creation of the world, divinity, and how he and other spirits fell; destroys and burns the enemies of the exorcist if desired; will not allow exorcist to be tempted. A consistent liar if not commanded into the triangle. | 212 |
| **Havvah** | ChWH | Eve. | 19 |
| **Hayayel** | HYYAL | Angel of 5th quinance of Cancer; angel by day of the 4 of Cups; also spelled Haiaiel. | 56 |
| **Hayeya** | HYY | 71st name of Shem Hamphorash, associated with 5th quinance of Cancer. | 25 |
| **Hazayel** | | See *Haziel.* | |
| **Haziel** | HZYAL | Angel of 3rd quinance of Virgo; angel by day of the 9 of Pentacles; also spelled Hazayel. | 53 |
| **He** | H | 5th letter of Hebrew alphabet; transliterated as H.<br>Spelled out, HH, "window" (10).<br>Corresponds to Aries (or Aquarius), the 15th Path (between Chokmah and Tipha- | 5 |

reth), and the Tarot Trump IV. The Emperor (or XVII. The Star); for additional correspondences, see *Taleh*.

| | | | |
|---|---|---|---|
| **He** | HA | Lo! | 6 |
| **Hebel** | HBL | Vapor, breath, vanity; son of Adam (Abel), slain by Cain. | 37 |
| **Hechashiah** | HChShYH | Angel of 3rd quinance of Aries; angel by day of the 3 of Wands; also spelled Hahaziah. | 328 |
| **Hed** | HD | Shout of joy. | 9 |
| **Hehah** | HHH | 41st name of Shem Hamphorash, associated with 5th quinance of Aquarius. | 15 |
| **Hehau** | HHO | 12th name of Shem Hamphorash, associated with 6th quinance of Virgo. | 80 |
| **Hekel** | HYKL | Temple, palace, mansion. | 65 |

In cabalism, seven palaces or mansions are said to be the original home of Adam and, after the Fall, the abode of saints. What relationship, if any, exists between these palaces and the seven heavens is unclear. Crowley (777) calls them Palaces of Briah. The palaces and the Sephiroth with which they are associated are as follows:

| | |
|---|---|
| **Supernals** | Hekel Qadosh Qadeshim (Palace of the Holy of Holies) |
| **Chesed** | Hekel Ahbah (Palace of Love) |
| **Geburah** | Hekel Zakoth (Palace of Merit) |
| **Tiphareth** | Hekel Ratzon (Palace of Delight) |
| **Netzach** | Hekel Etzem Shamaim (Palace of the Body of Heaven) |
| **Hod** | Hekel Gonah (Palace of Serenity) |
| **Yesod and Malkuth** | Hekel Lebanath ha-Saphir (Palace of the Pavement of Sapphire Stone) (Ex. XXIV:10) |

| | | | |
|---|---|---|---|
| **Hekel Ahbah** | HYKL AHBH | Palace of Love; heavenly manison corresponding to Chesed and to the Moslem Dar as-Salaam (House of Rest or Peace). | 78 |
| **Hekel Etzem Shamaim** | HYKL OTzM ShMYM | Palace of the Body of Heaven (Ex. XXIV: 10); heavenly mansion corresponding to Netzach and to the Moslem Jannat al-Naim (Garden of Delights). | 1775 1215 655 |
| **Hekel Gonah** | HYKL GWNH | Palace of Serenity; heavenly mansion corresponding to Hod and to the Moslem Jannat al-Firdaus (Garden of Paradise). | 129 |
| **Hekel Lebanath ha-Saphir** | HYKL LBNTh HSPYR | Palace of the Pavement of Sapphire Stone (Ex. XXIV:10); heavenly mansion corresponding to Yesod and Malkuth and to the Moslem Jannat al-'Adn (Garden of Eden) or Al-Karar (Everlasting Abode). | 902 |
| **Hekel Qadosh Qadeshim** | HYKL QDWSh QDShYM | Palace of the Holy of Holies; heavenly mansion corresponding to the three Supernal Sephiroth and to the Moslem Dar al-Jalal (House of Glory). | 1489 929 |
| **Hekel Ratzon** | HYKL RTzWN | Palace of Delight; heavenly mansion corresponding to Tiphareth and to the Moslem Jannat al-Khuld (Garden of Eternity). | 1061 411 |
| **Hekel Zakoth** | HYKL ZKWTh | Palace of Merit; heavenly mansion corresponding to Geburah and to the Moslem Jannat al-Maawa (Garden of Mansions). | 498 |
| **Hem** | HM | They. | 605 45 |
| **Hen** | HN | Lo!; whether, if. | 705 55 |
| **Herachiel** | HRChAL | Angel of 5th quinance of Taurus; angel by day of the 7 of Pentacles; also spelled Herochiel or Harahel. | 244 |
| **Heth** | | See *Cheth*. | |
| **Heylel** | HYLL | Brightness; morning star. | 75 |
| **Heylel ben Shachar** | HYLL BN ShChR | Morning Star, Son of the Dawn; Lucifer. | 1285 635 |
| **Hezi** | HZY | 9th name of Shem Hamphorash, associated with 3rd quinance of Virgo. | 22 |
| **Hi** | HY | Lamentation. | 15 |
| **Hiddikel** | HDQL | Tigris; a river of Eden, associated with Air. | 139 |

| | | | |
|---|---|---|---|
| **Hihayah** | HHOYH | Angel of 6th quinance of Virgo; angel by night of the 10 of Pentacles; also spelled Hiha'ayah or Hahiah. | 95 |
| **Hismael** | HSMAL | Spirit of Jupiter. | 136 |
| **Hod** | HWD | Splendor; the 8th Sephira. | 15 |
| | | Divine Name: Elohim Tzabaoth. | |
| | | Archangel: Michael. | |
| | | Choir of Angels: Beni Elohim; Archangels. | |
| | | Material World: Kokab, the Sphere of Mercury. | |
| **Hoqmiah** | | See *Haqmiah*. | |
| **Hu** | HWA | He; a name of God and title of Kether. | 12 |
| **Hua** | HWA | Avenging angel; angel of the Tarot. | 12 |
| **Husham** | HShM | A King of Edom, associated with Geburah. His land was Temani. | 905 345 |

| | | | |
|---|---|---|---|
| **I** | OY | Ruins. | 80 |
| **Iahhel** | | See *Yehohel*. | |
| **Ibri** | OBRY | Hebrew. | 282 |
| **Ibrim** | OBRYM | Hebrews. | 882 332 |
| **Iehuiah** | | See *Yechaviah*. | |
| **Ieiaiel** | | See *Yeyayel*. | |
| **Ieilael** | | See *Yeyalel*. | |
| **Ielael** | | See *Yezalel*. | |
| **Ielahiah** | | See *Yelahiah*. | |
| **Ieliel** | | See *Yelayel*. | |
| **Ierathel** | | See *Yerathel*. | |
| **Igrath** | | See *Agrath*. | |
| **Ihiazel** | | See *Yeyazel*. | |
| **Iibamiah** | | See *Yebamiah*. | |
| **Im** | OM | With, by, near. | 670 110 |
| **Imamiah** | | See *Amamiah*. | |

| | | | |
|---|---|---|---|
| **Iophiel** | YHOYAL | Intelligence of Jupiter. | 136 |
| **Ipos** | YPWSh | Goetic demon by day of 1st decanate of Scorpio.<br>Earl and Prince commanding 36 legions.<br>Appears as an angel with a lion's head, a goose's foot, and a hare's tail.<br>Powers: tells fortunes; makes men witty and bold. | 396 |
| **Irad** | OYRD | Son of Enoch and father of Mehujael; grandson of Cain. | 284 |
| **Iram** | | R.S.V. spelling of Eram (q.v.). | |
| **Isaac**<br>  **(Itzchaq)** | YTzChQ | Son of Abraham and father of Jacob. | 208 |
| **Ish** | AYSh | Man; a title of Tiphareth. | 311 |
| **Ishah** | AShH | Woman. | 306 |
| **Isheth**<br>  **Zenunim** | AShTh<br>ZNWNYM | Woman of Whoredom; Demon of Prostitution; Mother of Chioa, the Beast (Samael being the father), or Samael and Isheth Zenunim together are considered to be Chioa; arch-demon corresponding to Binah (777). | 1424<br>864 |
| **Ishmael** | YShMOAL | Son of Abraham and brother of Isaac. | 451 |
| **Israel** | YShRAL | Israel. | 541 |
| **Issachar** | YShShKR | A tribe of Israel, associated with Cancer. | 830 |
| **Iyar** | AYR | The 8th Hebrew month, April-May, corresponding roughly to the period when the Sun is in Taurus. | 211 |

| | | | |
|---|---|---|---|
| **Jabal** | YBL | Son of Lamech and Adah; "the father of such as dwell in tents, and of such as have cattle." | 79 |
| **Jachin** | YAChYN | One of the pillars in the Temple of Solomon (the other being Boaz); Jachin is the white pillar, on the left, corresponding to the male or Yang principle. | 729<br>79 |

| | | | |
|---|---|---|---|
| **Jacob (Yaaqob)** | YOQB | Son of Isaac and father of twelve sons from whom came the tribes of Israel. | 182 |
| **Jael** | | See *Yahel.* | |
| **Japheth (Yapheth)** | YPTh | Son of Noah. | 490 |
| **Jared** | YRD | Son of Mahalaleel and father of Enoch; great-great-grandfather of Noah; lived 962 years (460-1422 after Creation). | 214 |
| **Jehovah** | | See *Yahweh.* | |
| **Jericho (Yericho)** | YRChW | Jericho. | 224 |
| **Jesus** | | See *Joshua.* | |
| **Jetheth** | YThTh | A Duke of Edom, associated (with Timnah and Alvah) with Daath. | 810 |
| **Jethro** | YThRW | Moses' father-in-law, also known as Reuel. | 616 |
| **Jobab** | YWBB | A King of Edom, associated with Chesed; son of Zerah. His city was Bozrah. | 20 |
| **Jobab ben Zerah** | YWBB BN ZRCh | Jobab, son of Zerah. | 937 287 |
| **Jordan** | YRDN | Jordan. | 914 264 |
| **Joseph (Yoseph)** | YWSP | Son of Jacob. | 876 156 |
| **Joshua** | YHWShO | Son of Nun (Fish); Jesus. | 391 |
| **Jubal** | YWBL | Son of Lamech and Adah; "the father of all such as handle the harp and organ." | 48 |
| **Judah** | YHWDH | A tribe of Israel, associated with Leo. | 30 |

| | | | |
|---|---|---|---|
| **Kaamah** | KOMH | Some sort of infernal being associated with the northwest. | 135 |
| **Kad** | KD | Bucket, pail, vessel. | 24 |
| **Kael** | KOAL | Angel of 4th astrological house. | 121 |
| **Kahath** | KHTh | 8th name of Shem Hamphorash, associated with 2nd quinance of Virgo. | 425 |
| **Kalah** | KLH | Bride; a title of Malkuth, meaning the | 55 |

|  |  | Bride of Microprosopus. |  |
|---|---|---|---|
| **Kaliel** | KLYAL | Angel of 6th quinance of Libra; angel by night of the 4 of Swords; also spelled Kelial or Caliel. | 91 |
| **Kamael** | KMAL | Archangel associated with Geburah and with Mars; sometimes spelled Camael. | 91 |
| **Kambriel** | KAM-BRYAL | Archangel of Aquarius; also spelled Cambriel. | 304 |
| **Kamotz** | KMWTz | Angel of 1st decanate of Scorpio. | 966 156 |
| **Kaph** | K | 11th letter of Hebrew alphabet, transliterated as *k* or *kh*. Spelled out, KP, palm of hand (820 or 100). Corresponds to Jupiter, the 21st Path (between Chesed and Netzach), and the Tarot Trump X. The Wheel of Fortune; for additional correspondences, see *Tzedek*. | 20 500 |
| **Kashenyayah** | KShNYOYH | Angel of 10th astrological house. | 465 |
| **Kaspith** | KSPYTh | Mercury, the metal of Mercury. | 570 |
| **Kavar** | KBR | To make heavy; to make many, multiply. | 222 |
| **Kedamidi** | KDMDY | Angel of 1st decanate of Taurus (Regardie gives the Hebrew spelling as KRDMDY, 278). | 78 |
| **Kedemel** | QDMAL | Spirit of Venus. | 175 |
| **Kegadikesh** | KGDYKSh | The 13th through 18th letters of the 42-letter name of God, associated with Geburah. | 357 |
| **Kehethal** |  | See *Kehethel*. |  |
| **Kehethel** | KHThAL | Angel of 2nd quinance of Virgo; angel by night of the 8 of Pentacles; also spelled Kehethal or Cahethel. | 456 |
| **Keli** | KLY | Utensil, instrument, tool; 18th name of Shem Hamphorash, associated with 6th quinance of Libra. | 60 |
| **Kelial** |  | See *Kaliel*. |  |
| **Ken** | KN | Honest; so, thus, just so, such, so much. | 720 70 |
| **Kenan** |  | See *Cainan*. |  |
| **Kenaz** | QNZ | A Duke of Edom, associated with Netzach. | 157 |
| **Kerub** | KRWB | Ruler of Earth; also one of the Kerubim. | 228 |

| | | | |
|---|---|---|---|
| **Kerubim** | KRWBYM | Angelic Choir associated with Yesod and with the Sphere of the Moon; "The Kerubim are the Living Powers of Tetragrammaton on the Material Plane and the Presidents of the Four Elements. They operate through the Fixed or Kerubic Signs of the Zodiac and are thus symbolized and attributed: | 838 278 |

Kerub of Air—Man—Aquarius
Kerub of Fire—Lion—Leo
Kerub of Earth—Bull—Taurus
Kerub of Water—Eagle—Scorpio
(from a Golden Dawn knowledge lecture; Regardie: *The Golden Dawn*, Llewellyn).

| | | | |
|---|---|---|---|
| **Kes** | KS | Throne. | 80 |
| **Kesep** | KSP | Silver, the metal of the Moon. | 880 160 |
| **Kesil** | KSYL | Fool. | 120 |
| **Kesilim** | KSYLYM | Fools; the constellation Orion. | 730 170 |
| **Kether** | KThR | Crown; the 1st Sephira. | 620 |

Divine Name: Ehyeh.
Archangel: Metatron.
Choir of Angels: Chayoth ha-Qadesh (Holy Living Creatures); Seraphim.
Material World: Rashith ha-Gilgalim, the Primum Mobile.
Additional titles of Kether are Arik Anpin, Long of Nose, The Greater Countenance, Macroprosopus, The Vast Countenance; Atiqa, The Ancient One; Atiqa de-Atiqin, The Ancient of the Ancient Ones; Atiqa Qadisha, The Most Holy Ancient One; Arik Apim, Long of Face; Ehyeh Asher Ehyeh, Existence of Existences, I AM WHAT AM; Elyon, The Most High; Hu, He; Neqedah Peshutah, The Simple Point; Neqedah Rishonah, The Primordial Point; Or Mopla, The Hidden Light; Or Penimi, The Internal Light; Or Pashot,

The Simple Light; Pele, The Wonder; Risha, The Head; Risha Dela, The Head Which Is Not; Risha Havurah, The White Head; Rom Maalah, The Inscrutable Height; Temira de-Temirin, The Concealed of the Concealed; Tath Zel, The Profuse Giver; etc. All these are called "titles of Kether," but they are likewise (and therefore) appellations of God.

| | | | |
|---|---|---|---|
| Kevar | KBR | Long; extent; long ago, already. | 222 |
| Keveq | KWQ | 35th name of Shem Hamphorash, associated with 5th quinance of Capricorn. | 126 |
| Keveqiah | KWQYH | Angel of 5th quinance of Capricorn; angel by day of the 4 of Pentacles; also spelled Chavakiah. | 141 |
| Khebar | KBR | A river in Mesopotamia. | 222 |
| Ki | KY | Brand; that, so that, because, when, for. | 30 |
| Kimaris | KYMAWR | Goetic demon by night of 3rd decanate of Capricorn; also spelled Cimejes or Cimeies. | 277 |
| | | Marquis commanding 20 legions. | |
| | | Appears as a valiant warrior riding a goodly black horse. | |
| | | Powers: teaches grammar, logic, and rhetoric; discovers treasures and things lost or hidden. | |
| | | Rules over all spirits in Africa. | |
| Kinnim | KNYM | Vermin; the 3rd of the 10 plagues of Egypt. | 680 120 |
| Kislev | KSLW | The 3rd Hebrew month, November-December, corresponding roughly to the period when the Sun is in Sagittarius. | 116 |
| Koch | KCh | Strength. | 28 |
| Kochmah | KChMH | Power of Yetzirah; a title of Chokmah. | 73 |
| Koh | KH | Thus, so; here, there. | 25 |
| Kohen | KHN | Priest. | 725 75 |
| Koheneth | KHNTh | Priestess. | 475 |
| Koheneth ha-Gadhol | KHNTh HGDWL | High Priestess. | 523 |

| | | | |
|---|---|---|---|
| **Kohen ha-** | KHN | High Priest. | 773 |
| **Gadhol** | HGDWL | | 123 |
| **Kokab** | KWKB | Star; Mercury. | 48 |

The Sphere of Mercury corresponds to Hod.
The planet Mercury corresponds to Beth and the 12th Path.
Archangel: Michael.
Angel: Raphael.
Intelligence: Tiriel.
Spirit: Taphthartharath.
Olympic Spirit: Ophiel.
Metal: Mercury.
Color: Yellow.
Stone: Opal, Agate.
Scent: Mastic, White Sandal, Mace, Storax, all Fugitive Odors.
Tarot Trump: I. The Magician.
Rules Gemini and Virgo.
Exalted in Virgo.
Detriment in Sagittarius and Pisces.
Fall in Pisces.

| | | | |
|---|---|---|---|
| **Kol** | KL | All. | 50 |
| **Korsia** | KWRSYA | Throne; a title of Binah. | 297 |
| **Korson** | KWRSWN | Demon King of the West (according to the Goetia). | 992 |
| | | | 342 |
| **Kuzu** | KWZW | A name of God by Temurah. | 39 |

**L**

| | | | |
|---|---|---|---|
| **Lach** | LCh | Moist, fresh, green. | 38 |
| **Lamech** | LMK | 1. Son of Methusael of the line of Cain and father of Jabal, Jubal, Tubal-Cain, and Naamah; 2. Son of Methuselah and father of Noah; lived 777 years (874-1651 after Creation. | 570 |
| | | | 90 |
| **Lamed** | L | The 12th letter of the Hebrew alphabet; | 30 |

its transliteration is *l*.

Spelled out, LMD, "ox-goad" (74).

Corresponds to Libra, the 22nd Path (between Geburah and Tiphareth), and the Tarot Trump VIII. Justice; for additional correspondences, see *Moznayim.*

| | | | |
|---|---|---|---|
| **Laslara** | LSLRA | Lord of Triplicity by Day for Virgo. | 321 |
| **Lau** | LAW | 17th name of Shem Hamphorash; associated with 5th quinance of Libra. | 37 |
| **Lauiah** | | See *Laviah.* | |
| **Lav** | LAW | 11th name of Shem Hamphorash, associated with 5th quinance of Virgo. | 37 |
| **Lavan** | LBN | White. | 732 |
| | | | 82 |
| **Laviah** | LAWYH | Angel of 5th quinance of Virgo; angel by day of the 10 of Pentacles; also spelled Lauiah; angel of 5th quinance of Libra; angel by day of the 4 of Swords; also spelled Leviah. | 52 |
| **Laylah** | LYLH | Night. | 75 |
| **Leah** | LAH | First wife of Jacob; mother of Reuben, Simeon, Levi, Judah, Issachar, and Zebulun. | 36 |
| **Leb** | LB | Heart; center. | 32 |
| **Lebarmim** | LBRMYM | Lord of Triplicity by Night for Sagittarius. | 882 |
| | | | 322 |
| **Lecabel** | | See *Lekabel.* | |
| **Lehach** | LHCh | 34th name of Shem Hamphorash, associated with 4th quinance of Capricorn. | 43 |
| **Lehachiah** | LHChYH | Angel of 4th quinance of Capricorn; angel by night of the 3 of Pentacles; also spelled Lehahiah. | 58 |
| **Lekab** | LKB | 31st name of Shem Hamphorash, associated with 1st quinance of Capricorn. | 52 |
| **Lekabel** | LKBAL | Angel of 1st quinance of Capricorn; angel by day of the 2 of Pentacles; also spelled Lecabel. | 83 |
| **Lelah** | LLH | 6th name of Shem Hamphorash, associated with 6th quinance of Leo. | 65 |
| **Lelahel** | LLHAL | Angel of 6th quinance of Leo; angel by night of the 7 of Wands. | 96 |

| | | | |
|---|---|---|---|
| **Leraje** | LRAYK | Goetic demon by day of 2nd decanate of Leo; also spelled Leraikha or Leraie. Marquis commanding 30 legions. Appears as an archer clad in green carrying a bow and quiver. Powers: causes great battles and contests; festers arrow wounds. | 741 261 |
| **Letz** | LTz | Mocker. | 930 120 |
| **Leuuiah** | | See *Luviah*. | |
| **Levanah** | LBNH | The Moon. The Sphere of the Moon corresponds to Yesod. The Moon itself corresponds to Gimel and the 13th Path. Archangel and Angel: Gabriel. Intelligence: Malka be-Tarshishim we-ad be-Ruah Shehakim. Spirit: Chashmodai; Shed Barshemath ha-Sharthathan. Olympic Spirit: Phul. Metal: Silver. Color: Blue. Stone: Moonstone, Pearl, Crystal. Scent: Menstrual Blood, Camphor, Aloes, all Sweet Virginal Odors. Tarot Trump: II. The High Priestess. Rules Cancer. Exalted in Taurus. Detriment in Capricorn. Fall in Scorpio. | 87 |
| **Levi** | LWY | A son of Jacob; the Israelite tribe appointed the priestly caste during the Exodus. | 46 |
| **Leviah** | | See *Laviah*. | |
| **Leviathan** | LWYThN | The great sea-monster of Hebrew mythology; equivalent to the Greek Typhon. | 1146 496 |
| **Levim** | LWYM | Levites; the priest-tribe. | 646 86 |
| **Levo** | LWW | 19th name of Shem Hamphorash, associated with 1st quinance of Scorpio. | 42 |
| **Lilith** | LYLYTh | Queen of the Night, Queen of Demons, | 480 |

|  |  | wife of Samael, wife of Asmodai, first wife (before Eve) of Adam, arch-demon corresponding to Yesod. |  |
| **Livayah** |  | See *Luviah*. |  |
| **Lo** | LA | Not, no. | 31 |
| **Lo** | LW | Not, no. | 36 |
| **Loa** | LO | Throat. | 100 |
| **Lod** | LD | Lydda, a town in Benjamin. | 34 |
| **Log** | LG | Basin. | 33 |
| **Losanahar** | LWSNHR | Angel of 1st decanate of Leo. | 351 |
| **Lot** | LWT | Lot (of the Bible). | 45 |
| **Lot** | LT | Laudanum. | 39 |
| **Lucifer** |  | See *Heylel ben Shachar*. |  |
| **Lucifuge** |  | Arch-demon corresponding to Binah (Mathers, Waite) or to Chesed (Crowley, 777); no Hebrew spelling. |  |
| **Luviah** | LWWYH | Angel of 1st quinance of Scorpio; angel by day of the 5 of Cups; also spelled Livayah or Leuuiah. | 57 |
| **Lydda (Lod)** | LD | A town in Benjamin. | 34 |

| **Maarab** | MORB | West; see also *Maim*. | 312 |
| **Mabeh** | MBH | 55th name of Shem Hamphorash, associated with 1st quinance of Taurus. | 47 |
| **Macroprosopus** |  | See *Arik Anpin*. |  |
| **Mad** | MD | Garment. | 44 |
| **Madim** | MDYM | Mars. | 654 |
|  |  | The Sphere of Mars corresponds to Geburah. | 94 |
|  |  | The planet Mars corresponds to Pe and the 27th Path. |  |
|  |  | Archangel: Kamael. |  |
|  |  | Angel: Zamael. |  |
|  |  | Intelligence: Graphiel. |  |
|  |  | Spirit: Bartzabel. |  |

Olympic Spirit: Phaleg.
Metal: Iron.
Color: Red.
Stone: Ruby, any Red Stone.
Scent: Pepper, Dragon's Blood, all Hot
    Pungent Odors.
Tarot Trump: XVI. The Tower.
Rules Aries and Scorpio.
Exalted in Capricorn.
Detriment in Taurus and Libra.
Fall in Cancer.

| | | | |
|---|---|---|---|
| **Mag** | MG | Magus. | 43 |
| **Magdiel** | MGDYAL | A Duke of Edom, associated (with Mibzar) with Yesod. | 88 |
| **Magog** | MGWG | Magog; see also *Gog*. | 52 |
| **Mah** | MH | What? Which? Why? How?; anything, something; the secret name of the World of Yetzirah. | 45 |
| **Mahalaleel** | MHLLAL | Son of Cainan and father of Jared; great-great-grandson of Adam; lived 895 years (395-1290 after Creation). | 136 |
| **Mahalath** | MChLTh | Daughter of Ishmael, wife of Esau; later considered a major demon, mother of Agrath (q.v.). | 478 |
| **Mahash** | MHSh | 5th name of Shem Hamphorash, associated with 5th quinance of Leo. | 345 |
| **Mahashiah** | MHShYH | Angel of 5th quinance of Leo; angel by day of the 7 of Wands; also spelled Mahasiah. | 360 |
| **Mahazael** | MHZAL | Demon Prince of Earth. | 83 |
| **Maim** | MYM | Water, one of the four elements, associated with Mem and the 23rd Path. | 650 |

Cardinal Point: West (Maarab).
Tetramorph: Eagle.
Evangelist: John.
Color: Blue.
Properties: Cold and Moist.
Elementals: Undines.
Letter of Tetragrammaton: He.
Cabalistic World: Briah.
Archangel: Gabriel.

Angel: Taliahad.
Ruler: Tharsis.
King: Nichsa.
Supreme Elemental King (Enochian):
  THAHEBYOBEAATAN.
Demon Prince: Azael.
Demon King: Ariton.
Demon King (Goetia): Korson.
River of Eden: Gihon.
Infernal River: Styx.
Tarot Trump: XII. The Hanged Man.
Tarot Suit: Cups.
Tarot Court Cards: Queens.
Enochian Word: HCOMA.
Enochian Divine Names: MPH ARSL
  GAIOL.
Tattwa: Apas (Silver Crescent).
Scent: Myrrh.
Humor: Blood.
Jungian Function: Intuition.
Chinese System: North, Black, Tortoise.

| | | | |
|---|---|---|---|
| **Makath be-Khoroth** | MKTh BKWRWTh | The Slaying of the Firstborn; the 10th of the 10 plagues of Egypt. | 1094 |
| **Makhon** | MKWN | Emplacement; the 6th Heaven, corresponding to Chesed. | 766 116 |
| **Malak** | MLAK | Angel. | 571 91 |
| **Malak ha-Elohim** | MLAK HALHYM | Angel of God. | 1222 742 662 182 |
| **Malak ha-Mash-chith** | MLAK HMSh-ChYTh | Angel of Destruction. | 1329 849 |
| **Malchidial** | | See *Malkidiel.* | |
| **Malka be-Tarshishim we-ad be-Ruah Shehaqim** | MLKA BThR-ShYShYM WOD BRWH ShHQYM | Intelligence of the Intelligences of the Moon; final *M* in ShHQYM counted as 700; Regardie (*The Golden Dawn*) gives, as a restored spelling, Malka be-Tarshisim we-ad Ruachoth Shechalim (MLKA BThRShYSYM WOD RWChWTh ShCh- | 3321 |

LYM), which adds to 3321 naturally. The best translation I can make out of the latter is "Queen of the Chrysolites and the Eternal Spirits of the Lions." Both phrases are, however, essentially untranslatable and have been made up to equal 3321, the sum of all the numbers on the magic square of the Moon.

| | | | |
|---|---|---|---|
| **Malkah** | MLKH | Queen; a title of Malkuth. | 95 |
| **Malkidiel** | MLKYDAL | Archangel of Aries. | 135 |
| **Malkuth** | MLKWTh | Kingdom; the 10th Sephira. | 496 |

Divine Name: Adonai ha-Eretz.

Archangel: Sandalphon.

Choir of Angels: Eshim.

Material World: Cholam Yesodoth, The Breaker of Foundations, or Olam Yesodoth, World of Foundations; the Sphere of the Elements.

Associated with the final He of Tetragrammaton.

Additional titles of Malkuth are Malkah, The Queen; Kalah, The Bride; Shekinah, The Divine Presence; Shar or Throa, The Gate; and Betulah, The Virgin.

| | | | |
|---|---|---|---|
| **Malphas** | MALP | Goetic demon by night of 3rd decanate | 871 |
| | | of Aries. | 151 |

President commanding 40 legions.

Appears as a crow; assumes human form upon request; speaks hoarsely.

Powers: builds houses and high towers; reveals thoughts and desires of enemies; gives good familiars.

| | | | |
|---|---|---|---|
| **Man** | MN | Manna. | 740 |
| | | | 90 |
| **Manasseh** | MNShH | A tribe of Israel, associated with Gemini. | 395 |
| **Maon** | MOWN | Residence; the 5th Heaven, corresponding | 816 |
| | | to Geburah. | 166 |
| **Maq** | MQ | Rottenness. | 140 |
| **Maqqel** | MQL | Wand. | 170 |
| **Maqqeloth** | MQLWTh | Wands; Tarot suit associated with Fire. | 576 |
| **Mar** | MR | Drop; bitter, sad; fierce, violent, wild; | 240 |

|            |          | bitterness, sadness. |      |
|------------|----------|----------------------|------|
| **Marax**  | MARATz   | Goetic demon by day of 3rd decanate of Libra; also spelled Morax.<br>Earl and President commanding 30 legions.<br>Appears as a bull with a man's face.<br>Powers: teaches astronomy and other liberal sciences; gives good familiars who are wise, knowing the virtues of precious herbs and stones. | 1142<br>332 |
| **Marbas** | MARB     | Goetic demon by day of 2nd decanate of Taurus.<br>President commanding 36 legions.<br>Appears as a great lion; changes to human form upon request.<br>Powers: gives true answers on secret matters; causes and cures diseases; teaches mechanical arts; changes men into other shapes. | 243 |
| **Marchosias** | MRChWSh | Goetic demon by day of 2nd decanate of Pisces.<br>Marquis commanding 30 legions.<br>Appears as a wolf or ox with griffin's wings and a serpent's tail, vomiting flames; after a while, assumes human form on command.<br>Powers: "He is a strong fighter."<br>Formerly of the Order of Dominations; told Solomon he hoped to return to the 7th throne after 1200 years. If his hopes were fulfilled, he has already done so some time ago. | 554 |
| **Mas** | MS | A suffering, discouraged one; tax. | 100 |
| **Mashchith** | MShChYTh | The Destroyer (Ex. XII:23). | 758 |
| **Masrekah** | MShRQH | A city of Edom; city of King Samlah. | 645 |
| **Matbea** | MTBO | Coin. | 121 |
| **Matbeoth** | MTBOWTh | Coins; Tarot suit associated with Earth. | 527 |
| **Mathravash** | MThRAWSh | Angel of 1st decanate of Cancer. | 947 |
| **Matred** | MTRD | Mother of Mehetable, wife of Hadar, a King of Edom; daughter of Mezahab. | 253 |
| **Mattah** | MTH | Tribe; branch, twig, rod, staff, stick, sceptre, spear. | 54 |

The 12 Tribes of Israel and the astrological signs with which they are associated are as follows:

| | |
|---|---|
| **Gad** | Aries |
| **Ephraim** | Taurus |
| **Manasseh** | Gemini |
| **Issachar** | Cancer |
| **Judah** | Leo |
| **Naphtali** | Virgo |
| **Asher** | Libra |
| **Dan** | Scorpio |
| **Benjamin** | Sagittarius |
| **Zebulun** | Capricorn |
| **Reuben** | Aquarius |
| **Simeon** | Pisces |

| | | | |
|---|---|---|---|
| **Matz-Patz** | MTzPTz | A name of God by Temurah. | 1110 |
| | | | 300 |
| **Maveth** | MWTh | Death. | 446 |
| **Maziq** | MZYQ | Demon; injurer. | 157 |
| **Mazloth** | MZLWTh | Constellations; the Sphere of the Zodiac; the part of the material world corresponding to Chokmah. | 483 |
| **Meach** | MCh | Fat. | 48 |
| **Meah** | MAH | Hundred. | 46 |
| **Mebah** | MBH | 14th name of Shem Hamphorash, associated with 2nd quinance of Libra. | 47 |
| **Mebahel** | MBHAL | Angel of 2nd quinance of Libra; angel by night of the 2 of Swords. | 78 |
| **Mebahiah** | MBHYH | Angel of 1st quinance of Taurus; angel by day of the 5 of Pentacles; also spelled Mibahiah. | 62 |
| **Mechi** | MChY | Battering ram; 64th name of Shem Hamphorash, associated with 4th quinance of Gemini. | 58 |
| **Mehetabel** | MHYTBAL | Wife of Hadar, a King of Edom; daughter of Matred, the daughter of Mezahab. | 97 |
| **Mehujael** | MChWYAL | Son of Irad and father of Methusael; great-grandson of Cain. | 95 |
| **Mekeshar** | MKShR | Sorceress. | 560 |

| | | | |
|---|---|---|---|
| **Mekshepah** | MKShPH | Sorcerer. | 445 |
| **Melah** | MLH | 23rd name of Shem Hamphorash, associated with 5th quinance of Scorpio. | 75 |
| **Melahel** | MLHAL | Angel of 5th quinance of Scorpio; angel by day of the 7 of Cups; also spelled Melchal. | 106 |
| **Melek** | MLK | King; a title of Tiphareth; one of the Melekim. | 570 90 |
| **Melekim** | MLKYM | Kings; Angelic Choir associated with Tiphareth and with the Sphere of the Sun. | 700 140 |
| **Mem** | M | 13th letter of Hebrew alphabet, transliterated as *m*. Spelled out, MYM, "water" (650 or 90). Corresponds to the element Water, the 23rd Path (between Geburah and Hod), and the Tarot Trump XII. The Hanged Man; for additional correspondences, see *Maim*. | 40 600 |
| **Men** | MN | Portion. | 740 90 |
| **Menad** | MND | Prickly; 36th name of Shem Hamphorash, associated with 6th quinance of Capricorn. | 94 |
| **Menaq** | MNQ | 66th name of Shem Hamphorash, associated with 6th quinance of Gemini. | 190 |
| **Mendel** | MNDAL | Angel of 6th quinance of Capricorn; angel by night of the 4 of Pentacles; also spelled Mendial or Monadel. | 125 |
| **Menkl** | | See *Menqel*. | |
| **Menorah** | MNRH | Candlestick; specifically, the seven-branched candlestick in the Temple. | 295 |
| **Menqel** | MNQAL | Angel of 6th quinance of Gemini; angel by night of the 10 of Swords; also spelled Menkl. | 221 |
| **Merkabah** | MRKBH | Chariot. | 267 |
| **Messiah (Mashiach)** | MShYCh | Messiah. | 358 |
| **Metatron** | MTTRWN | Angel of the Presence; World-Prince; Archangel associated with Kether. | 964 314 |
| **Meth** | MTh | Dead. | 440 |
| **Methusael** | MThWShAL | Son of Mehujael and father of Lamech of the generation of Cain. | 777 |

| Methuselah | MThW-ShLCh | Son of Enoch and father of Lamech; grandfather of Noah; lived 969 years, dying in the year of the Deluge (1656 after Creation). | 784 |
| Metzar | MTzR | Distress; isthmus. | 330 |
| Metzer | MTzR | Boundary; 60th name of Shem Hamphorash, associated with 6th quinance of Taurus. | 330 |
| Mevamiah | MWMYH | Angel of 6th quinance of Cancer; angel by night of the 4 of Cups; also spelled Mevamayah or Mevamaih. | 101 |
| Mezahab | MY ZHB | Mother of Matred, mother of Mehetabel, wife of Hadar, a King of Edom. | 64 |
| Meziqim | MZYQYM | Demons; injurers. | 767 / 207 |
| Mi | MY | Who? Which?; whoever; every one. | 50 |
| Miah | MYH | 48th name of Shem Hamphorash, associated with 6th quinance of Pisces. | 55 |
| Mibahiah | | See *Mebahiah.* | |
| Mibzar | MBTzR | A Duke of Edom, associated (with Magdiel) with Yesod. | 332 |
| Michael | MYKAL | 1. Archangel associated with Hod, with Mercury, with the South, and with Fire; 2. Angel ruling the Sun and Sunday; 3. Angel of 6th quinance of Aquarius; angel by night of the 7 of Swords. | 101 |
| Midian | MDYN | A biblical land. | 754 / 104 |
| Mihael | MYHAL | Angel of 6th quinance of Pisces; angel by night of the 10 of Cups; also spelled Mihal. | 86 |
| Mik | MYK | 42nd name of Shem Hamphorash, associated with 6th quinance of Aquarius. | 550 / 70 |
| Milah | MYLH | Circumcision. | 85 |
| Milah | MLH | Word. | 75 |
| Milchamah | MLChMH | War. | 123 |
| Minacharai | MNChRAY | Angel of 2nd decanate of Taurus. | 315 |
| Miriam | MRYM | Sister of Moses; Mary. | 850 / 290 |
| Mishkan | MShKN | Tabernacle. | 1060 / 410 |
| Mishpar | MShPR | Angel of 3rd decanate of Virgo; Regardie | 620 |

|  |  | gives the Hebrew spelling as MSPR, 380. |  |
|---|---|---|---|
| **Mishrath** | MShRATh | Angel of 1st decanate of Sagittarius; Regardie gives the Hebrew spelling as MShRYTh, 950. | 941 |
| **Misnin** | MSNYN | Angel of 1st decanate of Capricorn. | 860 |
|  |  |  | 210 |
| **Mitzrael** | MTzRAL | Angel of 6th quinance of Taurus; angel by night of the 7 of Pentacles; also spelled Mizrael. | 361 |
| **Mitzraim** | MTzRYM | Egypt. | 940 |
|  |  |  | 380 |
| **Mizrach** | MZRCh | East; see *Ruach.* | 255 |
| **Mizrael** |  | See *Mitzrael.* |  |
| **Moab** | MWAB | A biblical land. | 49 |
| **Moach** | MCh | Marrow. | 48 |
| **Mochayel** | MChYAL | Angel of 4th quinance of Gemini; angel by night of the 9 of Swords; also spelled Mochael. | 89 |
| **Moloch** | MLK | Arch-demon corresponding (with Satan) to Kether; according to the *Encyclopaedia Britannica,* it is no accident that Moloch has the same Hebrew spelling as *Melek,* "king." | 570 |
|  |  |  | 90 |
| **Monadel** |  | See *Mendel.* |  |
| **Moph** | MP | Memphis, Egypt. | 840 |
|  |  |  | 120 |
| **Mor** | MR | Myrrh. | 240 |
| **Moses (Mosheh)** | MShH | Moses. | 345 |
| **Motz** | MTz | Chaff. | 940 |
|  |  |  | 130 |
| **Moznaim** | MAZNYM | Scales; Libra. | 708 |
|  |  | Corresponds to Lamed and the 22nd Path. | 148 |
|  |  | Archangel: Zuriel. | 254 |
|  |  | Angel: Chedeqiel. | 153 |
|  |  | Lord of Triplicity by Day: Thergebon. | 1311 |
|  |  |  | 661 |
|  |  | Lord of Triplicity by Night: Achodraon. | 926 |
|  |  |  | 276 |
|  |  | Angel Ruling 7th House: Yahel. | 46 |
|  |  | Angel of 1st Decanate: Tarasni. | 329 |

Angel of 1st Quinance: Yezalel.                               78
Angel of 2nd Quinance: Mebahel.                              78
Angel of 2nd Decanate: Saharnatz.                         1215
                                                           405
Angel of 3rd Quinance: Hariel.                             246
Angel of 4th Quinance: Haqmiah.                            160
Angel of 3rd Decanate: Shachdar.                           512
Angel of 5th Quinance: Laviah.                              52
Angel of 6th Quinance: Kaliel.                              91
Qlippoth: Abiriron (The Clayish Ones).                    1198
                                                           548

Goetic Demons by Day:
   1st Decanate: Sallas (Saleos)                         637
   2nd Decanate: Purson                                1292
                                                           592
   3rd Decanate: Marax (Morax).                        1142
                                                           332

Goetic Demons by Night:
   1st Decanate: Orobas                                 216
   2nd Decanate: Gamori (Gremory)                       249
   3rd Decanate: Voso (Ose, Oso).                       312
Color: Green.
Scent: Galbanum.
Tarot Trump: VIII. Justice.
Tarot Cards associated with Decanates:
   1st Decanate: 2 of Swords.
   2nd Decanate: 3 of Swords.
   3rd Decanate: 4 of Swords.
Direction: Northwest.
Tribe of Israel: Asher.
Apostle: Bartholomew.
Geomantic Figure: Puella.
Mystic Number of 22nd Path: 253.
Ruling Planet: Venus.
Planet Exalted in: Saturn.
Planet in Detriment in: Mars.
Planet in Fall in: Sun.

| | | | |
|---|---|---|---|
| **Muhammad** | MHMMD | "The highly praised one"; the founder of Islam | 132 |
| **Mum** | MWM | Blemish; 72nd name of Shem Hamphorash, associated with 6th quinance of Cancer. | 646 |
| | | | 86 |
| **Muriel** | MWRYAL | Archangel of Cancer. | 287 |
| **Murmus** | MWRM | Goetic demon by night of 3rd decanate | 846 |

of Virgo; also spelled Murmur or Murmux.    286
Duke and Earl commanding 30 legions.
Appears as a warrior riding a griffin and
wearing a ducal crown; preceded by min-
isters sounding trumpets.
Powers: teaches philosophy; constrains
the souls of the dead to appear and
answer questions.
Formerly partly of the Order of Thrones
and partly of the Order of Angels.

| | | | |
|---|---|---|---|
| **Na** | NA | Please, pray; raw, rare; a name of God. | 51 |
| **Naam** | NOM | To be lovely, pleasant. | 720 |
| | | | 160 |
| **Naamah** | NOMH | The Lovely One; sister of Tubal-Cain; a queen of demons; arch-demon corresponding to Malkuth. | 165 |
| **Naberius** | NBR | Goetic demon by day of 3rd decanate of Scorpio. Marquis commanding 19 legions. Appears as a black crane fluttering about the circle; speaks hoarsely. Powers: makes men cunning in arts and sciences, especially rhetoric; restores lost dignities and honors. | 252 |
| **Nachash** | NChSh | Snake, serpent. | 358 |
| **Nachashiron** | NCh-ShYRWN | The Snaky Ones; Qlippoth of Sagittarius. | 1274 |
| | | | 624 |
| **Nahema** | | See *Naamah*. | |
| **Naher** | NHR | River. | 255 |
| **Nahor** | NChWR | 1. Son of Serug and father of Terah; grandfather of Abraham; lived 148 years (1849-1997 after Creation); 2. Son of Terah and brother of Abraham, born in the year 1948 after Creation. | 264 |

| | | | |
|---|---|---|---|
| **Nakhiel** | NKYAL | Intelligence of the Sun. | 111 |
| **Nanael** | NNAAL | Angel of 5th quinance of Aries; angel by day of the 4 of Wands. | 132 |
| **Naphtali** | NPThLY | A tribe of Israel, associated with Virgo. | 570 |
| **Naphula** | NPWL | Goetic demon by night of 3rd decanate of Scorpio; also spelled Vapula. Duke commanding 36 legions. Appears as a lion with griffin's wings. Powers: teaches handicrafts, professions, philosophy, and other sciences. | 166 |
| **Nashim** | NShYM | Women, wives. | 960 400 |
| **Nashimiron** | NShY-MYRWN | Malignant Women; Qlippoth of Pisces. | 1316 666 |
| **Nathdorinel** | NTh-DWRYNAL | Lord of Triplicity by Night for Pisces. | 751 |
| **Navi** | NBYA | Prophet. | 63 |
| **Ned** | ND | Heap, wall. | 54 |
| **Necheshethi** | NChShThY | Coppery, brassy. | 768 |
| **Necheshiron** | | See *Nachashiron*. | |
| **Nechesh-thiron** | NChShThY-RWN | The Brazen Ones; Qlippoth of Scorpio. | 1674 1024 |
| **Nechsheth** | NChShTh | Copper, brass; metal of Venus. | 758 |
| **Negep** | NGP | Plague. | 853 |
| | | The 10 plagues of Egypt were as follows:<br>1. Dam: Blood<br>2. Tzephardea: Frogs<br>3. Kinnim: Vermin<br>4. Arov: Wild Beasts<br>5. Dever: Murrain<br>6. Shechin: Boils<br>7. Barad: Hail<br>8. Arbeh: Locusts<br>9. Choshek: Darkness<br>10. Makath be-Khoroth: Slaying of the Firstborn<br>These are abbreviated DTzK ODSh BAChB, Detzak Adhash Beachav. | 133 |
| **Nelak** | NLK | 21st name of Shem Hamphorash, associated with 3rd quinance of Scorpio. | 580 100 |
| **Nelakiel** | NLKAL | Angel of 3rd quinance of Scorpio; angel | 131 |

|  |  | by day of the 6 of Cups; also spelled Nelokhiel or Nelchael. |  |
|---|---|---|---|
| **Nemamiah** | NMMYH | Angel of 3rd quinance of Taurus; angel by day of the 6 of Pentacles; also spelled Nemamaih. | 145 |
| **Nemem** | NMM | 57th name of Shem Hamphorash, associated with 3rd quinance of Taurus. | 690 130 |
| **Nena** | NNA | 53rd name of Shem Hamphorash, associated with 5th quinance of Aries. | 101 |
| **Nephesh** | NPSh | Lowest part of the tripartite soul, representing the animal instincts. | 430 |
| **Nephilim** | NPLYM | "Giants" (Gen. VI:4). | 770 210 |
| **Neqedah Peshutah** | NQDH PShWTH | The Simple Point; a title of Kether. | 559 |
| **Neqedah Rishonah** | NQDH RAShWNH | The Primordial Point; a title of Kether. | 721 |
| **Ner** | NR | Lamp; prosperity; instruction. | 250 |
| **Nes** | NS | Banner, sign, standard. | 110 |
| **Neshamah** | NShMH | Highest part of the tripartite soul. Neshamah is referred to the Supernal Sephiroth, represents "the highest aspirations of the soul," and is itself divided into three parts: Yechidah: Kether. Chiah: Chokmah. Neshamah: Binah. | 395 |
| **Nesher** | NShR | Eagle, bird of prey. | 550 |
| **Neshiah** | NShYH | Oblivion; one of the seven earths, corresponding to Tiphareth. | 365 |
| **Nethah** | NThH | 25th name of Shem Hamphorash, associated with 1st quinance of Sagittarius. | 455 |
| **Netz** | NTz | Flower; hawk. | 950 140 |
| **Netzach** | NTzCh | Victory; the 7th Sephira. Divine Name: Yahweh Tzabaoth. Archangel: Haniel. Choir of Angels: Elohim; Tarshishim; Principalities. Material World: Nogah, the Sphere of Venus. | 148 |
| **Ni** | NY | Lament. | 60 |

| | | | |
|---|---|---|---|
| **Nimrod** | NMRD | The mighty hunter; son of Cush; founder of many Mesopotamian cities (Gen. X:8-12); a city of ancient Mesopotamia. | 294 |
| **Nineveh** | NYNWH | A city of ancient Mesopotamia. | 121 |
| **Nisan** | NYSN | The 7th Hebrew month, March-April, corresponding roughly to the period when the Sun is in Aries. | 820 170 |
| **Nisetar** | NSThR | Secret, hidden. | 710 |
| **Nith** | NYTh | 54th name of Shem Hamphorash, associated with 6th quinance of Aries. | 460 |
| **Nithael** | NYThAL | Angel of 6th quinance of Aries; angel by night of the 4 of Wands; also spelled Nithal. | 491 |
| **Nithahiah** | NThHYH | Angel of 1st quinance of Sagittarius; angel by day of the 8 of Wands; also spelled Nithhaiah. | 470 |
| **Nithal** | | See *Nithael.* | |
| **Nithhaiah** | | See *Nithahiah.* | |
| **No** | NA | Thebes, Egypt. | 51 |
| **Noah (Noach)** | NCh | Builder of the ark. | 58 |
| **Noah** | NH | Splendor, eminence. | 55 |
| **Nob** | NB | A town in Benjamin. | 52 |
| **Nod** | NWD | The land where Cain went after murdering Abel. | 60 |
| **Nogah** | NWGH | Venus. | 64 |

The Sphere of Venus corresponds to Netzach.

The planet Venus corresponds to Daleth and the 14th Path.

Archangel: Haniel.

Angel: Anael.

Intelligence: Hagiel.

Spirit: Kedemel.

Olympic Spirit: Hagith.

Metal: Copper.

Color: Green.

Stone: Emerald, turquoise.

Scent: Sandalwood, Myrtle, all Soft Voluptuous Odors.

Tarot Trump: III, The Empress.

Rules Taurus and Libra.

|  |  | Exalted in Pisces. Detriment in Aries and Scorpio. Fall in Virgo. |  |
|---|---|---|---|
| **Noph** | NP | Memphis, Egypt. | 850 130 |
| **Notariqon** | NWTRY-QWN | The cabalistic theory that words may meaningfully be taken as acronyms for phrases and vice-versa (e.g., ChN, "grace," and ChKMH NSThRH, "secret wisdom"). | 1081 431 |
| **Nu** | NW | Egyptian sky goddess; see *The Book of the Law.* | 56 |
| **Nuit** | NWYTh | Egyptian sky goddess; see *The Book of the Law.* | 466 |
| **Nun** | N | 14th letter of Hebrew alphabet, transliterated as *n.* Spelled out, NYN, "fish"; father of Joshua (756 or 106). Corresponds to Scorpio, the 24th Path (between Tiphareth and Netzach), and the Tarot Trump XIII. Death; for additional correspondences, see *Akrab.* | 50 700 |
| **Nundohar** | NYNDWHR | Angel of 2nd decanate of Scorpio. | 325 |

| **'O** | AW | Or. | 7 |
|---|---|---|---|
| **Och** | AWCh | Olympic Planetary Spirit of the Sun. | 15 |
| **Oel** | OWAL | Angel of 5th astrological house. | 107 |
| **Ogarman** | OWGRMON | Lord of Triplicity by Night for Gemini. | 1089 439 |
| **Ogiel** | OWGYAL | The Hinderers; Qlippoth of Chokmah; variously spelled Ghagiel (Crowley), Chaigidel (Mathers), Ghogiel (Regardie), Chaigidiel (Waite). | 120 |
| **Oholibamah** |  | R.S.V. spelling of Aholibamah. |  |
| **Ol** | OL | Yoke. | 100 |
| **Ol** | OWAL | See *Oel.* |  |

| | | | |
|---|---|---|---|
| **Olam** | OWLM | World; also spelled Olahm. | 701 |
| | | | 141 |
| **Olam** | OWLM | The World of Atziluth; the World of | 1243 |
| **Atziluth** | ATzY- | Nobility; the World of Archetypes; see | 683 |
| | LWTh | *Atziluth.* | |
| **Olam ha-** | OWLM | The World of Assiah; the World of Action; | 1091 |
| **Assiah** | HOShYH | the Material World; see *Assiah.* | 531 |
| **Olam ha-** | OWLM | The World of Briah; the World of Crea- | 924 |
| **Briah** | HBRYAH | tion; see *Briah.* | 364 |
| **Olam ha-** | OWLM | The World of Shells; the World of | 1337 |
| **Qlippoth** | HQLY- | Demons; see *Qlippoth.* | 777 |
| | PWTh | | |
| **Olam ha-** | OWLM | The World of Yetzirah; the World of For- | 1021 |
| **Yetzirah** | HYTzYRH | mation; see *Yetzirah.* | 461 |
| **Olam** | OWLM | The World of Foundations; the Sphere of | 1192 |
| **Yesodoth** | YSWDWTh | the Elements; the part of the material | 632 |
| | | world corresponding to Malkuth; tradi- | |
| | | tionally given as Cholam Yesodoth, the | |
| | | Breaker of Foundations; Olam Yesodoth | |
| | | is the restored spelling promulgated by | |
| | | Regardie in *The Golden Dawn.* | |
| **Olmiah** | | See *Elemiah.* | |
| **Omael** | | See *Avamel.* | |
| **On** | AWN | Strength; wealth; sorrow. | 707 |
| | | | 57 |
| **Onan** | AWNN | Son of Judah; condemned by God for fail- | 757 |
| | | ing to do his duty to his dead brother's wife. | 107 |
| **Ophan** | AWPN | Wheel; one of the Ophanim. | 787 |
| | | | 137 |
| **Ophanim** | AWPNYM | Wheels (Ez. I:16); Angelic Choir associ- | 747 |
| | | ated with Chokmah and with the Sphere | 187 |
| | | of the Zodiac; also spelled Auphanim. | |
| **Ophiel** | AWPYAL | Olympic Planetary Spirit of Mercury. | 128 |
| **Ophir** | OPYR | Earth. | 360 |
| **Or** | AWR | Light; also spelled Aor, Aur, etc. | 207 |
| **Oreb** | ORB | Raven, crow. | 272 |
| **Oreb Zaraq** | ORB ZRQ | The Raven of Dispersion; Qlippoth of | 579 |
| | | Netzach; variously given as A'arab Zaraq | |
| | | (Crowley), Harab-Serapel (Mathers), | |
| | | Gharab Tzerek (Regardie), Harab Serap | |
| | | (Waite). | |

| Oriax | WRYATz | Goetic demon by night of 2nd decanate of Scorpio; also spelled Orias. | 1117 307 |
| | | Marquis commanding 30 legions. | |
| | | Appears as a lion with a serpent's tail, riding a mighty, strong horse and holding two great hissing serpents in his right hand. | |
| | | Powers: teaches the virtues of the stars and planets; transforms men; gives dignities, prelacies, and the confirmation thereof; gives favor with friends and foes. | |
| Orions | | Demon King of Air; no Hebrew spelling. | |
| Or Mopla | AWR MWPLA | The Hidden Light; a title of Kether. | 364 |
| Orobas | AWRAWB | Goetic demon by night of 1st decanate of Libra. | 216 |
| | | Prince commanding 20 legions. | |
| | | Appears as a horse; assumes human form upon command. | |
| | | Powers: tells fortunes; gives dignities, prelacies, and the favor of friends and foes; gives true answers concerning divinity and the creation of the world. | |
| | | Very faithful to the exorcist; will not allow him to be tempted by any spirit. | |
| Or Pashot | AWR PShWT | The Simple Light; a title of Kether. | 602 |
| Or Penimi | AWR PNMY | The Internal Light; a title of Kether. | 397 |
| Oz | OZ | Strength; violence; glory. | 77 |

| Pach | PCh | Danger. | 88 |
| Pachad | PChD | Fear; a title of Geburah. | 92 |
| Pag | PG | Unripe fig. | 83 |
| Pahaliah | PHLYH | Angel of 2nd quinance of Scorpio; angel | 130 |

| | | | |
|---|---|---|---|
| | | by night of the 5 of Cups; also spelled Pehilyah. | |
| **Pahel** | PHL | 20th name of Shem Hamphorash, associated with 2nd quinance of Scorpio. | 115 |
| **Paimon** | PAYMWN | Demon King of Fire and Goetic demon by day of 3rd decanate of Gemini. | 837 |
| | | | 187 |
| | | To be observed toward the West. | |
| | | Appears as a man sitting on a dromedary with a glorious crown preceded by a host of spirits like men with trumpets, cymbals, and other musical instruments; roars upon appearing; inarticulate unless compelled to speak clearly. | |
| | | Powers: teaches all arts and sciences and anything else the exorcist wishes to know; gives and confirms dignity; binds any man and makes him subject to the exorcist; gives good familiars who can teach all arts. Formerly of the Order of Dominations. | |
| | | His legions of spirits are partly of the Order of Angels and partly of the Order of Potentates. | |
| | | If called Paimon only, the exorcist must make him an offering; he will then be attended by two Kings called Labal and Abalim, other spirits of the Order of Potentates, and 25 legions of infernal spirits. | |
| **Pak** | PK | Flask, bottle. | 580 |
| | | | 100 |
| **Pakiel** | PKYAL | Angel of Cancer. | 141 |
| **Par** | PR | Bull; victim; offering. | 280 |
| **Parush** | PRWSh | Hermit. | 586 |
| **Pas** | PS | Extremity. | 140 |
| **Pash** | PSh | Folly. | 380 |
| **Pasiel** | PShYAL | Angel of 12th astrological house. | 421 |
| **Path** | PTh | Bit, morsel. | 480 |
| **Pau** | POW | A city of Edom; city of King Hadar. | 156 |
| **Paz** | PZ | Pure gold. | 87 |
| **Pe** | P | 17th letter of Hebrew alphabet, transliterated as *p*, *ph*, or *f*. | 80 |
| | | | 800 |

| | | | |
|---|---|---|---|
| | | Spelled out, PH, "mouth" (85). | |
| | | Corresponds to Mars, the 27th Path (between Netzach and Hod), and the Tarot Trump XVI. The Tower; for additional correspondences, see *Madim*. | |
| Pehilyah | | See *Pahaliah*. | |
| Pele | PLA | The Wonder; a title of Kether. | 111 |
| Peleg | PLG | Son of Eber and father of Reu; great-great-grandson of Shem; lived 239 years (1757-1996 after Creation). | 113 |
| Pen | PN | Lest. | 780 |
| | | | 130 |
| Phaleg | PLG | Olympic Planetary Spirit of Mars. | 113 |
| Pharaoh | PROH | King of Egypt. | 355 |
| Phenex | PANTz | Goetic demon by night of 1st decanate of Aries; also spelled Pheynix. | 1031 |
| | | | 121 |
| | | Marquis commanding 20 legions. | |
| | | Appears as a phoenix with the voice of a child. | |
| | | Powers: speaks on all wonderful sciences; writes poetry. | |
| | | The exorcist must ignore his beautiful singing and ask him to assume human form after a while. | |
| | | Told Solomon he hoped to return to the 7th Throne after another 1200 years. | |
| Phorlakh | PWRLAK | Angel of Earth. | 817 |
| | | | 337 |
| Phrath | PRTh | Euphrates; a river of Eden, associated with Earth. | 680 |
| Phul | PWL | Olympic Planetary Spirit of the Moon. | 116 |
| Pinon | PYNN | A Duke of Edom, associated with Tiphareth. | 840 |
| | | | 190 |
| Pison | PYShWN | A river of Eden, associated with Fire. | 1096 |
| | | | 446 |
| Poi | PWY | 56th name of Shem Hamphorash, associated with 2nd quinance of Taurus. | 96 |
| Poiel | | See *Poyel*. | |
| Polayan | PLAYN | Lord of Triplicity by Night for Aquarius. | 821 |
| | | | 171 |
| Pooyal | | See *Poyel*. | |

| Poth | PTh | Opening; pudenda. | 480 |
| Poyel | PWYAL | Angel of 2nd quinance of Taurus; angel by night of the 5 of Pentacles; also spelled Pooyal or Poiel. | 127 |
| Puk | PWK | Antimony. | 586 |
|  |  |  | 106 |
| Pul | PWL | A King of Assyria (Tiglath-Pileser III). | 116 |
| Purson | PWRShWN | Goetic demon by day of 2nd decanate of Libra. | 1292 |
|  |  |  | 592 |

King commanding 22 legions, partly of the Order of Virtues and partly of the Order of Thrones.

Appears as a comely man with a lion's face, riding a bear and carrying a viper; preceded by many trumpets blowing.

Powers: knows all hidden things; discovers treasure; tells fortunes; can assume a body either human or aerial; answers truly concerning all earthly things, both secret and divine, and the creation of the world; brings good familiars.

| Qab | QB | Unit of measure. | 102 |
| Qabalah |  | See *Cabala*. |  |
| Qadesh | QDSh | Holiness. | 404 |
| Qadesh la-Yahweh | QDSh LYHWH | Holy to the Lord (emblazoned on the mitre of the High Priest). | 460 |
| Qadosh | QDWSh | Holy. | 410 |
| Qadosh Qadeshim | QDWSh QDShYM | Holy of Holies; Sancti Sanctorum. | 1424 |
|  |  |  | 864 |
| Qaftzaphoni | QPTzPWNY | Prince and King of Heaven, husband of Mehetabel, father of Lilith the Younger. | 416 |
| Qal | QL | Swift. | 130 |
| Qalb | QLB | Heart *(Arabic)*. | 132 |
| Qamat | QMT | To make wrinkled. | 149 |
| Qar | QR | Cold; quiet. | 300 |

| Qash | QSh | Straw, chaff. | 400 |
| Qasshat | QShTh | Bow; Sagittarius. | 800 |

It is written that the Lord placed Qasshat in the heavens as a sign of His covenant: *Eth qasshati nathathi beanan we-ha-yethah loth berith beyn u-beyn ha-aretz*: (Gen. IX:13).

Sagittarius corresponds to Samkeh and the 25th Path.

| | |
|---|---|
| Archangel: Advakiel. | 72 |
| Angel: Saritiel (Regardie has Sameqiel, reversing Sagittarius and Capricorn). | 320 |
| Lord of Triplicity by Day: Ahoz. | 19 |
| Lord of Triplicity by Night: Lebarmim. | 882 |
| | 322 |
| Angel Ruling 9th House: Soyasel. | 237 |
| Angel of 1st Decanate: Mishrath. | 941 |
| Angel of 1st Quinance: Nithahiah. | 470 |
| Angel of 2nd Quinance: Haayah. | 22 |
| Angel of 2nd Decanate: Vehrin. | 921 |
| | 271 |
| Angel of 3rd Quinance: Yerathel. | 641 |
| Angel of 4th Quinance: Sahiah. | 321 |
| Angel of 3rd Decanate: Aboha. | 15 |
| Angel of 5th Quinance: Reyayel. | 251 |
| Angel of 6th Quinance: Avamel. | 78 |
| Qlippoth: Nachashiron (The Snaky Ones) | 1274 |
| (from *Nachash*, "snake," "serpent"). | 624 |
| Goetic Demons by Day: | |
| 1st Decanate: Glasya-Labolas | 162 |
| 2nd Decanate: Bimé (Buné, Bim) | 612 |
| | 52 |
| 3rd Decanate: Ronové. | 272 |
| Goetic Demons by Night: | |
| 1st Decanate: Zagan | 711 |
| | 61 |
| 2nd Decanate: Valu (Volac, Valak, Ualac) | 37 |
| 3rd Decanate: Andras. | 255 |
| Color: Blue. | |
| Scent: Lign-aloes. | |

Tarot Trump: XIV. Temperance.
Tarot Cards associated with Decanates:
   1st Decanate: 8 of Wands.
   2nd Decanate: 9 of Wands.
   3rd Decanate: 10 of Wands.
Direction: West, above.
Tribe of Israel: Benjamin.
Apostle: James, son of Zebedee.
Geomantic Figure: Acquisitio.
Mystic Number of 25th Path: 325.
Ruling Planet: Jupiter.
Exalted in: Descending Node.
Planet in Detriment in: Mercury.
In Fall in: Ascending Node.

| | | | |
|---|---|---|---|
| **Qat** | QT | Small. | 109 |
| **Qaw** | QW | Line; chord; norm. | 106 |
| **Qayitz** | QYTz | Summer. | 1010 |
| | | | 200 |
| **Qe** | QA | Vomit. | 101 |
| **Qedem** | QDM | Before; the East; ancient things. | 704 |
| | | | 144 |
| **Qelalah** | QLLH | Curse. | 165 |
| **Qemetiel** | QMTYAL | The Crowd of Gods; Qlippoth of Ain. | 190 |
| **Qen** | QN | Nest. | 800 |
| | | | 150 |
| **Qerashamen** | QROShMN | The 7th through 12th letters of the 42-letter name of God, associated with Chesed. | 760 |
| **Qetz** | QTz | End. | 1000 |
| | | | 190 |
| **Qi** | QYA | Vomit. | 111 |
| **Qlippoth** | QLYPWTh | Shells; demons. | 626 |

The Infernal Orders of Qlippoth more or less correspond to the Orders of Angels. They are:

| | | |
|---|---|---|
| **Ain** | Qemetiel | The Crowd of Gods |
| **Ain Soph** | Belial | Without God |
| **Ain Soph Or** | Athiel | Uncertainty |

| Kether | Thaumiel | Twins of God |
|---|---|---|
| Chokmah | Ogiel | The Hinderers |
| Binah | Satariel | The Concealers |
| Chesed | Gasheklah | The Smiters |
| Geburah | Golachab | The Arsonists |
| Tiphareth | Tageriron | The Hagglers |
| Netzach | Oreb Zaraq | The Raven of Dispersion |
| Hod | Samael | Poison of God |
| Yesod | Gamaliel | The Obscene Ones |
| Malkuth | Lilith | Queen of the Night |
| Aries | Beiriron | The Herd |
| Taurus | Adimiron | The Bloody Ones |
| Gemini | Tzeli-limiron | The Clangers |
| Cancer | Shichiriron | The Black Ones |
| Leo | Shalhe-biron | The Flaming Ones |
| Virgo | Tzaphiriron | The Scratchers |
| Libra | Abiriron | The Clayish Ones |
| Scorpio | Nechesh-thiron | The Brazen Ones |
| Sagittarius | Nacha-shiron | The Snakey Ones |
| Capricorn | Dagdagiron | The Fishy Ones |
| Aquarius | Bahimiron | The Bestial Ones |
| Pisces | Nashimiron | Malignant Women |

The Qlippoth of the planets are the same as those of the corresponding Sephiroth.

**Qoph**  Q  19th letter of Hebrew alphabet, transliterated as *q* or *k*.  100
Spelled out, QWP, "back of head" (906 or 186).
Corresponds to Pisces, the 29th Path (between Netzach and Malkuth), and the Tarot Trump XVIII. The Moon; for additional correspondences, see *Dagim*.

**Qotz**  QWTz  Thorn.  1006
196

| | | | |
|---|---|---|---|
| Ra | RO | Evil. | 270 |
| Raadar | RODR | Lord of Triplicity by Day for Cancer. | 474 |
| Raah | RAH | To see, observe, perceive, consider; 69th name of Shem Hamphorash, associated with 3rd quinance of Cancer. | 206 |
| Raah | ROH | Evil. | 275 |
| Rab | RB | Many, much; great, mighty. | 202 |
| Racham | RChM | Vulture. | 808 |
| | | | 248 |
| Rachel | RChL | Wife of Jacob; mother of Joseph and Benjamin. | 238 |
| Rahadetz | RHDTz | Angel of 2nd Decanate of Cancer; Regardie gives the Hebrew spelling as RHDO, 279. | 1109 |
| | | | 299 |
| Rahael | RAHAL | Angel of 3rd quinance of Cancer; angel by day of the 3 of Cups; also spelled Rochel. | 237 |
| Ra-Hoor | RA HWWR | Ra-Horus, an Egyptian god; see *The Book of the Law.* | 418 |
| Rakav | RKB | To ride, drive; horseman, driver. | 222 |
| Ram | RM | Ram (Job XXXII:2). | 800 |
| | | | 240 |
| Ramara | RMRA | Lord of Triplicity by Day for Pisces. | 441 |
| Rameses | ROMSS | A King of Egypt; a district of Egypt. | 430 |
| Raphael | RPAL | "God's Healing"; archangel associated with Tiphareth, with the Sun, with the East, and with Air; angel ruling Mercury and Wednesday. | 311 |
| Raq | RQ | Thin; only. | 300 |
| Raqia | RQYO | Firmament; the 2nd Heaven, corresponding to Hod. | 380 |
| Rashith | RAShYTh | Beginning. | 911 |
| Rashith ha-Gilgalim | RAShYTh HGLGLYM | The Beginning of Revolvings; the Primum Mobile, the part of the material world corresponding to Kether. | 1592 1032 |
| Ratz | RTz | Piece. | 1100 |
| | | | 290 |

| | | | |
|---|---|---|---|
| **Ratzon** | RTzWN | Delight, favor. | 996 |
| | | | 346 |
| **Räum** | RAWM | Goetic demon by night of 1st decanate of | 807 |
| | | Taurus. | 247 |
| | | Earl commanding 30 legions. | |
| | | Appears as a crow; assumes human form upon command. | |
| | | Powers: steals treasures from kings' houses and takes it where he is told; destroys men's cities and dignities; tells fortunes; causes love between friends and foes. | |
| | | Formerly of the Order of Thrones. | |
| **Ravak** | RBK | To be mixed, mingled. | 702 |
| | | | 222 |
| **Rayadyah** | RAYDYH | Angel of 2nd decanate of Virgo; Regardie gives the Hebrew spelling as RAYHYH, 231. | 230 |
| **Raydel** | RAYDAL | Lord of Triplicity by Day for Taurus. | 246 |
| **Raziel** | RZYAL | Archangel associated with Chokmah and with the Sphere of the Zodiac. | 248 |
| **Rea** | RO | Friend. | 270 |
| **Rebekah** (Ribeqah) | RBQH | Wife of Isaac; mother of Jacob. | 307 |
| **Reha** | RHO | 39th name of Shem Hamphorash, associated with 3rd quinance of Aquarius. | 275 |
| **Rehael** | RHOAL | Angel of 3rd quinance of Aquarius; angel by day of the 6 of Swords; also spelled Reha'ayel. | 306 |
| **Rehoboth** | RHBYTh | A city of Edom; city of King Saul. | 617 |
| **Rekev** | RKB | Vehicle. | 222 |
| **Reiiel** | | See *Reyayel.* | |
| **Resh** | R | 20th letter of Hebrew alphabet, transliterated as *r*. | 200 |
| | | Spelled out, RYSh, "head" (510). | |
| | | Corresponds to the Sun, to the 30th Path (between Hod and Yesod), and to the Tarot Trump XIX. The Sun; for additional correspondences, see *Shemesh.* | |
| **Retzeltoth** | | Francis Barrett's misprint for TzLMWTh, Tzal-Maweth, q.v. | |

reserved for pagans and idolaters.

| | | | |
|---|---|---|---|
| **Reu** | ROW | Son of Peleg and father of Serug; great-great-grandfather of Abraham; lived 239 years (1787-2026 after Creation). | 276 |
| **Reuben** | RAWBN | A tribe of Israel, associated with Aquarius. | 909 259 |
| **Reuel** | ROWAL | Friend of God; Moses' father-in-law, also called Jethro. | 307 |
| **Reyayel** | RYYAL | Angel of 5th quinance of Sagittarius; angel by day of the 10 of Wands; also spelled Reiiel. | 251 |
| **Ri** | RY | Rushing water. | 210 |
| **Risha** | RYShA | Head; a title of Kether. | 511 |
| **Risha Dela** | RYShA DLA | The Head Which Is Not; a title of Kether. | 546 |
| **Risha Havurah** | RYShA HWWRH | The White Head; a title of Kether. | 733 |
| **Riyi** | RYY | 29th name of Shem Hamphorash, associated with 5th quinance of Sagittarius. | 220 |
| **Rob** | RB | Multitude, abundance. | 202 |
| **Rochel** | | See *Rahael.* | |
| **Rok** | RK | Softness. | 700 220 |
| **Rom Maalah** | ROM MOLH | The Inscrutable Height; a title of Kether. | 951 |
| **Ron** | RN | Shout, rejoicing. | 900 250 |
| **Ronove** | RYNWW | Goetic demon by day of 3rd decanate of Sagittarius. Marquis and Earl commanding 19 legions. Appears as a monster. Powers: teaches rhetoric; gives good servants, knowledge of tongues, and favors with friends or foes. | 272 |
| **Roq** | RQ | Saliva. | 300 |
| **Ruach** | RWCh | Breath, wind, spirit; middle part of the tripartite soul, representing "the mind and reasoning powers"; Air, one of the four elements, associated with Aleph and the 11th Path. Cardinal Point: East (Mizrach). Tetramorph: Man. | 214 |

Evangelist: Matthew.

Color: Yellow.

Properties: Hot and Moist.

Elementals: Sylphs.

Letter of Tetragrammaton: Waw.

Cabalistic World: Yetzirah.

Archangel: Raphael.

Angel: Chassan.

Ruler: Ariel.

King: Paralda.

Supreme Elemental King (Enochian): TAHOELOJ.

Demon Prince: Azazel.

Demon King: Orions.

Demon King (Goetia): Amaymon.

River of Eden: Hiddikel (Tigris).

Infernal River: Cocytus.

Tarot Trump: 0. The Fool.

Tarot Suit: Swords.

Tarot Court Cards: Kings; Princes.

Enochian Word: EXARP.

Enochian Divine Names: ORO IBAH AOZPI.

Tattwa: Vayu (blue circle).

Scent: Galbanum.

Humor: Phlegm.

Jungian Function: Thinking.

Chinese System: East, Blue (or Turquoise), Dragon.

| | | | |
|---|---|---|---|
| **Sabbath** | ShBTh | Day of Rest. | 702 |
| **Sabnock** | ShBNWK | Goetic demon by night of 1st decanate | 858 |
| | | of Gemini; also spelled Savnok. | 378 |
| | | Marquis commanding 50 legions. | |
| | | Appears as an armed soldier with a lion's | |

head, riding a pale horse.

Powers: builds and arms high towers, castles, and cities; afflicts men for many days with wounds and sores rotten and full of worms; gives good familiars. Crowley, 777, gives the Hebrew spelling as ShBNYK, 862 or 382, but this is probably a misprint.

| | | | |
|---|---|---|---|
| Sachiel | SChYAL | Angel ruling Jupiter and Thursday. | 109 |
| Sad | SD | Stocks. | 64 |
| Sadhe | Tz | 18th letter of Hebrew alphabet, transliterated as *tz*, *ts*, or *ṣ*; also spelled Tzaddi. | 90<br>900 |

Spelled out, TzDY, "fish-hook" (104). Corresponds to Aquarius (or Aries), the 28th Path (between Netzach and Yesod), and the Tarot Trump XVII. The Star (or IV. The Emperor); for additional correspondences, see *Deli*.

The confusion as to the attribution of the astrological sign and Tarot Trump to Sadhe is due to *The Book of the Law*, which says that Sadhe "is not the Star."

| | | | |
|---|---|---|---|
| Sael | SAL | 45th name of Shem Hamphorash, associated with 3rd quinance of Pisces. | 91 |
| Sagarash | SGRSh | Angel of 1st decanate of Gemini. | 563 |
| Sahaqnab | SHQNB | Lord of Triplicity by Night for Scorpio. | 217 |
| Saharnatz | SHRNTz | Angel of 2nd decanate of Libra. | 1215<br>405 |
| Sahiah | ShAHYH | Angel of 4th quinance of Sagittarius; angel by night of the 9 of Wands; also spelled Seehiah. | 321 |
| Sahiber | SHYBR | Angel of 3rd decanate of Leo; Regardie gives the Hebrew spelling as SHYBH, 82. | 277 |
| Sair | ShOYR | Hairy one; he-goat; demon; hairy. | 580 |
| Saitel | | See *Sitael*. | |
| Saitziel | SAYTzYAL | Angel of Scorpio. | 202 |
| Sak | SK | Crowd. | 560<br>80 |
| Sal | SL | Basket. | 90 |
| Salah<br>(Shelah) | ShLCh | Son of Arphaxad and father of Eber; grandson of Shem; lived 433 years (1693- | 338 |

|  |  | 2126 after Creation). |  |
|---|---|---|---|
| **Saliah** | SALYH | Angel of 3rd quinance of Pisces; angel by day of the 9 of Cups; also spelled Sealiah. | 106 |
| **Sallos** | ShALWSh | Goetic demon by day of 1st decanate of Libra; also spelled Saleos.<br>Duke commanding 30 legions.<br>Appears as a gallant soldier riding a crocodile and wearing a ducal crown, "but peaceably."<br>Powers: procures love. | 637 |
| **Sam** | SM | Spice; drug; poison. | 660<br>100 |
| **Samael** | SMAL | "Poison of God"; Angel of Death; the Prince of Demons, equated with Satan; in particular, the demon prince of Fire; husband of Isheth Zenunim, the Woman of Whoredom, the Demon of Prostitution, and father of Chioa, the Beast; the husband of Lilith; Qlippoth of Hod; according to 777, arch-demon corresponding to Chokmah. | 131 |
| **Samekh** | S | 15th letter of Hebrew alphabet, transliterated as *s*.<br>Spelled out, SMK, "prop or support" (600 or 120).<br>Corresponds to Sagittarius, the 25th Path (between Tiphareth and Yesod), and the Tarot Trump XIV. Temperance; for additional correspondences, see *Qasshat*. | 60 |
| **Sameqiel** | SMQYAL | Angel of Capricorn. | 241 |
| **Samlah** | ShMLH | A King of Edom, associated with Netzach; his city was Masrekah. | 375 |
| **Samuel (Shemuel)** | ShMWAL | Samuel | 377 |
| **Sanahem** | SNHM | Lord of Triplicity by Day for Leo. | 715<br>155 |
| **Sandali** | SNDLOY | Lord of Triplicity by Day for Capricorn. | 224 |
| **Sandalphon** | SNDLPWN | Archangel associated with Malkuth. | 930<br>280 |
| **Sansenoy** | SNSNWY | One of the three angels invoked against Lilith, the other two being Senoy and | 236 |

|          |          | Semangeloph. | |
|----------|----------|-----------------------------------------------|------|
| **Sapatawi** | SPOTAWY | Lord of Triplicity by Night for Aries. | 236 |
| **Saph** | SP | Threshold, entrance. | 860 |
|          |          |                                               | 140 |
| **Saq** | ShQ | Sack. | 400 |
| **Sar** | SR | Ill-humored. | 260 |
| **Sar** | ShR | Master, prince, head, chief. | 500 |
| **Sarah** | ShRH | Wife of Abraham. | 505 |
| **Sarai** | ShRY | Wife of Abram. | 510 |
| **Sarash** | SORSh | Lord of Triplicity by Day for Gemini. | 630 |
| **Sarayel** | SRAYAL | Angel of Gemini. | 302 |
| **Saritiel** | SRYTYAL | Angel of Sagittarius. | 320 |
| **Sarton** | SRTN | Crab; Cancer. | 969 |
|          |          | Corresponds to Cheth and the 18th Path. | 319 |
|          |          | Archangel: Muriel. | 287 |
|          |          | Angel: Pakiel. | 141 |
|          |          | Lord of Triplicity by Day: Raadar. | 474 |
|          |          | Lord of Triplicity by Night: Akel. | 121 |
|          |          | Angel Ruling 4th House: Kael. | 121 |
|          |          | Angel of 1st Decanate: Mathravash. | 947 |
|          |          | Angel of 1st Quinance: Ayoel. | 112 |
|          |          | Angel of 2nd Quinance: Chabuyah. | 31 |
|          |          | Angel of 2nd Decanate: Rahadetz. | 1109 |
|          |          |                                               | 299 |
|          |          | Angel of 3rd Quinance: Rahael. | 237 |
|          |          | Angel of 4th Quinance: Yebamiah. | 67 |
|          |          | Angel of 3rd Decanate: Alinkir. | 321 |
|          |          | Angel of 5th Quinance: Hayayel. | 56 |
|          |          | Angel of 6th Quinance: Mevamiah. | 101 |
|          |          | Qlippoth: Shichiriron (The Black Ones). | 1434 |
|          |          |                                               | 784 |
|          |          | Goetic Demons by Day: | |
|          |          | 1st Decanate: Buer. | 209 |
|          |          | 2nd Decanate: Gusion. | 785 |
|          |          |                                               | 135 |
|          |          | 3rd Decanate: Sitri. | 529 |
|          |          | Goetic Demons by Night: | |
|          |          | 1st Decanate: Bifrons. | 298 |
|          |          | 2nd Decanate: Uvall (Vual). | 38 |
|          |          | 3rd Decanate: Haagente. | 528 |
|          |          | Color: Amber (Orange-Yellow). | |

Scent: Onycha.
Tarot Trump: VII. The Chariot.
Tarot Cards associated with Decanates:
    1st Decanate: 2 of Cups.
    2nd Decanate: 3 of Cups.
    3rd Decanate: 4 of Cups.
Direction: East, below.
Tribe of Israel: Issachar.
Apostle: John.
Geomantic Figures: Populus and Via.
Mystic Number of 18th Path: 171.
Ruling Planet: Moon.
Planet Exalted in: Jupiter.
Planet in Detriment in: Saturn.
Planet in Fall in: Mars.

| | | | |
|---|---|---|---|
| **Sas** | SS | Moth. | 120 |
| **Saspam** | SSPM | Angel of 1st decanate of Aquarius. | 800 |
| | | | 240 |
| **Satan** | ShTN | Adversary, accuser; arch-demon corresponding (with Moloch) to Kether; Prince of Demons, King of Hell, etc. | 1009 359 |
| **Satander** | STNDR | Angel of 3rd decanate of Aries. | 323 |
| **Satariel** | SAThA-RYAL | The Concealers; Qlippoth of Binah. | 703 |
| **Sateraton** | STROTN | Lord of Triplicity by Day for Aries. | 1048 398 |
| **Sathariel** | | See *Satariel.* | |
| **Satrip** | STRYP | Angel of 3rd decanate of Pisces. | 1079 359 |
| **Saul** | ShAWL | A King of Edom, associated with Hod; his city was Rehoboth; Saul, later Paul, of the New Testament. | 337 |
| **Seach** | ShCh | Thought, meditation. | 308 |
| **Sealiah** | | See *Saliah.* | |
| **Seehiah** | | See *Sahiah.* | |
| **Seere** | ShAR | Goetic demon by night of 1st decanate of Pisces; also spelled Sear or Seir. Prince commanding 26 legions. Under Amaymon, King of the East. Appears as a beautiful man riding a winged horse. | 501 |

Powers: runs errands, a task facilitated by the fact that he can traverse the entire earth instantly; brings many things to pass suddenly; tells truly about theft, hidden treasure, and many other things. Good-natured and cooperative.

| | | | |
|---|---|---|---|
| **Seg** | SG | Secret name of the World of Briah. | 63 |
| **Seh** | ShH | Sheep, goat. | 305 |
| **Seir Anpin** | ShOYR ANPYN | The Bearded Countenance; a title of Tiphareth. | 1421 771 |
| **Seirim** | ShOYRYM | Hairy ones; he-goats; demons. | 1190 630 |
| **Sek** | ShK | Thorn; enclosure. | 800 320 |
| **Sellam** | SLM | Ladder. | 690 130 |
| **Semangeloph** | SMNGLWP | One of the three angels invoked against Lilith, the other two being Senoy and Sansenoy. | 989 269 |
| **Senoy** | SNWY | One of the three angels invoked against Lilith, the other two being Sansenoy and Semangeloph. | 126 |
| **Sephalim** | SPLYM | Cups; Tarot suit associated with Water. | 780 220 |
| **Sephel** | SPL | Cup. | 170 |
| **Sepher** | SPR | Book. | 340 |
| **Sepher ha-Torah** | SPR HThWRH | Book of the Law; the Pentateuch. | 956 |
| **Sepher ha-Zohar** | SPR HZHR | Book of Splendor, a basic text of cabalism. | 557 |
| **Sepher Yetzirah** | SPR YTzYRH | Book of Formation, a basic text of cabalism. | 655 |
| **Sephira** | SPYRH | Number; sphere; emanation. | 355 |
| **Sephiroth** | SPYRWTh | Numbers; spheres; emanations. | 756 |
| **Seraph** | ShRP | Flaming Serpent; one of the Seraphim; Ruler of Fire. | 1300 580 |
| **Seraphim** | ShRPYM | Flaming Serpents (Isaiah VI:6); Angelic Choir associated with Geburah and with the Sphere of Mars. | 1190 630 |
| **Serug** | ShRWG | Son of Reu and father of Nahor; great-grandfather of Abraham; lived 230 years | 509 |

|          |          | (1819-2049 after Creation).                                |       |
|----------|----------|-----------------------------------------------------------|-------|
| Set      | ST       | Transgression, error, sin.                                | 69    |
| Set      | ShT      | Transgression.                                            | 309   |
| Seth     | ShTh     | Son of Adam and Eve; father of Enos; lived 912 years (130-1042 after Creation). | 700   |
| Sethav   | SThW     | Autumn.                                                    | 466   |
| Shaah    | ShAH     | To lay waste, devastate; 28th name of Shem Hamphorash, associated with 4th quinance of Sagittarius. | 306   |
| Shaah    | ShOH     | Hour.                                                      | 375   |
| Shaare-Maweth | ShORY- | Gates of Death; the 3rd hell, corresponding to Netzach and to the Islamic *Hutamah* reserved for Jews. | 1026  |
| Shabbathai | ShBThAY | Saturn. | 713 |

The Sphere of Saturn corresponds to
Binah.
The planet Saturn corresponds to Taw
and the 32nd Path.
Archangel: Tzaphqiel.
Angel: Cassiel.
Intelligence: Agiel.
Spirit: Zazel.
Olympic Spirit: Arathron.
Metal: Lead.
Color: Indigo (Blue-Violet).
Stone: Onyx.
Scent: Storax, all Dull and Heavy Odors.
Tarot Trump: XXI. The World.
Rules Capricorn and Aquarius.
Exalted in Libra.
Detriment in Cancer and Leo.
Fall in Aries.

| Shach    | ShCh     | Depressed.                                                | 308   |
| Shachar  | ShChR    | Dawn.                                                     | 508   |
| Shachdar | ShChDR   | Angel of 3rd decanate of Libra; Regardie gives the Hebrew spelling as ShHDR, 509. | 512   |
| Shachor  | ShChWR   | Black.                                                    | 514   |
| Shad     | ShD      | Teat.                                                     | 304   |
| Shaddai  | ShDY     | The Almighty.                                             | 314   |
| Shaddai El Chai | ShDY AL ChY | Almighty Living God; divine name associated with Yesod, with Air, and with the East. | 363   |

| Shagal | ShGL | To be sexually aroused, to lie with. | 333 |
|---|---|---|---|
| Shai | ShY | Gift, tribute. | 310 |
| Shakanom | ShKAGNM | A title of Tiphareth. | 977 |
| | | | 417 |
| Shal | ShL | Transgression, fault, crime. | 330 |
| Shalag | ShLG | To snow. | 333 |
| Shalehbiron | | See *Shalhebiron.* | |
| Shalhebeth | ShLHBTh | Flame. | 737 |
| Shalhebiron | ShLH-BYRWN | The Flaming Ones; Qlippoth of Leo. | 1253 |
| | | | 603 |
| Shalom | ShLWM | Peace. | 936 |
| | | | 376 |
| Sham | ShM | There, then. | 900 |
| | | | 340 |
| Shamaim | ShMYM | Heaven, firmament, sky. | 950 |
| | | In cabalism, there are (usually) seven heavens, just as there are seven hells: | 390 |

| Supernals | Arabhoth | Plains | 7th |
|---|---|---|---|
| Chesed | Makhon | Emplacement | 6th |
| Geburah | Maon | Residence | 5th |
| Tiphareth | Zebhul | Dwelling | 4th |
| Netzach | Shechaqim | Clouds | 3rd |
| Hod | Raqia | Firmament | 2nd |
| Yesod and Malkuth | Tebel Wilon | Veil of the Shamaim (or simply Wilon) | Firmament (or Veil) | 1st |

| Shanah | ShNH | Year. | 355 |
|---|---|---|---|
| Shar | ShOR | Gate; a title of Malkuth. | 570 |
| Sharatiel | ShRTYAL | Angel of Leo. | 550 |
| Sharhiel | ShRHYAL | Angel of Aries. | 546 |
| Shath | ShTh | Pillar; prince. | 700 |
| Shaul | ShAWL | Saul, q.v. | 337 |
| Shavua | ShBWO | Week. | 378 |
| Shax | ShTz | Goetic demon by night of 2nd decanate of Gemini; also spelled Shan, Shaz, or Shass.<br>Marquis commanding 30 legions.<br>Appears as a stock-dove with a hoarse but subtle voice.<br>Powers: deprives anyone of sight, hearing, | 1200<br>390 |

or understanding; steals money from kings' houses and carries it again in 1200 years; fetches horses or anything else; discovers hidden things not kept by evil spirits; sometimes gives good familiars.
Lies if not commanded into a triangle.

| | | | |
|---|---|---|---|
| **Sheba** | ShBA | A Biblical land. | 303 |
| **Shechaqim** | ShChQYM | Clouds; the 3rd Heaven, corresponding to Netzach. | 1018 458 |
| **Shechin** | ShChYN | Boils; the 6th of the 10 plagues of Egypt. | 1018 368 |
| **Shed** | ShD | Demon, idol; originally a specific storm demon. | 304 |
| **Shed Barshemath ha- Sharthathan** | ShD BRSh- MOTh HShRTh- ThN | The Spirit of the Spirits of the Moon; Regardie gives Shedbarshehmath Sharthathan, ShDBRShHMOTh ShRThThN, 3321; the phrase is essentially untranslatable, having been constructed to equal 3321, the sum of all the numbers in the magic square of the Moon. | 3321 |
| **Shedim** | ShDYM | Demons. | 914 354 |
| **Shegal** | ShGL | Royal paramour. | 333 |
| **Shehadani** | ShHDNY | Angel of 2nd decanate of Gemini. | 369 |
| **Shekinah** | ShKYNH | Divine Presence, personified in Hebrew mythology into a goddess; a title of Malkuth. | 385 |
| **Shelah** | | See *Salah.* | |
| **Shelathiel** | ShLThYAL | Angel of Virgo. | 771 |
| **Sheleg** | ShLG | Snow. | 333 |
| **Shelshah** | ShLShH | Three. | 635 |
| **Shelshah- Asar** | ShLShH- OShR | Thirteen. | 1205 |
| **Shelshim** | ShLShYM | Thirty. | 1240 680 |
| **Shem** | ShM | Sign; name; son of Noah. | 900 340 |
| **Shemesh** | ShMSh | The Sun. | 640 |

The Sphere of the Sun corresponds to Tiphareth.
The Sun itself corresponds to Resh and

the 30th Path.
Archangel: Raphael.
Angel: Michael.
Intelligence: Nakhiel.
Spirit: Sorath.
Olympic Spirit: Och.
Metal: Gold.
Color: Orange.
Stone: Crysoleth.
Scent: Frankincense, Cinnamon, all Glorious Odors.
Tarot Trump: XX. The Sun.
Rules Leo.
Exalated in Aries.
Detriment in Aquarius.
Fall in Libra.

**Shem Hamphorash**   ShM   HMPRSh

Name of Extension; the Name of God; Tetragrammaton; specifically, the 72-fold name of God contained in Exodus XIV: 19-21. Each of these three verses contains, in the Hebrew, 72 letters. When they are written in boustrophedon, 72 three-letter names of God are obtained. When Yah (YH) or El (AL) is added to each combination, the names of 72 angels are obtained. Each angelic name contains one of the names of God, wherefore it is written, "My angel shall go before thee; observe him, for my name is in him." These angels rule over the quinances of the Zodiac, the Tarot cards of the minor arcana, and the joints of the body; they are associated with the 72 seniors of the synagogue and 72 disciples of Christ. The verses from Exodus are as follows:

1525
965

*19. And the angel of God, which went before the camp of Israel, removed and went behind them; and the pillar of the cloud went from before their face, and stood behind them: 20. And it came between the camp of the Egyptians and the*

camp of Israel; and it was a cloud and
darkness to them, but it gave light by
night to these: so that the one came not
near the other all the night. 21. And
Moses stretched out his hand over the sea;
and the Lord caused the sea to go back
by a strong east wind all that night, and
made the sea dry land, and the waters
were divided.

In transliterated Hebrew:

*19. Wa-yi-sa malak ha-Elohim ha-holek
liphney machaneh Israel wa-yi-lek meacharehem wa-yi-sa amud he-anan mipnehem
wa-ya-amod meacharehem: 20. Wa-ya-bo
beyn machaneh Mitzraim u-beyn machaneh Israel wa-yehi he-anan we-ha-choshek
wa-yi-er eth-ha-laylah welo-qarab zeh el-
zeh bal-ha-laylah: 21. Wa-yet Mosheh eth-
yado ol-ha-yam wa-yolek YHWH eth-ha-
yam be-ruach qadim azah kal-ha-laylah
wa-ya-shem eth-ha-yam lecharabah wa-yi-
baqu ha-maim:*

The Hebrew consonants only, from which
the 72 names are derived:

*19. WYSO MLAK HALHYM HHLK LPNY
MChNH YShRAL WYLK MAChR YHM
WYSO OMWD HONN MPNYHM WYOMD
MAChR YHM: 20. WYBA BYN MChNH
MTzRYM WBYN MChNH YShRAL WYHY
HONN WHChShK WYAR ATh-HLYLH
WLA-QRB ZH AL-ZH KL-HLYLH: 21.
WYT MShH ATh-YDW OL-HYM WYWLK
YHWH ATh-HYM BRWCh QDYM OZH
KL-HLYLH WYShM ATh-HYM LChRBH
WYBQOW HMYM:*

From this, one obtains the names of
Shem Hamphorash, which are assigned to

the quinances of the Zodiac, beginning
with the first quinance of Leo.

| | | | |
|---|---|---|---|
| **1. WHW** | Vehu | Vahaviah | Leo |
| **2. YLY** | Yeli | Yelayel | |
| **3. SYT** | Sit | Sitael | |
| **4. OLM** | Alem | Elemiah | |
| **5. MHSh** | Mahash | Mahashiah | |
| **6. LLH** | Lelah | Lelahel | |
| **7. AKA** | Aka | Akaiah | Virgo |
| **8. KHTh** | Kahath | Kehethel | |
| **9. HZY** | Hezi | Haziel | |
| **10. ALD** | Elad | Aldiah | |
| **11. LAW** | Lav | Laviah | |
| **12. HHO** | Hahau | Hihayah | |
| **13. YZL** | Yezel | Yezalel | Libra |
| **14. MBH** | Mebah | Mebahel | |
| **15. HRY** | Hari | Hariel | |
| **16. HQM** | Haqem | Haqmiah | |
| **17. LAW** | Lau | Laviah | |
| **18. KLY** | Keli | Kaliel | |
| **19. LWW** | Levo | Luviah | Scorpio |
| **20. PHL** | Pahel | Pahaliah | |
| **21. NLK** | Nelak | Nelakiel | |
| **22. YYY** | Yeyaya | Yeyayel | |
| **23. MLH** | Melah | Melahel | |
| **24. ChHW** | Chaho | Chahaviah | |
| **25. NThH** | Nethah | Nithahiah | Sagit-<br>tarius |
| **26. HAA** | Haa | Haayah | |
| **27. YRTh** | Yereth | Yerathel | |
| **28. ShAH** | Shaah | Sahiah | |
| **29. RYY** | Riyi | Reyayel | |
| **30. AWM** | Aum | Avamel | |
| **31. LKB** | Lekab | Lekabel | Capricorn |
| **32. WShR** | Vesher | Veshriah | |
| **33. YChW** | Yecho | Yechaviah | |
| **34. LHCh** | Lehach | Lehachiah | |
| **35. KWQ** | Keveq | Keveqiah | |
| **36. MND** | Menad | Mendel | |
| **37. ANY** | Ani | Aniel | Aquarius |
| **38. ChOM** | Cham | Chamiah | |

| | | | |
|---|---|---|---|
| 39. RHO | Reha | Rehael | |
| 40. YYZ | Yeyaz | Yeyazel | |
| 41. HHH | Hehah | Hahahel | |
| 42. MYK | Mik | Michael | |
| 43. WWL | Vaval | Vavaliah | Pisces |
| 44. YLH | Yelah | Yelahiah | |
| 45. SAL | Sael | Saliah | |
| 46. ORY | Eri | Ariel | |
| 47. OShL | Ashel | Asaliah | |
| 48. MYH | Miah | Mihael | |
| 49. WHW | Vaho | Vehuel | Aries |
| 50. DNY | Dani | Daniel | |
| 51. HChSh | Hachash | Hechashiah | |
| 52. OMM | Amem | Amamiah | |
| 53. NNA | Nena | Nanael | |
| 54. NYTh | Nith | Nithael | |
| 55. MBH | Mabeh | Mebahiah | Taurus |
| 56. PWY | Poi | Poyel | |
| 57. NMM | Nemem | Nemamiah | |
| 58. YYL | Yeyal | Yeyalel | |
| 59. HRCh | Herach | Herachiel | |
| 60. MTzR | Metzer | Mitzrael | |
| 61. WMB | Vameb | Vemibael | Gemini |
| 62. YHH | Yehah | Yehohel | |
| 63. ONW | Anu | Anevel | |
| 64. MChY | Mechi | Mochayel | |
| 65. DMB | Dameb | Damabiah | |
| 66. MNQ | Menaq | Menqel | |
| 67. AYO | Aya | Ayoel | Cancer |
| 68. ChBW | Chebo | Chabuyah | |
| 69. RAH | Raah | Rahael | |
| 70. YBM | Yebem | Yebamiah | |
| 71. HYY | Hayeya | Hayayel | |
| 72. MWM | Mum | Mevamiah | |

It is interesting to note the resemblance between some of these names and various names of God from different, unrelated religions: for example, No. 15, Hari, and the Hindu *Hare*, "Lord"; No. 18, Keli, and the Hindu goddess Kali; No. 30,

Aum, and the Hindu holy word *Aum* or *Om*; No. 54, Nith, and the Egyptian goddess Neith; No. 69, Raah, and the Egyptian god Ra; and so on.

The sum of the 72 names, if the finals be counted as such, is 14,583. If none of the finals be counted as such, the sum is 9,623, the same, of course, as the sum of the letters of the verses if finals are not counted as such. Otherwise, the verses add to 20,303.

| | | | |
|---|---|---|---|
| **Shemonah** | ShMNH | Eight. | 395 |
| **Shemonah-Asar** | ShMNH-OShR | Eighteen. | 965 |
| **Shemonim** | ShMNYM | Eighty. | 1000 440 |
| **Shen** | ShN | Tooth. | 1000 350 |
| **Shenaim** | ShNYM | Two. | 960 400 |
| **Shenaim-Asar** | ShNYM-OShR | Twelve. | 1530 970 |
| **Sheol** | ShAWL | Depth of the Earth; the 7th and lowest hell, corresponding to the three Supernal Sephiroth and to the Islamic *Ha'wijah,* reserved for hypocrites. | 337 |
| **Shephet** | ShPT | Judgment. | 389 |
| **Sheqi** | ShQY | The penultimate three letters of the 42-letter name of God, associated with Yesod. | 410 |
| **Shesh** | ShSh | White marble. | 600 |
| **Sheth** | ShTh | Buttocks; noise. | 700 |
| **Shethiqah** | ShThYQH | Silence. | 815 |
| **Shevet** | ShBT | The 5th Hebrew month, January-February, corresponding roughly to the period when the Sun is in Aquarius. | 311 |
| **Shevil** | ShBYL | Path. | 342 |
| **Shevilim** | ShBYLYM | Paths. | 952 392 |
| **Shevil he-Chalav** | ShBYL HChLB | Milky Way. | 387 |

| | | | |
|---|---|---|---|
| **Shichiriron** | ShYChRY-<br>RWN | The Black Ones; Qlippoth of Cancer. | 1434<br>784 |
| **Shin** | Sh | 21st letter of Hebrew alphabet, transliterated as *sh* or *s*; sometimes differentiated into two separate letters, Shin (*sh*) and Sin (*s*), the difference being indicated by a mark at the top of the letter.<br>Spelled out, ShYN, "tooth" (1010 or 360).<br>Corresponds to the element Fire, to the 31st Path (between Hod and Malkuth), and to the Tarot Trump XX. Judgment; for additional correspondences, see *Esh.* | 300 |
| **Shinanim** | ShNANYM | Angelic Choir sometimes associated with Tiphareth and the Sphere of the Sun, although this slot is usually given to the Melekim. | 1011<br>451 |
| **Shishah** | ShShH | Six. | 605 |
| **Shishah-Asar** | ShShH-<br>OShR | Sixteen. | 1175 |
| **Shishim** | ShShYM | Sixty. | 1210<br>650 |
| **Shivah** | ShBOH | Seven. | 377 |
| **Shivah-Asar** | ShBOH-<br>OShR | Seventeen. | 947 |
| **Shivim** | ShBOYM | Seventy. | 982<br>422 |
| **Sho** | ShA | Destruction. | 301 |
| **Shod** | ShD | Violence, ruin. | 304 |
| **Shor** | ShWR | Ox, bull; Taurus. | 506 |
| | | Corresponds to Waw and the 16th Path. | |
| | | Archangel: Asmodel. | 142 |
| | | Angel: Araziel. | 249 |
| | | Lord of Triplicity by Day: Raydel. | 246 |
| | | Lord of Triplicity by Night: Totath. | 424 |
| | | Angel Ruling 2nd House: Toel. | 46 |
| | | Angel of 1st Decanate: Kedamidi. | 78 |
| | | Angel of 1st Quinance: Mebahiah. | 62 |
| | | Angel of 2nd Quinance: Poyel. | 127 |
| | | Angel of 2nd Decanate: Minacharai. | 315 |
| | | Angel of 3rd Quinance: Nemamiah. | 145 |

Angle of 4th Quinance: Yeyalel.     81
Angel of 3rd Decanate: Yakasaganotz.     1049
    239
Angel of 5th Quinance: Herachiel.     244
Angel of 6th Quinance: Mitzrael.     361
Qlippoth: Adimiron (The Bloody Ones).     971
    321

Goetic Demons by Day:
    1st Decanate: Gamigin (Samigin).     766
    116

    2nd Decanate: Marbas.     243
    3rd Decanate: Valefor.     317
Goetic Demons by Night:
    1st Decanate: Räum.     807
    247

    2nd Decanate: Focalor.     342
    3rd Decanate: Vepar.     287
Color: Red-Orange.
Scent: Storax.
Tarot Trump: V. The Hierophant.
Tarot Cards associated with Decanates:
    1st Decanate: 5 of Pentacles.
    2nd Decanate: 6 of Pentacles.
    3rd Decanate: 7 of Pentacles.
Direction: Southeast.
Tribe of Israel: Ephraim.
Apostle: Thaddeus.
Geomantic Figure: Amissio.
Mystic Number of 16th Path: 136.
Ruling Planet: Venus.
Planet Exalted in: Moon.
Planet in Detriment in: Mars.
Planet in Fall in: Pluto.

| | | | |
|---|---|---|---|
| **Shor** | ShR | Navel. | 500 |
| **Shotheq** | ShWThQ | Silent. | 806 |
| **Simeon** | ShMOWN | A tribe of Israel, associated with Pisces. | 1116 |
| | | | 466 |
| **Sin** | | See *Shin.* | |
| **Sinai** | SYNY | Sinai. | 130 |
| **Sit** | SYT | 3rd name of Shem Hamphorash, associated with 3rd quinance of Leo. | 79 |

| | | | |
|---|---|---|---|
| **Sitael** | SYTAL | Angel of 3rd quinance of Leo; angel by day of the 6 of Wands; also spelled Saitel. | 110 |
| **Sitri** | ShYTRY | Goetic demon by day of 3rd decanate of Cancer.<br>Prince commanding 60 legions.<br>Appears as a being with the head of a leopard and the wings of a griffin; assumes "very beautiful" human form upon request.<br>Powers: procures love; causes a desired person to show himself or herself naked. | 529 |
| **Sivan** | SYWN | The 9th Hebrew month, May-June, corresponding roughly to the period when the Sun is in Gemini. | 776<br>126 |
| **Sizajasel** | | See *Soyasel*. | |
| **Sodom** | SDM | Sodom. | 664<br>104 |
| **Sodom we-**<br>   **Amorah** | SDM<br>   WOMRH | Sodom and Gomorah. | 985<br>425 |
| **Solomon**<br>   **(Shelomoh)** | ShLMH | Solomon. | 375 |
| **Sorath** | SWRTh | Spirit of the Sun. | 666 |
| **Sosul** | SWSWL | Angel of 8th astrological house; also spelled Sosol. | 162 |
| **Soyasel** | SWYOSAL | Angel of 9th astrological house; also given as Sizajasel (SZYOSAL, 238). | 237 |
| **Stolas** | ShTWLWSh | Goetic demon by day of 3rd decanate of Pisces; also spelled Stolos.<br>Prince commanding 26 legions.<br>Appears as a mighty raven; later, as a man.<br>Powers: teaches astronomy and the virtues of herbs and precious stones. Crowley's spelling: YShTWLWSh, 666. | 651 |

| | | | |
|---|---|---|---|
| **Ta** | TA | To sweep away. | 10 |
| **Ta** | ThA | Room. | 401 |

| | | | |
|---|---|---|---|
| **Tagaririm** | | See *Tageriron*. | |
| **Tageran** | ThGRN | Haggler. | 1303 |
| | | | 653 |
| **Tageriron** | ThGRYRWN | The Hagglers; Qlippoth of Tiphareth; variously given as Thagiriron (Crowley), Tagaririm (Mathers), Tagiriron (Regardie), or Togarini (Waite). | 1519 869 |
| **Tal** | TL | Dew. | 39 |
| **Taleh** | TLH | Lamb; Aries. | 44 |

Corresponds to He (or Sadhe) and the 15th Path (or 28th).

| | |
|---|---|
| Archangel: Malkidiel. | 135 |
| Angel: Sharhiel. | 546 |
| Lord of Triplicity by Day: Sateraton. | 1048 |
| | 398 |
| Lord of Triplicity by Night: Sapatawi. | 236 |
| Angel Ruling 1st House: Ayel. | 42 |
| Angel of 1st Decanate: Zazer. | 214 |
| Angel of 1st Quinance: Vehuel. | 48 |
| Angel of 2nd Quinance: Daniel. | 95 |
| Angel of 2nd Decanate: Behahemi. | 62 |
| Angel of 3rd Quinance: Hechashiah. | 328 |
| Angel of 4th Quinance: Amamiah. | 165 |
| Angel of 3rd Decanate: Satander. | 323 |
| Angel of 5th Quinance: Nanael. | 132 |
| Angel of 6th Quinance: Nithael. | 491 |
| Qlippoth: Beiriron (The Herd) (from *Beir*, "beast," "cattle"). | 1198 548 |
| Goetic Demons by Day: | |
| 1st Decanate: Bael. | 33 |
| 2nd Decanate: Agares (Agreas). | 205 |
| 3rd Decanate: Vassago. | 316 |
| Goetic Demons by Night: | |
| 1st Decanate: Phenex (Pheynix). | 1031 |
| | 121 |
| 2nd Decanate: Halphas (Malthas, Malthus, Malthous). | 836 116 |
| 3rd Decanate: Malphas. | 871 |
| | 151 |

Color: Red.
Scent: Dragon's Blood.

Tarot Trump: IV. The Emperor.
Tarot Cards associated with Decanates:
    1st Decanate: 2 of Wands.
    2nd Decanate: 3 of Wands.
    3rd Decanate: 4 of Wands.
Direction: Northeast.
Tribe of Israel: Gad.
Apostle: Matthias.
Geomantic Figure: Puer.
Mystic Number of 15th Path: 120.
Ruling Planet: Mars.
Planet Exalted in: Sun.
Planet in Detriment in: Venus.
Planet in Fall in: Saturn.

| | | | |
|---|---|---|---|
| **Taliahad** | TLYHD | Angel of Water. | 58 |
| **Talmud** | ThLMWD | Teaching. | 480 |
| **Tam** | ThM | Whole, complete; simple, pious, innocent, sincere, mild, perfect. | 1000 440 |
| **Tammuz** | ThMWZ | The 10th Hebrew month, June-July, corresponding roughly to the period when the Sun is in Cancer. | 453 |
| **Tan** | ThN | Jackal. | 1100 450 |
| **Taph** | TP | Children. | 809 89 |
| **Taphthar-tharath** | ThPThR-ThRTh | Spirit of Mercury. | 2080 |
| **Tarasni** | TRSNY | Angel of 1st decanate of Libra. | 329 |
| **Tarshish** | ThRShYSh | 1. Tarsis, a city in Spain; 2. Chrysolite, precious stone. | 1210 |
| **Tarshishim** | ThR-ShYShYM | Chrysolites, precious stones; Angelic Choir sometimes associated with Netzach and the Sphere of Venus, although this slot is usually assigned to the Elohim. | 1820 1260 |
| **Tath Zal** | ThTh ZL | The Profuse Giver; a title of Kether. | 837 |
| **Taw** | Th | 22nd letter of the Hebrew alphabet, transliterated as *th* or *t*; sometimes spelled Tau. Spelled out, ThW, Tau cross (406). Corresponds to Saturn, to the 32nd Path (between Yesod and Malkuth), and to the Tarot Trump XXI. The World; for addi- | 400 |

| | | | |
|---|---|---|---|
| | | tional correspondences, see *Shabbatai*. | |
| **Tebah** | ThBH | Ark (Noah's). | 407 |
| **Tebel Wilon** | TBL | Veil of the Firmament; the 1st Heaven, | 1743 |
| **Shamaim** | WYLWN | corresponding to Yesod and Malkuth. | 1093 |
| | ShMYM | | 533 |
| **Tebhel** | ThBL | World; one of the seven earths; with Cheled, corresponding to Yesod and Malkuth. | 432 |
| **Tehom** | ThHWM | Abyss, "deep" (Gen. I:2); in Hebrew mythology, Queen of the Waters of the Deep, the Mesopotamian goddess Tiamat. | 1011 451 |
| **Tekheleth** | ThKLTh | Purple. | 850 |
| **Tel** | ThL | Mound. | 430 |
| **Teman** | ThYMN | A Duke of Edom, associated with Hod. | 1150 500 |
| **Temani** | ThYMNY | The land of King Husham of Edom. | 510 |
| **Temira de-** | TMYRA | The Concealed of the Concealed; a title | 1233 |
| **Temirin** | DTMYRYN | of Kether. | 583 |
| **Temurah** | ThMWRH | The cabalistic theory that words may be related to other words by means of one of several pre-established codes; see *Aiq Bekar* as one example. | 651 |
| **Teomim** | ThAWMYM | Twins; Gemini. | 1057 |
| | | Corresponds to Zayin and the 17th Path. | 497 |
| | | Archangel: Ambriel. | 284 |
| | | Angel: Sarayel. | 302 |
| | | Lord of Triplicity by Day: Sarash. | 630 |
| | | Lord of Triplicity by Night: Ogarman. | 1089 439 |
| | | Angel Ruling 3rd House: Giel. | 44 |
| | | Angel of 1st Decanate: Sagarash. | 563 |
| | | Angel of 1st Quinance: Vemibael. | 79 |
| | | Angel of 2nd Quinance: Yehohel. | 51 |
| | | Angel of 2nd Decanate: Shehadani. | 369 |
| | | Angel of 3rd Quinance: Anevel. | 157 |
| | | Angel of 4th Quinance: Mochayel. | 89 |
| | | Angel of 3rd Decanate: Bethon. | 918 468 |
| | | Angel of 5th Quinance: Damabiah. | 61 |
| | | Angel of 6th Quinance: Menqel. | 221 |
| | | Qlippoth: Tzelilimiron (The Clangers) | 1126 |

|  |  | (from *Tzelil*, "ring"; "sound," "tone"). | 476 |
|---|---|---|---|
|  |  | Goetic Demons by Day: |  |
|  |  | 1st Decanate: Amon. | 747 |
|  |  |  | 97 |
|  |  | 2nd Decanate: Barbatos. | 519 |
|  |  | 3rd Decanate: Paimon. | 837 |
|  |  |  | 187 |
|  |  | Goetic Demons by Night: |  |
|  |  | 1st Decanate: Sabnock (Savnok). | 862 |
|  |  |  | 382 |
|  |  | 2nd Decanate: Shax (Shan, Shaz, Shass). | 1200 |
|  |  |  | 390 |
|  |  | 3rd Decanate: Viné (Vinea). | 67 |

Color: Orange.

Scent: Wormwood.

Tarot Trump: VI. The Lovers.

Tarot Cards associated with Decanates:

1st Decanate: 8 of Swords.

2nd Decanate: 9 of Swords.

3rd Decanate: 10 of Swords.

Direction: East, above.

Tribe of Israel: Manasseh.

Apostle: Simon.

Geomantic Figure: Albus.

Mystic Number of 17th Path: 153.

Ruling Planet: Mercury.

Exalted in: Ascending Node.

Planet in Detriment in: Jupiter.

In Fall in: Descending Node.

| **Terah** | ThRCh | Son of Nahor and father of Abraham, Nahor, and Haran; lived 205 years (1878-2083 after Creation). | 608 |
|---|---|---|---|
| **Teth** | T | 9th letter of Hebrew alphabet, transliterated as *t* or *ṭ*. | 9 |
|  |  | Spelled out, TYTh, "serpent" (419). |  |
|  |  | Corresponds to Leo, to the 19th Path (between Chesed and Geburah), and to the Tarot Trump XI. Strength; for additional correspondences, see *Ari*. |  |
| **Tevet** | TBTh | The 4th Hebrew month, December-January, corresponding roughly to the period | 411 |

| | | | |
|---|---|---|---|
| | | when the Sun is in Capricorn. | |
| **Thagiriron** | | See *Tageriron.* | |
| **Thamiel** | | See *Thaumiel.* | |
| **Tharsis** | ThRShYS | Ruler of Water. | 970 |
| **Thaumiel** | ThAW-MYAL | Twins of God; Qlippoth of Kether. | 488 |
| **Theli** | ThLY | Dragon; Satan. | 440 |
| **Thergebon** | ThRGBWN | Lord of Triplicity by Day for Libra. | 1311 661 |
| **Thetz** | ThTz | The third two letters in the 42-letter name of God, associated with Binah. | 490 |
| **Thoabath** | ThWOBTh | Abomination. | 878 |
| **Throa** | ThROA | Gate; a title of Malkuth. | 671 |
| **Thummim** | ThMYM | One of two objects (the other being the Urim) carried by the High Priest and supposedly used for divination. | 1050 490 |
| **Tiger** | ThGR | To haggle. | 603 |
| **Timnah** | ThMWO | A Duke of Edom, associated (with Alvah and Jetheth) with Daath. | 516 |
| **Tiphareth** | ThPARTh | Beauty; the 6th Sephira. | 1081 |
| | | Divine Name: Yahweh Eloah wa-Daath. | |
| | | Archangel: Raphael. | |
| | | Choir of Angels: Melekim; Shinanim; Virtues. | |
| | | Material World: Shemesh, the Sphere of the Sun. | |
| | | Associated with Waw of Tetragrammaton. Additional titles of Tiphareth are Zauir Anpin, The Lesser Countenance, Microprosopus; Melek, The King; Seir Anpin, The Bearded Countenance; Adam; Ben, The Son; Ish, the Man; and Shakanom. | |
| **Tiriel** | TYRYAL | Intelligence of Mercury. | 260 |
| **Tishah** | ThShOH | Nine. | 775 |
| **Tishah-Asar** | ThShOH-OShR | Nineteen. | 1345 |
| **Tishim** | ThShOYM | Ninety. | 1380 820 |
| **Tishri** | ThShRY | The 1st Hebrew month, September-October, corresponding roughly to the period when the Sun is in Libra. | 910 |

| Tit-ha-yawen | TYTHYWN | Mire of Mud; the 4th hell, corresponding to Tiphareth and to the Islamic *Sa'ir*, reserved for Sabians. | 749<br>99 |
| Tob | TWB | Good. | 17 |
| Toel | TWAL | Angel of 2nd astrological house; also spelled Tual. | 46 |
| Togarini | | See *Tageriron*. | |
| To'hu | ThHW | Desolation ("without form"–Gen. I:2). | 411 |
| Tok | ThK | Oppression. | 900<br>420 |
| Tom | ThM | Wholeness; simplicity, piety, innocence, sincerity, mildness, perfection. | 1000<br>440 |
| Toph | ThP | Hand-drum; bezel. | 1200<br>480 |
| Torah | ThWRH | Law; the Pentateuch. | 611 |
| Totath | TWTTh | Lord of Triplicity by Night for Taurus. | 424 |
| Tual | | See *Toel*. | |
| Tubal-Cain | ThWBL QYN | Son of Lamech and Zillah; "an instructor of every artificer in brass and iron." | 1248<br>598 |
| Tzab | TzB | Litter. | 92 |
| Tzach | TzCh | Bright. | 98 |
| Tzad | TzD | Side. | 94 |
| Tzaddi | | See *Sadhe*. | |
| Tzadiq-Yesod-Olam | TzDYQ-YSWD-OWLM | The Righteous is the Foundation of the World; a title of Yesod. | 990<br>430 |
| Tzadqiel | TzDQYAL | God's Justice; Archangel associated with Chesed and with Jupiter; sometimes spelled Tsadkiel. | 235 |
| Tzahov | TzHB | Yellow. | 97 |
| Tzakmiqiel | TzKMQYAL | Angel of Aquarius. | 291 |
| Tzal | TzL | Shadow; shelter. | 120 |
| Tzal Maweth | TzLMWTh | Shadow of death; the 2nd hell, corresponding to Hod and to the Islamic *Laza*, reserved for Christians. The valley of Tzal-Maweth is mentioned in the 23rd Psalm. | 566 |
| Tzalalimiron | | See *Tzelilimiron*. | |
| Tzaphiriron | TzPRYRWN | The Scratchers; Qlippoth of Virgo. | 1286<br>636 |
| Tzaphon | TzPWN | North; see also *Eretz*. | 876<br>226 |
| Tzaphoni | TzPWNY | The Northern One; Lilith. | 236 |

| | | | |
|---|---|---|---|
| **Tzaphqiel** | TzPQYAL | Archangel associated with Binah and with the Sphere of Saturn; also spelled Tsaphkiel. | 311 |
| **Tzar** | TzR | Persecutor, enemy; distress, danger; stone. | 290 |
| **Tzaw** | TzW | Statute. | 96 |
| **Tzedek** | TzDQ | Jupiter. | 194 |

The Sphere of Jupiter corresponds to Chesed.

The planet Jupiter corresponds to Kaph and the 21st Path.

Archangel: Tzadqiel.
Angel: Sachiel.
Intelligence: Iophiel.
Spirit: Hismael.
Olympic Spirit: Bethor.
Metal: Tin.
Color: Violet.
Stone: Amethyst, Lapis Lazuli.
Scent: Saffron, all Generous Odors.
Tarot Trump: X. The Wheel of Fortune.
Rules Sagittarius and Pisces.
Exalted in Cancer.
Detriment in Gemini and Virgo.
Fall in Capricorn.

| | | | |
|---|---|---|---|
| **Tzela** | TzLO | Rib, such as the one from which Eve was made. | 190 |
| **Tzelil** | TzLYL | Ring; sound, tone. | 160 |
| **Tzelilimiron** | TzLYLYMY-RWN | The Clangers; Qlippoth of Gemini; given in 777 as Tzalalimiron, with the Hebrew spelling as TzLLDMYRWN (1110, 460) (probably a misprint); from *Tzelil*, "ring"; sound, tone. | 1126 476 |
| **Tzen** | TzN | Thorn. | 790 140 |
| **Tzephardea** | TzPRDO | Frogs; the 2nd of the 10 plagues of Egypt. | 444 |
| **Tzeva** | TzBO | Color. | 162 |
| **Tzi** | TzY | Dryness; ship. | 100 |
| **Tziah** | TzYH | Dryness; one of the seven earths, corresponding to Tiphareth or, according to others, to Netzach. | 105 |
| **Tzoq** | TzWQ | Narrowness; oppression. | 196 |

| Umabel | | See *Vemibael.* | |
|---|---|---|---|
| Ur | AWR | A city of Mesopotamia; Abraham's birthplace. | 207 |
| Urim | AWRYM | One of two objects (the other being the Thummim) carried by the High Priest and supposedly used for divination. | 817 257 |
| Ur Kasdim | AWR KShDYM | Ur of the Chaldees; a city of Mesopotamia; birthplace of Abraham. | 1141 581 |
| Uriel | AWRYAL | Archangel associated with North and Earth. | 248 |
| Uthrodiel | WThRW DYAL | Angel of 3rd decanate of Scorpio; Regardie gives the Hebrew spelling as NThRW-DYAL, 701. | 657 |
| Uvall | AWAL | Goetic demon by night of 2nd decanate of Cancer; also spelled Vual or Voval. Duke commanding 37 legions. Appears as a mighty dromedary; assumes human form upon command. Powers: speaks Egyptian (poorly); procures love; tells fortunes; obtains friendship between friends and foes. Formerly of the Order of Potestates or Powers. | 38 |

| Vahaviah | WHWYH | Angel of 1st quinance of Leo; angel by day of the 5 of Wands; also spelled Vehuiah. | 32 |
| Vaho | WHW | 49th name of Shem Hamphorash, associated with 1st quinance of Aries. | 17 |
| Vakabiel | WKBYAL | Angel of Pisces. | 69 |

| | | | |
|---|---|---|---|
| **Valefor** | WALPR | Goetic demon by day of 3rd decanate of Taurus. | 317 |
| | | Duke commanding 10 legions. | |
| | | Appears as a lion with the head of an ass, bellowing. | |
| | | Powers: a good familiar, but tempts to steal. | |
| **Valu** | WAL | Goetic demon by night of 2nd decanate of Sagittarius; also spelled Volac, Valak, or Ualac. | 37 |
| | | President commanding 38 legions. | |
| | | Appears as a child with angel's wings, riding a two-headed dragon. | |
| | | Powers: tells about hidden treasures; tells where serpents may be seen and brings them to the exorcist. | |
| **Vameb** | WMB | 61st name of Shem Hamphorash, associated with 1st quinance of Gemini. | 48 |
| **Vasariah** | | See *Veshriah.* | |
| **Vassago** | WShAGW | Goetic demon by day of 3rd decanate of Aries. | 316 |
| | | Prince commanding 26 legions. | |
| | | Appears as an old, fair man riding on a crocodile and carrying a goshawk on his fist. | |
| | | Powers: tells fortunes; finds hidden or lost objects. | |
| | | Good natured. | |
| **Vau, Vav** | | See *Waw.* | |
| **Vaval** | WWL | 43rd name of Shem Hamphorash, associated with 1st quinance of Pisces. | 42 |
| **Vavaliah** | WWLYH | Angel of 1st quinance of Pisces; angel by day of the 8 of Cups; also spelled Vevaliah. | 73 |
| **Veadar** | WADR | The Hebrew intercalary month, in March, between Adar and Nisan. | 211 |
| **Vehooel** | | See *Vehuel.* | |
| **Vehrin** | WHRYN | Angel of 2nd decanate of Sagittarius. | 921 |
| | | | 271 |
| **Vehu** | WHW | 1st name of Shem Hamphorash, associated with 1st quinance of Leo. | 17 |
| **Vehuel** | WHWAL | Angel of 1st quinance of Aries; angel by | 48 |

|  |  | day of the 2 of Wands; also spelled Vehooel. |  |
|---|---|---|---|
| **Vehuiah** |  | See *Vahaviah*. |  |
| **Vemibael** | WMBAL | Angel of 1st quinance of Gemini; angel by day of the 8 of Swords; also spelled Umabel. | 79 |
| **Vepar** | WPAR | Goetic demon by night of 3rd decanate of Taurus; also spelled Vephar. | 287 |
|  |  | Duke commanding 29 legions. |  |
|  |  | Appears as a mermaid. |  |
|  |  | Powers: governs the waters; guides ships carrying war materials; causes stormy seas; creates the illusion that the sea is full of ships; kills men in three days as the result of putrefying wounds or sores in which he causes worms to breed. |  |
| **Verkiel** | WRKYAL | Archangel of Leo; also spelled Verchiel. | 267 |
| **Vesher** | WShR | 32nd name of Shem Hamphorash, associated with 2nd quinance of Capricorn. | 506 |
| **Veshiriah** |  | See *Veshriah*. |  |
| **Veshriah** | WShRYH | Angel of 2nd quinance of Capricorn; angel by night of the 2 of Pentacles; also spelled Veshiriah or Vasariah. | 521 |
| **Vevaliah** |  | See *Vavaliah*. |  |
| **Veyel** | WYAL | Angel of 6th astrological house; also spelled Voil. | 47 |
| **Vine** | WYNA | Goetic demon by night of 3rd decanate of Gemini; also spelled Vinea. | 67 |
|  |  | King and Earl commanding 36 legions. |  |
|  |  | Appears as a lion riding a black horse and carrying a viper. |  |
|  |  | Powers: discovers hidden things, witches, and wizards; tells fortunes; builds towers; demolishes great stone walls; makes waves. |  |
| **Vitriol** | WYThRY-OL | Acronym for the alchemical formula *Visita interiora terrae rectificando invenies occultum lapidem* ("Visit the interior of the earth; by rectification, you shall find | 726 |

the hidden stone"). As C. G. Jung so well understood, the true meaning of this aphorism is "Get in touch with your unconscious; by integrating the various parts of your psyche, you will discover your Self." The Self is the divine spark within every person, the Hindu atman, the jewel in the lotus, Tiphareth, the Holy Guardian Angel. The Hebrew spelling and enumeration are Crowley's.

**Voil**            See *Veyel.*

**Voso**    WShW    Goetic demon by night of 3rd decanate    312
of Libra; also spelled Osé or Oso.
President commanding 30 legions.
Appears as a leopard; later, a man.
Powers: teaches liberal sciences; gives true answers concerning divine and secret matters; changes men into any shape so that the person changed really thinks he *is* that creature or thing.

**Waw**    W    6th letter of Hebrew alphabet; transliterated as *w*, *v*, *u*, or *o*; also spelled Vav or Vau.    6
Spelled out, WW, "nail," peg (12).
Corresponds to Taurus, the 16th Path (between Chokmah and Chesed), and the Tarot Trump V. The Hierophant; for additional correspondences, see *Shor.*

**Wilon**    WYLWN    Veil; the 1st Heaven, corresponding to    752
Yesod and Malkuth; sometimes given as    102
Tebel Wilon Shamaim, Veil of the Firmament.

| Ya | YO | Shovel. | 80 |
|---|---|---|---|
| Yabam | YBM | Brother-in-law. | 612 |
| | | | 52 |
| Yabbashah | YBShH | Dry land; one of the seven earths, corresponding to Netzach. | 317 |
| Yadashchom | YDOShChWM | Francis Barrett's misprint for ShORYMWTh (?), Shaare-Maweth. q.v. | |
| Yadid | YDYD | One beloved. | 28 |
| Yaglepzeq | YGLPZQ | The 31st through 36th letters of the 42-letter name of God, associated with Hod. | 230 |
| Yah | YH | Divine name associated with Chokmah. | 15 |
| Yahel | YHAL | Angel of 7th astrological house; also spelled Jael. | 46 |
| Yahweh | YHWH | Jehovah; Tetragrammaton, name of God associated with Air and with the East in magic ritual; the usual name of the chief god of the Hebrews, translated "Lord" or "the Lord." | 26 |
| Yahweh Eloah wa-Daath | YHWH ALWH WDOTh | Lord God of Knowledge; divine name associated with Tiphareth. | 548 |
| Yahweh Elohim | YHWH ALHYM | Lord God; divine name associated with Binah. | 672 |
| | | | 112 |
| Yahweh Ish Milchamah | YHWH AYSh MLChMH | The Lord is a man of war (Ex. XV:3). | 460 |
| Yahweh Ish Milchamah Yahweh Shemo | YHWH AYSh MLChMH YHWH ShMW | The Lord is a man of war; Yahweh is His Name (Ex. XV:3). | 832 |
| Yahweh Shemo | YHWH ShMW | Yahweh is His Name. | 372 |
| Yahweh Tzabaoth | YHWH TzBAWTh | Lord of Hosts; divine name associated with Netzach, with Fire, and with the South. | 525 |

| Yakasaganotz | YKSGNWTz | Angel of 3rd decanate of Taurus; Regardie gives the Hebrew spelling as YSGNZN, 830 or 180. | 1049 239 |
| Yam | YM | Sea. | 610 50 |
| Yasgedibaro-diel | YSGDYB-RWDYAL | Angel of 3rd decanate of Capricorn; 777 gives YSNDYBRWDYAL, 387; *Sephir Sephiroth* gives the present spelling. | 340 |
| Yasyasyah | YSYSYH | Angel of 2nd decanate of Capricorn. | 155 |
| Yebamiah | YBMYH | Angel of 4th quinance of Cancer; angel by night of the 3 of Cups; also spelled Yebomayah or Iibamiah. | 67 |
| Yebem | YBM | 70th name of Shem Hamphorash, associated with 4th quinance of Cancer. | 612 52 |
| Yebomayah | | See *Yebamiah.* | |
| Yecho | YChW | 33rd name of Shem Hamphorash, associated with 3rd quinance of Capricorn. | 24 |
| Yehah | YHH | 62nd name of Shem Hamphorash, associated with 2nd quinance of Gemini. | 20 |
| Yechaviah | YChWYH | Angel of 3rd quinance of Capricorn; angel by day of the 3 of Pentacles; also spelled Yechavah or Iehuiah. | 39 |
| Yechidah | YChYDH | Part of the soul referred to Kether; see also *Neshamah.* | 37 |
| Yedidiah | YDYDYH | One beloved by God; Solomon. | 43 |
| Yehohel | YHHAL | Angel of 2nd quinance of Gemini; angel by night of the 8 of Swords; also spelled Iahhel. | 51 |
| Yelayel | YLYAL | Angel of 2nd quinance of Leo; angel by night of the 5 of Wands; also spelled Ieliel. | 81 |
| Yelah | YLH | 44th name of Shem Hamphorash, associated with 2nd quinance of Pisces. | 45 |
| Yelahiah | YLHYH | Angel of 2nd quinance of Pisces; angel by night of the 8 of Cups; also spelled Ielahiah. | 60 |
| Yeli | YLY | 2nd name of Shem Hamphorash, associated with 2nd quinance of Leo. | 50 |
| Yerathel | YRThAL | Angel of 3rd quinance of Sagittarius; angel by day of the 9 of Wands; also spelled Yirthiel or Ierathel. | 641 |
| Yereth | YRTh | 27th name of Shem Hamphorash, associ- | 610 |

|  |  | ated with 3rd quinance of Sagittarius. |  |
|---|---|---|---|
| **Yesh** | YSh | Existence; there is/are. | 310 |
| **Yesod** | YSWD | Foundation; the 9th Sephira. | 80 |

Divine Name: Shaddai El Chai.
Archangel: Gabriel.
Choir of Angels: Kerubim; Angels.
Material World: Levanah, the Sphere of
the Moon.
An additional title of Yesod is Tzadiq-
Yesod-Olam, The Righteous is the Foun-
dation of the World.

| **Yetzirah** | YTzYRH | Formation; the Angelic or Formative | 315 |
|---|---|---|---|

World, the third of the four cabalistic
worlds, associated with the Waw of Tetragrammaton. The names of the angelic
choirs associated with the Sephiroth are
also associated with the world of Yetzirah, also called Olam ha-Yetzirah. The
secret name of Yetzirah is Mah. The
Sepher Yetzirah (q.v.) is the Book of
Formation.
The Angelic Choirs of Yetzirah are as follows:

| Sephira | Hebrew | Christian |
|---|---|---|
| Kether | Chayoth ha-Qadesh (Holy Living Creatures) | Seraphim |
| Chokmah | Ophanim (Wheels) | Cherubim |
| Binah | Aralim (Mighty Ones) | Thrones |
| Chesed | Chashmalim (Brilliant Ones) | Dominations |
| Geburah | Seraphim (Flaming Serpents) | Powers |
| Tiphareth | Melekim (Kings) | Virtues |
| Netzach | Elohim (Gods) | Principalities |
| Hod | Beni Elohim (Sons of the Gods) | Archangels |
| Yesod | Kerubim (Cherubs) | Angels |

| | Malkuth | Eshim (Flames) | Souls of the Re-deemed |
|---|---|---|---|

| | | | |
|---|---|---|---|
| **Yeya** | YY | A name of God. | 20 |
| **Yeyal** | YYL | 58th name of Shem Hamphorash, associated with 4th quinance of Taurus. | 50 |
| **Yeyalel** | YYLAL | Angel of 4th quinance of Taurus; angel by night of the 6 of Pentacles; also spelled Yeyelal or Ieilael. | 81 |
| **Yeyaya** | YYY | 22nd name of Shem Hamphorash, associated with 4th quinance of Scorpio. | 30 |
| **Yeyayel** | YYYAL | Angel of 4th quinance of Scorpio; angel by night of the 6 of Cups; also spelled Ieiaiel. | 61 |
| **Yeyaz** | YYZ | 40th name of Shem Hamphorash, associated with 4th quinance of Aquarius. | 27 |
| **Yeyazel** | YYZAL | Angel of 4th quinance of Aquarius; angel by night of the 6 of Swords; also spelled Yeyeziel or Ihiazel. | 58 |
| **Yeyelal** | | See *Yeyalel.* | |
| **Yeyeziel** | | See *Yeyazel.* | |
| **Yezalel** | YZLAL | Angel of 1st quinance of Libra; angel by day of the 2 of Swords; also spelled Ielael. | 78 |
| **Yezel** | YZL | 13th name of Shem Hamphorash, associated with 1st quinance of Libra. | 47 |
| **Yirthiel** | | See *Yerathel.* | |
| **Yod** | Y | 10th letter of Hebrew alphabet, transliterated as *y*, *i*, or *j*. Spelled out, YWD, "hand" (20). Corresponds to Virgo, the 20th Path (between Chesed and Tiphareth), and the Tarot Trump IX. The Hermit; for additional correspondences, see *Betulah.* | 10 |
| **Yod He Waw** | YWD HH WW | The three consonants in Tetragrammaton, spelled out; see *Forty-two letter Name,* section II. | 42 |
| **Yod He Waw He** | YWD HH WW HH | The consonants of Tetragrammaton spelled out; the expanded name. | 52 |

| Yod H Waw H | YWD H WW H | Tetragrammaton with the Yod and Waw spelled out; see *Forty-two letter Name*, section II. | 42 |
| Yom | YWM | Day. | 616 56 |
| Yonah | YWNH | Dove; Jonah. | 71 |

# Z

| Zachi | ZChOY | Angel of 2nd decanate of Leo. | 95 |
| Zag | ZG | Skin of grapes. | 10 |
| Zagan | ZAGN | Goetic demon by night of 1st decanate of Sagittarius. | 711 61 |
| | | King and President commanding 33 legions. | |
| | | Appears as a bull with griffin's wings; later, as a human being. | |
| | | Powers: makes men witty; turns wine into water and blood into wine; turns any metal into coins appropriate thereto; makes even fools wise. | |
| Zahab | ZHB | Gold, the metal of the Sun; in alchemy, the Self. | 14 |
| Zahob | ZHWB | Golden. | 20 |
| Zak | ZK | Pure, clear, transparent, innocent. | 507 27 |
| Zakoth | ZKWTh | Merit, privilege, right. | 433 |
| Zalbarhith | ZLBRHYTh | Lord of Triplicity by Night for Leo. | 654 |
| Zamael | ZMAL | Angel ruling Mars and Tuesday; sometimes given as Camael, but this is more likely a variant spelling of Kamael, the archangel of Mars. | 78 |
| Zan | ZN | Species, kind. | 707 57 |
| Zar | ZR | Strange, foreign. | 207 |
| Zarach | ZRCh | To shine. | 215 |
| Zauir Anpin | ZAWYR ANPYN | The Lesser Countenance; Microprosopus; a title of Tiphareth, but also associated | 1065 415 |

| | | with Sephiroth 4 through 9, collectively. | |
|---|---|---|---|
| **Zayin** | Z | 7th letter of Hebrew alphabet, transliterated as *z*. | 7 |
| | | Spelled out, ZYN, "sword" (717 or 67). Corresponds to Gemini, the 17th Path (between Binah and Geburah), and the Tarot Trump VII. The Chariot; for additional correspondences, see *Teomim*. | |
| **Zazel** | ZAZL | Spirit of Saturn. | 45 |
| **Zazer** | ZZR | Angel of the 1st decanate of Aries. | 214 |
| **Zebhul** | ZBWL | Dwelling; the 4th Heaven, corresponding to Tiphareth. | 41 |
| **Zebulun** | ZBWLN | A tribe of Israel, associated with Capricorn. | 745 95 |
| **Zed** | ZD | Arrogant. | 11 |
| **Zeh** | ZH | This, that; who, which; here, there. | 12 |
| **Zepar** | ZPAR | Goetic demon by day of 1st decanate of Virgo. Duke commanding 26 legions. Appears as a soldier in red clothing and armor. Powers: procures love; makes women barren. | 288 |
| **Zeq** | ZQ | Chain; flaming arrow. | 107 |
| **Zer** | ZR | Border. | 207 |
| **Zerach** | ZRCh | Sunrise. | 215 |
| **Zerah** | ZRCh | Father of Jobab, a King of Edom. | 215 |
| **Zillah** (Tzillah) | TzLH | A wife of Lamech of the line of Cain; mother of Tubal-Cain and Naamah. | 125 |
| **Zilpah** | ZLPH | Leah's handmaiden; mother of Gad and Asher. | 122 |
| **Zimimay** | ZYMYMAY | Demon King of the North, according to the Goetia; also spelled Ziminair. | 118 |
| **Zipporah** (Tzipporah) | TzPRH | Wife of Moses. | 375 |
| **Ziv** | ZW | Glory, splendor. | 13 |
| **Zohar** | ZHR | Splendor; the Sepher ha-Zohar, Book of Splendor. | 212 |
| **Zuriel** | ZWRYAL | Archangel of Libra. | 254 |

# SECTION II

SECTION II

| Abomination | Thoabath | ThWOBTh | 878 |
| Air | Ruach | RWCh | 214 |
| All | Kol | KL | 50 |
| Almighty, The | Shaddai | ShDY | 314 |
| Almighty God | Elohim Gibor | ALHYM GBWR | 857 297 |
| | El Shaddai | AL ShDY | 345 |
| Angel | Malak | MLAK | 571 91 |
| Angelic Choirs | See *Yetzirah.* | | |
| Angel of God | Malak ha-Elohim | MLAK HALHYM | 1222 742 662 182 |
| Antimony | Puk | PWK | 586 106 |
| Aquarius | Deli ("bucket") | DLY | 44 |

**Arch-demons** There are several versions of the hierarchy of chief devils or arch-demons. Three of them are as follows:

| Sephira | Crowley (777) | Mathers | Waite |
|---|---|---|---|
| Kether | Satan and Moloch | Satan and Moloch | Satan and Moloch |
| Chokmah | Samael | Beelzebub | Adam Belial or Beelzebuth |
| Binah | Isheth Zenunim | Lucifuge | Lucifuge |

141

| | | | |
|---|---|---|---|
| **Chesed** | Lucifuge | Ashtaroth | Astaroth |
| **Geburah** | Ashtaroth | Asmodeus | Asmodeus |
| **Tiphareth** | Belphegor or Chioa | Belphegor | Belphegor |
| **Netzach** | Asmodai | Baal | Baal Cha-nan |
| **Hod** | Adramelek or Belial | Adramme-lech | Adramelek |
| **Yesod** | Lilith | Lilith | Lilith |
| **Malkuth** | Naamah | Nahema | None given |

| | | | |
|---|---|---|---|
| **Aries** | Taleh ("lamb") | TLH | 44 |
| **Ark (Noah's)** | Tebah | ThBH | 407 |
| **Ark (of the covenant)** | Aron | ARN | 901 251 |
| **Ark of the Testimony** | Aron ha-Edeth | ARWN HODTh | 1386 736 |
| **Assyria** | Ashur | AShWR | 507 |
| **Autumn** | Sethav | SThW | 466 |

| | | | |
|---|---|---|---|
| **Bear (n.)** | Dob | DB | 7 |
| **Beast** | Chioa | ChYWA | 25 |
| **Beauty** | Tiphareth | ThPARTh | 1081 |
| **Black** | Shachor | ShChWR | 514 |
| **Blessed** | Baruk | BRWK | 708 228 |
| **Blessing** | Berakah | BRKH | 227 |
| **Blood** | Dam | DM | 604 44 |
| **Bride** | Kalah | KLH | 55 |
| **Boils** | Shechin | ShChYN | 1018 368 |
| **Book** | Sepher | SPR | 340 |
| **Book of Formation** | Sepher Yetzirah | SPR YTzYRH | 655 |

| | | | |
|---|---|---|---|
| **Book of Splendor** | Sepher ha-Zohar | SPR HZHR | 557 |
| **Book of the Law** | Sepher ha-Torah | SPR HThWRH | 956 |
| **Bosom** | Chob | ChB | 10 |
| **Breast** | Dadh | DD | 8 |
| **Brother** | Ach | ACh | 9 |
| **Brother-in-law** | Yabam | YBM | 612 52 |
| **Bull** | Shor | ShWR | 506 |

| | | | |
|---|---|---|---|
| **Cancer** | Sarton ("crab") | SRTN | 969 319 |
| **Candlestick** | Menorah | MNRH | 295 |
| **Capricorn** | Gedi ("kid, young goat") | GDY | 17 |
| **Chariot** | Merkabah | MRKBH | 267 |
| **Circumcision** | Milah | MYLH | 85 |
| **Coin** | Matbea | MTBO | 121 |
| **Coins** | Matbeoth | MTBOWTh | 527 |
| **Color** | Tzeva | TzBO | 162 |
| **Copper** | Nechsheth | NChShTh | 758 |
| **Covenant** | Berith | BRYTh | 612 |
| **Creation** | Briah | BRYAH | 218 |
| **Crown** | Kether | KThR | 620 |
| **Cup** | Sephel | SPL | 170 |
| **Cups** | Sephalim | SPLYM | 780 220 |
| **Curse** | Qelalah | QLLH | 165 |
| **Cursed** | Arur | ARWR | 407 |

| | | | |
|---|---|---|---|
| **Darkness** | Choshek | ChShK | 808 328 |

| Daughter | Bath | BTh | 402 |
|---|---|---|---|
| Dawn | Shachar | ShChR | 508 |
| | Zerach | ZRCh | 215 |
| Day | Yom | YWM | 616 |
| | | | 56 |
| Dead | Meth | MTh | 440 |
| Death | Maveth | MWTh | 446 |
| Delight | Ratzon | RTzWN | 996 |
| | | | 346 |
| Demon | Shed | ShD | 304 |
| | Sair ("hairy one") | ShOYR | 580 |
| | Maziq | MZYQ | 157 |

**Demon Kings** The Demon Kings of the Elements and Cardinal Points are variously given as follows:

| Point | Element | Rabbinic | Grimoiric | Goetic |
|---|---|---|---|---|
| East | Air | Samael | Orions | Amaymon |
| West | Water | Azazel | Paimon | Corson |
| North | Earth | Azael | Ariton | Zimimay |
| South | Fire | Mahazael | Amaimon | Göap |

| Demons | Shedim | ShDYM | 914 |
|---|---|---|---|
| | | | 354 |
| | Seirim | ShOYRYM | 1190 |
| | | | 630 |
| | Meziqim | MZYQYM | 767 |
| | | | 207 |
| | Qlippoth ("shells") | QLYPWTh | 626 |
| Desolation | Tohu | ThHW | 411 |
| Dove | Yonah | YWNH | 71 |
| Dragon | Theli | ThLY | 440 |
| Duke | Alup | ALWP | 837 |
| | | | 117 |

| Eagle | Nesher | NShR | 550 |
|---|---|---|---|

| | | | |
|---|---|---|---|
| **Earth** | Eretz | ARTz | 1101 |
| | | | 291 |
| | Ophir | OPYR | 360 |
| | Adamah | ADMH | 50 |
| | Arqa | ARQA | 302 |
| **Egypt** | Mitzraim | MTzRYM | 940 |
| | | | 380 |
| **Eight** | Shemonah | ShMNH | 395 |
| **Eighteen** | Shemonah-Asar | ShMNH-OShR | 965 |
| **Eighty** | Shemonim | ShMNYM | 1000 |
| | | | 440 |
| **Eleven** | Achad-Asar | AChD-OShR | 583 |
| **Eternity** | Ad | OD | 74 |
| **Evening** | Ereb | ORB | 272 |
| **Evil** | Ra | RO | 270 |
| | Raah | ROH | 275 |

| | | | |
|---|---|---|---|
| **Fall (autumn)** | Sethav | SThW | 466 |
| **Father** | Ab | AB | 3 |
| **Father-in-law** | Cham | ChM | 608 |
| | | | 48 |
| **Fear** | Pachad | PChD | 92 |
| **Fifty** | Chamishim | ChMShYM | 958 |
| | | | 398 |
| **Fifteen** | Chamishah-Asar | ChMShH-OShR | 923 |
| **Fire** | Esh | ASh | 301 |
| **Fish** | Dag | DG | 7 |
| **Five** | Chamishah | ChMShH | 353 |
| **Fool** | Kesil | KSYL | 120 |
| **Foreskin** | Arlah | ORLH | 305 |
| **Formation** | Yetzirah | YTzYRH | 315 |
| **Fortune** | Gad | GD | 7 |
| **Forty** | Arbaim | ARBOYM | 883/323 |

**Forty-two-letter name**
The 42-fold name of God is based on the idea that the three consonants in YHWH (Tetragrammaton), when spelled out, add to 42 (YWD HH WW or YWD H WW H). The letters of the expanded name are the initials (Notariqon) of 42 attributes of God. The 42-letter name is: ABGYThTz-QROShMNKGDYKShBMRTzThGHQM-MNOYGLPZQShQYOYTh. I have had the presumption to anglicize this spelling into "Ab-gi-thetz-qerashamen-kegadikesh-bamratztag-haqamamna-yaglepzeq-sheqi-ayeth," the hyphens based on the division of the name into groups of 2, 2, 2, 6, 6, 6, 6, 6, 3, and 3 for assignment to the Sephiroth, per Crowley (777), as follows:

3783

| Kether | AB | Ab |
|---|---|---|
| Chokmah | GY | Gi |
| Binah | ThTz | Thetz |
| Chesed | QROShMN | Qerashamen |
| Geburah | KGDYKSh | Kegadikesh |
| Tiphareth | BMRTzThG | Bamratztag |
| Netzach | HQMMNO | Haqamamna |
| Hod | YGLPZQ | Yaglepzeq |
| Yesod | ShQY | Sheqi |
| Malkuth | OYTh | Ayeth |

| | | | |
|---|---|---|---|
| **Foundation** | Yesod | YSWD | 80 |
| **Four** | Arbaah | ARBOH | 278 |
| **Fourteen** | Arbaah-Asar | ARBOH-OShR | 848 |
| **Frogs** | Tzephardea | TzPRDO | 444 |

| | | | |
|---|---|---|---|
| **Garden** | Gan | GN | 703 |
|  |  |  | 53 |

| | | | |
|---|---|---|---|
| **Garden of Eden** | Gan Eden | GN ODN | 1477 |
| | | | 827 |
| | | | 177 |
| **Gemini** | Teomim ("twins") | ThAWMYM | 1057 |
| | | | 497 |
| **Goat** | Ez | OZ | 77 |
| **God** | El | AL | 31 |
| | Elil | ALYL | 71 |
| | Eloah | ALH | 36 |
| | | ALWH | 42 |
| | Elohim | ALHYM | 646 |
| | | | 86 |
| | Yahweh | YHWH | 26 |
| **God Almighty** | El Shaddai | AL ShDY | 345 |
| **Goddess** | Elah | ALH | 36 |
| | Alilah | ALYLH | 76 |

**Goetic Demons**  *Goetia: The Book of Evil Spirits* is part of *The Lesser Key of Solomon*, the oldest extant copy of which is of the 17th century and in French. It contains the names and descriptions of 72 demons under the authority of Amaimon (East), Korson (or Corson) (West), Zimimay (North), and Göap (South). There is no established Hebrew spelling of these names; I have used that of Crowley (777), with a few obvious corrections, constructing the spelling myself for the four kings. As to the correctness of the numerology involved, one should bear in mind that all such constructed spellings are by their nature somewhat arbitrary, as is the assignment of the demons to the decanates of the Zodiac (in which I have also followed Crowley). For the names of the demons, see the individual signs of the Zodiac in section I.

| | | | |
|---|---|---|---|
| **Gold** | Zahab | ZHB | 14 |
| **Golden** | Zahob | ZHWB | 20 |
| **Good** | Tob | TWB | 17 |
| **Grace** | Chen | ChN | 708 |
| | | | 58 |

| Great | Gadhol | GDWL | 43 |

# H

| Hail | Barad | BRD | 206 |
| Hawk | Netz | NTz | 950 |
| | | | 140 |
| Heaven | Shamaim | ShMYM | 950 |
| | | | 390 |
| Hebrew | Ibri | OBRY | 282 |
| Hebrews | Ibrim | OBRYM | 882 |
| | | | 322 |
| Hell | Gehenna; Ge-Hinnom. | GYHNWM | 674 |
| | | | 114 |
| Hermetic Order of the Golden Dawn | Chevrah Zerach Boqer Or (Society of the Shining Light of Dawn) | ChBRH ZRCh BQR AWR | 939 |
| Hermit | Parush | PRWSh | 586 |
| High Priest | Kohen ha-Gadhol | KHN | 773 |
| | | HGDWL | 123 |
| High Priestess | Koheneth ha-Gadhol | KHNTh | 523 |
| | | HGDWL | |
| Holiness | Qadesh | QDSh | 404 |
| Holy | Qadosh | QDWSh | 410 |
| Holy Living Creatures | Chayoth ha-Qadesh | ChYWTh HQDSh | 833 |
| Holy of Holies | Qadosh Qadeshim | QDWSh QDShYM | 1424 864 |
| Hour | Shaah | ShOH | 375 |
| Hundred | Meah | MAH | 46 |

# I

| Infinity | Ain-Soph | AYN-SWP | 1577 |
| | | | 927 |
| | | | 207 |

| | | | |
|---|---|---|---|
| **Innocence** | Bor | BR | 202 |
| | Tom | ThM | 1000 |
| | | | 440 |
| **Innocent** | Chaph | ChP | 808 |
| | | | 88 |
| | Zak | ZK | 507 |
| | | | 27 |
| **Iron** | Barzel | BRZL | 239 |

# J

| | | | |
|---|---|---|---|
| **Jackal** | Tan | ThN | 1100 |
| | | | 450 |
| **Judgment** | Shephet | ShPT | 389 |
| **Jupiter** | Tzedek | TzDQ | 194 |
| **Justice** | Din | DYN | 714 |
| | | | 64 |

# K

| | | | |
|---|---|---|---|
| **King** | Melek | MLK | 570 |
| | | | 90 |
| **Kingdom** | Malkuth | MLKWTh | 496 |
| **Knowledge** | Daath | DOTh | 474 |
| | Dea | DO | 74 |

# L

| | | | |
|---|---|---|---|
| **Ladder** | Sellam | SLM | 690 |
| | | | 130 |

| | | | |
|---|---|---|---|
| **Law** | Torah | ThWRH | 611 |
| **Lead** | Abar | ABR | 203 |
| **Leo** | Ari ("lion") | ARYH | 216 |
| **Libra** | Moznaim ("scales") | MAZNYM | 708 |
| | | | 148 |
| **Life** | Chayim | ChYYM | 628 |
| | | | 68 |
| **Light** | Or | AWR | 207 |
| **Lion** | Ari | ARY | 211 |
| | Ari | ARYH | 216 |
| **Living** | Chai | ChY | 18 |
| **Locusts** | Arbeh | ARBH | 208 |
| **Lord** | Baal | BOL | 102 |
| | Yahweh | YHWH | 26 |
| **Love** | Ahab | AHB | 8 |
| | Ahbah | AHBH | 13 |

| | | | |
|---|---|---|---|
| **Macro-prosopus** | Arik Anpin | ARYK ANPYN | 1551 1072 |
| | | | 422 |
| **Magician** | Chartom | ChRTM | 817 |
| | | | 257 |
| **Magus** | Mag | MG | 43 |
| **Man** | Adam | ADM | 605 |
| | | | 45 |
| | Ish | AYSh | 311 |
| **Manna** | Man | MN | 740 |
| | | | 90 |
| **Mars** | Madim | MDYM | 654 |
| | | | 94 |
| **Mary** | Miriam | MRYM | 850 |
| | | | 290 |

| | | | |
|---|---|---|---|
| **Memphis** | Moph | MP | 840 |
| (Egypt) | | | 120 |
| | Noph | NP | 750/130 |
| **Mercury** | Kokab | KWKB | 48 |
| (the planet) | | | |
| **Mercury** | Kaspith | KSPYTh | 570 |
| (the metal) | | | |
| **Mercy** | Chesed | ChSD | 72 |
| **Merit** | Zakoth | ZKWTh | 433 |
| **Micro-** | Zauir Anpin | ZAWYR | 1065 |
| prosopus | | ANPYN | 415 |
| **Milk** | Chalav | ChLB | 40 |
| **Milky Way** | Shevil ha-Chalav | ShBYL | 387 |
| | | HChLB | |
| **Month** | Chodesh | ChDSh | 312 |
| **Moon** | Levanah | LBNH | 87 |
| **Morning** | Boqer | BQR | 302 |
| **Mother** | Em | AM | 601 |
| | | | 41 |
| **Mountain** | Har | HR | 205 |
| **Mount Sinai** | Har Sinai | HR SYNY | 335 |
| **Murrain** | Dever | DBR | 206 |
| **Muse** | Bath Shir | Bth ShYR | 912 |
| **Myrrh** | Mor | MR | 240 |

| | | | |
|---|---|---|---|
| **Night** | Laylah | LYLH | 75 |
| **Nine** | Tishah | ThShOH | 775 |
| **Nineteen** | Tishah-Asar | ThShOH- | 1345 |
| | | OShR | |
| **Ninety** | Tishim | ThShOYM | 1380 |
| | | | 820 |
| **North** | Tzaphon | TzPWN | 876 |
| | | | 226 |
| **Nothing** | Ayn | AYN | 711/61 |

| Olympic Planetary Spirits | These spirits are from the 16th-century *Arbatel of Magic*, which is in Latin; hence, there are no established Hebrew spellings of the names. Nevertheless, I have constructed what seem to me to be the most likely Hebrew spellings of the names. The spirits are: |

| | | | |
|---|---|---|---|
| **Moon** | Phul | PWL | 116 |
| **Mercury** | Ophiel | AWPYAL | 128 |
| **Venus** | Hagith | ChGYTh | 421 |
| **Sun** | Och | AWCh | 15 |
| **Mars** | Phaleg | PLG | 113 |
| **Jupiter** | Bethor | BYThWR | 618 |
| **Saturn** | Arathron | ARAThRWN | |
| | | | 1508 |
| | | | 858 |

| | | | |
|---|---|---|---|
| **One** | Echad | AChD | 13 |
| **Orion** | Kesilim ("fools") | KSYLYM | 730 |
| | | | 170 |
| **Ox** | Aleph | ALP | 831 |
| | | | 111 |
| | Shor | ShWR | 506 |

| | | | |
|---|---|---|---|
| **Palace** | Hekel | HYKL | 65 |
| **Path** | Shevil | ShBYL | 342 |
| **Paths** | Shevilim | ShBYLYM | 952 |
| | | | 392 |
| **Peace** | Shalom | ShLWM | 936 |
| | | | 376 |

| Pearl | Dar | DR | 204 |
|---|---|---|---|
| Pisces | Dagim ("fishes") | DGYM | 617 |
| | | | 57 |
| Plague | Negep | NGP | 853 |
| | | | 133 |
| Priest | Kohen | KHN | 725 |
| | | | 75 |
| Priestess | Koheneth | KHNTh | 475 |
| Prophet | Navi | NBYA | 63 |
| Pure | Chaph | ChP | 808 |
| | | | 88 |
| | Zak | ZK | 507 |
| | | | 27 |
| Purity | Bor | BR | 202 |
| Purple | Tekheleth | ThKLTh | 850 |

| Queen | Malkah | MLKH | 95 |
|---|---|---|---|

| Raven | Oreb | ORB | 272 |
|---|---|---|---|
| Red | Adhom | ADM | 605 |
| | | | 45 |
| River | Naher | NHR | 255 |

| Sagittarius | Qasshat ("bow") | QShTh | 800 |
|---|---|---|---|

| | | | |
|---|---|---|---|
| Saturn | Shabbathai | ShBThAY | 713 |
| Scorpio | Akrab ("scorpion") | OQRB | 372 |
| Sea | Yam | YM | 610 |
| | | | 50 |
| Secret (adj.) | Nisetar | NSThR | 710 |
| Secret Wisdom | Chokmah Nisetarah | ChKMH NSThRH | 788 |
| Serpent | Nachash | NChSh | 358 |
| Seven | Shivah | ShBOH | 377 |
| Seventeen | Shivah-Asar | ShBOH-OShR | 947 |
| Seventy | Shivim | ShBOYM | 982 |
| | | | 422 |
| Severity | Geburah | GBWRH | 216 |
| Shells | Qlippoth | QLYPWTh | 626 |
| Silence | Demamah | DMMH | 89 |
| | Dumiah | DWMYH | 65 |
| | Shethiqah | ShThYQH | 815 |
| Silent | Domem | DWMM | 650 |
| | | | 90 |
| | Shotheq | ShWThQ | 806 |
| Silver | Kesep | KSP | 880 |
| | | | 160 |
| Sin | Hattaah | HTAH | 20 |
| | Set | ST | 69 |
| Sister | Achoth | AChWTh | 415 |
| Six | Shishah | ShShH | 605 |
| Sixteen | Shishah-Asar | ShShH-OShR | 1175 |
| Sixty | Shishim | ShShYM | 1210 |
| | | | 650 |
| Slaying of the Firstborn | Makath be-Khoroth | MKTh BKWRWTh | 1094 |
| Society (organization) | Chevrah | ChBRH | 215 |
| Son | Ben | BN | 702 |
| | | | 52 |
| | Bar | BR | 202 |
| Sorceress | Mekeshar | MKShR | 560 |
| Sorceror | Mekshepah | MKShPH | 445 |

| | | | |
|---|---|---|---|
| **South** | Darom | DRWM | 810 |
| | | | 250 |
| **Splendor** | Hod | HWD | 15 |
| | Noah | NH | 55 |
| | Ziv | ZW | 11 |
| **Spring** | Abib | ABYB | 15 |
| **Star** | Kokab | KWKB | 48 |
| **Strength** | Koch | KCh | 28 |
| | Ez | OZ | 77 |
| | On | AWN | 707 |
| | | | 57 |
| **Summer** | Qayitz | QYTz | 1010 |
| | | | 200 |
| **Sun** | Shemesh | ShMSh | 640 |
| **Sword** | Cherev | ChRB | 210 |
| **Swords** | Charavoth | ChRBWTh | 616 |

| | | | |
|---|---|---|---|
| **Tabernacle** | Mishkan | MShKN | 1060 |
| | | | 410 |
| **Taurus** | Shor ("ox," "bull") | ShWR | 506 |
| **Ten** | Asarah | OShRH | 575 |
| **Testimony** | Edeth | ODTh | 474 |

**Tetragram-**  The Holy Ineffable Name of God, YHWH,
**maton**  Yahweh, Jehovah, etc.; the Name of Four
Letters; the letters correspond to the four
elements, the four worlds of cabalism, ad
infinitum; e.g.:

| | | | |
|---|---|---|---|
| **Yod** | Fire | Atziluth (Nobility) | Father |
| **He** | Water | Briah (Creation) | Mother |
| **Waw** | Air | Yetzirah (Formation) | Son |
| **He** | Earth | Assiah (Action) | Daughter |

| | | | |
|---|---|---|---|
| **Thebes (Egypt)** | No | NA | 51 |
| **Thirteen** | Shelshah-Asar | ShLShH-OShR | 1205 |
| **Thirty** | Shelshim | ShLShYM | 1240 |
| | | | 680 |
| **Thousand** | Elep | ALP | 831 |
| | | | 111 |
| **Three** | Shelshah | ShLShH | 635 |
| **Throne** | Kes | KS | 80 |
| | Korsia | KWRSYA | 297 |
| **Tigris** | Hiddikel | HDQL | 139 |
| **Tin** | Bedil | BDYL | 46 |
| **Tradition** | Cabala | QBLH | 137 |
| **Transgression** | Set | ST | 69 |
| | Set | ShT | 309 |
| | Shal | ShL | 330 |
| **Tree** | Etz | OTz | 970 |
| | | | 160 |
| **Tree of Knowledge** | Etz ha-Daath | OTz HDOTh | 1449 639 |
| **Tree of Life** | Etz ha-Chayim | OTz HChYYM | 1603 793 |
| | | | 233 |
| **Tree of the Knowledge of Good and Evil** | Etz ha-Daath Tob wa-Ra | OTz HDOTh TWB WRO | 1742 932 |
| **Tribe** | Mattah | MTH | 54 |
| **Truth** | Emeth | AMTh | 441 |
| **Twelve** | Shenaim-Asar | ShNYM-OShR | 1530 970 |
| **Twenty** | Esrim | OShRYM | 1180 620 |
| **Twenty-one** | Esrim we-Echad | OShRYM WAChD | 1199 639 |
| **Twenty-two** | Esrim u-Shenaim | OShRYM WShNYM | 2146 1586 |
| | | | 1026 |

| Two | Shenaim | ShNYM | 960 |
| | | | 400 |

**U**

| Under- standing | Binah | BYNH | 67 |
| Unity | Echad | AChD | 13 |
| Ur of the Chaldees | Ur Kasdim | AWR KShDYM | 1141 581 |
| Ursa Major | Ayish | OYSh | 380 |
| Ursa Minor | Ben Ayish | BN OYSh | 1082 432 |

**V**

| Valley | Gay | GY | 13 |
| | Gaye | GYA | 14 |
| Valley of the Shadow of Death | Gey-Tzalmaweth | GYA- TzLMWTh | 580 |
| Veil | Wilon | WYLWN | 752 102 |
| Venus | Nogah | NWGH | 64 |
| Vermin | Kinnim | KNYM | 680 120 |
| Victory | Netzach | NTzCh | 148 |
| Virgo | Betulah (Virgin) | BThWLH | 443 |
| Void (Gen. 1:2) | Bohu | BHW | 13 |
| Vulture | Racham | RChM | 808 248 |

# W

| Wand | Maqqel | MQL | 170 |
| Wands | Maqqeloth | MQLWTh | 576 |
| War | Milchamah | MLChMH | 123 |
| Waste | Bohu | BHW | 13 |
| Water | Maim | MYM | 650 |
| | | | 90 |
| Week | Shavua | ShBWO | 378 |
| West | Maarab | MORB | 312 |
| Wheel | Ophan | AWPN | 787 |
| | | | 137 |
| White | Lavan | LBN | 732 |
| | | | 82 |
| Wild Beasts | Arov | ORWB | 278 |
| Winter | Choreph | ChRP | 1008 |
| | | | 288 |
| Wisdom | Chokmah | ChKMH | 73 |
| | Dea | DO | 74 |
| Woman | Ishah | AShH | 306 |
| Word | Milah | MLH | 75 |
| | Davar | DBR | 206 |
| World | Olam | OWLM | 701 |
| | | | 141 |
| | Cheled | ChLD | 42 |
| | Tebhel | ThBL | 432 |

# Y

| Year | Shanah | ShNH | 355 |
| Yellow | Tzahov | TzHB | 97 |
| Yoke | Ol | OL | 100 |

# Z

**Zodiac**      Mazloth                  MZLWTh      483

The Signs of the Zodiac in Hebrew are as follows:

| | |
|---|---|
| **Aries** | Taleh ("lamb") |
| **Taurus** | Shor ("ox," "bull") |
| **Gemini** | Teomim ("twins") |
| **Cancer** | Sarton ("crab") |
| **Leo** | Ari ("lion") |
| **Virgo** | Betulah ("virgin") |
| **Libra** | Moznaim ("scales") |
| **Scorpio** | Akrab ("scorpion") |
| **Sagittarius** | Qasshat ("bow") |
| **Capricorn** | Gedi ("kid," "young goat") |
| **Aquarius** | Deli ("bucket") |
| **Pisces** | Dagim ("fishes") |

# SECTION III

SECTION III

# ℵ A

**ALEPH**

| | | | |
|---|---|---|---|
| A | Aleph | 1st letter of Hebrew alphabet. | 1 |
| AB | Ab | Father; a title of Chokmah; the first two letters of the 42-letter name of God, associated with Kether. | 3 |
| | Av | The 11th Hebrew month. | |
| ABBA | Abba | The Supernal Father; a title of Chokmah. | 6 |
| ABGYThTzQRO-ShMNKGDYKSh-BMRTzThGHQ-MMNOYGLPZQ-ShQYOYTh | Ab-gi-thetz-qerashamen-kegadikesh-bamratztag-haqamamna-yaglepzeq-sheqi-ayeth | The name of God of 42 letters. | 3783 |
| ABDWN | Abaddon | Destruction; the angel of the bottomless pit; the 6th hell, corresponding to Chesed. | 713 63 |
| ABDRWN | Abdaron | Angel of 2nd decanate of Aquarius. | 913 263 |
| ABWHA | Aboha | Angel of 3rd decanate of Sagittarius. | 15 |
| ABWZ | Aboz | According to Francis Barrett, the 2nd hell; evidently a misprint for ABDWN. | 16 |
| ABYB | Abib | Spring. | 15 |
| ABYMLK | Abimelech | A King of the Philistines. | 583 103 |
| ABYR | Abir | The Almighty. | 213 |
| ABR | Abar | Lead, the metal of Saturn. | 203 |
| ABRAHADABRA | Abrahadabra | Crowley's spelling of Abracadabra. | 418 |
| ABRAKALA | Abrakala | The original form of Abracadabra. | 526 |
| ABRHM | Abraham | Abraham. | 808 248 |
| ABRM | Abram | Abraham's original name. | 803 243 |

| AGAR | Agar | Agares, Goetic demon by day of 2nd decanate of Aries. | 205 |
| AGYAL | Agiel | Intelligence of Saturn. | 45 |
| AGLA | Agla | A name of God; acronym for Ateh Gibor le-Olam Adonai (AThH GBWR LOWLM ADNY), "Thou art mighty forever, O Lord." | 35 |
| AGRTh | Agrath | See *AGRTh BTh MChLTh.* | 604 |
| AGRTh BTh MChLTh | Agrath bath Mahalath | Agrath, daughter of Mahalath; a queen of demons; one of the three wives of Samael. | 1484 |
| AD | Edh | Vapor, mist. | 5 |
| ADWKYAL | Advakiel | Archangel of Sagittarius. | 72 |
| ADWM | Edom | Edom. | 611/51 |
| ADM | Adam Adhom | Adam; man; a title of Tiphareth Red. | 605/45 |
| ADM BLYAL | Adam Belial | Arch-demon corresponding to Chokmah (Waite). | 678 118 |
| ADMH | Adamah | Earth; one of the seven earths, corresponding to Chesed. | 50 |
| ADM QDMWN | Adam Qadmon | The archetypal man. | 1455 895 245 |
| ADNY | Adonai | A name of God originally used as a euphemism for YHWH. | 65 |
| ADNY HARTz | Adonai ha-Eretz | Lord of the Earth; divine name associated with Malkuth, with Earth, and with the North. | 1171 361 |
| ADYMYRWN | Admiron | The Bloody Ones; Qlippoth of Taurus. | 971 321 |
| ADYRYRWN | Adiryaron | "The Mighty One sings"; a title of Tiphareth. | 1131 481 |
| ADR | Adar | The 6th Hebrew month. | 205 |
| AHB | Ahab | Love. | 8 |
| AHBH | Ahbah | Love, beloved. | 13 |
| AHWZ | Ahoz | Lord of Triplicity by Day for Sagittarius. | 19 |
| AHYH | Ehyeh | "I AM" (Ex. III:14); divine name associated with Kether. | 21 |
| AHYH AShR AHYH | Ehyeh Asher Ehyeh | Existence of Existences; "I AM WHAT AM" (Ex. XIII:14); a title of Kether. | 543 |

| | | | |
|---|---|---|---|
| **AHYHWH** | Ehyahweh | The combination of AHYH and YHWH, the microcosm and the macrocosm. | 32 |
| **AHLYBMH** | Aholibamah | A Duke of Edom, associated with Chesed. | 93 |
| **AHRN** | Aaron | Brother of Moses. | 906/256 |
| **AW** | 'O | Or. | 7 |
| **AWAL** | Uvall | Goetic demon by night of 2nd decanate of Cancer. | 38 |
| **AWCh** | Och | Olympic Planetary Spirit of the Sun. | 15 |
| **AWM** | Aum | 30th name of Shem Hamphorash, associated with 6th quinance of Sagittarius. | 607 47 |
| **AWMAL** | Avamel | Angel of 6th quinance of Sagittarius; angel by night of the 10 of Wands. | 78 |
| **AWN** | Avan | Avnas, Goetic demon by night of 1st decanate of Scorpio. | 707 57 |
| | On | Strength; wealth; sorrow. | |
| **AWNN** | Onan | Onan. | 757/107 |
| **AWPYAL** | Ophiel | Olympic Planetary Spirit of Mercury. | 128 |
| **AWPN** | Ophan | Wheel; one of the Ophanim. | 787/137 |
| **AWPNYM** | Ophanim | Wheels (Ez. I:16); Angelic Choir associated with Chokmah and with the Sphere of the Zodiac. | 747 187 |
| **AWR** | Or | Light. | 207 |
| | Ur | A city of Mesopotamia, birthplace of Abram. | |
| **AWRAWB** | Orob | Orobas, Goetic demon by night of 1st decanate of Libra. | 216 |
| **AWRWN** | Avron | Angel of 2nd decanate of Pisces. | 913 263 |
| **AWRYAL** | Uriel | Archangel associated with North and Earth. | 248 |
| **AWRYM** | Urim | One of two devices carried by the High Priest and used for divination. | 817 257 |
| **AWR KShDYM** | Ur Kasdim | Ur of the Chaldees; a city of Mesopotamia, birthplace of Abram. | 1141 581 |
| **AWR MWPLA** | Or Mopla | The Hidden Light; a title of Kether. | 364 |
| **AWR PNYMY** | Or Penimi | The Internal Light; a title of Kether. | 397 |
| **AWR PShWT** | Or Pashot | The Simple Light; a title of Kether. | 602 |

| | | | |
|---|---|---|---|
| AZ | Az | Then. | 8 |
| ACh | Ach | Brother. | 9 |
| AChD | Echad | One; unity. | 13 |
| AChD HWA ALHYM | Echad Hua Elohim | He is One God. | 111 |
| AChD-OShR | Achad-Asar | Eleven. | 583 |
| AChD RASh AChDWThW RASh YChWDW ThMWRHZW AChD | Echad Rosh Achdotho Rosh Ichudo Temurahzo Echad | One is His beginning, one is His individuality, His permutation is one; usually abbreviated Ararita and used as a name of God. | 2151 |
| AChWDRAWN | Achodraon | Lord of Triplicity by Night for Libra. | 926 276 |
| AChWTh | Achoth | Sister. | 415 |
| AChTh RWCh ACLYM ChYYM | Achath Ruach Elohim Chayyim | One is the Spirit of the Living God. | 840 300 |
| AT | At | Whisper (n.). | 10 |
| AY | Ay | Where?; island. | 11 |
| AYAL | Ayel | Angel of 1st astrological house. | 42 |
| AYWAS | Aiwass | The supposed author of *The Book of the Law.* | 78 |
| AYL | Ayyal | Hart; a title of Malkuth. | 41 |
| AYM | Aim | Goetic demon by day of 2nd decanate of Scorpio. | 611 51 |
| AYMA | Aima | The Supernal Mother; a title of Binah. | 52 |
| AYN | Ain | Nothing. | 711/61 |
| AYN-SWP | Ain-Soph | Infinity. | 1577/927/207 |
| AYN-SWP AWR | Ain-Soph Or | The Limitless Light. | 1784/1134/414 |
| AYO | Aya | 67th name of Shem Hamphorash, associated with 1st quinance of Cancer. | 81 |
| AYOAL | Ayoel | Angel of 1st quinance of Cancer; angel by day of the 2 of Cups. | 112 |
| AYQ BKR | Aiq Bekar | The cabala of the nine chambers. | 333 |
| AYR | Iyar | The 8th Hebrew month. | 211 |
| AYSh | Ish | Man; a title of Tiphareth. | 311 |
| AK | Ak | But, only, surely, indeed. | 501/21 |
| AKA | Aka | 7th name of Shem Hamphorash, associated with 1st quinance of Virgo. | 22 |

| AKAYH | Akaiah | Angel of 1st quinance of Virgo; angel by day of the 8 of Pentacles. | 37 |
|---|---|---|---|
| AKD | Akkad | Dynasty of ancient Mesopotamia. | 25 |
| AL | El | Divine name associated with Chesed. | 31 |
| ALD | Elad | 10th name of Shem Hamphorash, associated with 4th quinance of Virgo. | 35 |
| ALDYH | Aldiah | Angel of 4th quinance of Virgo; angel by night of the 9 of Pentacles. | 50 |
| ALH | Eloah | God. | 36 |
| | Elah | Goddess; a Duke of Edom, associ- ed with Geburah. | |
| ALHY ABRHM | Elohi Abraham | The God of Abraham. | 854 294 |
| ALHY ABRHM ALHY YTzChQ WALHY YOQB | Elohi Abra- ham Elohi Itzchaq we- Elohi Yaaqob | The God of Abraham, the God of Isaac, and the God of Jacob. | 1342 782 |
| ALHY HOBRYM | Elohi ha-Ibrim | God of the Hebrews. | 933 373 |
| ALHY YOQB | Elohi Yaaqob | The God of Jacob. | 228 |
| ALHY YTzChQ | Elohi Itzchaq | The God of Isaac. | 254 |
| ALHYM | Elohim | A name of God; Angelic Choir asso- ciated with Netzach and with the Sphere of Venus; usually enumerat- ed with the final M as 40. | 646 86 |
| ALHYM GBWR | Elohim Gibor | Almighty God; divine name asso- ciated with Geburah. | 857 297 |
| ALHYM TzBAWTh | Elohim Tzabaoth | God of Hosts; divine name associ- ated with Hod, with Water, and with the West. | 1145 585 |
| ALWYR | Aloyar | Lord of Triplicity by Night for Capricorn. | 247 |
| ALWK | Allok | Alloces, Goetic demon by night of 1st decanate of Virgo. | 537 57 |
| ALWL | Elul | The 12th Hebrew month. | 67 |
| ALWP | Alup | Chief; "duke." | 837 117 |
| ALYGWSh | Eligos | Goetic demon by day of 3rd deca- nate of Leo. | 350 |
| ALYL | Elil | God. | 71 |

| ALLH | Allah | Name of God in Islam *(Arabic)*. | 66 |
|---|---|---|---|
| ALYLH | Elihah | Goddess. | 76 |
| ALYNKYR | Alinkir | Angel of 3rd decanate of Cancer. | 321 |
| ALP | Aleph | Ox; 1st letter of Hebrew alphabet. | 831 |
|  | Elep | Thousand. | 111 |
| AL QNA | El Qanna | A jealous God (Ex. XX:5). | 182 |
| AL ShDY | El Shaddai | God Almighty. | 345 |
| AM | Em | Mother. | 601 |
|  |  |  | 41 |
| AMA | Ama | Mother; a title of Binah. | 42 |
| AMAYMWN | Amaimon | Demon King of Earth and the North; according to the Goetia, Demon King of the East. | 798 148 |
| AMBRYAL | Ambriel | Archangel of Gemini. | 284 |
| AMDWK | Amduk | Amdukias, Goetic demon by night of 1st decanate of Aquarius. | 551 71 |
| AMWN | Amon | Goetic demon by day of 1st decanate of Gemini; chief god of the Egyptians. | 747 97 |
| AMN | Amen | Firm, faithful; so be it!; a title of Kether. | 741 91 |
| AMNYTzYAL | Amnitziel | Archangel of Pisces. | 232 |
| AMth | Emeth | Truth | 441 |
| AN | An | Where? | 701/51 |
| ANAL | Anael | Angel ruling Venus and Friday. | 82 |
| ANDR | Andar | Andras; Goetic demon by night of 3rd decanate of Sagittarius. | 255 |
| ANDRALP | Andrealph | Andrealphus, Goetic demon by night of 2nd decanate of Capricorn. | 1086 366 |
| ANDRWMAL | Andromal | Andromalius, Goetic demon by night of 3rd decanate of Pisces. | 332 |
| ANWSh | Enosh | Enos. | 357 |
| ANY | Ani | I; fleet (of ships); 37th name of Shem Hamphorash, associated with 1st quinance of Aquarius. | 61 |
| ANYAL | Aniel | Angel of 1st quinance of Aquarius; angel by day of the 5 of Swords. | 92 |
| ANNAWRH | Ananaurah | Angel of 1st decanate of Virgo. | 313 |
| ANKY YHWH ALHYK | Anoki Yahweh Eloheka | I am the Lord thy God. | 173 |
| ANSWAL | Ansuel | Angel of 11th astrological house. | 148 |
| ASYMWN | Asimon | Old coin; telephone token; infernal being associated with the northwest. | 817 167 |

| ASMWDAY | Asmodai | Asmodeus; arch-demon corresponding to Geburah (Mathers and Waite) or to Netzach (Crowley); Goetic demon by day of 2nd decanate of Aquarius. | 122 |
|---|---|---|---|
| ASMWDAL | Asmodel | Archangel of Taurus. | 142 |
| AP | Aph | Also. | 801 |
| | | | 81 |
| APWD | Ephod | Part of the paraphernalia of the High Priest. | 91 |
| APRAYM | Ephraim | A tribe of Israel, associated with Taurus. | 892 |
| | | | 332 |
| ATzYLWTh | Atziluth | Nobility; the Divine or Archetypal World. | 537 |
| ARAL | Aral | Angel of Fire. | 232 |
| ARALYM | Aralim | Mighty Ones; Angelic Choir associated with Binah and with the Sphere of Saturn. | 842 |
| | | | 282 |
| ARARYThA | Ararita | A name of God; acronym for Echad Rosh Achdotho Rosh Ichudo Temurahzo Echad (AChD RASh AChDWThW RASh YChWDW ThMWRHZW AChD), "One is His beginning, one is His individuality, his permutation is one." | 813 |
| ARAThRWN | Arathron | Olympic Planetary Spirit of Saturn. | 1508 |
| | | | 858 |
| ARBH | Arbeh | Locusts; the 8th of the 10 plagues of Egypt. | 208 |
| ARBOH | Arbaah | Four. | 278 |
| ARBOH-OShR | Arbaah-Asar | Fourteen. | 848 |
| ARBOYM | Arbaim | Forty. | 883 |
| | | | 323 |
| ARWN HODTh | Aron ha-Edeth | Ark of the Testimony. | 1386 |
| | | | 736 |
| ARWR | Arur | Cursed. | 407 |
| ARZYAL | Araziel | Angel of Taurus. | 249 |
| ARYAL | Ariel | Ruler of Air. | 242 |
| ARY | Ari | Lion. | 211 |
| ARYH | Ari | Lion; Leo. | 216 |

| | | | |
|---|---|---|---|
| **ARYTWN** | Ariton | Demon King of Water and the West. | 926 |
| | | | 276 |
| **ARYK ANPYN** | Arik Anpin | The Vast Countenance; The Greater Countenance; Macroprosopus; Long of Nose; a title of Kether. | 1552 |
| | | | 1072 |
| **ARYK APYM** | Arik Apim | Long of Face; a title of Kether. | 1402 |
| | | | 922 |
| | | | 362 |
| **ARK** | Erech | Uruk, a city of ancient Mesopotamia. | 701 |
| | | | 221 |
| **ARN** | Aron | Ark (of the covenant). | 901 |
| | | | 251 |
| **ARPKShD** | Arphaxad | Arphaxad. | 605 |
| **ARTz** | Eretz | Earth; one of the four elements; one of the seven earths, corresponding to the three Supernal Sephiroth. | 1101 |
| | | | 291 |
| **ARQA** | Arqa | Earth; one of the seven earths, corresponding to Hod. | 302 |
| **ARR** | Arar | To curse. | 401 |
| **ASh** | Esh | Fire. | 301 |
| **AShH** | Ishah | Woman. | 306 |
| **AShWR** | Ashur | Assyria. | 507 |
| **AShYM** | Eshim | Flames; Angelic Choir associated with Malkuth. | 911 |
| | | | 351 |
| **AShMDAY** | Asmodai | A variant spelling; usually ASMW-DAY. | 356 |
| **AShR** | Asher | A tribe of Israel, associated with Libra. | 501 |
| **AShRH** | Asherah | Phoenician goddess of prosperity. | 506 |
| **AShTh ZNWNYM** | Isheth Zenunim | Woman of Whoredom; Demon of Prostitution; according to Crowley, arch-demon corresponding to Binah. | 1424 |
| | | | 864 |
| **AShThRWTh** | Ashtaroth | Arch-demon corresponding to Chesed (Mathers and Waite) or to Geburah (Crowley); Goetic demon by day of 2nd decanate of Capricorn. | 1307 |
| **ATh** | Eth | Word used in Hebrew to indicate a direct object; no English equivalent; used by the Golden Dawn adepts to mean "essence" and to designate | 401 |

the fifth element, Spirit.

| | | | |
|---|---|---|---|
| AThH GBWR | Ateh Gibor | "Thou art mighty forever, O Lord"; | 1418 |
| LOWLM ADNY | le-Olam Adonai | usually abbreviated Agla and used as a name of God. | 858 |

BETH

| | | | |
|---|---|---|---|
| B | Beth | 2nd letter of Hebrew alphabet. | 2 |
| BABALON | Babalon | Figure in Crowley's mythology. | 806/156 |
| BADShChTh | Badshechath | According to Francis Barrett, the 4th hell; evidently a misprint for BARShChTh. | 715 |
| BAL | Bael | Goetic demon by day of 1st decanate of Aries. | 33 |
| BARShChTh | Bar Shachath | Pit of Ruin; the 5th hell, corresponding to Geburah. | 911 |
| BAThYN | Bathin | Goetic demon by day of 3rd decanate of Virgo. | 1113 463 |
| BAR | Beer | Well; a title of Malkuth. | 203 |
| BBL | Babel | Babel. | 34 |
| BG | Bag | Food. | 5 |
| BD | Bad | White linen. | 6 |
| BDD | Bedad | Father of Hadad, a King of Edom. | 10 |
| BDYL | Bedil | Tin, the metal of Jupiter. | 46 |
| BHHMY | Behahemi | Angel of the 2nd decanate of Aries. | 62 |
| BHW | Bohu | Waste; "void" (Gen. I:2). | 13 |
| BHYMYRWN | Bahimiron | The Bestial Ones; Qlippoth of Aquarius. | 973 323 |
| BHLMY | Bihelami | Angel of 1st decanate of Pisces. | 87 |
| BHMWTh | Behemoth | The great land-monster of Hebrew mythology. | 453 |
| BWAR | Buer | Goetic demon by day of 1st decanate of Cancer. | 209 |
| BWTYSh | Botis | Goetic demon by day of 2nd decanate of Virgo. | 327 |
| BZ | Baz | Booty; prey. | 9 |
| BY | Bi | Please, pray. | 12 |
| BYM | Bim | Bimé, Goetic demon by day of 2nd | 612 |

| | | decanate of Sagittarius. | 52 |
|---|---|---|---|
| BYNH | Binah | Understanding; the 3rd Sephira. | 67 |
| BYPRW | Bifro | Bifrons, Goetic demon by night of 1st decanate of Cancer. | 298 |
| BYTh | Beth | House; 2nd letter of Hebrew alphabet. | 412 |
| BYTh-AL | Bethel | House of God. | 443 |
| BYThWN | Bethon | Angel of 3rd decanate of Gemini. | 918 468 |
| BYThWR | Bethor | Olympic Planetary Spirit of Jupiter. | 618 |
| BYThChWN | Bethchon | Lord of Triplicity by Day for Scorpio. | 1126 476 |
| BKR | Beker | Young male camel. | 222 |
| BL | Bal | Not. | 32 |
| | Bel | Chief god of the Babylonians. | |
| BLATh | Beleth | Goetic demon by day of 1st decanate of Leo. | 433 |
| BLHH | Bilhah | Rachel's handmaiden; mother of Dan and Naphtali. | 42 |
| BLYAL | Belial | An arch-demon; according to Crowley, corresponds to Hod; Qlippoth of Ain-Soph; Goetic demon by night of 2nd decanate of Aquarius. | 73 |
| BLO | Bela | A King of Edom, associated with Daath. | 102 |
| BLO BN BOWR | Bela ben Beor | Bela, son of Beor. | 1082/432 |
| BLOM | Balaam | Balaam. | 702/142 |
| BMRTzThG | Bamratztag | The 19th through 24th letters of the 42-letter name of God, associated with Tiphareth. | 735 |
| BN | Ben | Son; a title of Tiphareth; the secret name of the World of Assiah. | 702 52 |
| BNY ALHYM | Beni Elohim | Sons of the Gods; Angelic Choir associated with Hod and with the Sphere of Mercury. | 708 148 |
| BNYMN | Benjamin | A tribe of Israel, associated with Sagittarius. | 802 152 |
| BN OYSh | Ben Ayish | Son of Ayish; Ursa Minor. | 1082 432 |
| BOWR | Beor | Father of Bela, a King of Edom. | 278 |
| BOZ | Boaz | One of the pillars in the Temple of Solomon. | 79 |
| BOYR | Beir | Beast, cattle. | 282 |

| | | | |
|---|---|---|---|
| **BOYRYRWN** | Beiriron | The Herd; Qlippoth of Aries. | 1198 |
| | | | 548 |
| **BOL** | Baal | Lord, owner; according to Mathers, arch-demon corresponding to Netzach. | 102 |
| **BOLZBWB** | Beelzebub | Lord of the Flies; arch-demon corresponding to Chokmah. | 119 |
| **BOL ChNN** | Baal-Hanan | A King of Edom, associated with Yesod; arch-demon corresponding to Netzach (Waite). | 860 |
| | | | 210 |
| **BOL ChNN BN OKBWR** | Baal-Hanan ben Achbor | Baal-Hanan, son of Achbor. | 1860 |
| | | | 1210 |
| | | | 560 |
| **BOLM** | Balam | Goetic demon by night of 3rd decanate of Leo. | 702 |
| | | | 142 |
| **BTz** | Botz | Mud. | 902 |
| | | | 92 |
| **BTzRH** | Bozrah | A city of Edom; city of King Jobab. | 297 |
| **BQR** | Boqer | Morning. | 302 |
| **BR** | Bar | Corn, grain; son; chosen, pure, empty. | 202 |
| | Bor | Purity, innocence. | |
| **BRA** | Bara | Created. | 203 |
| **BRAShYTh** | Bereshith | In the beginning. | 2911 |
| **BRBTWSh** | Barbatos | Goetic demon by day of 2nd decanate of Gemini. | 519 |
| **BRD** | Barad | Hail; the 7th of the 10 plagues of Egypt. | 206 |
| **BRWK** | Baruk | Blessed. | 708 |
| | | | 228 |
| **BRZL** | Barzel | Iron, the metal of Mars. | 239 |
| **BRYAH** | Briah | Creation; the Archangelic or Creative World. | 218 |
| **BRYTh** | Berith | Covenant; Goetic demon by day of 1st decanate of Capricorn. | 612 |
| **BRK** | Barak | To kneel, bless. | 702 |
| | Berek | Knee, lap. | 222 |
| **BRKH** | Berakah | Blessing. | 227 |
| **BRKYAL** | Barkiel | Archangel of Scorpio. | 263 |
| **BRTzBAL** | Bartzabel | Spirit of Mars. | 325 |
| **BTh** | Bath | Daughter. | 402 |

| BThWLH | Betulah | Virgin; a title of Malkuth; Virgo. | 443 |
| BTh ShYR | Bath Shir | Song-maiden; muse. | 912 |

# G ↗ GIMEL

| G | Gimel | 3rd letter of Hebrew alphabet. | 3 |
| GA | Ge | Proud. | 4 |
| GB | Gab | Elevation, top. | 5 |
| | Geb | Pit, water-hole. | |
| GBWRH | Geburah | Severity; the 5th Sephira. | 216 |
| GBRYAL | Gabriel | Archangel associated with Yesod, with the Moon, with the West, and with Water. | 246 |
| GG | Gag | Flat roof; cover of an altar. | 6 |
| GD | Gad | A tribe of Israel, associated with Aries; good luck, fortune; Babylonian god of fortune. | 7 |
| GDWL | Gadhol | Great. | 43 |
| GDWLH | Gedulah | Greatness, magnificence; a title of Chesed. | 48 |
| GDY | Gedi | Kid, young goat; Capricorn. | 17 |
| GW | Gav | Back (n.) | 9 |
| GWAP | Göap | Demon King of the South (Goetia). | 810 90 |
| GWG | Gog | Gog. | 12 |
| GWG WMGWG | Gog we-Magog | Gog and Magog. | 70 |
| GWLChB | Golachab | The Arsonists; Qlippoth of Geburah. | 49 |
| GWNH | Gonah | Serenity. | 64 |
| GWSYWN | Gusion | Goetic demon by day of 2nd decanate of Cancer. | 785 135 |
| GZ | Gez | Fleece. | 10 |
| GY | Gi | The 2nd two letters of the 42-letter name of God, associated with Chokmah. | 13 |
| | Gay | Valley. | |
| GYA | Gaye | Valley; one of the seven earths, corresponding to Geburah. | 14 |

| | | | |
|---|---|---|---|
| GYAL | Giel | Angel of 3rd astrological house. | 44 |
| GYA-<br>TzLMWTh | Gey-<br>Tzalmaweth | Valley of the Shadow of Death. | 580 |
| GYHBM | Gihebem | Acccrding to Francis Barrett, the 7th hell; evidently a misprint for GYHNWM. | 620<br>60 |
| GYHWN | Gihon | A river of Eden, associated with Water. | 724<br>74 |
| GYNNWM | Ge-Hinnom | The Valley of Hinnom; Gehenna; hell; specifically, the 1st hell, corresponding to Yesod and Malkuth. | 674<br>114 |
| GL | Gal<br>Gel<br>Gol | Ruins; well; fountain; wave.<br>Dung.<br>Oil vessel. | 33 |
| GLASLBWL | Glaslabol | Glasya-Labolas, Goetic demon by day of 1st decanate of Sagittarius. | 162 |
| GLGLTh | Gelgoleth | Golgoltha; skull, head. | 466 |
| GLOD | Gilead | Gilead. | 107 |
| GLSh | Galash | To lie down. | 333 |
| GM | Gam | Together; also. | 603<br>43 |
| GMWR | Gamor | Gamori, Goetic demon by night of 2nd decanate of Libra. | 249 |
| GMTRYA | Gematria | Hebrew numerology. | 263 |
| GMYGYN | Gamigin | Goetic demon by day of 1st decanate of Taurus. | 766<br>116 |
| GML | Gimel | Camel; 3rd letter of Hebrew alphabet. | 73 |
| GMLYAL | Gamaliel | The Obscene Ones; Qlippoth of Yesod. | 114 |
| GN | Gan | Garden. | 703<br>53 |
| GN ODN | Gan Eden | Garden of Eden. | 1477<br>827<br>177 |
| GOP | Gäap | Goetic demon by day of 3rd decanate of Aquarius. | 873<br>153 |
| GOSh | Gash | Quaking. | 373 |
| GOShKLH | Gasheklah | The Smiters; the Disturbers of All Things; the Breakers in Pieces; Qlippoth of Chesed. | 428 |
| GP | Gaph | Back, top; body, person. | 803<br>83 |

| GR | Gar | Dwelling. | 203 |
| GRAPYAL | Graphiel | Intelligence of Mars. | 325 |
| GRWDYAL | Gerodiel | Angel of 3rd decanate of Aquarius. | 254 |
| GTh | Gath | Winepress. | 403 |

# D T DALETH

| D | Daleth | 4th letter of Hebrew alphabet. | 4 |
| DB | Dob | Bear (n.). | 7 |
| DBYR | Devir | Sanctuary of the Temple. | 216 |
| DBR | Davar | Word, thing. | 206 |
| | Dever | Murrain; the 5th of the 10 plagues of Egypt. | |
| DG | Dag | Fish. | 7 |
| DGDGYRWN | Dagdagiron | The Fishy Ones; Qlippoth of Capricorn. | 930 280 |
| DGWN | Dagon | Philistine fish god. | 713 63 |
| DGYM | Dagim | Fishes; Pisces. | 617 57 |
| DD | Dadh | Breast. | 8 |
| DWD | David | David. | 14 |
| DWMYH | Dumiah | Silence, quietness. | 65 |
| DWMM | Domem | Silent. | 650 90 |
| DY | Day | Sufficiency, plenty. | 14 |
| DYN | Din | Justice; a title of Geburah. | 714 64 |
| DK | Dak | Oppressed. | 504/24 |
| DKAWRAB | Decarab | Decarabia, Goetic demon by night of 3rd decanate of Aquarius. | 234 |
| DL | Dal | Wretched. | 34 |
| DLY | Deli | Bucket; Aquarius. | 44 |
| DLTh | Daleth | Door; 4th letter of Hebrew alphabet. | 434 |
| DM | Dam | Blood; the 1st of the 10 plagues of Egypt. | 604 44 |

| DMB | Dameb | 65th name of Shem Hamphorash, associated with 5th quinance of Gemini. | 46 |
| DMBYH | Damabiah | Angel of 5th quinance of Gemini; angel by day of the 10 of Swords. | 61 |
| DMMH | Demamah | Silence, whisper. | 89 |
| DMShQ | Damesq | Damascus. | 444 |
| DN | Dan | A tribe of Israel, associated with Scorpio. | 704 54 |
| DNHBH | Dinhabah | A city of Edom; city of King Bela. | 66 |
| DNTAL | Dantal | Dantalian, Goetic demon by night of 2nd decanate of Pisces. | 94 |
| DNY | Dani | 50th name of Shem Hamphorash, associated with 2nd quinance of Aries. | 64 |
| DNYAL | Daniel | Angel of 2nd quinance of Aries; angel by night of the 2 of Wands. | 95 |
| DO | Dea | Knowledge, wisdom. | 74 |
| DOTh | Daath | Knowledge. | 474 |
| DTzK ODSh BAChB | Detzak Ad-hash Bea-chav | The 10 plagues of Egypt, taking the first letter of each. | 981 501 |
| DQ | Daq | Crushed, fine, thin. | 104 |
| DR | Dar | Pearl. | 204 |
| DRWM | Darom | South. | 810 250 |
| DTh | Dath | Royal command, law. | 404 |

**HE**

| H | He | 5th letter of Hebrew alphabet. | 5 |
| HA | He | Lo! | 6 |
| HAA | Haa | 26th name of Shem Hamphorash, associated with 2nd quinance of Sagittarius. | 7 |
| HAAYH | Haayah | Angel of 2nd quinance of Sagittarius; angel by night of the 8 of Wands. | 22 |

| | | | |
|---|---|---|---|
| **HAWR** | Haur | Haures, Goetic demon by night of 1st decanate of Capricorn. | 212 |
| **HALP** | Halph | Halphas, Goetic demon by night of 2nd decanate of Aries. | 836 116 |
| **HANYAL** | Haniel | Archangel associated with Netzach and with Venus. | 97 |
| **HBL** | Hebel | Abel, son of Adam, slain by Cain; vapor, breath; vanity. | 37 |
| **HGYAL** | Hagiel | Intelligence of Venus. | 49 |
| **HGR** | Hagar | Sarai's maid; mother of Ishmael. | 208 |
| **HD** | Hed | Shout of joy. | 9 |
| **HDD** | Hadad | A King of Edom, associated with Tiphareth. | 13 |
| **HDD BN BDD** | Hadad ben Bedad | Hadad, son of Bedad. | 725 75 |
| **HDQL** | Hiddikel | Tigris; a river of Eden, associated with Air. | 139 |
| **HDR** | Hadar | A King of Edom, associated with Malkuth. | 209 |
| **HH** | He | Window; 5th letter of Hebrew alphabet. | 10 |
| | Hah | Alas! | |
| **HHH** | Hehah | 41st name of Shem Hamphorash, associated with 5th quinance of Aquarius. | 15 |
| **HHHAL** | Hahahel | Angel of 5th quinance of Aquarius; angel by day of the 7 of Swords. | 46 |
| **HHO** | Hehau | 12th name of Shem Hamphorash, associated with 6th quinance of Virgo. | 80 |
| **HHOYH** | Hihayah | Angel of 6th quinance of Virgo; angel by night of the 10 of Pentacles. | 95 |
| **HWA** | Hu | He; a name of God and title of Kether. | 12 |
| **HWD** | Hod | Splendor; the 8th Sephira. | 15 |
| **HZY** | Hezi | 9th name of Shem Hamphorash, associated with 3rd quinance of Virgo. | 22 |
| **HZYAL** | Haziel | Angel of 3rd quinance of Virgo; angel by day of the 9 of Pentacles. | 53 |
| **HChSh** | Hachash | 51st name of Shem Hamphorash, associated with 3rd quinance of Aries. | 313 |

| | | | |
|---|---|---|---|
| **HChShYH** | Hechashiah | Angel of 3rd quinance of Aries; angel by day of the 3 of Wands. | 328 |
| **HTAH** | Hattaah | Sin. | 20 |
| **HY** | Hi | Lamentation. | 15 |
| **HYY** | Hayeya | 71st name of Shem Hamphorash, associated with 5th quinance of Cancer. | 25 |
| **HYYAL** | Hayayel | Angel of 5th quinance of Cancer; angel by day of the 4 of Cups. | 56 |
| **HYKL** | Hekel | Temple, palace, mansion. | 65 |
| **HYKL AHBH** | Hekel Ahbah | Palace of Love; Heavenly Mansion corresponding to Chesed. | 78 |
| **HYKL GWNH** | Hekel Gonah | Palace of Serenity; Heavenly Mansion corresponding to Hod. | 129 |
| **HYKL ZKWTh** | Hekel Zakoth | Palace of Merit; Heavenly Mansion corresponding to Geburah. | 498 |
| **HYKL LBNTh HSPYR** | Hekel Lebanath ha-Saphir | Palace of the Pavement of Sapphire Stone (Ex. XXIV:10); Heavenly Mansion corresponding to Yesod and Malkuth. | 902 |
| **HYKL OTzM ShMYM** | Hekel Etzem Shamaim | Palace of the Body of Heaven (Ex. XXIV:10); Heavenly Mansion corresponding to Netzach. | 1775 1215 |
| **HYKL QDWSh QDShYM** | Hekel Qadosh Qadeshim | Palace of the Holy of Holies; Heavenly Mansion corresponding to the three Supernal Sephiroth. | 1489 929 |
| **HYKL RTzWN** | Hekel Ratzon | Palace of Delight; Heavenly Mansion corresponding to Tiphareth. | 1061 411 |
| **HYLL** | Heylel | Brightness; morning star. | 75 |
| **HYLL BN ShChR** | Heylel ben Shachar | Morning Star, Son of the Dawn; Lucifer. | 1285 635 |
| **HLLWYH** | Haleluyah | Hallelujah; praise the Lord. | 86 |
| **HM** | Hem | They. | 605 45 |
| **HMLYAL** | Hamaliel | Archangel of Virgo. | 116 |
| **HN** | Hen | Lo!; whether, if. | 705 55 |
| **HNAL** | Hanael | Archangel of Capricorn. | 86 |
| **HS** | Has | Silence! | 65 |
| **HSMAL** | Hismael | Spirit of Jupiter. | 136 |
| **HOGNTh** | Haagent | Haagenti, Goetic demon by night of 3rd decanate of Cancer. | 528 |

| HQBH | Haqabah | A name of God; acronym for Ha-qadosh Baruk Hu (HQDWSh BRWK HWA), "The Holy One, blessed be He." | 112 |
| HQDWSh BRWK HWA | Ha-qadosh Baruk Hu | The Holy One, blessed be He. | 1135 655 |
| HQM | Haqem | 16th name of Shem Hamphorash, associated with 4th quinance of Libra. | 705 145 |
| HQMYH | Haqmiah | Angel of 4th quinance of Libra; angel by night of the 3 of Swords. | 160 |
| HQMMNO | Haqamamna | The 25th through 30th letters of the 42-letter name of God, associated with Netzach. | 305 |
| HR | Har | Mountain. | 205 |
| HRCh | Harach | 59th name of Shem Hamphorash, associated with 5th quinance of Taurus. | 213 |
| HRChAL | Herachiel | Angel of 5th quinance of Taurus; angel by day of the 7 of Pentacles. | 244 |
| HRY | Hari | Aspect, characteristic; 15th name of Shem Hamphorash, associated with 3rd quinance of Libra. | 215 |
| HRYAL | Hariel | Angel of 3rd quinance of Libra; angel by day of the 3 of Swords. | 246 |
| HRN | Haran | Haran. | 905 255 |
| HR SYNY | Har Sinai | Mount Sinai. | 335 |
| HShM | Ha-Shem | The Name; Tetragrammaton. | 905 |
|  | Husham | A King of Edom, associated with Geburah. | 345 |

WAW

| W | Waw | 6th letter of Hebrew alphabet. | 6 |
| WADR | Veadar | The Hebrew intercalary month. | 211 |
| WAL | Val | Valu, Goetic demon by night of | 37 |

|  |  | 2nd decanate of Sagittarius. |  |
|---|---|---|---|
| **WALPR** | Valefor | Goetic demon by day of 3rd decanate of Taurus. | 317 |
| **WHW** | Vehu | 1st name of Shem Hamphorash, associated with 1st quinance of Leo. | 17 |
|  | Vaho | 49th name of Shem Hamphorash, associated with 1st quinance of Aries. |  |
| **WHWAL** | Vehuel | Angel of 1st quinance of Aries; angel by day of the 2 of Wands. | 48 |
| **WHWYH** | Vahaviah | Angel of 1st quinance of Leo; angel by day of the 5 of Wands. | 32 |
| **WHRYN** | Vehrin | Angel of 2nd decanate of Sagittarius. | 921 271 |
| **WW** | Waw | Nail, peg; 6th letter of Hebrew alphabet. | 12 |
| **WWL** | Vaval | 43rd name of Shem Hamphorash, associated with 1st quinance of Pisces. | 42 |
| **WWLYH** | Vavaliah | Angel of 1st quinance of Pisces; angel by day of the 8 of Cups. | 73 |
| **WYAL** | Veyel | Angel of 6th astrological house. | 47 |
| **WYLWN** | Wilon | Veil; the 1st Heaven, corresponding to Yesod and Malkuth. | 752 102 |
| **WYNA** | Viné | Goetic demon by night of 3rd decanate of Gemini. | 67 |
| **WYThRYOL** | Vitriol | Acronym for the alchemical formula *Visita interiora terrae rectificando invenies occultum lapidem.* ("Visit the interior of the earth; by rectification, you shall find the hidden stone"). | 726 |
| **WKBYAL** | Vakabiel | Angel of Pisces. | 69 |
| **WMB** | Vameb | 61st name of Shem Hamphorash, associated with 1st quinance of Gemini. | 48 |
| **WMBAL** | Vemibael | Angel of 1st quinance of Gemini; angel by day of the 8 of Swords. | 79 |
| **WPAR** | Vepar | Goetic demon by night of 3rd decanate of Taurus. | 287 |
| **WRYATz** | Oriatz | Oriax, Goetic demon by night of | 1117 |

| | | | |
|---|---|---|---|
| | | 2nd decanate of Scorpio. | 307 |
| WRKYAL | Verkiel | Archangel of Leo. | 267 |
| WShAGW | Vassago | Goetic demon by day of 3rd decanate of Aries. | 316 |
| WShW | Voso | Goetic demon by night of 3rd decanate of Libra. | 312 |
| WShR | Vesher | 32nd name of Shem Hamphorash, associated with 2nd quinance of Capricorn. | 506 |
| WShRYH | Veshriah | Angel of 2nd quinance of Capricorn; angel by night of the 2 of Pentacles. | 521 |
| WThRWDYAL | Uthrodiel | Angel of 3rd decanate of Scorpio. | 657 |

## ZAYIN

| | | | |
|---|---|---|---|
| Z | Zayin | 7th letter of Hebrew alphabet. | 7 |
| ZAGN | Zagan | Goetic demon by night of 1st decanate of Sagittarius. | 711 61 |
| ZAWYR ANPYN | Zauir Anpin | The Lesser Countenance; Microprosopus; a title of Tiphareth. | 1065 415 |
| ZAZL | Zazel | Spirit of Saturn. | 45 |
| ZBWL | Zebhul | Dwelling; the 4th Heaven, corresponding to Tiphareth. | 41 |
| ZBWLN | Zebulun | A tribe of Israel, associated with Capricorn. | 745 95 |
| ZG | Zag | Skin of grapes. | 10 |
| ZD | Zed | Arrogant. | 11 |
| ZH | Zeh | This, that; who, which; here, there. | 12 |
| ZHB | Zahab | Gold, the metal of the Sun. | 14 |
| ZHWB | Zahob | Golden. | 20 |
| ZHR | Zohar | Splendor; the Sepher ha-Zohar. | 212 |
| ZHRARYAL | Zoharariel | A title of Tiphareth. | 454 |
| ZW | Ziv | Glory, splendor. | 13 |
| ZWRYAL | Zuriel | Archangel of Libra. | 254 |
| ZZR | Zazer | Angel of 1st decanate of Aries. | 214 |
| ZChOY | Zachi | Angel of 2nd decanate of Leo. | 95 |
| ZYMYMAY | Zimimay | Demon King of the North (Goetia). | 118 |

| ZYN | Zayin | Sword; 7th letter of Hebrew alphabet. | 717 |
| | | | 67 |
| ZK | Zak | Pure, clear, transparent, innocent. | 507 |
| | | | 27 |
| ZKWTh | Zakoth | Merit, privilege, right. | 433 |
| ZLBRHYTh | Zalbarhith | Lord of Triplicity by Night for Leo. | 654 |
| ZLPH | Zilpah | Leah's handmaiden; mother of Gad and Asher. | 122 |
| ZMAL | Zamael | Angel ruling Mars and Tuesday. | 78 |
| ZN | Zan | Species, kind. | 707 |
| | | | 57 |
| ZPAR | Zepar | Goetic demon by day of 1st decanate of Virgo. | 288 |
| ZQ | Zeq | Chain; flaming arrow. | 107 |
| ZR | Zar | Strange, foreign. | 207 |
| | Zer | Border. | |
| ZRCh | Zerah | Father of Jobab, a King of Edom. | 215 |
| | Zarach | To shine. | |
| | Zerach | Sunrise. | |

## CHETH ∏CH

| Ch | Cheth | 8th letter of Hebrew alphabet. | 8 |
| ChB | Chob | Bosom. | 10 |
| ChBW | Chebo | 68th name of Shem Hamphorash, associated with 2nd quinance of Cancer. | 16 |
| ChBWYH | Chabuyah | Angel of 2nd quinance of Cancer; angel by night of the 2 of Cups. | 31 |
| ChBRH | Chevrah | Society, organization. | 215 |
| ChBRH ZRCh BQR AWR | Chevrah Zerach Boqer Or | "Society of the Shining Light of Dawn"; official Hebrew name of the Hermetic Order of the Golden Dawn. | 939 |
| ChG | Chag | Feast. | 11 |
| ChGYTh | Haggith | A wife of David; mother of Adonijah. | 421 |
| | Hagith | Olympic Planetary Spirit of Venus. | |

| | | | |
|---|---|---|---|
| ChD | Chad | Sharp. | 12 |
| ChDQYAL | Chedeqiel | Angel of Libra. | 153 |
| ChDSh | Chodesh | Month. | 312 |
| ChHW | Chaho | 24th name of Shem Hamphorash, associated with 6th quinance of Scorpio. | 19 |
| ChHWYH | Chahaviah | Angel of 6th quinance of Scorpio; angel by night of the 7 of Cups. | 34 |
| ChWH | Chavvah | Eve. | 19 |
| ChCh | Chach | Hook, brooch, ring. | 16 |
| ChY | Chai | Living. | 18 |
| ChYH | Chiah | Part of the soul referred to Chokmah. | 23 |
| ChYWA | Chioa | The Beast; the union or offspring of Samael, Prince of Demons, and Isheth Zenunim, Demon of Prostitution; according to Crowley, the arch-demon corresponding to Tiphareth. | 25 |
| ChYWTh | Chayoth | Living Creatures (Ez. I). | 424 |
| ChYWTh HQDSh | Chayoth ha-Qadesh | Holy Living Creatures; Angelic Choir associated with Kether. | 833 |
| ChYYM | Chayim | Life. | 628<br>68 |
| ChYTh | Cheth | Fence, enclosure; 8th letter of Hebrew alphabet. | 418 |
| ChK | Chek | Palate. | 508<br>28 |
| ChKMH | Chokmah | Wisdom; the 2nd Sephira. | 73 |
| ChKMH NSThRH | Chokmah Nisetarah | Secret Wisdom. | 788 |
| ChL | Chel<br>Chol | Bulwark, wall, rampart.<br>Profane, unholy. | 38 |
| ChLB | Chalav | Milk. | 40 |
| ChLD | Cheled | World; one of the seven earths; with Tebhel, corresponds to Yesod and Malkuth; our own earth. | 42 |
| ChLM YSWDWTh | Cholam Yesodoth | The Breaker of Foundations; the Sphere of the Elements, the part of the material world corresponding to Malkuth. | 1124<br>564 |

| ChM | Cham | Ham, son of Noah; father-in-law; warm, hot; warmth, heat. | 608 48 |
| ChMShH | Chamishah | Five. | 353 |
| ChMShH-OShR | Chamishah-Asar | Fifteen. | 923 |
| ChMShYM | Chamishim | Fifty. | 958 398 |
| ChN | Chen | Grace, charm. | 708 58 |
| ChNWK | Chanok | Enoch. | 564 84 |
| ChSD | Chesed | Mercy; love; the 4th Sephira. | 72 |
| ChOM | Cham | 38th name of Shem Hamphorash, associated with 2nd quinance of Aquarius. | 678 118 |
| ChOMYH | Chamiah | Angel of 2nd quinance of Aquarius; angel by night of the 5 of Swords. | 133 |
| ChP | Chaph | Pure, innocent. | 808 88 |
| ChTz | Chetz | Arrow; lightning; punishment, wound. | 908 98 |
| ChQ | Choq | Statute; share; task; boundary. | 108 |
| ChR | Chor | Hole. | 208 |
| ChRB | Cherev | Sword. | 210 |
| ChRBH | Charabhah | Parched Land; one of the seven earths, corresponding to Geburah. | 215 |
| ChRBWTh | Charavoth | Swords. | 616 |
| ChRTM | Chartom | Magician. | 817 257 |
| ChRP | Choreph | Winter. | 1008 288 |
| ChShWN | Cheshvan | The 2nd Hebrew month. | 1014 364 |
| ChShK | Choshek | Darkness; the 9th of the 10 plagues of Egypt. | 808 328 |
| ChShMWDAY | Chashmodai | Spirit of the Moon. | 369 |
| ChShMLYM | Chashmalim | Brilliant Ones; Angelic Choir associated with Chesed and with the Sphere of Jupiter. | 988 428 |
| ChTh | Chath | Broken; terrified. | 408 |
| ChShN | Chassan | Angel of Air. | 1008 |

Choshen      Breastplate of the High Priest.      358

**TETH**

| T | Teth | 9th letter of Hebrew alphabet. | 9 |
|---|---|---|---|
| TA | Ta | To sweep away. | 10 |
| TBL WYLWN | Tebel Wilon | Veil of the Firmament; the 1st | 1743 |
| ShMYM | Shamaim | Heaven, corresponding to Yesod | 1093 |
| | | and Malkuth. | 533 |
| TBTh | Tevet | The 4th Hebrew month. | 411 |
| TWAL | Toel | Angel of 2nd astrological house. | 46 |
| TWB | Tob | Good. | 17 |
| TWTTh | Totath | Lord of Triplicity by Night for | 424 |
| | | Taurus. | |
| TYTHYWN | Tit-ha-yawen | Mire of Mud; the 4th hell, corre- | 749 |
| | | sponding to Tiphareth. | 99 |
| TYRYAL | Tiriel | Intelligence of Mercury. | 260 |
| TYTh | Teth | Serpent; 9th letter of Hebrew | 419 |
| | | alphabet. | |
| TL | Tal | Dew. | 39 |
| TLH | Taleh | Lamb; Aries. | 44 |
| TLYHD | Taliahad | Angel of Water. | 58 |
| TMYRA | Temira de- | The Concealed of the Concealed; | 1233 |
| DTMYRYN | Temirin | a title of Kether. | 583 |
| TP | Taph | Children. | 809 |
| | | | 89 |
| TRSNY | Tarasni | Angel of 1st decanate of Libra. | 329 |

**YOD**

| Y | Yod | 10th letter of Hebrew alphabet. | 10 |
|---|---|---|---|
| YAChYN | Jachin | One of the pillars in the Temple of | 729 |
| | | Solomon. | 79 |

| YBL | Jabal | Jabal. | 79 |
|---|---|---|---|
| YBM | Yabam | Brother-in-law. | 612 |
| | Yebem | 70th name of Shem Hamphorash; associated with 4th quinance of Cancer. | 52 |
| YBMYH | Yebamiah | Angel of 4th quinance of Cancer; angel by night of the 3 of Cups. | 67 |
| YBShH | Yabbashah | Dry Land; one of the seven earths, corresponding to Netzach. | 317 |
| YGLPZQ | Yaglepzeq | The 31st through 36th letters of the 42-letter name of God, associated with Hod. | 230 |
| YDYD | Yadid | One beloved. | 28 |
| YDYDYH | Yedidiah | One beloved by God; Solomon. | 43 |
| YDOShChWM | Yadashchom | According to Francis Barrett, the 5th hell; evidently a misprint (for ShORYMWTh?). | 998 438 |
| YH | Yah | Divine name associated with Chokmah. | 15 |
| YHAL | Yahel | Angel of 7th astrological house. | 46 |
| YHH | Yehah | 62nd name of Shem Hamphorash, associated with 2nd quinance of Gemini. | 20 |
| YHHAL | Yehohel | Angel of 2nd quinance of Gemini; angel by night of the 8 of Swords. | 51 |
| YHWDH | Judah | A tribe of Israel, associated with Leo. | 30 |
| YHWH | Yahweh | Tetragrammaton; Jehovah; the Lord. | 26 |
| YHWH AChD | Yahweh Echad | Yahweh is One. | 38 |
| YHWH AYSh MLChMH | Yahweh Ish Milchamah | The Lord is a man of war. | 460 |
| YHWH AYSh MLChMH YHWH ShMW | Yahweh Ish Milchamah Yahweh Shemo | The Lord is a man of war; Yahweh is His Name (Ex. XV:3). | 832 |
| YHWH ALHYM | Yahweh Elohim | The Lord God; divine name associated with Binah. | 672 112 |
| YHWH ALWH WDOTh | Yahweh Eloah wa-Daath | Lord God of Knowledge; divine name associated with Tiphareth. | 548 |
| YHWH TzBAWTh | Yahweh Tzabaoth | Lord of Hosts; divine name associated with Netzach, with Fire, and | 525 |

|  |  | with the South. |  |
|---|---|---|---|
| **YHWH ShMW** | Yahweh Shemo | Yahweh is His Name. | 372 |
| **YHWShO** | Yehosha | Joshua; Jesus. | 391 |
| **YHY AWR** | Yehi Or | Let there be light. | 232 |
| **YHPYAL** | Iophiel | Intelligence of Jupiter. | 136 |
| **YWBB** | Jobab | A King of Edom, associated with Chesed. | 20 |
| **YWBB BN ZRCh** | Jobab ben Zerah | Jobab, son of Zerah. | 937 287 |
| **YWBL** | Jubal | Jubal | 48 |
| **YWD** | Yod | Hand; 10th letter of Hebrew alphabet. | 20 |
| **YWD HH WW** | Yod He Waw | The three consonants in Tetragrammaton. | 42 |
| **YWD HH WW HH** | Yod He Waw He | The consonants of Tetragrammaton spelled out; the expanded name. | 52 |
| **YWD H WW H** | Yod H Waw H | Tetragrammaton with the Yod and Waw spelled out. | 42 |
| **YWM** | Yom | Day. | 616 56 |
| **YWNH** | Yonah | Dove; Jonah. | 71 |
| **YWSP** | Yoseph | Joseph. | 876 156 |
| **YZL** | Yezel | 13th name of Shem Hamphorash, associated with 1st quinance of Libra. | 47 |
| **YZLAL** | Yezalel | Angel of 1st quinance of Libra; angel by day of the 2 of Swords. | 78 |
| **YChW** | Yecho | 33rd name of Shem Hamphorash, associated with 3rd quinance of Capricorn. | 24 |
| **YChWYH** | Yechaviah | Angel of 3rd quinance of Capricorn; angel by day of the 3 of Pentacles. | 39 |
| **YChYDH** | Yechidah | Part of the soul referred to Kether. | 37 |
| **YYZ** | Yeyaz | 40th name of Shem Hamphorash, associated with 4th quinance of Aquarius. | 27 |
| **YYZAL** | Yeyazel | Angel of 4th quinance of Aquarius; angel by night of the 6 of Swords. | 58 |

| YYY | Yeyaya | 22nd name of Shem Hamphorash, associated with 4th quinance of Scorpio. | 30 |
|---|---|---|---|
| YYYAL | Yeyayel | Angel of 4th quinance of Scorpio; angel by night of the 6 of Cups. | 61 |
| YYL | Yeyal | 58th name of Shem Hamphorash, associated with 4th quinance of Taurus. | 50 |
| YYLAL | Yeyalel | Angel of 4th quinance of Taurus; angel by night of the 6 of Pentacles. | 81 |
| YKSGNWTz | Yakasaganotz | Angel of 3rd decanate of Taurus. | 1049 239 |
| YLH | Yelah | 44th name of Shem Hamphorash, associated with 2nd quinance of Pisces. | 45 |
| YLHYH | Yelahiah | Angel of 2nd quinance of Pisces; angel by night of the 8 of Cups. | 60 |
| YLY | Yeli | 2nd name of Shem Hamphorash, associated with 2nd quinance of Leo. | 50 |
| YLYAL | Yelayel | Angel of 2nd quinance of Leo; angel by night of the 5 of Wands. | 81 |
| YM | Yam | Sea. | 610 50 |
| YSWD | Yesod | Foundation; the 9th Sephira. | 80 |
| YSYSYH | Yasyasyah | Angel of 2nd decanate of Capricorn. | 155 |
| YSGDYBRW-DYAL | Yasgedibaro-diel | Angel of 3rd decanate of Capricorn. | 340 |
| YO | Ya | Shovel. | 80 |
| YOQB | Yaaqob | Jacob. | 182 |
| YPWSh | Ipos | Goetic demon by day of 1st decanate of Scorpio. | 396 |
| YPTh | Yapheth | Japheth; son of Noah. | 490 |
| YTzChQ | Itzchaq | Isaac. | 208 |
| YTzYRH | Yetzirah | Formation; the Angelic or Formative World. | 315 |
| YRD | Yared | Jared. | 214 |
| YRDN | Yordan | Jordan. | 914 264 |
| YRChW | Yericho | Jericho | 224 |

| | | | |
|---|---|---|---|
| YRTh | Yereth | 27th name of Shem Hamphorash, associated with 3rd quinance of Sagittarius. | 610 |
| YRThAL | Yerathel | Angel of 3rd quinance of Sagittarius; angel by day of the 9 of Wands. | 641 |
| YSh | Yesh | Existence; there is/are. | 310 |
| YShMOAL | Ishmael | Ishmael. | 451 |
| YShRAL | Israel | Israel. | 541 |
| YShShKR | Issachar | A tribe of Israel, associated with Cancer. | 830 |
| YThRW | Yithero | Jethro. | 616 |
| YThTh | Jetheth | A Duke of Edom, associated with Daath. | 810 |

KAPH

| | | | |
|---|---|---|---|
| K | Kaph | 11th letter of Hebrew alphabet. | 20<br>500 |
| KAYN | Kain | Camio, Goetic demon by night of 2nd decanate of Virgo. | 731<br>81 |
| KAMBRYAL | Kambriel | Archangel of Aquarius. | 304 |
| KBR | Kavar | To make heavy; to make many, multiply. | 222 |
| | Kevar | Long; extent; long ago, already. | |
| | Khebar | A river in Mesopotamia. | |
| KGDYKSh | Kegadikesh | The 13th through 18th letters of the 42-letter name of God, associated with Geburah. | 357 |
| KD | Kad | Bucket, pail, vessel. | 24 |
| KDMDY | Kedamidi | Angel of 1st decanate of Taurus. | 78 |
| KH | Koh | Thus, so; here, there. | 25 |
| KHN | Kohen | Priest. | 725<br>75 |
| KHN HGDWL | Kohen ha-Gadhol | High Priest. | 773<br>123 |
| KHNTh | Koheneth | Priestess. | 475 |

| | | | |
|---|---|---|---|
| **KHNTh HGDWL** | Koheneth ha-Gadhol | High Priestess. | 523 |
| **KHTh** | Kahath | 8th name of Shem Hamphorash, associated with 2nd quinance of Virgo. | 425 |
| **KHThAL** | Kehethel | Angel of 2nd quinance of Virgo; angel by night of the 8 of Pentacles. | 456 |
| **KWZW** | Kuzu | A name of God by Temurah. | 39 |
| **KWKB** | Kokab | Star; Mercury. | 48 |
| **KWQ** | Keveq | 35th name of Shem Hamphorash, associated with 5th quinance of Capricorn. | 126 |
| **KWQYH** | Keveqiah | Angel of 5th quinance of Capricorn; angel by day of the 4 of Pentacles. | 141 |
| **KWRSWN** | Korson | Demon King of the West (Goetia). | 992 342 |
| **KWRSYA** | Korsia | Throne; a title of Binah. | 297 |
| **KWSh** | Kush | Cush. | 326 |
| **KCh** | Koch | Strength. | 28 |
| **KChMH** | Kochmah | A title of Chokmah. | 73 |
| **KY** | Ki | Brand; that, so that, because, when, for. | 30 |
| **KYMAWR** | Kimar | Kimaris, Goetic demon by night of 3rd decanate of Capricorn. | 277 |
| **KL** | Kol | All. | 50 |
| **KLH** | Kalah | Bride; a title of Malkuth. | 55 |
| **KLY** | Keli | Utensil, instrument, tool; 18th name of Shem Hamphorash, associated with 6th quinance of Libra. | 60 |
| **KLYAL** | Kaliel | Angel of 6th quinance of Libra; angel by night of the 4 of Swords. | 91 |
| **KMAL** | Kamael | Archangel associated with Geburah and with Mars. | 91 |
| **KMWTz** | Kamotz | Angel of 1st decanate of Scorpio. | 966 156 |
| **KN** | Ken | Honest; so, thus, just so, such, so much. | 720 70 |
| **KNYM** | Kinnim | Vermin; the 3rd of the 10 plagues of Egypt. | 680 120 |
| **KNON** | Kanaan | Canaan. | 840 190 |

| | | | |
|---|---|---|---|
| **KS** | Kes | Throne. | 80 |
| **KSYAL** | Kassiel | Cassiel, angel ruling Saturn and Saturday. | 121 |
| **KSYL** | Kesil | Fool. | 120 |
| **KSYLYM** | Kesilim | Fools; Orion. | 730 170 |
| **KSLW** | Kislev | The 3rd Hebrew month. | 116 |
| **KSP** | Kesep | Silver, the metal of the Moon. | 880 160 |
| **KSPYTh** | Kaspith | Mercury, the metal of the planet Mercury. | 570 |
| **KOAL** | Kael | Angel of 4th astrological house. | 121 |
| **KOMH** | Kaamah | Some sort of infernal being associated with the Northwest (a misprint for NOMH, "Naamah"?) | 135 |
| **KP** | Kaph | Palm of hand; 11th letter of Hebrew alphabet. | 820 100 |
| **KRWB** | Kerub | Ruler of Earth; one of the Kerubim. | 228 |
| **KRWBYM** | Kerubim | Angelic Choir associated with Yesod and with the Sphere of the Moon. | 838 278 |
| **KRWKL** | Crocell | Goetic demon by night of 1st decanate of Leo. | 276 |
| **KShNYOYH** | Kashenyayah | Angel of 10th astrological house. | 465 |
| **KThR** | Kether | Crown; the 1st Sephira. | 620 |

**LAMED**

| | | | |
|---|---|---|---|
| **L** | Lamed | 12th letter of Hebrew alphabet. | 30 |
| **LA** | Lo | Not, no. | 31 |
| **LAH** | Leah | First wife of Jacob; mother of Reuben, Simeon, Levi, Judah, Issachar, and Zebulun. | 36 |
| **LAW** | Lav | 11th name of Shem Hamphorash, associated with 5th quinance of Virgo. | 37 |
| | Lau | 17th name of Shem Hamphorash, | |

| | | | |
|---|---|---|---|
| | | associated with 5th quinance of Libra. | |
| **LAWYH** | Laviah | Angel of 5th quinance of Virgo; angel by day of the 10 of Pentacles; angel of 5th quinance of Libra; angel by day of the 4 of Swords. | 52 |
| **LB** | Leb | Heart, center. | 32 |
| **LBN** | Lavan | White. | 732 |
| | | | 82 |
| **LBNH** | Levanah | The Moon. | 87 |
| **LBRMYM** | Lebarmim | Lord of Triplicity by Night for Sagittarius. | 882 |
| | | | 322 |
| **LG** | Log | Basin. | 33 |
| **LD** | Lod | Lydda, a town in Benjamin. | 34 |
| **LHCh** | Lehach | 34th name of Shem Hamphorash, associated with 4th quinance of Capricorn. | 43 |
| **LHChYH** | Lehachiah | Angel of 4th quinance of Capricorn; angel by night of the 3 of Pentacles. | 58 |
| **LW** | Lo | Not, no. | 36 |
| **LWW** | Levo | 19th name of Shem Hamphorash, associated with 1st quinance of Scorpio. | 42 |
| **LWWYH** | Luviah | Angel of 1st quinance of Scorpio; angel by day of the 5 of Cups. | 57 |
| **LWT** | Lot | Lot. | 45 |
| **LWY** | Lewi | Levi. | 46 |
| **LWYM** | Levim | Levites; the priest tribe. | 646 |
| | | | 86 |
| **LWYThN** | Leviathan | The great sea-monster of Hebrew mythology. | 1146 |
| | | | 496 |
| **LWSNHR** | Losanahar | Angel of 1st decanate of Leo. | 351 |
| **LCh** | Lach | Moist, fresh, green. | 38 |
| **LT** | Lot | Laudanum. | 39 |
| **LYLH** | Laylah | Night. | 75 |
| **LYLYTh** | Lilith | Queen of the Night; Queen of Demons; wife of Samael; wife of Asmodai; first wife (before Eve) of Adam; arch-demon corresponding to Yesod. | 480 |

| LKB | Lekab | 31st name of Shem Hamphorash, associated with 1st quinance of Capricorn. | 52 |
| LKBAL | Lekabel | Angel of 1st quinance of Capricorn; angel by day of the 2 of Pentacles. | 83 |
| LLH | Lelah | 6th name of Shem Hamphorash, associated with 6th quinance of Leo. | 65 |
| LLHAL | Lelahel | Angel of 6th quinance of Leo; angel by night of the 7 of Wands. | 96 |
| LMD | Lamed | Ox goad; 12th letter of Hebrew alphabet. | 74 |
| LMK | Lamek | Lamech. | 570 90 |
| LSLRA | Laslara | Lord of Triplicity by Day for Virgo. | 321 |
| LO | Loa | Throat. | 100 |
| LTz | Letz | Mocker. | 930 120 |
| LRAYK | Leraik | Leraje, Goetic demon by day of 2nd decanate of Leo. | 741 261 |

MEM

| M | Mem | 13th letter of Hebrew alphabet. | 40 600 |
| MAH | Meah | Hundred | 46 |
| MAZNYM | Moznaim | Scales; Libra. | 708 148 |
| MALP | Malph | Malphas, Goetic demon by night of 3rd decanate of Aries. | 871 151 |
| MARATz | Maratz | Marax, Goetic demon by day of 3rd decanate of Libra. | 1142 332 |
| MARB | Marb | Marbas, Goetic demon by day of 2nd decanate of Taurus. | 243 |
| MBH | Mebah | 14th name of Shem Hamphorash, associated with 2nd quinance of Libra. | 47 |

|  | Mabeh | 55th name of Shem Hamphorash, associated with 1st quinance of Taurus. | |
| MBHAL | Mebahel | Angel of 2nd quinance of Libra; angel by night of the 2 of Swords. | 78 |
| MBHYH | Mebahiah | Angel of 1st quinance of Taurus; angel by day of the 5 of Pentacles. | 62 |
| MBTzR | Mibzar | A Duke of Edom, associated (with Magdiel) with Yesod. | 332 |
| MG | Mag | Magus. | 43 |
| MGDYAL | Magdiel | A Duke of Edom, associated (with Mibzar) with Yesod. | 88 |
| MGWG | Magog | Magog. | 52 |
| MD | Mad | Garment. | 44 |
| MDYM | Madim | Mars. | 654 94 |
| MDYN | Midian | Midian. | 754 104 |
| MH | Mah | What?, Which?, Why?, How?; anything, something; the secret name of the World of Yetzirah. | 45 |
| MHZAL | Mahazael | Demon Prince of Earth. | 83 |
| MHYTBAL | Mehetabel | Wife of Hadar, a King of Edom. | 97 |
| MHLLAL | Mahalaleel | Mahalaleel. | 136 |
| MHMMD | Muhammad | The prophet of Islam *(Arabic)*. | 132 |
| MHSh | Mahash | 5th name of Shem Hamphorash, associated with 5th quinance of Leo. | 345 |
| MHShYH | Mahashiah | Angel of 5th quinance of Leo; angel by day of the 7 of Wands. | 360 |
| MWAB | Moab | Moab. | 49 |
| MWM | Mum | Blemish; 72nd name of Shem Hamphorash, associated with 6th quinance of Cancer. | 646 86 |
| MWMYH | Mevamiah | Angel of 6th quinance of Cancer; angel by night of the 4 of Cups. | 101 |
| MWRYAL | Muriel | Archangel of Cancer. | 287 |
| MWRM | Murm | Murmus, Goetic demon by night of 3rd decanate of Virgo. | 846 286 |
| MWTh | Maveth | Death. | 446 |
| MZYQ | Maziq | Demon; injurer. | 157 |
| MZYQYM | Meziqim | Demons; injurers. | 767 207 |

| | | | |
|---|---|---|---|
| **MZLWTh** | Mazloth | Constellations; the Sphere of the Zodiac; the part of the material world corresponding to Chokmah. | 483 |
| **MZRCh** | Mizrach | East. | 255 |
| **MCh** | Meach Moach | Fat. Marrow. | 48 |
| **MChWYAL** | Mehujael | Mehujael. | 95 |
| **MChY** | Mechi | Battering ram; 64th name of Shem Hamphorash, associated with 4th quinance of Gemini. | 58 |
| **MChYAL** | Mochayel | Angel of 4th quinance of Gemini; angel by night of the 9 of Wands. | 89 |
| **MChLTh** | Mahalath | Daughter of Ishmael; wife of Esau; later considered a major demon; mother of Agrath. | 478 |
| **MTBO** | Matbea | Coin. | 121 |
| **MTBOWTh** | Matbeoth | Coins. | 527 |
| **MTH** | Mattah | Tribe; branch, twig, rod, staff, stick, sceptre, spear. | 54 |
| **MTTRWN** | Metatron | Archangel associated with Kether. | 964 314 |
| **MTRD** | Matred | Mother of Mehetabel, wife of Hadar, a King of Edom. | 253 |
| **MY** | Mi | Who?, Which?; whoever, every one. | 50 |
| **MYH** | Miah | 48th name of Shem Hamphorash, associated with 6th quinance of Pisces. | 55 |
| **MYHAL** | Mihael | Angel of 6th quinance of Pisces; angel by night of the 10 of Cups. | 86 |
| **MY ZHB** | Mezahab | Mother of Matred, mother of Mehetabel, wife of Hadar, a King of Edom. | 64 |
| **MYK** | Mik | 42nd name of Shem Hamphorash, associated with 6th quinance of Aquarius. | 550 70 |
| **MYKAL** | Michael | 1. Archangel associated with Hod, with Mercury, with the South, and with Fire; 2. Angel ruling the Sun and Sunday; 3. Angel of 6th quinance of Aquarius; angel by night of the 7 of Swords. | 101 |

| | | | |
|---|---|---|---|
| **MYLH** | Milah | Circumcision. | 85 |
| **MYM** | Mem | Water; 13th letter of Hebrew | 650 |
| | | alphabet. | 90 |
| | Maim | Water. | |
| **MKWN** | Makhon | Emplacement; the 6th Heaven, | 766 |
| | | corresponding to Chesed. | 116 |
| **MKShPH** | Mekshepah | Sorceror. | 445 |
| **MKShR** | Mekeshar | Sorceress. | 560 |
| **MKTh** | Makath be- | The Slaying of the Firstborn; the | 1094 |
| **BKWRWTh** | Khoroth | 10th of the 10 plagues of Egypt. | |
| **MLAK** | Malak | Angel. | 571 |
| | | | 91 |
| **MLAK HALHYM** | Malak ha- | Angel of God. | 1222 |
| | Elohim | | 742 |
| | | | 662 |
| | | | 182 |
| **MLAK HMSh-** | Malak ha- | Angel of Destruction. | 1329 |
| **ChYTh** | Mashchith | | 849 |
| **MLH** | Melah | 23rd name of Shem Hamphorash, | 75 |
| | | associated with 5th quinance of | |
| | | Scorpio. | |
| | Milah | Word. | |
| **MLHAL** | Melahel | Angel of 5th quinance of Scorpio; | 106 |
| | | angel by day of the 7 of Cups. | |
| **MLChMH** | Milchamah | War. | 123 |
| **MLK** | Melek | King; a title of Tiphareth; one of | 570 |
| | | the Melekim. | 90 |
| | Moloch | Arch-demon corresponding (with | |
| | | Satan) to Kether. | |
| **MLKA BThRSh-** | Malka be- | The Intelligence of the Intelli- | 3321 |
| **YShYM WOD** | Tarshishim | gences of the Moon; final M in | |
| **BRWH ShHQYM** | we-ad be- | ShHQYM, counted as 700. | |
| | Ruah | | |
| | Shehaqim | | |
| **MLKH** | Malkah | Queen; a title of Malkuth. | 95 |
| **MLKWTh** | Malkuth | Kingdom; the 10th Sephira. | 496 |
| **MLKYDAL** | Malkidiel | Archangel of Aries. | 135 |
| **MLKYM** | Melekim | Kings; Angelic Choir associated | 700 |
| | | with Tiphareth and with the Sphere | 140 |
| | | of the Sun. | |
| **MN** | Man | Manna. | 740 |

|        | Men       | Portion.                                                                          | 90   |
|--------|-----------|-----------------------------------------------------------------------------------|------|
| MND    | Menad     | Prickly; 36th name of Shem Hamphorash; associated with 6th quinance of Capricorn.  | 94   |
| MNDAL  | Mendel    | Angel of 6th quinance of Capricorn; angel by night of the 4 of Pentacles.          | 125  |
| MNChRAY | Minacharai | Angel of 2nd decanate of Taurus.                                                  | 315  |
| MNQ    | Menaq     | 66th name of Shem Hamphorash, associated with 6th quinance of Gemini.              | 190  |
| MNQAL  | Menqel    | Angel of 6th quinance of Gemini; angel by night of the 10 of Swords.               | 221  |
| MNRH   | Menorah   | Candlestick.                                                                      | 295  |
| MNShH  | Manasseh  | A tribe of Israel, associated with Gemini.                                         | 395  |
| MS     | Mas       | A suffering, discouraged one; tax.                                                 | 100  |
| MSNYN  | Misnin    | Angel of 1st decanate of Capricorn.                                                | 860  |
|        |           |                                                                                   | 210  |
| MOWN   | Maon      | Residence; the 5th Heaven, corresponding to Geburah.                               | 816  |
|        |           |                                                                                   | 166  |
| MORB   | Maarab    | West.                                                                             | 312  |
| MP     | Moph      | Memphis (Egypt).                                                                  | 840  |
|        |           |                                                                                   | 120  |
| MTz    | Motz      | Chaff.                                                                            | 940  |
|        |           |                                                                                   | 130  |
| MTzPTz | Matz-Patz | A name of God by Temurah.                                                          | 1110 |
|        |           |                                                                                   | 300  |
| MTzR   | Metzar    | Distress; isthmus.                                                                | 330  |
|        | Metzer    | Boundary; 60th name of Shem Hamphorash, associated with 6th quinance of Taurus.   |      |
| MTzRAL | Mitzrael  | Angel of 6th quinance of Taurus; angel by night of the 7 of Pentacles.            | 361  |
| MTzRYM | Mitzraim  | Egypt.                                                                            | 940  |
|        |           |                                                                                   | 380  |
| MQ     | Maq       | Rottenness.                                                                       | 140  |
| MQL    | Maqqel    | Wand.                                                                             | 170  |
| MQLWTh | Maqqeloth | Wands.                                                                            | 576  |
| MR     | Mar       | Drop; bitter, sad; fierce, violent, wild; bitterness, sadness.                    | 240  |
|        | Mor       | Myrrh.                                                                            |      |

| | | | |
|---|---|---|---|
| MRChWSh | Marchos | Marchosias, Goetic demon by day of 2nd decanate of Pisces. | 554 |
| MRYM | Miriam | Miriam; Mary. | 850 |
| | | | 290 |
| MRKBH | Merkabah | Chariot. | 267 |
| MShH | Mosheh | Moses. | 345 |
| MShChYTh | Mashchith | The Destroyer (Ex. XII:23). | 758 |
| MShYCh | Mashiach | Messiah. | 358 |
| MShKN | Mishkan | Tabernacle. | 1060 |
| | | | 410 |
| MShPR | Mishpar | Angel of 3rd decanate of Virgo. | 620 |
| MShRATh | Mishrath | Angel of 1st decanate of Sagittarius. | 941 |
| MShRQH | Masrekah | A city of Edom; city of King Samlah. | 645 |
| MTh | Meth | Dead. | 440 |
| MThWShAL | Methusael | Methusael. | 777 |
| MThWShLCh | Methushelach | Methuselah. | 784 |
| MThRAWSh | Mathravash | Angel of 1st decanate of Cancer. | 947 |

NUN

| | | | |
|---|---|---|---|
| N | Nun | 14th letter of Hebrew alphabet. | 50 |
| | | | 700 |
| NA | Na | Please, pray; raw. | 51 |
| | No | Thebes. | |
| NB | Nob | A town in Benjamin. | 52 |
| NBYA | Navi | Prophet. | 63 |
| NBR | Naber | Naberius, Goetic demon by day of 3rd decanate of Scorpio. | 252 |
| NGP | Negep | Plague. | 853 |
| | | | 133 |
| ND | Ned | Heap, wall. | 54 |
| NH | Noah | Splendor, eminence. | 55 |
| NHR | Naher | River. | 255 |
| NW | Nu | Egyptian goddess. | 56 |
| NWGH | Nogah | Venus. | 64 |
| NWD | Nod | Nod. | 60 |

| NWTRYQWN | Notariqon | The cabalistic theory of acronyms. | 1081 |
| | | | 431 |
| NWYTh | Nuit | Egyptian sky goddess. | 466 |
| NCh | Noach | Noah. | 58 |
| NChWR | Nachor | Nahor. | 264 |
| NChSh | Nachash | Snake, serpent. | 358 |
| NChShYRWN | Nachashiron | The Snakey Ones; Qlippoth of | 1274 |
| | | Sagittarius. | 624 |
| NChShTh | Nechsheth | Copper, brass; the metal of Venus. | 758 |
| NChShThY | Necheshethi | Coppery, brassy. | 768 |
| NChShThYRWN | Necheshthi-ron | The Brazen Ones; Qlippoth of Scorpio. | 1674 1024 |
| NY | Ni | Lament. | 60 |
| NYN | Nun | Fish; 14th letter of Hebrew alphabet; father of Joshua. | 756 106 |
| NYNDWHR | Nundohar | Angel of 2nd decanate of Scorpio. | 325 |
| NYNWH | Nineveh | Nineveh. | 121 |
| NYSN | Nisan | The 7th Hebrew month. | 820 |
| | | | 170 |
| NYTh | Nith | 54th name of Shem Hamphorash, associated with 6th quinance of Aries. | 460 |
| NYThAL | Nithael | Angel of 6th quinance of Aries; angel by night of the 4 of Wands. | 491 |
| NKYAL | Nakhiel | Intelligence of the Sun. | 111 |
| NLK | Nelak | 21st name of Shem Hamphorash, associated with 3rd quinance of Scorpio. | 580 100 |
| NLKAL | Nelakiel | Angel of 3rd quinance of Scorpio; angel by day of the 6 of Cups. | 131 |
| NMM | Nemem | 57th name of Shem Hamphorash, associated with 3rd quinance of Taurus. | 690 130 |
| NMMYH | Nemamiah | Angel of 3rd quinance of Taurus; angel by day of the 6 of Pentacles. | 145 |
| NMRD | Nimrod | Nimrod. | 294 |
| NNA | Nena | 53rd name of Shem Hamphorash, associated with 5th quinance of Aries. | 101 |
| NNAAL | Nanael | Angel of 5th quinance of Aries; angel by day of the 4 of Wands. | 132 |

| NS | Nes | Banner, sign, standard. | 110 |
|---|---|---|---|
| NSThR | Nisetar | Hidden, secret. | 710 |
| NOM | Naam | To be lovely, pleasant. | 720 |
| | | | 160 |
| NOMH | Naamah | A queen of demons; arch-demon corresponding to Malkuth; sister of Tubal-Cain. | 165 |
| NP | Noph | Memphis (Egypt). | 850 |
| | | | 130 |
| NPWL | Naphul | Naphula, Goetic demon by night of 3rd decanate of Scorpio. | 166 |
| NPLYM | Nephilim | Giants (Gen. VI:4). | 770 |
| | | | 210 |
| NPSh | Nephesh | Lowest part of the tripartite soul. | 430 |
| NPThLY | Naphtali | A tribe of Israel, associated with Virgo. | 570 |
| NTz | Netz | Flower; hawk. | 950 |
| | | | 140 |
| NTzCh | Netzach | Victory; the 7th Sephira. | 148 |
| NQDH PShWTH | Neqedah Peshutah | The Simple Point; a title of Kether. | 559 |
| NQDH RAShWNH | Neqedah Rishonah | The Primordial Point; a title of Kether. | 721 |
| NR | Ner | Lamp; prosperity; instruction. | 250 |
| NShYH | Neshiah | Oblivion; one of the seven earths, corresponding to Tiphareth. | 365 |
| NShYM | Nashim | Women, wives. | 960 |
| | | | 400 |
| NShYMYRWN | Nashimiron | Malignant Women; Qlippoth of Pisces. | 1316 |
| | | | 666 |
| NShMH | Neshamah | The highest part of the soul. | 395 |
| NShR | Nesher | Eagle, bird of prey. | 550 |
| NThDWRYNAL | Nathdorinel | Lord of Triplicity by Night for Pisces. | 751 |
| NThH | Nethah | 25th name of Shem Hamphorash, associated with 1st quinance of Sagittarius. | 455 |
| NThHYH | Nithahiah | Angel of 1st quinance of Sagittarius; angel by day of the 8 of Wands. | 470 |

# S□

**SAMEKH**

| | | | |
|---|---|---|---|
| **S** | Samekh | 15th letter of Hebrew alphabet. | 60 |
| **SAYTzYAL** | Saitziel | Angel of Scorpio. | 202 |
| **SAL** | Sael | 45th name of Shem Hamphorash; associated with 3rd quinance of Pisces. | 91 |
| **SALYH** | Saliah | Angel of 3rd quinance of Pisces; angel by day of the 9 of Cups. | 106 |
| **SAThARYAL** | Satariel | The Concealers; Qlippoth of Binah. | 703 |
| **SG** | Seg | Secret name of the World of Briah. | 63 |
| **SGRSh** | Sagarash | Angel of 1st decanate of Gemini. | 563 |
| **SD** | Sad | Stocks. | 64 |
| **SDM** | Sodom | Sodom. | 664 |
| | | | 104 |
| **SDM WOMRH** | Sodom we-Amorah | Sodom and Gomorah. | 985 |
| | | | 425 |
| **SHYBR** | Sahiber | Angel of 3rd decanate of Leo. | 277 |
| **SHQNB** | Sahaqnab | Lord of Triplicity by Night for Scorpio. | 217 |
| **SHRNTz** | Saharnatz | Angel of 2nd decanate of Libra. | 1215 |
| | | | 405 |
| **SWYOSAL** | Soyasel | Angel of 9th astrological house. | 237 |
| **SWSWL** | Sosul | Angel of 8th astrological house. | 162 |
| **SWRTh** | Sorath | Spirit of the Sun. | 666 |
| **SChYAL** | Sachiel | Angel ruling Jupiter and Thursday. | 109 |
| **ST** | Set | Transgression, error, sin. | 69 |
| **STNDR** | Satander | Angel of 3rd decanate of Aries. | 323 |
| **STRYP** | Satrip | Angel of 3rd decanate of Pisces. | 1079 |
| | | | 359 |
| **STROTN** | Sateraton | Lord of Triplicity by Day for Aries. | 1048 |
| | | | 398 |
| **SYWN** | Sivan | The 9th Hebrew month. | 776 |
| | | | 126 |
| **SYT** | Sit | 3rd name of Shem Hamphorash, associated with 3rd quinance of Leo. | 79 |
| **SYTAL** | Sitael | Angel of 3rd quinance of Leo; angel by day of the 6 of Wands. | 110 |

| | | | |
|---|---|---|---|
| **SYNY** | Sinai | Sinai. | 130 |
| **SK** | Sak | Crowd. | 560 |
| | | | 80 |
| **SL** | Sal | Basket. | 90 |
| **SLM** | Sellam | Ladder. | 690 |
| | | | 130 |
| **SM** | Sam | Spice; drug; poison. | 660 |
| | | | 100 |
| **SMAL** | Samael | Angel of Death; Prince of Demons, equated with Satan; Demon Prince of Fire; Qlippoth of Hod; according to Crowley, arch-demon corresponding to Chokmah. | 131 |
| **SMK** | Samekh | Prop, support; 15th letter of Hebrew alphabet. | 600 |
| | | | 120 |
| **SMNGLWP** | Semangeloph | One of the three angels invoked against Lilith. | 989 |
| | | | 269 |
| **SMQYAL** | Sameqiel | Angel of Capricorn. | 241 |
| **SNDLOY** | Sandali | Lord of Triplicity by Day for Capricorn. | 224 |
| **SNDLPWN** | Sandalphon | Archangel associated with Malkuth. | 930 |
| | | | 280 |
| **SNHM** | Sanahem | Lord of Triplicity by Day for Leo. | 715 |
| | | | 155 |
| **SNWY** | Senoy | One of the three angels invoked against Lilith. | 126 |
| **SNSNWY** | Sansenoy | One of the three angels invoked against Lilith. | 236 |
| **SS** | Sas | Moth. | 120 |
| **SSPM** | Saspam | Angel of 1st decanate of Aquarius. | 800 |
| | | | 240 |
| **SORSh** | Sarash | Lord of Triplicity by Day for Gemini. | 630 |
| **SP** | Saph | Threshold, entrance. | 860 |
| | | | 140 |
| **SPYRH** | Sephira | Number; sphere; emanation. | 355 |
| **SPYRWTh** | Sephiroth | Numbers; spheres; emanations. | 756 |
| **SPL** | Sephel | Cup. | 170 |
| **SPLYM** | Sephalim | Cups. | 780 |
| | | | 220 |
| **SPOTAWY** | Sapamawi | Lord of Triplicity by Night for Aries. | 236 |

| | | | |
|---|---|---|---|
| **SPR** | Sepher | Book. | 340 |
| **SPR HZHR** | Sepher ha-Zohar | Book of Splendor. | 557 |
| **SPR HThWRH** | Sepher ha-Torah | Book of the Law. | 956 |
| **SPR YTzYRH** | Sepher Yetzirah | Book of Formation. | 655 |
| **SR** | Sar | Ill-humored. | 260 |
| **SRAYAL** | Sarayel | Angel of Gemini. | 302 |
| **SRTN** | Sarton | Crab; Cancer. | 969 |
| | | | 319 |
| **SRYTYAL** | Saritiel | Angel of Sagittarius. | 320 |
| **SThW** | Sethav | Autumn. | 466 |

AYIN

| | | | |
|---|---|---|---|
| **O** | Ayin | 16th letter of Hebrew alphabet. | 70 |
| **OB** | Ab | Secret name of the World of Atziluth; density; thicket; darkness; cloud. | 72 |
| **OBYRYRWN** | Abiriron | The Clayish Ones; Qlippoth of Libra. | 1198 548 |
| **OBR** | Eber | Eber. | 272 |
| **OBRY** | Ibri | Hebrew. | 282 |
| **OBRYM** | Ibrim | Hebrews. | 882 322 |
| **OD** | Ad | Eternity, duration; during; booty. | 74 |
| | Ed | Witness, proof; ruler. | |
| **ODH** | Adah | A wife of Lamech. | 79 |
| **ODN** | Eden | Eden. | 774 124 |
| **ODTh** | Edeth | Testimony. | 474 |
| **OWAL** | Oel | Angel of 5th astrological house. | 107 |
| **OWGYAL** | Ogiel | The Hinderers; Qlippoth of Chokmah. | 120 |
| **OWGRMON** | Ogarman | Lord of Triplicity by Night for Gemini. | 1089 439 |

| | | | |
|---|---|---|---|
| OWYTh | Avith | A city of Edom; city of King Hadad. | 486 |
| OWLM | Olam | World. | 706 |
| | | | 146 |
| OWLM | Olam | The World of Nobility; the Divine | 1243 |
| ATzYLWTh | Atziluth | or Archetypal World. | 683 |
| OWLM | Olam | The World of Creation; the Archan- | 929 |
| HBRYAH | ha-Briah | gelic or Creative World. | 369 |
| OWLM | Olam | The World of Action; the Material | 1096 |
| HOShYH | ha-Assiah | World. | 536 |
| OWLM | Olam | The World of Formation; the An- | 1026 |
| HYTzYRH | ha-Yetzirah | gelic or Formative World. | 466 |
| OWLM | Olam | The World of Shells or Demons. | 1337 |
| HQLYPWTh | ha-Qlippoth | | 777 |
| OWLM | Olam | The World of Foundations; the | 1192 |
| YSWDWTh | Yesodoth | Sphere of the Elements; the part of | 632 |
| | | the material world corresponding to | |
| | | Malkuth. | |
| OZ | Ez | Goat. | 77 |
| | Oz | Strength; violence; glory. | |
| OZA | Ezah | A giant chained in Arqa. | 78 |
| OZAZL | Azazel | Demon Prince of Air. | 115 |
| OZAL | Azael | Demon Prince of Water. | 108 |
| | Ezal | A giant chained in Arqa. | |
| OT | Et | Writing instrument. | 79 |
| OY | Ay | A town near Bethel. | 80 |
| | I | Ruins. | |
| OYN | Ayin | Eye; 16th letter of Hebrew alpha- | 780 |
| | | bet. | 130 |
| OYRD | Irad | Irad. | 284 |
| OYRM | Eram | A Duke of Edom, associated with | 880 |
| | | Malkuth. | 320 |
| OYSh | Ayish | Ursa Major. | 380 |
| OYTh | Ayeth | The last three letters of the 42-let- | 480 |
| | | ter name of God, associated with | |
| | | Malkuth. | |
| OKAL | Akel | Lord of Triplicity by Night for Can- | 121 |
| | | cer. | |
| OKBWR | Achbor | Father of Baal-Hanan, a King of | 298 |
| | | Edom. | |
| OL | Al | Upper part; on, above, over, to, to- | 100 |
| | | wards, after, because. | |

| | Ol | Yoke. | |
|---|---|---|---|
| **OLWH** | Alvah | A Duke of Edom, associated with Daath. | 111 |
| **OLYWN** | Elyon | The Most High; a title of Kether. | 816 |
| | | | 166 |
| **OLM** | Alem | 4th name of Shem Hamphorash, associated with 4th quinance of Leo. | 700 |
| | | | 140 |
| **OLMYH** | Elemiah | Angel of 4th quinance of Leo; angel by night of the 6 of Wands. | 155 |
| **OM** | Am | Nation, populace. | 670 |
| | Em | With, by, near. | 110 |
| **OMM** | Amem | 52nd name of Shem Hamphorash, associated with 4th quinance of Aries. | 710 |
| | Amam | To darken, dim. | |
| **OMMYH** | Amamiah | Angel of 4th quinance of Aries; angel by night of the 3 of Wands. | 165 |
| **OMRH** | Amorah | Gomorah. | 315 |
| **ON** | An | A name of God. | 120 |
| **ONW** | Anu | 63rd name of Shem Hamphorash, associated with 3rd quinance of Gemini. | 126 |
| | Anaw | Humble, afflicted. | |
| **ONWAL** | Anevel | Angel of 3rd quinance of Gemini; angel by day of the 9 of Swords. | 157 |
| **ONQ** | Anaq | Anak, a giant. | 220 |
| **ONTh** | Anath | Semitic goddess similar to Astarte. | 520 |
| **OPYR** | Ophir | Earth. | 360 |
| **OTz** | Etz | Tree. | 970/160 |
| **OTz HDOTh** | Etz ha-Daath | Tree of Knowledge. | 1449 |
| | | | 639 |
| **OTz HDOTh TWB WRO** | Etz ha-Daath Tob wa-Ra | Tree of the Knowledge of Good and Evil. | 1742 |
| | | | 932 |
| **OTz HChYYM** | Etz ha-Chayim | Tree of Life. | 1603 |
| | | | 793 |
| | | | 233 |
| **OTzM** | Etzem | Bone, substance, essence, body. | 760 |
| | | | 200 |
| **OQRB** | Akrab | Scorpion; Scorpio. | 372 |
| **OR** | Ar | Enemy. | 270 |
| **ORB** | Arab | To exchange, pawn; to grow dark; | 272 |

|  |  |  |  |
|---|---|---|---|
|  | Areb | poplar, willow; Arabia.<br>Sweet, pleasant. |  |
|  | Ereb | Evening. |  |
|  | Oreb | Raven, crow. |  |
| ORBWTh | Arabhoth | Plains; the 7th Heaven, corresponding to the three Supernal Sephiroth. | 678 |
| ORB ZRQ | Oreb Zaraq | Raven of Dispersion; Qlippoth of Netzach. | 579 |
| ORWB | Arov | Wild Beasts; the 4th of the 10 plagues of Egypt. | 278 |
| ORY | Eri | 46th name of Shem Hamphorash, associated with 4th quinance of Pisces. | 280 |
| ORYAL | Ariel | Angel of 4th quinance of Pisces; angel by night of the 9 of Cups. | 311 |
| ORLH | Arlah | Foreskin. | 305 |
| OShW | Esau | Esau. | 376 |
| OShYH | Assiah | Action; the Material World. | 385 |
| OShL | Ashel | 47th name of Shem Hamphorash, associated with 5th quinance of Pisces. | 400 |
| OShLYH | Asaliah | Angel of 5th quinance of Pisces; angel by day of the 10 of Cups. | 415 |
| OShRH | Asarah | Ten. | 575 |
| OShRYM | Esrim | Twenty. | 1180<br>620 |
| OShRYM WAChD | Esrim we-Echad | Twenty-one. | 1199<br>639 |
| OShRYM WShNYM | Esrim u-Shenaim | Twenty-two. | 2146<br>1586<br>1026 |
| OShThRTh | Ashtoreth | Astarte, a Phoenician goddess. | 1370 |
| OTh | Eth | Time, season. | 470 |
| OThWR | Athor | Lord of Triplicity by Day for Aquarius. | 676 |
| OThYAL | Athiel | "Uncertainty"; Qlippoth of Ain Soph Or. | 511 |
| OThYK YWMYN | Atik Yomin | The Ancient of Days; a title of Kether. | 1746<br>1266<br>616 |
| OThYQA | Atiqa | The Ancient One; a title of Kether. | 581 |

| OThYQA | Atiqa | The Ancient of the Ancient Ones; a | 1875 |
| DOThYQYN | de-Atiqin | title of Kether. | 1225 |
| OThYQA | Atiqa | The Most Holy Ancient One; a title | 996 |
| QDYShA | Qadisha | of Kether. | |

**PE**

| P | Pe | 17th letter of Hebrew alphabet. | 80 |
| | | | 800 |
| PAYMWN | Paimon | Demon King of Fire; Goetic demon | 837 |
| | | by day of 3rd decanate of Gemini. | 187 |
| PG | Pag | Unripe fig. | 83 |
| PANTz | Phenetz | Phenex, Goetic demon by night of | 1031 |
| | | 1st decanate of Aries. | 121 |
| PH | Pe | Mouth; 17th letter of Hebrew al-phabet. | 85 |
| PHL | Pahel | 20th name of Shem Hamphorash, associated with 2nd quinance of Scorpio. | 115 |
| PHLYH | Pahaliah | Angel of 2nd quinance of Scorpio; angel by night of the 5 of Cups. | 130 |
| PWY | Poi | 56th name of Shem Hamphorash, associated with 2nd quinance of Taurus. | 96 |
| PWYAL | Poyel | Angel of 2nd decanate of Taurus; angel by night of the 5 of Penta-cles. | 127 |
| PWK | Puk | Antimony. | 586 |
| | | | 106 |
| PWKLWR | Phokalor | Focalor, Goetic demon by night of 2nd decanate of Taurus. | 342 |
| PWL | Pul | A king of Assyria. | 116 |
| | Phul | Olympic Planetary Spirit of the Moon. | |
| PWRK | Phurk | Furcas, Goetic demon by night of | 786 |

|  |  |  |  |
|---|---|---|---|
|  |  | 2nd decanate of Leo. | 306 |
| PWRASh | Phoras | Foras, Goetic demon by day of 1st decanate of Aquarius. | 587 |
| PWRLAK | Phorlakh | Angel of Earth. | 817 |
|  |  |  | 337 |
| PWRNASh | Phornas | Forneus, Goetic demon by day of 3rd decanate of Capricorn. | 637 |
| PWRPWR | Phurphur | Furfur, Goetic demon by day of 1st decanate of Pisces. | 572 |
| PWRShWN | Purson | Goetic demon by day of 2nd decanate of Libra. | 1292 |
|  |  |  | 592 |
| PZ | Paz | Pure gold. | 87 |
| PCh | Pach | Danger. | 88 |
| PChD | Pachad | Fear; a title of Geburah. | 92 |
| PYNN | Pinon | A Duke of Edom, associated with Tiphareth. | 840 |
|  |  |  | 190 |
| PYShWN | Pison | A river of Eden, associated with Fire. | 1096 |
|  |  |  | 446 |
| PK | Pak | Flask, bottle. | 580 |
|  |  |  | 100 |
| PKYAL | Pakiel | Angel of Cancer. | 141 |
| PLA | Pele | The Wonder; a title of Kether. | 111 |
| PLAYN | Polayan | Lord of Triplicity by Night for Aquarius. | 821 |
|  |  |  | 171 |
| PLG | Peleg | Son of Eber; father of Reu. | 113 |
|  | Phaleg | Olympic Planetary Spirit of Mars. |  |
| PN | Pen | Lest. | 780/130 |
| PNYN | Panin | Pearl; a title of Malkuth. | 840/190 |
| PS | Pas | Extremity. | 140 |
| POW | Pau | A city of Edom; city of King Hadar. | 156 |
| PR | Par | Bull; victim; offering. | 280 |
| PRWSh | Parush | Hermit. | 586 |
| PROH | Pharaoh | Pharaoh. | 355 |
| PRTh | Phrath | Euphrates; a river of Eden, associated with Earth. | 680 |
| PSh | Pash | Folly. | 380 |
| PShYAL | Pasiel | Angel of 12th astrological house. | 421 |
| PTh | Path | Bit, morsel. | 480 |
|  | Poth | Opening; pudenda. |  |

# Tzx

SADHE

| Tz | Sadhe | 18th letter of Hebrew alphabet. | 90 |
| | | | 900 |
| TzB | Tzab | Litter. | 92 |
| TzBO | Tzeva | Color. | 162 |
| TzD | Tzad | Side. | 94 |
| TzDY | Sadhe | Fish-hook; 18th letter of Hebrew alphabet. | 104 |
| TzDYQ-YSWD-OWLM | Tzadiq-Yesod-Olam | The Righteous Is the Foundation of the World; a title of Yesod. | 990 430 |
| TzDQ | Tzedek | Jupiter; righteousness. | 194 |
| TzDQYAL | Tzadqiel | Archangel associated with Chesed and with Jupiter. | 235 |
| TzHB | Tzahov | Yellow. | 97 |
| TzW | Tzaw | Statute. | 96 |
| TzWQ | Tzoq | Narrowness; oppression. | 196 |
| TzCh | Tzach | Bright. | 98 |
| TzY | Tzi | Dryness; ship. | 100 |
| TzYH | Tziah | Dryness; one of the seven earths, corresponding to Tiphareth or to Netzach. | 105 |
| TzYWN | Tzion | Zion. | 806/156 |
| TzKMQYAL | Tzakmiqiel | Angel of Aquarius. | 291 |
| TzL | Tzal | Shadow; shelter. | 120 |
| TzLH | Tzillah | Zillah, a wife of Lamech. | 125 |
| TzLYL | Tzelil | Ring; sound; tone. | 160 |
| TzLYLYMYRWN | Tzelilimiron | The Clangers; Qlippoth of Gemini. | 1126 476 |
| TzLMWTh | Tzal-Maweth | Shadow of Death; the 2nd hell, corresponding to Yesod. | 566 |
| TzLO | Tzela | Rib. | 190 |
| TzN | Tzen | Thorn. | 790/140 |
| TzPWN | Tzaphon | North. | 876 226 |
| TzPWNY | Tzaphoni | The Northern One; Lilith. | 236 |
| TzPQYAL | Tzaphqiel | Archangel associated with Binah and with Saturn. | 311 |
| TzPRDO | Tzephardea | Frogs; the 2nd of the 10 plagues of Egypt. | 444 |

| | | | |
|---|---|---|---|
| **TzPRH** | Tziporah | Zipporah. | 375 |
| **TzPRYRWN** | Tzaphiriron | The Scratchers; Qlippoth of Virgo. | 1286 |
| | | | 636 |
| **TzR** | Tzar | Persecutor, enemy; distress, danger; stone. | 290 |

**QOPH**

| | | | |
|---|---|---|---|
| **Q** | Qoph | 19th letter of Hebrew alphabet. | 100 |
| **QA** | Qe | Vomit. | 101 |
| **QLB** | Qalb | Heart *(Arabic)*. | 132 |
| **QB** | Qab | Unit of measure. | 102 |
| **QBLH** | Qabalah | Cabala; tradition. | 137 |
| **QDWSh** | Qadosh | Holy. | 410 |
| **QDWSh QDShYM** | Qadosh Qadeshim | Holy of Holies. | 1424<br>864 |
| **QDM** | Qedem | Before; the east; ancient things. | 704<br>144 |
| **QDMAL** | Qedemel | Kedemel, the Spirit of Venus. | 175 |
| **QDSh** | Qadesh | Holiness. | 404 |
| **QDSh LYHWH** | Qadesh la-Yahweh | Holy to the Lord. | 460 |
| **QW** | Qaw | Line; chord; norm. | 106 |
| **QWP** | Qoph | Back of head; 19th letter of Hebrew alphabet. | 906<br>186 |
| **QWTz** | Qotz | Thorn. | 1006<br>196 |
| **QT** | Qat | Small. | 109 |
| **QYA** | Qi | Vomit. | 111 |
| **QYN** | Qayin | Cain. | 810<br>160 |
| **QYNN** | Cainan | Kenan. | 860<br>210 |
| **QYTz** | Qayitz | Summer. | 1010<br>200 |
| **QL** | Qal | Swift. | 130 |
| **QLYPWTh** | Qlippoth | Shells; demons. | 626 |
| **QLLH** | Qelalah | Curse. | 165 |

| QMT | Qamat | To make wrinkled. | 149 |
| QMTYAL | Qemetiel | The Crowd of Gods; Qlippoth of Ain. | 190 |
| QN | Qen | Nest. | 800 |
| | | | 150 |
| QNZ | Qenaz | Kenaz, a Duke of Edom, associated with Netzach. | 157 |
| QPTzPWNY | Qaftzaphoni | Prince and King of Heaven; husband of Mehetabel; father of Lilith the Younger. | 416 |
| QTz | Qetz | End. | 1000 |
| | | | 190 |
| QR | Qar | Cold; quiet. | 300 |
| QROShMN | Qerashamen | The 7th through 12th letters of the 42-letter name of God, associated with Chesed. | 760 |
| QSh | Qash | Straw, chaff. | 400 |
| QShTh | Qasshat | Bow; Sagittarius. | 800 |

**RESH**

| R | Resh | 20th letter of Hebrew alphabet. | 200 |
| RAH | Raah | To see, observe, perceive, consider; 69th name of Shem Hamphorash, associated with 3rd quinance of Cancer. | 206 |
| RAHAL | Rahael | Angel of 3rd quinance of Cancer; angel by day of the 3 of Cups. | 237 |
| RA HWWR | Ra-Hoor | Ra-Horus, an Egyptian god. | 418 |
| RAWBN | Reuben | A tribe of Israel, associated with Aquarius. | 909 |
| | | | 259 |
| RAWM | Räum | Goetic demon by night of 1st decanate of Taurus. | 807 |
| | | | 247 |
| RAYDAL | Raydel | Lord of Triplicity by Day for Taurus. | 246 |
| RAYDYH | Rayadyah | Angel of 2nd decanate of Virgo. | 231 |
| RAShYTh HGLGLYM | Rashith ha-Gilgalim | The Beginning of Revolvings; the Primum Mobile. | 1592 |
| | | | 1032 |

| RB | Rab | Many, much; great, mighty. | 202 |
|---|---|---|---|
| | Rob | Multitude; abundance. | |
| RBK | Ravak | To be mixed, mingled. | 702/222 |
| RBQH | Ribeqah | Rebekah. | 307 |
| RHBYTh | Rehoboth | A city of Edom; city of King Saul. | 617 |
| RHDTz | Rahadetz | Angel of 2nd decanate of Cancer. | 1109 |
| | | | 299 |
| RHO | Reha | 39th name of Shem Hamphorash, associated with 3rd quinance of Aquarius. | 275 |
| RHOAL | Rehael | Angel of 3rd quinance of Aquarius; angel by day of the 6 of Swords. | 306 |
| RWCh | Ruach | Breath, wind, spirit; middle part of the tripartite soul; the element of Air. | 214 |
| RWCh ALHYM | Ruach Elohim | The Spirit of God. | 860/300 |
| RWM MOLH | Rom Maalah | The Inscrutable Height; a title of Kether. | 951 |
| RZYAL | Raziel | Archangel associated with Chokmah and with the Sphere of the Zodiac. | 248 |
| RChL | Rachel | Wife of Jacob; mother of Joseph and Benjamin. | 238 |
| RChM | Racham | Vulture. | 808 |
| | | | 248 |
| RY | Ri | Rushing water. | 210 |
| RYY | Riyi | 29th name of Shem Hamphorash, associated with 5th quinance of Sagittarius. | 220 |
| RYYAL | Reyayel | Angel of 5th quinance of Sagittarius; angel by day of the 10 of Wands. | 251 |
| RYNWW | Ronow | Ronové, Goetic demon by day of 3rd decanate of Sagittarius. | 272 |
| RYSh | Resh | Head; 20th letter of Hebrew alphabet. | 510 |
| RYShA | Risha | Head; a title of Kether. | 511 |
| RYShA DLA | Risha Dela | The Head Which Is Not; a title of Kether. | 546 |
| RYShA HWWRH | Risha Havurah | The White Head; a title of Kether. | 733 |
| RK | Rok | Softness. | 700 |
| | | | 220 |
| RKB | Rakav | To ride, drive; horseman, driver. | 222 |

|  | Rekev | Vehicle. |  |
|---|---|---|---|
| RM | Ram | Ram (Job XXXII:2). | 800 |
|  |  |  | 240 |
| RMRA | Ramara | Lord of Triplicity by Day for Pisces. | 441 |
| RN | Ron | Shout, rejoicing. | 900 |
|  |  |  | 250 |
| RO | Ra | Evil. | 270 |
|  | Rea | Friend. |  |
| RODR | Raadar | Lord of Triplicity by Day for Cancer. | 474 |
| ROH | Raah | Evil. | 275 |
| ROW | Reu | Reu. | 276 |
| ROWAL | Reuel | Reuel. | 307 |
| ROMSS | Rameses | Rameses. | 430 |
| RPAL | Raphael | 1. Archangel associated with Tiphareth, with the Sun, with the East, and with Air; 2. Angel ruling Mercury and Wednesday. | 311 |
| RTz | Ratz | Piece. | 1100 |
|  |  |  | 290 |
| RTzLTWTh | Retzeltoth | According to Francis Barrett, the 6th hell; evidently a misprint for TzLMWTh. | 435 |
| RTzWN | Ratzon | Delight, favor. | 996 |
|  |  |  | 346 |
| RQ | Raq | Thin; only. | 300 |
|  | Roq | Saliva. |  |
| RQYO | Raqia | Firmament; the 2nd Heaven, corresponding to Hod. | 380 |

# SHẅ SHIN

| Sh | Shin | 21st letter of Hebrew alphabet. | 300 |
|---|---|---|---|
| ShA | Sho | Destruction. | 301 |
| ShAH | Shaah | To lay waste, devastate; 28th name of Shem Hamphorash, associated with 4th quinance of Sagittarius. | 306 |
|  | Shah | Calamity, devastation, ruin. |  |

| | | | |
|---|---|---|---|
| **ShAHYH** | Sahiah | Angel of 4th quinance of Sagittari-us; angel by night of the 9 of Wands. | 321 |
| **ShAWL** | Sheol | Depth of the Earth; the 7th and lowest hell, corresponding to the three Supernal Sephiroth. | 337 |
| | Saul | A King of Edom, associated with Hod; Saul of the New Testament. | |
| **ShALWSh** | Sallos | Goetic demon by day of 1st deca-nate of Libra. | 637 |
| **ShAR** | Seer | Seere, Goetic demon by night of 1st decanate of Pisces. | 501 |
| **ShBA** | Sheba | Sheba. | 303 |
| **ShBWO** | Shavua | Week. | 378 |
| **ShBT** | Shevet | The 5th Hebrew month. | 311 |
| **ShBYL** | Shevil | Path. | 342 |
| **ShBYLYM** | Shevilim | Paths. | 952 392 |
| **ShBYL HChLB** | Shevil ha-Chalav | Milky Way. | 387 |
| **ShBNWK** | Sabnok | Sabnock, Goetic demon by night of 1st decanate of Gemini. | 858 378 |
| **ShBOH** | Shivah | Seven. | 377 |
| **ShBOH-OShR** | Shivah-Asar | Seventeen. | 947 |
| **ShBOYM** | Shivim | Seventy. | 982 422 |
| **ShBTh** | Sabbath | Day of Rest. | 702 |
| **ShBThAY** | Shabbathai | Saturn. | 713 |
| **ShGL** | Shagal Shegal | To be sexually aroused; to lie with. Royal paramour. | 333 |
| **ShD** | Shad Shed Shod | Teat. Demon, idol. Violence, ruin. | 304 |
| **ShD BRShMOTh HShRThThN** | Shed Barshe-math ha-Sharthathan | Spirit of the Spirits of the Moon. | 3321 |
| **ShDY** | Shaddai | The Almighty. | 314 |
| **ShDY AL ChY** | Shaddai El Chai | Almighty Living God; divine name associated with Yesod, with Air, and with the East. | 363 |
| **ShDYM** | Shedim | Demons. | 914 354 |

| ShH | Seh | Sheep, goat. | 305 |
| ShHDNY | Shehadani | Angel of 2nd decanate of Gemini. | 369 |
| ShWR | Shor | Ox, bull; Taurus. | 506 |
| ShWThQ | Shotheq | Silent. | 806 |
| ShCh | Seach | Thought, meditation. | 308 |
| | Shach | Depressed. | |
| ShChDR | Shachdar | Angel of 3rd decanate of Libra. | 512 |
| ShChWR | Shachor | Black. | 514 |
| ShChYN | Shechin | Boils; the 6th of the 10 plagues of | 1018 |
| | | Egypt. | 368 |
| ShChQYM | Shechaqim | Clouds; the 3rd Heaven, corre- | 1018 |
| | | sponding to Netzach. | 458 |
| ShChR | Shachar | Dawn. | 508 |
| ShT | Set | Transgression. | 309 |
| ShTWLWSh | Stolas | Goetic demon by day of 3rd deca- | 651 |
| | | nate of Pisces. | |
| ShTN | Satan | Adversary, accuser; arch-demon | 1009 |
| | | corresponding (with Moloch) to | 359 |
| | | Kether. | |
| ShY | Shai | Gift, tribute. | 310 |
| ShYChRYRWN | Shichiriron | The Black Ones; Qlippoth of Can- | 1434 |
| | | cer. | 784 |
| ShYTRY | Sitri | Goetic demon by day of 3rd deca- | 529 |
| | | nate of Cancer. | |
| ShYN | Shin | Tooth; 21st letter of Hebrew alpha- | 1010 |
| | | bet. | 360 |
| ShK | Sek | Thorn; enclosure. | 800 |
| | | | 320 |
| ShKANWM | Shakanom | A title of Tiphareth. | 977 |
| | | | 417 |
| ShKYNH | Shekinah | The Divine Presence; a title of Mal- | 385 |
| | | kuth. | |
| ShL | Shal | Transgression, fault, crime. | 330 |
| ShLG | Shalag | To snow. | 333 |
| | Sheleg | Snow. | |
| ShLHBYRWN | Shalhebiron | The Flaming Ones; Qlippoth of Leo. | 1253 |
| | | | 603 |
| ShLHBTh | Shalhebeth | Flame. | 737 |
| ShLWM | Shalom | Peace. | 936 |
| | | | 376 |
| ShLCh | Shelah | Salah. | 338 |

| | | | |
|---|---|---|---|
| **ShLMH** | Shelomoh | Solomon. | 375 |
| **ShLShH** | Shelshah | Three. | 635 |
| **ShLShH-OShR** | Shelshah-Asar | Thirteen. | 1205 |
| **ShLShYM** | Shelshim | Thirty. | 1240 |
| | | | 680 |
| **ShLThYAL** | Shelathiel | Angel of Virgo. | 771 |
| **ShM** | Sham | There, then. | 900 |
| | Shem | Sign; name; son of Noah. | 340 |
| **ShMH** | Shamah | Horror, desolation. | 345 |
| **ShM HMPRSh** | Shem Hamphorash | The Name of God; Tetragrammaton; the 72-fold name of God. | 1525 965 |
| **ShMWAL** | Shemuel | Samuel. | 377 |
| **ShMYM** | Shamaim | Heaven, firmament, sky. | 950/390 |
| **ShMLH** | Samlah | A King of Edom, associated with Netzach. | 375 |
| **ShMNH** | Shemonah | Eight. | 395 |
| **ShMNH-OShR** | Shemonah-Asar | Eighteen. | 965 |
| **ShMNYM** | Shemonim | Eighty. | 1000 440 |
| **ShMOWN** | Simeon | A tribe of Israel, associated with Pisces. | 1116 466 |
| **ShMSh** | Shemesh | The Sun. | 640 |
| **ShN** | Shen | Tooth. | 1000 350 |
| **ShNANYM** | Shinanim | Angelic Choir sometimes associated with Tiphareth and the Sphere of the Sun. | 1011 451 |
| **ShNH** | Shanah | Year. | 355 |
| **ShNYM** | Shenaim | Two. | 960 400 |
| **ShNYM-OShR** | Shenaim-Asar | Twelve. | 1530 970 |
| **ShOH** | Shaah | Hour. | 375 |
| **ShOYR** | Sair | Hairy one; he-goat; demon; hairy. | 580 |
| **ShOYR ANPYN** | Seir Anpin | The Bearded Countenance; a title of Tiphareth. | 1421 771 |
| **ShOYRYM** | Seirim | Hairy ones; he-goats; demons. | 1190 630 |
| **ShOR** | Shar | Gate; a title of Malkuth. | 570 |
| **ShORYMWTh** | Shaare-Maweth | Gates of Death; the 3rd hell, corresponding to Netzach. | 1026 |
| **ShPT** | Shephet | Judgment. | 389 |

| | | | |
|---|---|---|---|
| **ShTz** | Shatz | Shax, Goetic demon by night of 2nd decanate of Gemini. | 1200 390 |
| **ShQ** | Saq | Sack. | 400 |
| **ShQY** | Sheqi | The penultimate three letters of the 42-letter name of God, associated with Yesod. | 410 |
| **ShR** | Sar | Master, prince, head, chief. | 500 |
| | Shor | Navel. | |
| **ShRH** | Sarah | Abraham's wife. | 505 |
| **ShRHYAL** | Sharhiel | Angel of Aries. | 546 |
| **ShRWG** | Serug | Serug. | 509 |
| **ShRTYAL** | Sharatiel | Angel of Leo. | 550 |
| **ShRY** | Sarai | Abram's wife. | 510 |
| **ShRP** | Seraph | Flaming Serpent; Ruler of Fire; one of the Seraphim. | 1300 580 |
| **ShRPYM** | Seraphim | Flaming Serpents; Angelic Choir associated with Geburah and with the Sphere of Mars. | 1190 630 |
| **ShSh** | Shesh | White marble. | 600 |
| **ShShH** | Shishah | Six. | 605 |
| **ShShH-OShR** | Shishah-Asar | Sixteen. | 1175 |
| **ShShYM** | Shishim | Sixty. | 1210 650 |
| **ShTh** | Seth | Son of Adam. | 700 |
| | Shath | Pillar; prince. | |
| | Sheth | Buttocks; noise. | |
| **ShThYQH** | Shethiqah | Silence. | 815 |

TAW

| | | | |
|---|---|---|---|
| **Th** | Taw | 22nd letter of Hebrew alphabet. | 400 |
| **ThA** | Ta | Room. | 401 |
| **ThAWMYAL** | Thaumiel | Twins of God; Qlippoth of Kether. | 488 |
| **ThAWMYM** | Teomim | Twins; Gemini. | 1057 497 |
| **ThBH** | Tebah | Ark (Noah's). | 407 |
| **ThBL** | Tebhel | World; one of the seven earths; cor- | 432 |

|  |  | responding (with Cheled) to Yesod and Malkuth. |  |
|---|---|---|---|
| ThGR | Tiger | To haggle. | 603 |
| ThGRYRWN | Tageriron | The Hagglers; Qlippoth of Tiphareth. | 1519 |
|  |  |  | 869 |
| ThGRN | Tageran | Haggler. | 1303 |
|  |  |  | 653 |
| ThHW | Tohu | Desolation; "without form" (Gen. I:2). | 411 |
| ThHWM | Tehom | Abyss, "deep" (Gen. I:2). | 1011 |
|  |  |  | 451 |
| ThW | Taw | Tau cross; 22nd letter of Hebrew alphabet. | 406 |
| ThWBL QYN | Tubal-Cain | Tubal-Cain. | 1248 |
|  |  |  | 598 |
| ThWOBTh | Thoabath | Abomination. | 878 |
| ThWRH | Torah | Law. | 611 |
| ThMYM | Thummim | One of two devices carried by the High Priest and used for divination. | 1050 |
|  |  |  | 490 |
| ThYMN | Teman | A Duke of Edom, associated with Hod. | 1150 |
|  |  |  | 500 |
| ThYMNY | Temani | The land of King Husham of Edom. | 510 |
| ThK | Tok | Oppression. | 900 |
|  |  |  | 420 |
| ThKLTh | Tekheleth | Purple. | 850 |
| ThL | Tel | Mound. | 430 |
| ThLY | Theli | Dragon; Satan. | 440 |
| ThLMWD | Talmud | Teaching. | 480 |
| ThM | Tam | Whole, complete; simple, pious, innocent, sincere, mild, perfect. | 1000 |
|  |  |  | 440 |
|  | Tom | Wholeness; simplicity, piety, innocence, sincerity, mildness, perfection. |  |
| ThMWZ | Tammuz | The 10th Hebrew month. | 453 |
| ThMWO | Timnah | A Duke of Edom, associated with Daath. | 516 |
| ThMWRH | Temurah | Permutation; the cabalistic theory of cryptography. | 651 |
| ThN | Tan | Jackal. | 1100 |
|  |  |  | 450 |
| ThP | Toph | Hand-drum; bezel. | 1200 |
|  |  |  | 480 |

| | | | |
|---|---|---|---|
| **ThPARTh** | Tiphareth | Beauty; the 6th Sephira. | 1081 |
| **ThPThRThRTh** | Taphthar-<br>tharath | Spirit of Mercury. | 2080 |
| **ThTz** | Thetz | The third two letters in the 42-letter name of God, associated with Binah. | 490 |
| **ThRGBWN** | Thergebon | Lord of Triplicity by Day for Libra. | 1311<br>661 |
| **ThRCh** | Terach | Terah. | 608 |
| **ThROA** | Throa | Gate; a title of Malkuth. | 671 |
| **ThRShYS** | Tharsis | Ruler of Water. | 970 |
| **ThRShYSh** | Tarshish | Tarsis, a city in Spain; chrysolite, precious stone. | 1210 |
| **ThRShYShYM** | Tarshishim | Chrysolites; Angelic Choir sometimes associated with Netzach and the Sphere of Venus. | 1820<br>1260 |
| **ThShOH** | Tishah | Nine. | 775 |
| **ThShOH-OShR** | Tishah-Asar | Nineteen. | 1345 |
| **ThShOYM** | Tishim | Ninety. | 1380<br>820 |
| **ThShRY** | Tishri | The 1st Hebrew month. | 910 |
| **ThTh ZL** | Tath Zal | The Profuse Giver; a title of Kether. | 837 |

# SECTION IV

Prime numbers are designated by a "p."

# 1

The 1st Path is the Sephira Kether, Crown.
Unity; the monad.
Mystic number of 1st Path (Kether).

**A**    Aleph    1st letter of Hebrew alphabet.

# 2 p

The 2nd Path is the Sephira Chokmah, Wisdom.
Duality; the duad.

**B**    Beth    2nd letter of Hebrew alphabet.

# 3 p

The 3rd Path is the Sephira Binah, Understanding.
The triangle; the triad.
The number of alchemical elements (sulfur, mercury, salt).
The number of mother letters (Aleph, Mem, Shin).
Mystic number of 2nd Path (Chokmah).

**G**    Gimel    3rd letter of Hebrew alphabet.
**AB**    Ab    Father; a title of Chokmah; the first two letters of the 42-letter name of God, associated with Kether.
     Av    The 11th Hebrew month.

# 4 $2^2$

The 4th Path is the Sephira Chesed, Mercy.
The square; the tetrad.
The number of elements (Fire, Water, Air, Earth).
The number of cardinal points.
The number of letters in Yahweh.
The number of human limbs.

**D**    Daleth    4th letter of Hebrew alphabet.
**GA**    Ge    Proud.

# 5 p

The 5th Path is the Sephira Geburah, Severity.
The pentagon; the pentad.
The number of elements including Spirit.
The number of *lataif* in Sufism.
The number of senses.
The number of fingers on one hand.
The number of toes on one foot.
The number of human limbs counting the head.
The number of lumbar vertabrae in the human spine.

**H** He 5th letter of Hebrew alphabet.
**AD** Edh Vapor, mist.
**BG** Bag Food.
**GB** Gab Elevation, top.
Geb Pit, water-hole.

# 6 Perfect

The 6th Path is the Sephira Tiphareth, Beauty.
The hexagon; the hexad.
Mystic number of 3rd Path (Binah).

**W** Waw 6th letter of Hebrew alphabet.
**ABBA** Abba The Supernal Father; a title of Chokmah.
**BD** Bad White linen.
**GG** Gag Flat roof; cover of an altar.
**HA** He Lo!

# 7 p

The 7th Path is the Sephira Netzach, Victory.
The heptagon; the heptad.
The number of traditional planets.
The number of days in the week.
The number of vertebrae in the human neck.
The number of spinal chakras in Yoga.

**Z** Zayin 7th letter of Hebrew alphabet.
**GD** Gad Tribe of Israel associated with Aries; fortune, good luck; Babylonian god of fortune.
**DG** Dag Fish.
**AW** 'O Or.
**DB** Dob Bear (n.).
**HAA** Haa 26th name of Shem Hamphorash, associated with 2nd quinance of Sagittarius.

# 8 2³

The 8th Path is the Sephira Hod, Splendor.
The octagon; the ogdoad.
The number of trigrams in the *I Ching*.
The number of Sephiroth on the Sufi Tree of Life.

**Ch** Cheth 8th letter of Hebrew alphabet.
**AHB** Ahab Love.
**AZ** Az Then.
**DD** Dadh Breast.

# 9 3²

The 9th Path is the Sephira Yesod,
 Foundation.
The number of squares in the magic
 square of Saturn.

**T**   Teth   9th letter of Hebrew
 alphabet.
**ACh**   Ach   Brother.
**BZ**   Baz   Booty; prey.
**GW**   Gav   Back (n.).
**HD**   Hed   Shout of joy.

# 10

The 10th Path is the Sephira
 Malkuth, Kingdom.
The decagon; the decad.
Mystic number of 4th Path (Chesed).
The number of Sephiroth.
The number of fingers.
The number of toes.

**Y**   Yod   10th letter of Hebrew
 alphabet.
**HH**   He   Window; 5th letter of
 Hebrew alphabet.
    Hah   Alas!
**BDD**   Bedad   Father of Hadad, a
 King of Edom.
**AT**   At   Whisper (n.).
**GZ**   Gez   Fleece.
**ZG**   Zag   Skin of grapes.
**ChB**   Chob   Bosom.
**TA**   Ta   To sweep away.

# 11 p

The 11th Path is between Kether and
 Chokmah and corresponds to
 Aleph and Air.
The number of magic (according to
 Crowley).

**AY**   Ay   Where?; island.
**ZD**   Zed   Arrogant.
**ChG**   Chag   Feast.

# 12

The 12th Path is between Kether and
 Binah and corresponds to Beth
 and Mercury.
The number of signs in the Zodiac.
The number of pairs of ribs in the
 human body.
The number of thoracic vertebrae in
 the human spine.

**WW**   Waw   Nail, peg; 6th letter of
 Hebrew alphabet.
**HWA**   Hu   He; a name of God
 and title of Kether.
**GWG**   Gog   Gog.
**BY**   Bi   Please, pray.
**ZH**   Zeh   This, that; who, which;
 here, there.
**ChD**   Chad   Sharp.

# 13 p

The 13th Path is between Kether and
 Tiphareth and corresponds to

Gimel and the Moon.
The Sephiroth of the Pillar of Mercy
are 2+4+7=13.

**AHBH**  Ahbah  Love, beloved.
**AChD**  Echad  One; unity.
**BHW**  Bohu  Waste; "void."
**HDD**  Hadad  A King of Edom,
associated with Tiphareth.
**GY**  Gi  The second two letters
of the 42-letter name of God, as-
sociated with Chokmah.
   Gay  Valley.
**ZW**  Ziv  Glory, splendor.

# 14

The 14th Path is between Chokmah
and Binah and corresponds to
Daleth and Venus.
The number of phalanges in the
human hand.
The number of phalanges in the
human foot.
The number of bones in the human
face.

**DWD**  David  King of Israel.
**ZHB**  Zahab  Gold, the metal of
the Sun.
**GYA**  Gaye  Valley; one of the
seven earths, corresponding to
Geburah.
**DY**  Day  Sufficiency, plenty.

# 15

The 15th Path is between Chokmah

and Tiphareth and corresponds to
He and Aries (or Aquarius).
Mystic number of 5th Path
(Geburah).
Magic sum of the magic square of
Saturn.

**YH**  Yah  Divine name associated
with Chokmah.
**HWD**  Hod  Splendor; the 8th
Sephira.
**ABYB**  Abib  Spring.
**HY**  Hi  Lamentation.
**ABWHA**  Aboha  Angel of 3rd
decanate of Sagittarius.
**HHH**  Hehah  41st name of Shem
Hamphorash, associated with 5th
quinance of Aquarius.
**AWCh**  Och  Olympic Planetary
Spirit of the Sun.

# 16 4²

The 16th Path is between Chokmah
and Chesed and corresponds to
Waw and Taurus.
The number of geomantic figures.
The number of squares in the magic
square of Jupiter.
The Sephiroth of the Pillar of
Severity are 3+5+8=16.

**ChBW**  Chebo  68th name of
Shem Hamphorash, associated
with 2nd quinance of Cancer.
**ChCh**  Chach  Hook, brooch, ring.
**AHWD**  Ehud  The second judge
of Israel.

# 17 p

The 17th Path is between Binah and Tiphareth and corresponds to Zayin and Gemini.
According to Crowley, the "masculine unity," the trinity of A, W, and Y.

**GDY** Gedi Kid, young goat; Capricorn.
**TWB** Tob Good.
**WHW** Vehu 1st name of Shem Hamphorash, associated with 1st quinance of Leo.
Vaho 49th name of Shem Hamphorash, associated with 1st quinance of Aries.

# 18

The 18th Path is between Binah and Geburah and corresponds to Cheth and Cancer.

**ChY** Chai Living.

# 19 p

The 19th Path is between Chesed and Geburah and corresponds to Teth and Leo.
19 solar years=235 lunar months=1 "year of Meton."

**ChWH** Chavvah Eve.

**AhWZ** Ahoz Lord of Triplicity by Day for Sagittarius.
**ChHW** Chaho 24th name of Shem Hamphorash, associated with 6th quinance of Scorpio.
**AYWB** Iyyob Job.

# 20

The 20th Path is between Chesed and Tiphareth and corresponds to Yod and Virgo.
The number of fingers and toes.

**K** Kaph 11th letter of Hebrew alphabet.
**YWD** Yod Hand; 10th letter of Hebrew alphabet.
**YWBB** Jobab A King of Edom, associated with Chesed.
**ZHWB** Zahob Golden.
**HTAH** Hattaah Sin.
**YHH** Yehah 62nd name of Shem Hamphorash, associated with 2nd quinance of Gemini.

# 21

The 21st Path is between Chesed and Netzach and corresponds to Kaph and Jupiter.
Mystic number of 6th Path (Tiphareth).

**AHYH** Ehyeh "I AM"; name of God associated with Kether.
**ChGY** Chaggai Haggai.

**AK** (K=20)  Ak  But, only, surely, indeed.

# 22

The 22nd Path is between Geburah and Tiphareth and corresponds to Lamed and Libra.
The number of letters in the Hebrew alphabet.
The number of Tarot trumps.

**AKA**  Aka  7th name of Shem Hamphorash, associated with 1st quinance of Virgo.
**HZY**  Hezi  9th name of Shem Hamphorash, associated with 3rd quinance of Virgo.
**HAAYH**  Haayah  Angel of 2nd quinance of Sagittarius; angel by night of the 8 of Wands.

# 23 P

The 23rd Path is between Geburah and Hod and corresponds to Mem and Water.

**ChYH**  Chiah  Part of the soul referred to Chokmah.

# 24

The 24th Path is between Tiphareth and Netzach and corresponds to

Nun and Scorpio.
The number of hours in a day.
The number of elders before the Throne.
The number of ribs in the human body.
The number of vertebrae in the human spine.

**KD**  Kad  Bucket, pail, vessel.
**YChW**  Yecho  33rd name of Shem Hamphorash, associated with 3rd quinance of Capricorn.
**DK** (K=20)  Dak  Oppressed.

# 25 5²

The 25th Path is between Tiphareth and Yesod and corresponds to Samekh and Sagittarius.
The number of squares in the magic square of Mars.

**ChYWA**  Chioa  The Beast; the union or offspring of Samael and Isheth Zenunim; arch-demon corresponding to Tiphareth (according to Crowley).
**HYY**  Hayeya  71st name of Shem Hamphorash, associated with 5th quinance of Cancer.
**AKD**  Akkad  Dynasty of ancient Mesopotamia.
**KH**  Koh  Thus, so; here, there.

# 26

The 26th Path is between Tiphareth and Hod and corresponds to Ayin and Capricorn.

The Sephiroth of the Middle Pillar are 1+6+9+10=26.

**YHWH**   Yahweh   Tetragrammaton; Jehovah.

# 27 $3^3$

The 27th Path is between Netzach and Hod and corresponds to Pe and Mars.

The number of books in the New Testament.

**YYZ**   Yeyaz   40th name of Shem Hamphorash, associated with 4th quinance of Aquarius.

**ZK** (K=20)   Zak   Pure, clear, transparent, innocent.

# 28 Perfect

The 28th Path is between Netzach and Yesod and corresponds to Sadhe and Aquarius (or Aries).

The height in cubits of the curtains in the Tabernacle in the Wilderness.

Mystic number of 7th Path (Netzach)

Number of letters in the Arabic alphabet.

**YDYD**   Yadid   One beloved.

**KCh**   Koch   Strength.

**ChK** (K=20)   Chek   Palate.

# 29 p

The 29th Path is between Netzach and Malkuth and corresponds to Qoph and Pisces.

According to Crowley, the number of magic force.

The number of talents of gold used in the construction of the Tabernacle in the Wilderness.

# 30

The 30th Path is between Hod and Yesod and corresponds to Resh and the Sun.

**L**   Lamed   12th letter of Hebrew alphabet.

**YHWDH**   Judah   A tribe of Israel, associated with Leo.

**YYY**   Yeyaya   22nd name of Shem Hamphorash, associated with 4th quinance of Scorpio.

**KY**   Ki   Brand; that, so that, because, when, for.

# 31 p

The 31st Path is between Hod and Malkuth and corresponds to Shin and Fire.

**AL**   El   Divine name associated with Chesed.

**ChBWYH**   Chabuyah   Angel of 2nd quinance of Cancer; angel by night of the 2 of Cups.

**LA**   Lo   Not, no.

# 32 $2^5$

The 32nd Path is between Yesod and Malkuth and corresponds to Taw and Saturn.

The number of Paths of Wisdom.

The number of human teeth.

**BL**   Bal   Not.
   Bel   Chief God of the Babylonians.

**LB**   Leb   Heart, center.

**WHWYH**   Vahaviah   Angel of 1st quinance of Leo; angel by day of the 5 of Wands.

**AHYHWH**   Ehyahweh   Combination of Ehyeh and Yahweh, macrocosm and microcosm.

# 33

**BAL**   Bael   Goetic demon by day of 1st decanate of Aries.

**GL**   Gal   Ruins; well; fountain; wave.
   Gel   Dung.
   Gol   Oil Vessel.

**LG**   Log   Basin.

# 34

Magic sum of the magic square of Jupiter.

**BBL**   Babel   Babylon.

**ChHWYH**   Chahaviah   Angel of 6th quinance of Scorpio; angel by night of the 7 of Cups.

**DL**   Dal   Wretched.

**LD**   Lod   Lydda, a town in Benjamin.

# 35

**AGLA**   Agla   A name of God; acronym for Ateh Gibor le-Olam Adonai, "Thou art mighty forever, O Lord."

**ALD**   Elad   10th name of Shem Hamphorash, associated with 4th quinance of Virgo.

# 36 $6^2$

Mystic number of 8th Path (Hod).

The number of decanates in the Zodiac.

The number of squares in the magic square of the Sun.

**ALH**   Elah   Goddess; a Duke of Edom, associated with Geburah.
   Eloah   God.

**LAH**   Leah   First wife of Jacob;

mother of Reuben, Simeon, Levi, Judah, Issachar, and Zebulun.

**LW**  Lo  Not, no.

**AYKH**  Ekah  How; Hebrew title of the book of Lamentations.

# 37 p

**HBL**  Hebel  Abel, son of Adam; vapor, breath, vanity.

**YChYDH**  Yechidah  Part of the soul referred to Kether.

**AKAYH**  Akaiah  Angel of 1st quinance of Virgo; angel by day of the 8 of Pentacles.

**WAL**  Valu  Goetic demon by night of 2nd decanate of Sagittarius.

**LAW**  Lav  11th name of Shem Hamphorash, associated with 5th quinance of Virgo.

Lau  17th name of Shem Hamphorash, associated with 5th quinance of Libra.

# 38

**AWAL**  Uvall  Goetic demon by night of 2nd decanate of Cancer.

**ChL**  Chel  Bulwark, wall, rampart.

Chol  Profane, unholy.

**LCh**  Lach  Moist, fresh, green.

# 39

The number of books in the Old Testament in the Protestant Bible.

**YChWYH**  Yechaviah  Angel of 3rd quinance of Capricorn; angel by day of the 3 of Pentacles.

**KWZW**  Kuzu  A name of God by Temurah.

**TL**  Tal  Dew.

**LT**  Lot  Laudanum

**YHWH AChD**  Yahweh Echad  Yahweh is One.

# 40

**M**  Mem  13th letter of Hebrew alphabet.

**ChLB**  Chalav  Milk.

# 41 p

**AM**  Em  Mother.

**ZBWL**  Zebhul  Dwelling; the 4th Heaven, corresponding to Tiphareth.

**AYL**  Ayyal  Hart; a title of Malkuth.

# 42

The number of children of Azmaveth

who returned from exile (Ezra II:24).

**AMA** Ama Mother; a title of Binah.

**AYAL** Ayel Angel of 1st astrological house.

**LWW** Levo 19th name of Shem Hamphorash, associated with 1st quinance of Scorpio.

**WWL** Vaval 43rd name of Shem Hamphorash, associated with 1st quinance of Pisces.

**ChLD** Cheled World; one of the seven earths, corresponding (with Tebhel) to Yesod and Malkuth; our own Earth.

**BLHH** Bilhah Rachel's handmaiden; mother of Dan and Naphtali.

**YWD HH WW** Yod He Waw The three consonants in Tetragrammaton.

**YWD H WW H** Yod H Waw H Tetragrammaton with the Yod and Waw spelled out.

# 43 p

**GDWL** Gadhol Great.

**YDYDYH** Yedidiah One beloved by God; Solomon.

**MG** Mag Magus.

**LHCh** Lehach 34th name of Shem Hamphorash, associated with 4th quinance of Capricorn.

**GM** (M=40) Gam Together; also.

# 44

**TLH** Taleh Lamb; Aries.

**DLY** Deli Bucket; Aquarius.

**GYAL** Giel Angel of 3rd astrological house.

**MD** Mad Garment.

**DM** (M=40) Dam Blood; the 1st of the 10 plagues of Egypt.

# 45

Mystic number of the 9th Path (Yesod).

The sum of all the numbers (1 to 9) in the magic square of Saturn.

**AGYAL** Agiel The Intelligence of Saturn.

**ZAZL** Zazel The Spirit of Saturn.

**LWT** Lot Lot.

**YLH** Yelah 44th name of Shem Hamphorash, associated with 2nd quinance of Pisces.

**MH** Mah What?, Which?, Why?, How?; anything, something; the secret name of the World of Formation.

**ADM** (M=40) Adam Man; a title of Tiphareth.

Adhom Red.

**HM** (M=40) Hem They.

# 46

**TWAL** Toel Angel of 2nd astrological house.
**YHAL** Yahel Angel of 7th astrological house.
**DMB** Dameb 65th name of Shem Hamphorash, associated with 5th quinance of Gemini.
**HHHAL** Hahahel Angel of 5th quinance of Aquarius; angel by day of the 7 of Swords.
**BDYL** Bedil Tin, the metal of Jupiter.
**LWY** Levi The priest tribe of Israel.
**MAH** Meah Hundred.

# 47 p

**WYAL** Veyel Angel of 6th astrological house.
**YWAL** Yoel Joel.
**YZL** Yezel 13th name of Shem Hamphorash, associated with 1st quinance of Libra.
**MBH** Mebah 14th name of Shem Hamphorash, associated with 2nd quinance of Libra.
Mabeh 55th name of Shem Hamphorash, associated with 1st quinance of Taurus.
**AWM** (M=40) Aum 30th name of Shem Hamphorash, associated with 6th quinance of Sagittarius.

# 48

**GDWLH** Gedulah Greatness, magnificence; a title of Chesed.
**KWKB** Kokab Star; Mercury.
**WHWAL** Vehuel Angel of 1st quinance of Aries; angel by day of the 2 of Wands.
**WMB** Vameb 61st name of Shem Hamphorash, associated with 1st quinance of Gemini.
**YWBL** Jubal Jubal.
**MCh** Meach Fat.
Moach Marrow.
**ChM** (M=40) Cham Ham, son of Noah; father-in-law; warm, hot; warmth, heat.

# 49 7²

The number of squares in the magic square of Venus.

**HGYAL** Hagiel The Intelligence of Venus.
**MWAB** Moab Moab.
**GWLChB** Golachab The Arsonists; Qlippoth of Geburah.

# 50

**N** Nun 14th letter of Hebrew alphabet.
**KL** Kol All.
**ADMH** Adamah Earth; one of the seven earths, corresponding to Chesed.

**ALDYH**    Aldiah    Angel of 4th
quinance of Virgo; angel by night
of the 9 of Pentacles.

**YLY**    Yeli    2nd name of Shem
Hamphorash, associated with 2nd
quinance of Leo.

**YYL**    Yeyal    58th name of Shem
Hamphorash, associated with 4th
quinance of Taurus.

**MY**    Mi    Who?, Which?; whoever,
every one.

**YM** (M=40)    Yam    Sea.

# 51

**NA**    Na    Please; raw; a name of
God.
    No    Thebes.

**YHHAL**    Yehohel    Angel of 2nd
quinance of Gemini; angel by
night of the 8 of Swords.

**AN** (N=50)    An    Where?

**ADWM** (M=40)    Edom    Edom.

**AYM** (M=40)    Aim    Goetic
demon by day of 2nd decanate of
Scorpio.

# 52

The number of children of Nebo who
returned from exile (Ezra II:29).

**AYMA**    Aima    The Supernal
Mother; a title of Binah.

**YWD HH WW HH**    Yod He Waw He
The consonants of Tetragrammaton spelled out; the expanded

Name.

**MGWG**    Magog    Magog.

**NB**    Nob    A town in Benjamin.

**LKB**    Lekab    31st name of Shem
Hamphorash, associated with 1st
quinance of Capricorn.

**LAWYH**    Laviah    Angel of 5th
quinance of Virgo; angel by day
of the 10 of Pentacles; angel of
5th quinance of Libra; angel by
day of the 4 of Swords.

**BN** (N=50)    Ben    Son; a title of
Tiphareth; the secret name of the
World of Action.

**YBM** (M=40)    Yabam    Brother-
in-law.
    Yebem    70th name
of Shem Hamphorash, associated
with 4th quinance of Cancer.

**BYM** (M=40)    Bimé    Goetic
demon by day of 2nd decanate of
Sagittarius.

# 53 P

**HZYAL**    Haziel    Angel of 3rd
quinance of Virgo; angel by day
of the 9 of Pentacles.

**GN** (N=50)    Gan    Garden.

# 54

**MTH**    Mattah    Tribe; branch,
twig, rod, staff, stick, sceptre,
spear.

**ND**    Ned    Heap, wall.

**DN** (N=50)    Dan    A tribe of

Israel, associated with Scorpio.

# 55

Mystic number of 10th Path (Malkuth).

**KLH** Kalah Bride; a title of Malkuth.

**MYH** Miah 48th name of Shem Hamphorash, associated with 6th quinance of Pisces.

**NH** Noah Splendor, eminence.

**HN** (N=50) Hen Lo!; whether, if.

# 56

The number of men of Netophah who returned from exile (Ezra II:22).

**RYYAL** Rayayel Angel of 5th quinance of Cancer; angel by day of the 4 of Cups.

**NW** Nu Egyptian goddess.

**YWM** (M=40) Yom Day.

# 57

**LWWYH** Luviah Angel of 1st quinance of Scorpio; angel by day of the 5 of Cups.

**DGYM** (M=40) Dagim Fishes; Pisces.

**ALWK** (K=20) Alloces Goetic demon by night of 1st decanate of Virgo.

**AWN** (N=50) Avnas Goetic demon by night of 1st decanate of Scorpio. On Strength; wealth; sorrow.

**ZN** (N=50) Zan Species, kind.

# 58

**NCh** Noach Noah.

**TLYHD** Taliahad Angel of Water.

**MChY** Mechi Battering ram; 64th name of Shem Hamporash, associated with 4th quinance of Gemini.

**LHChYH** Lehachiah Angel of 4th quinance of Capricorn; angel by night of the 3 of Pentacles.

**YYZAL** Yeyazel Angel of 4th quinance of Aquarius; angel by night of the 6 of Swords.

**ChN** (N=50) Chen Grace, charm.

# 60

**S** Samekh 15th letter of Hebrew alphabet.

**KLY** Keli Utensil, instrument, tool; 18th name of Shem Hamphorash, associated with 6th quinance of Libra.

**YLHYH** Yelahiah Angel of 2nd

quinance of Pisces; angel by night
of the 8 of Cups.

**NWD**   Nod   Nod.

**NY**   Ni   Lament

# 61 p

**ANY**   Ani   I; fleet of ships; 37th
name of Shem Hamphorash, associated with 1st quinance of
Aquarius.

**DMBYH**   Damabiah   Angel of
5th quinance of Gemini; angel by
day of the 10 of Swords.

**YYYAL**   Yeyayel   Angel of 4th
quinance of Scorpio; angel by
night of the 6 of Cups.

**AYN** (N=50)   Ain   Nothing.

**ZAGN** (N=50)   Zagan   Goetic
demon by night of 1st decanate
of Sagittarius.

# 62

**BHHMY**   Behahemi   Angel of
2nd decanate of Aries.

**MBHYH**   Mebahiah   Angel of 1st
quinance of Taurus; angel by day
of the 5 of Pentacles.

# 63

**SG**   Seg   The secret name of the
World of Creation.

**NBYA**   Navi   Prophet.

**ABDWN** (N=50)   Abaddon
Destruction; the angel of the
bottomless pit; the 6th hell; corresponding to Chesed.

**DGWN** (N=50)   Dagon
Philistine fish god.

# 64 8²

The number of hexagrams in the
*I Ching*.

The number of squares in the magic
square of Mercury.

**NWGH**   Nogah   Venus.

**GWNH**   Gonah   Serenity.

**MY ZHB**   Mezahab   Mother of
Matred, mother of Mehetabel,
wife of Hadar, a King of Edom.

**DNY**   Dani   50th name of Shem
Hamphorash, associated with 2nd
quinance of Aries.

**SD**   Sad   Stocks.

**DYN** (N=50)   Din   Justice; a title
of Geburah.

**ChWYM**   Chivim   Hivites.

# 65

The magic sum of the magic square
of Mars.

**ADNY**   Adonai   A name of God.

HYKL   Hekel   Temple, palace, mansion. (From this, says the Zohar, we learn that Adonai is the palace of Yahweh.)

LLH   Lelah   6th name of Shem Hamphorash, associated with 6th quinance of Leo.

HS   Has   Silence!

DWMYH   Dumiah   Silence, quietness.

# 68

ChYYM (M=40)   Chayim   Life.

# 69

VKBYAL   Vakabiel   Angel of Pisces.

ST   Set   Transgression, error, sin.

# 66

Mystic number of the 11th Path (between Kether and Chokmah; Aleph; Air).

The number of books in the Protestant Bible.

DNHBH   Dinhabah   A city of Edom; city of King Bela.

# 67 p

BYNH   Binah   Understanding; the 3rd Sephira.

YBMYH   Yebamiah   Angel of 4th quinance of Cancer; angel by night of the 3 of Cups.

WYNA   Viné   Goetic demon by night of 3rd decanate of Gemini.

ALWL   Elul   The 12th Hebrew month.

# 70

O   Ayin   16th letter of Hebrew alphabet.

GWG WMGWG   Gog we-Magog   Gog and Magog.

MYK (K=20)   Mik   42nd name of Shem Hamphorash, associated with 6th quinance of Aquarius.

KN (N=50)   Ken   Honest; so, thus, just so, such, so much.

# 71 p

ALYL   Elil   God.

YWNH   Yonah   Dove; Jonah.

AMDWK (K=20)   Amdukias   Goetic demon by night of 1st decanate of Aquarius.

# 72

The number of quinances in the

Zodiac.
The number of names of Shem
Hamphorash.
The number of Goetic demons.
The number of joints in the human
body, according to cabalists.

**ChSD**    Chesed    Mercy; the 4th
Sephira.
**OB**    Ab    The secret name of the
World of Nobility; density;
thicket; darkness; cloud.
**ADWKYAL**    Advakiel    Archangel
of Sagittarius.

# 73 p

**ChKMH**    Chokmah    Wisdom; the
2nd Sephira.
**KChMH**    Kochmah    A title of
Chokmah.
**GML**    Gimel    Camel; the 3rd
letter of Hebrew alphabet.
**WWYLYH**    Vavaliah    Angel of
1st quinance of Pisces; angel by
day of the 8 of Cups.
**BLYAL**    Belial    An arch-demon
corresponding (according to
Crowley) to Hod; Qlippoth of Ain
Soph; Goetic demon by night of
2nd decanate of Aquarius.

# 74

The number of Levites who returned
from exile (Ezra II:40).

**LMD**    Lamed    Ox goad; 12th
letter of Hebrew alphabet.
**DO**    Dea    Knowledge, wisdom.
**OD**    Ad    Eternity, duration;
during; booty.
     Ed    Witness, proof; ruler.
**GYWHN** (N=50)    Gihon    A river
of Eden, associated with Water.

# 75

**LYLH**    Laylah    Night.
**HYLL**    Heylel    Brightness;
morning star.
**MYKH**    Mikah    Micah.
**MLH**    Melah    23rd name of Shem
Hamphorash, associated with 5th
quinance of Scorpio.
     Milah    Word.
**KHN** (N=50)    Kohen    Priest.
**HDD BN BDD** (N=50)    Hadad ben
Bedad    Hadad, son of Bedad; a
King of Edom, associated with
Tiphareth.

# 76

**ALYLH**    Elilah    Goddess.

# 77

**OZ**    Ez    Goat.
     Oz    Strength; violence; glory.

# 78

The number of Tarot cards.
Mystic number of 12th Path
(between Kether and Binah; Beth;
Mercury).

**AWMAL**   Avamel   Angel of 6th
quinance of Sagittarius; angel by
night of the 10 of Wands.
**AYWAS**   Aiwass   The supposed
author of *The Book of the Law.*
**HYKL AHBH**   Hekel Ahbah
Palace of Love; Heavenly Mansion
corresponding to Chesed.
**ZMAL**   Zamael   Angel ruling
Mars and Tuesday.
**YZLAL**   Yezalel   Angel of 1st
quinance of Libra; angel by day of
the 2 of Swords.
**KDMDY**   Kedamidi   Angel of 1st
decanate of Taurus.
**MBHAL**   Mebahel   Angel of 2nd
quinance of Libra; angel by night
of the 2 of Swords.
**OZA**   Ezah   A giant.

# 79 p

**YAChYN** (N=50)   Jachin   One of
the pillars in the Temple of
Solomon.
**BOZ**   Boaz   The other pillar in
the Temple of Solomon.
**SYT**   Sit   3rd name of Shem
Hamphorash, associated with 3rd
quinance of Leo.
**WMBAL**   Vemibael   Angel of 1st
quinance of Gemini; angel by day

of the 8 of Wands.
**ODH**   Adah   A wife of Lamech.
**YBL**   Jabal   Jabal.
**OT**   Et   Writing instrument.

# 80

**P**   Pe   17th letter of Hebrew
alphabet.
**YSWD**   Yesod   Foundation; the
9th Sephira.
**HHO**   Hehau   12th name of
Shem Hamphorash, associated
with 6th quinance of Virgo.
**YO**   Ya   Shovel.
**KS**   Kes   Throne.
**OY**   Ay   A town near Bethel.
**I**   Ruins.
**SK** (K=20)   Sak   Crowd.

# 81 9²

The number of squares in the magic
square of the Moon.

**AYO**   Aya   67th name of Shem
Hamphorash, associated with
1st quinance of Cancer.
**YYLAL**   Yeyalel   Angel of 4th
quinance of Taurus; angel by
night of the 6 of Pentacles.
**YLYAL**   Yelayel   Angel of 2nd
quinance of Leo; angel by night
of the 5 of Wands.
**KAYN** (N=50)   Camio   Goetic
demon by night of 1st decanate of
Virgo.

**AP** (P=80)   Aph   Also.

# 82

**ANAL**   Anael   Angel ruling
Venus and Friday.

**LBN** (N=50)   Lavan   White.

# 83 p

**MHZAL**   Mahazael   Demon
Prince of Earth.

**LKBAL**   Lekabel   Angel of 1st
quinance of Capricorn; angel by
day of the 2 of Pentacles.

**PG**   Pag   Unripe fig.

**GP** (P=80)   Gaph   Back, top;
body, person.

# 84

**ChNWK** (K=20)   Chanok   Enoch.

# 85

**PH**   Pe   Mouth; 17th letter of
Hebrew alphabet.

**MYLH**   Milah   Circumcision.

# 86

**ALHYM** (M=40)   Elohim   A
name of God; Angelic Choir associated with Netzach and with the
Sphere of Venus. (This is the
usual enumeration; i.e., not final
M as 600.)

**HLLWYH**   Haleluyah   Hallelujah;
praise the Lord.

**HNAL**   Hanael   Archangel of
Capricorn.

**MWM**   Mum   Blemish; 72nd
name of Shem Hamphorash, associated with 6th quinance of
Cancer.

**MYHAL**   Mihael   Angel of 6th
quinance of Pisces; angel by night
of the 10 of Cups.

**LWYM** (M=40)   Levim   Levites;
the priest tribe of Israel.

# 87

**LBNH**   Levanah   The Moon.

**BHLMY**   Bihelami   Angel of 1st
decanate of Pisces.

**PZ**   Paz   Pure gold.

**ALWN** (N=50)   Elon   The tenth
judge of Israel.

# 88

**PCh**   Pach   Danger.

**MGDYAL**   Magdiel   A Duke of
Edom, associated (with Mibzar)
with Yesod.

ChP (P=80)   Chaph   Pure, innocent.

# 89 p

MChYAL   Mochayel   Angel of 4th quinance of Gemini; angel by night of the 9 of Wands.
TP (P=80)   Taph   Children.
DMMH   Demamah   Silence, whisper; says Crowley, "The wrong kind of silence, that of the Black Brothers."

# 90

Tz   Sadhe   18th letter of Hebrew alphabet.
SL   Sal   Basket.
MYM (M=40)   Mem   Water; 13th letter of Hebrew alphabet.
MLK (K=20)   Melek   King; a title of Tiphareth; one of the Melekim.
   Moloch   Archdemon corresponding (with Satan) to Kether.
GWAP (P=80)   Göap   Demon King of the South (Goetia).
LMK (K=20)   Lamek   Lamech.
MN (N=50)   Man   Manna.
   Men   Portion.
DWMM (M=40)   Domem   Silent.

# 91

Mystic number of 13th Path (between Kether and Tiphareth; Gimel; Moon).

APWD   Ephod   Ephod.
OBDYH   Obadyah   Obadiah.
KMAL   Kamael   Archangel associated with Geburah and with Mars.
SAL   Sael   45th name of Shem Hamphorash, associated with 3rd quinance of Pisces.
KLYAL   Kaliel   Angel of 6th quinance of Libra; angel by night of the 4 of Swords.
AMN (N=50)   Amen   Firm, faithful; so be it!; a title of Kether.
MLAK (K=20)   Malak   Angel.

# 92

PChD   Pachad   Fear; a title of Geburah.
ANYAL   Aniel   Angel of 1st quinance of Aquarius; angel by day of the 5 of Swords.
TzB   Tzab   Litter.
BTz (Tz=90)   Botz   Mud.

# 93

AHLYBMH   Aholibamah   A Duke of Edom, associated with Chesed.

# 94

**MND** Menad Prickly; 36th name
of Shem Hamphorash, associated
with 6th quinance of Capricorn.
**DNTAL** Dantalion Goetic
demon by night of 2nd decanate
of Pisces.
**TzD** Tzad Side.
**MDYM** (M=40) Madim Mars.

# 95

The number of children of Gibbar
who returned from exile.
(Ezra II:20).

**MLKH** Malkah Queen; a title of
Malkuth.
**ZChOY** Zachi Angel of 2nd
decanate of Leo.
**DNYAL** Daniel Angel of 2nd
quinance of Aries; angel by night
of the 2 of Wands.
**HHOYH** Hihayah Angel of 6th
quinance of Virgo; angel by night
of the 10 of Pentacles.
**MChWYAL** Mehujael Mehujael.
**ZBWLN** (N=50) Zebulun A
tribe of Israel, associated with
Capricorn.

# 96

**PWY** Poi 56th name of Shem
Hamphorash, associated with 2nd
quinance of Taurus.

**LLHAL** Lelahel Angel of 6th
quinance of Leo; angel by night
of the 7 of Wands.
**TzW** Tzaw Statute.

# 97 p

**HANYAL** Haniel Archangel
associated with Netzach and with
Venus.
**MHYTBAL** Mehetabel Wife of
Hadar, a King of Edom.
**TzHB** Tzahov Yellow.
**AMWN** (N=50) Amon Goetic
demon by day of 1st decanate of
Gemini; chief god of the
Egyptians.

# 98

The number of children of Ater who
returned from exile (Ezra II:16).

**TzCh** Tzach Bright.
**ChTz** (Tz=90) Chetz Arrow;
lightning; punishment; wound.

# 99

**TYTHYWN** Tit-ha-yawen Mire
of Mud; the 4th hell, corresponding
to Tiphareth.

# I⊏O 10²

**Q** Qoph 19th letter of Hebrew alphabet.
**LO** Loa Throat.
**MS** Mas A suffering, discouraged one; tax.
**OL** Al Upper part; on, above, over, to, towards, after, because.
Ol Yoke.
**TzY** Tzi Dryness; ship.
**KP** (P=80) Kaph Palm of hand; 11th letter of Hebrew alphabet.
**NLK** (K=20) Nelak 21st name of Shem Hamphorash, associated with 3rd quinance of Scorpio.
**SM** (M=40) Sam Spice; drug; poison.
**PK** (K=20) Pak Flask, bottle.

# IOI p

**MYKAL** Michael 1. Archangel associated with Hod, with Mercury, with the South, and with Fire; 2. Angel ruling the Sun and Sunday; 3. Angel of 6th quinance of Aquarius; angel by night of the 7 of Swords.
**MLAKY** Meleaki Malachi.
**NNA** Nena 53rd name of Shem Hamphorash, associated with 5th quinance of Aries.
**MWMYH** Mevamiah Angel of 6th quinance of Cancer; angel by night of the 4 of Cups.
**QA** Qe Vomit.

# IO2

**BLO** Bela A King of Edom, associated with Daath.
**BOL** Baal Lord, owner; arch-demon corresponding to Netzach (according to Mathers).
**QB** Qab Unit of measure.
**WYLWN** (N=50) Wilon Veil; the 1st Heaven, corresponding to Yesod and Malkuth.

# IO3 p

**ABYMLK** (K=20) Abimelech A King of the Philistines.

# IO4

**TzDY** Sadhe Fishhook; 18th letter of Hebrew alphabet.
**DQ** Daq Crushed, fine, thin.
**MDYN** (N=50) Midian Midian.
**MLK DWD** (K=20) Melek David King David.
**NChWM** (M=40) Nachum Nahum.

# IO5

Mystic number of 14th Path (between Chokmah and Binah; Daleth; Venus).

**TzYH** Tziah Dryness; one of the

seven earths, corresponding to Tiphareth or Netzach.

# 106

**MLHAL**   Melahel   Angel of 5th quinance of Scorpio; angel by day of the 7 of Cups.

**SALYH**   Saliah   Angel of 3rd quinance of Pisces; angel by day of the 9 of Cups.

**QW**   Qaw   Line; chord; norm.

**NYN** (N=50)   Nun   Fish; 14th letter of Hebrew alphabet.

**PWK** (K=20)   Puk   Antimony.

# 107 p

**OWAL**   Oel   Angel of 5th astrological house.

**GLOD**   Gilead   Gilead.

**ZQ**   Zeq   Chain; flaming arrow.

**AWNN** (N=50)   Onan   Onan.

# 108

**OZAL**   Azael   Demon Prince of Water.

Ezal   A giant.

**ChQ**   Choq   Statute; share; task; boundary.

# 109 p

**SChYAL**   Sachiel   Angel ruling Jupiter and Thursday.

**QT**   Qat   Small.

# 110

The number of years Joseph lived (Gen. L:26).

**SYTAL**   Sitael   Angel of 3rd quinance of Leo; angel by day of the 6 of Wands.

**NS**   Nes   Banner, sign, standard.

**OM** (M=40)   Am   Nation, populace.

Em   With, by, near.

# 111

Magic sum of the magic square of the Sun.

**AChD HWA ALHYM**   Echad Hua Elohim   He is One God.

**NKYAL**   Nakhiel   The Intelligence of the Sun.

**PLA**   Pele   The Wonder; a title of Kether.

**OLWH**   Alvah   A Duke of Edom, associated with Daath.

**QYA**   Qi   Vomit.

**ALP** (P=80)   Aleph   Ox; 1st letter of Hebrew alphabet.

Elep   Thousand.

# 112

The number of children of Jorah who returned from exile (Ezra II:18).

**AYOAL**  Ayoel  Angel of 1st quinance of Cancer; angel by day of the 2 of Cups.

**HQBH**  Haqabah  A name of God; acronym for Ha-Qadosh Baruk Hu, "The Holy One, blessed be He."

**YHWH ALHYM** (M=40)  Yahweh Elohim  The Lord God; divine name associated with Binah.

# 113 p

**PLG**  Peleg  Son of Eber; father of Reu.

Phaleg  Olympic Planetary Spirit of Mars.

**NChMYH**  Nechemyah Nehemiah.

# 114

**GMLYAL**  Gamaliel  The Obscene Ones; Qlippoth of Yesod.

**GYHNWM** (M=40)  Ge-Hinnom Gehenna; Hell; the 1st hell, corresponding to Yesod and Malkuth.

# 115

**OZAZL**  Azazel  Demon Prince of Air.

**PHL**  Pahel  20th name of Shem Hamphorash, associated with 2nd quinance of Scorpio.

# 116

**HMLYAL**  Hamaliel  Archangel of Virgo.

**KSLW**  Kislev  The 3rd Hebrew month.

**PWL**  Phul  Olympic Planetary Spirit of the Moon.

Pul  A king of Assyria (Tiglath-Pileser III).

**HALP** (P=80)  Halphas  Goetic demon by night of 2nd decanate of Aries.

**GMYGYN** (N=50)  Gamigin Goetic demon by day of 1st decanate of Taurus.

**MKWN** (N=40)  Makhon Emplacement; the 6th Heaven, corresponding to Chesed.

# 117

**ALWP** (P=80)  Alup  Chief, "duke."

# 118

**ZYMYMAY** Zimimay Demon
King of the North (Goetia).
**ADM BLYAL** (M=40) Adam
Belial Arch-demon correspond-
ing to Chokmah (Waite).
**ChOM** (M=40) Cham 38th name
of Shem Hamphorash, associated
with 2nd quinance of Aquarius.

# 119

**BOLZBWB** Beelzebub Lord of
the Flies; arch-demon
corresponding to Chokmah.

# 120

Mystic number of 15th Path
(between Chokmah and Tiphareth;
He; Aries).

**OWGYAL** Ogiel The Hinderers;
Qlippoth of Chokmah.
**KSYL** Kesil Fool.
**SS** Sas Moth.
**TzL** Tzal Shadow; shelter.
**SMK** (K=20) Samekh Prop,
support; 15th letter of Hebrew
alphabet.
**LTz** (Tz=90) Letz Mocker.
**MP** (P=80) Moph Memphis
(Egypt).
**KNYM** (M=40) Kinnim Vermin;
the 3rd of the 10 plagues of
Egypt.

**ON** (N=50) An A name of God.

# 121 $11^2$

**KSYAL** Cassiel Angel ruling
Saturn and Saturday.
**OKAL** Akel Lord of Triplicity
by Night for Cancer.
**KOAL** Kael Angel of 4th astro-
logical house.
**MTBO** Matbea Coin.
**NYNWH** Nineveh Nineveh.
**PANTz** (Tz=90) Phenex Goetic
demon by night of 1st decanate of
Aries.

# 122

The number of men of Michmas who
returned from exile (Ezra II:27).

**ASMWDAY** Asmodai
Asmodeus; arch-demon
corresponding to Geburah or
Netzach; Goetic demon by day of
2nd decanate of Aquarius.
**ZLPH** Zilpah Leah's hand-
maiden; mother of Gad and
Asher.

# 123

The number of children of
Bethlehem who returned from
exile (Ezra II:21).

**MLChMH**  Milchamah  War.
**KHN HGDWL** (N=50)  Kohen ha-
Gadhol  High Priest.

# 124

**ODN** (N=50)  Eden  Eden.

# 125 5³

**MNDAL**  Mendel  Angel of 6th
quinance of Capricorn; angel by
night of the 4 of Pentacles.
**TzLH**  Tzillah  Zillah, a wife of
Lamech.

# 126

**SNWY**  Senoy  One of the three
angels invoked against Lilith.
**KWQ**  Keveq  35th name of
Shem Hamphorash, associated
with 5th quinance of Capricorn.
**ONW**  Anu  63rd name of Shem
Hamphorash, associated with 3rd
quinance of Gemini.
**SYWN** (N=50)  Sivan  The 9th
Hebrew month.

# 127 p

**PWYAL**  Poyel  Angel of 2nd
quinance of Taurus; angel by

night of the 5 of Pentacles.

# 128 2⁷

The number of letters in the ten
commandments.
The number of men of Anathoth
who returned from exile (Ezra
II:23).
The number of singers, children of
Asaph, who returned from exile
(Ezra II:41).

**AWPYAL**  Ophiel  Olympic
Planetary Spirit of Mercury.
**YBWSYM** (M=40)  Yebusim
Jebusites.

# 129

**HYKL GWNH**  Hekel Gonah
Palace of Serenity; Heavenly
Mansion corresponding to Hod.

# 130

**PHLYH**  Pahaliah  Angel of 2nd
quinance of Scorpio; angel by
night of the 5 of Cups.
**SYNY**  Sinai  Sinai.
**QL**  Qal  Swift.
**SLM** (M=40)  Sellam  Ladder.
(From the correspondence of
"ladder" and "Sinai," we learn
that the ladder to heaven—i.e.,

Jacob's ladder—is provided by the Law given on Sinai.)

**OYN** (N=50)  Ayin  Eye; 16th letter of Hebrew alphabet.

**NMM** (M=40)  Nemem  57th name of Shem Hamphorash, associated with 3rd quinance of Taurus.

**MTz** (Tz=90)  Motz  Chaff.

**NP** (P=80)  Noph  Memphis (Egypt).

**PN** (N=50)  Pen  Lest.

# 131 P

**SMAL**  Samael  Angel of Death; Prince of Demons; Demon Prince of Fire; Qlippoth of Hod; archdemon corresponding to Chokmah (Crowley).

**NLKAL**  Nelakiel  Angel of 3rd quinance of Scorpio; angel by day of the 6 of Cups.

# 132

**NNAAL**  Nanael  Angel of 5th quinance of Aries; angel by day of the 4 of Wands.

**OBDWN** (N=50)  Abon  The eleventh judge of Israel.

**MHMMD**  Muhammad *(Arabic)*.

**QLB**  Qalb  Heart *(Arabic)*.

# 133

**ChOMYH**  Chamiah  Angel of

2nd quinance of Aquarius; angel by night of the 5 of Swords.

**NGP** (P=80)  Negep  Plague.

**GDOWN** (N=50)  Gideon  The fifth judge of Israel.

# 135

**MLKYDAL**  Malkidiel  Archangel of Aries.

**KOMH**  Kaamah  Some sort of infernal being associated with the northwest (a misprint of NOMH?)

**GWSYWN** (N=50)  Gusion  Goetic demon by day of 2nd decanate of Cancer.

# 136

Mystic number of the 16th Path (between Chokmah and Chesed; Waw; Taurus).

The sum of all the numbers (1 to 16) of the magic square of Jupiter.

**YHPYAL**  Iophiel  The Intelligence of Jupiter.

**HSMAL**  Hismael  The Spirit of Jupiter.

**MHLLAL**  Mahalaleel  Mahalaleel.

# 137 P

The reciprocal of the fine structure constant.

The number of years that Ishmael
(Gen. XXV:17), Levi (Ex. VI:16),
and Amram (Ex. VI:20) lived.

**QBLH**   Cabala   Tradition.
**AWPN** (N=50)   Ophan   Wheel;
one of the Ophanim.

# 139 p

The children of the porters who
returned from exile (Ezra II:42).

**HDQL**   Hiddikel   Tigris; a river of
Eden, associated with Air.

# 140

**MQ**   Maq   Rottenness.
**PS**   Pas   Extremity.
**MLKYM** (M=40)   Melekim
Kings; Angelic Choir associated
with Tiphareth and with the
Sphere of the Sun; book of the
Bible.
**OLM** (M=40)   Alem   4th name of
Shem Hamphorash, associated
with 4th quinance of Leo.
**NTz** (Tz=90)   Netz   Flower;
hawk.
**SP** (P=80)   Saph   Threshold,
entrance.

**TzN** (N=50)   Tzen   Thorn.

# 141

**PKYAL**   Pakiel   Angel of Cancer.
**KWQYH**   Keveqiah   Angel of 5th
quinance of Capricorn; angel by
day of the 4 of Pentacles.
**OWLM** (M=40)   Olam   World.

# 142

**ASMWDAL**   Asmodel   Archangel
of Taurus.
**BLOM** (M=40)   Balaam   Balaam.
**BOLM** (M=40)   Balam   Goetic
demon by night of 3rd decanate
of Leo.

# 143

**ABTzN** (N=50)   Ibtzan   Ibzan,
the ninth judge of Israel.

# 144  12²

**QDM** (M=40)   Qedem   Before;
the east; ancient things.

# 145

**NMMYH**  Nemamiah  Angel of
3rd quinance of Taurus; angel by
day of the 6 of Pentacles.
**HQM** (M=40)  Haqem  16th
name of Shem Hamphorash, associated with 4th quinance of Libra.

# 148

**NTzCh**  Netzach  Victory; the
7th Sephira.
**ANSWAL**  Ansuel  Angel of 11th
astrological house.
**BNY ALHYM** (M=40)  Beni
Elohim  Sons of the Gods;
Angelic Choir associated with Hod
and with the Sphere of Mercury.
**MAZNYM** (M=40)  Moznaim
Scales; Libra.
**AMAYMWN** (N=50)  Amaimon
Demon King of Earth and the
North; according to the Goetia,
Demon King of the East.

# 149 p

**QMT**  Qamat  To make wrinkled.

# 150

**QN** (N=50)  Qen  Nest.
**OMM** (M=40)  Amem  52nd
name of Shem Hamphorash, associated with 4th quinance of Aries.
Amam  To
darken, dim.

# 151 p

**MALP** (P=80)  Malphas  Goetic
demon by night of 3rd decanate
of Aries.

# 152

**BNYMN** (N=50)  Benjamin  A
tribe of Israel, associated with
Sagittarius.

# 153

Mystic number of 17th Path
(between Binah and Tiphareth;
Zayin; Gemini).
The number of fishes caught by the
disciples when Jesus appeared to
them after the Resurrection
(John XXI:11).

**ChDQYAL**  Chedeqiel  Angel of
Libra.
**GOP** (P=80)  Gäap  Goetic
demon by day of 3rd decanate
of Aquarius.

# 155

**YSYSYH** Yasyasyah Angel of 2nd decanate of Capricorn.

**OLMYH** Elemiah Angel of 4th quinance of Leo; angel by night of the 6 of Wands.

**SNHM** (M=40) Sanahem Lord of Triplicity by Day for Leo.

# 156

The number of children of Magbish who returned from exile (Ezra II:30).

**POW** Pau A city of Edom; city of King Hadar.

**YChZQAL** Yechezqel Ezekiel.

**YSWP** (P=80) Yoseph Joseph.

**KMWTz** (Tz=90) Kamotz Angel of 1st decanate of Scorpio.

**TzYWN** (N=50) Zion Zion.

**BABALON** (N=50) Babalon An important figure in Aleister Crowley's mysticism.

# 157 P

**QNZ** Kenaz A Duke of Edom, associated with Netzach.

**ONWAL** Anevel Angel of 3rd quinance of Gemini; angel by day of the 9 of Swords.

**MZYQ** Maziq Demon; injurer.

# 160

**HQMYH** Haqmiah Angel of 4th quinance of Libra; angel by night of the 3 of Swords.

**TzLYL** Tzelil Ring; sound, tone.

**NOM** (M=40) Naam To be lovely, pleasant.

**KSP** (P=80) Kesep Silver, the metal of the Moon.

**OTz** (Tz=90) Etz Tree.

**QYN** (N=50) Qayin Cain.

# 162

**TzBO** Tzeva Color.

**SWSWL** Sosul Angel of 8th astrological house.

**GLASLBWL** Glasya-Labolas Goetic demon by day of 1st decanate of Sagittarius.

# 165

**NOMH** Naamah A queen of demons; arch-demon corresponding to Malkuth.

**OMMYH** Amamiah Angel of 4th quinance of Aries; angel by night of the 3 of Wands.

**QLLH** Qelalah Curse.

# 166

**NPWL** Naphula   Goetic demon by night of 3rd decanate of Scorpio.

**OLWYN** (N=50)   Elyon   The Most High; a name of God and title of Kether.

**MOWN** (N=50)   Maon Residence; the 5th Heaven, corresponding to Geburah.

# 167 P

**ASYMWN** (N=50)   Asimon   Old coin; telephone token; some sort of infernal being associated with the northwest.

# 168

**ChPP** (P=80)   Chapap   To cover, protect.

# 170

**SPL**   Sephel   Cup.
**MQL**   Maqqel   Wand.
**KSYLYM** (M=40)   Kesilim Orion; Fools.
**NYSN** (N=50)   Nisan   The 7th Hebrew month.

# 171

Mystic number of 18th Path (between Binah and Geburah; Cheth; Cancer).

**PLAYN** (N=50)   Polayan   Lord of Triplicity by Night for Aquarius.

# 173 P

**ANKY YHWH ALHYK** (K=20) Anoki Yahweh Eloheka   I am the Lord thy God.

# 175

Magic sum of the magic square of Venus.
The number of years Abraham lived (Gen. XXV:7).

**QDMAL**   Kedemel   The Spirit of Venus.

# 176

**OMWS**   Amos   Amos.

# 177

**GN ODN** (both N's=50)   Gan Eden Garden of Eden.

# 180

The number of years Isaac lived (Gen. XXXV:28).

# 182

**AL QNA**  El Qanna  A jealous god (Ex. XX:5).
**YOQB**  Yaaqob  Jacob.
**MLAK HALHYM** (K=20; M=40) Malak ha-Elohim  Angel of God.

# 186

**QWP** (P=80)  Qoph  Back of head; 19th letter of Hebrew alphabet.

# 187

**AWPNYM** (M=40)  Ophanim Wheels; Angelic Choir associated with Chokmah and with the Sphere of the Zodiac.
**PAYMWN** (N=50)  Paimon Demon King of Fire; Goetic demon by day of 3rd decanate of Gemini.

# 190

Mystic number of 19th Path

(between Chesed and Geburah; Teth; Leo).

**MNQ**  Menaq  66th name of Shem Hamphorash, associated with 6th quinance of Gemini.
**QMTYAL**  Qemetiel  The Crowd of Gods; Qlippoth of Ain.
**TzLO**  Tzela  Rib.
**PNYN** (N=50)  Panin  Pearl; a title of Malkuth.
**PYNN** (N=50)  Pinon  A Duke of Edom, associated with Tiphareth.
**KNON** (N=50)  Kenaan  Canaan.
**QTz** (Tz=90)  Qetz  End.

# 194

**TzDQ**  Tzedek  Jupiter; righteousness.

# 196  $14^2$

**TzWQ**  Tzoq  Narrowness; oppression.
**QWTz** (Tz=90)  Qotz  Thorn.

# 200

**R**  Resh  20th letter of Hebrew alphabet.
**OTzM** (M=40)  Etzem  Bone, substance, essence, body.
**QYTz** (Tz=90)  Qayitz  Summer.

# 202

**SAYTzYAL** Saitziel Angel of Scorpio.
**BR** Bar Corn, grain; son; chosen, pure, empty.
Bor Purity, innocence.
**RB** Rab Many, much; great, mighty.
Rob Multitude, abundance.

# 203

**ABR** Abar Lead, the metal of Saturn.
**BRA** Bara Created.
**GR** Gar Dwelling.
**BAR** Beer Well; a title of Malkuth.

# 204

**DR** Dar Pearl.

# 205

**HR** Har Mountain.
**ADR** Adar The 6th Hebrew month.
**AGAR** Agares Goetic demon by day of 2nd decanate of Aries.

# 206

**RAH** Raah To see, observe, perceive, consider; 69th name of Shem Hamphorash, associated with 3rd quinance of Cancer.
**DBR** Davar Word, thing.
Dever Murrain; the 5th of the 10 plagues of Egypt.
**BRD** Barad Hail; the 7th of the 10 plagues of Egypt.

# 207

**AWR** Or Light.
Ur A city of Mesopotamia, birthplace of Abram.
**ZR** Zar Strange, foreign.
Zer Border.
**AYN-SWP** (P=80) Ain-Soph Infinity.
**MZYQYM** (M=40) Meziqim Demons; injurers.

# 208

**YTzChQ** Itzchaq Isaac.
**HGR** Hagar Sarai's maid; mother of Ishmael.
**ChR** Chor Hole.
**ARBH** Arbeh Locusts; the 8th of the 10 plagues of Egypt.

## 209

**HDR**   Hadar   A King of Edom, associated with Malkuth.
**BWAR**   Buer   Goetic demon by day of 1st decanate of Cancer.

## 210

Mystic number of 20th Path (between Chesed and Tiphareth; Yod; Virgo).

**ChRB**   Cherev   Sword.
**RY**   Ri   Rushing water.
**BOL ChNN** (N=50)   Baal-Hanan A King of Edom, associated with Yesod; arch-demon corresponding to Netzach (Waite).
**MSNYN** (N=50)   Misnin   Angel of 1st decanate of Capricorn.
**NPLYM** (M=40)   Nephilim "Giants" (Gen. VI:4).
**QYNN** (N=50)   Cainan   Kenan.

## 211 ף

**ARY**   Ari   Lion.
**AYR**   Iyar   The 8th Hebrew month.
**WADR**   Veadar   The Hebrew intercalary month.

## 212

**ZHR**   Zohar   Splendor; the Sepher ha-Zohar.
**HAWR**   Haures   Goetic demon by night of 1st decanate of Capricorn.

## 213

**ABYR**   Abir   The Almighty.
**HRCh**   Harach   59th name of Shem Hamphorash, associated with 5th quinance of Taurus.

## 214

The number of bones in the human body.

**RWCh**   Ruach   Breath, wind, spirit; middle part of the tripartite soul; the element Air.
**ZZR**   Zazer   Angel of 1st decanate of Aries.
**YRD**   Yared   Jared.

## 215

**ChRBH**   Charabhah   Parched Land; one of the seven earths, corresponding to Geburah.
**ChBRH**   Chevrah   Society, organization.
**ZRCh**   Zerah   Father of Jobab, a

King of Edom.

    Zarach    To shine.

    Zerach    Sunrise.

**HRY**   Hari   Aspect, characteristic; 15th name of Shem Hamphorash, associated with 3rd quinance of Libra.

# 216 6³

**GBWRH**   Geburah   Severity; the 5th Sephira.

**DBYR**   Devir   Sanctuary of the Temple.

**ARYH**   Ari   Lion; Leo.

**AWRAWB**   Orobas   Goetic demon by night of 1st decanate of Libra.

**ChBQWQ**   Chabaqquq Habakkuk.

# 217

**SHQNB**   Sahaqnab   Lord of Triplicity by Night for Scorpio.

**DBWRH**   Deborah   The fourth judge of Israel.

# 218

**BRYAH**   Briah   Creation; the Archangelic or Creative World.

# 220

**RYY**   Riyi   29th name of Shem Hamphorash, associated with 5th quinance of Sagittarius.

**ONQ**   Anak   A giant.

**SPLYM** (M=40)   Sephalim   Cups.

**RK** (K=20)   Rok   Softness.

# 221

**MNQAL**   Menqel   Angel of the 6th quinance of Gemini; angel by night of the 10 of Swords.

**YAYR**   Yair   Jair, the seventh judge of Israel.

**ARK** (K=20)   Erech   Uruk; a city of ancient Mesopotamia.

# 222

**BKR**   Beker   Young male camel.

**KBR**   Kavar   To make heavy; to make many, multiply.

    Kevar   Long; extent; long ago, already.

    Khebar   A river in Mesopotamia.

**RKB**   Rakav   To ride, drive; horseman, driver.

    Rekev   Vehicle.

**BRK** (K=20)   Barak   To kneel, bless.

    Berek   Knee, lap.

**RBK** (K=20)   Ravak   To be mixed, mingled.

# 223 פ

The number of children of Hashum
who returned from exile (Ezra
II:19).
The number of men of Bethel and Ai
who returned from exile (Ezra
II:28).

# 230

**RAYDYH**  Rayadyah  Angel of
2nd decanate of Virgo.
**YGLPZQ**  Yaglepzeq  The 31st
through 36th letters of the
42-letter name of God, associated
with Hod.

# 224

**SNDLOY**  Sandali  Lord of
Triplicity by Day for Capricorn.
**YRChW**  Yericho  Jericho.

# 231

Mystic number of 21st Path
(between Chesed and Netzach;
Kaph; Jupiter).
The number of Gates of Wisdom,
according to the Sepher Yetzirah;
that is, the number of possible
combinations of two Hebrew
letters, disregarding order.

# 226

**TzPWN** (N=50)  Tzaphon  North.

# 227 פ

**BRKH**  Berakah  Blessing.

# 232

**AMNYTzYAL**  Amnitziel
Archangel of Pisces.
**ARAL**  Aral  Angel of Fire.
**YHY AWR**  Yehi Or  Let there
be light.

# 228

**KRWB**  Kerub  Ruler of Earth;
one of the Kerubim.
**ALHY YOQB**  Elohi Yaaqob
The God of Jacob.
**BRWK** (K=20)  Baruk  Blessed.

# 233 פ

**OTz HChYYM** (Tz=90; M=40)  Etz
ha-Chayim  Tree of Life.

# 234

**DKAWRAB** Decarabia Goetic demon by night of 3rd decanate of Aquarius.

# 235

235 lunar months=19 solar years= 1 "year of Meton."

**TzDQYAL** Tzadqiel Archangel associated with Chesed and with Jupiter.
**TzPNYH** Tzephanyah Zephaniah.

# 236

**SPOTAWY** Sapatawi Lord of Triplicity by Night for Aries.
**SNSNWY** Sansenoy One of the three angels invoked against Lilith.
**TzPWNY** Tzaphoni The Northern One; Lilith.

# 237

**SWYOSAL** Soyasel Angel of 9th astrological house.
**RAHAL** Rahael Angel of 3rd quinance of Cancer; angel by day of the 3 of Cups.

# 238

**RChL** Rachel Wife of Jacob; mother of Joseph and Benjamin.

# 239 p

**BRZL** Barzel Iron, the metal of Mars.
**YKSGNWTz** (Tz=90) Yakasaganotz Angel of 3rd decanate of Taurus.

# 240

**MR** Mar Drop; bitter, sad; fierce, violent, wild; bitterness, sadness.
Mor Myrrh.
**SSPM** (M=40) Saspam Angel of 1st decanate of Aquarius.
**RM** (M=40) Ram Ram (Job XXXII:2).
**KNONYM** (M=40) Kanannim Canaanites.

# 241 p

**SMQYAL** Sameqiel Angel of Capricorn.

# 242

**ARYAL** Ariel Ruler of Air.

ZKRYH   Zekaryah   Zechariah.          the 3 of Swords.

# 243 3⁵

**MARB**   Marbas   Goetic demon
by day of 2nd decanate of Taurus.
**ABRM** (M=40)   Abram   Abram.

# 244

**HRChAL**   Herachiel   Angel of
5th quinance of Taurus; angel by
day of the 7 of Pentacles.

# 245

The number of mules brought out of
exile (Ezra II:66).

**ADM QDMWN** (M=40; N=50)
Adam Qadmon   The archetypal
man.

# 246

**GBRYAL**   Gabriel   Archangel
associated with Yesod, with the
Moon, with the West, and with
Water.
**RAYDAL**   Raydel   Lord of
Triplicity by Day for Taurus.
**HRYAL**   Hariel   Angel of 3rd
quinance of Libra; angel by day of

# 247

**ALWYR**   Aloyar   Lord of
Triplicity by Night for Capricorn.
**RAWM** (M=40)   Raüm   Goetic
demon by night of 1st decanate of
Taurus.

# 248

**RZYAL**   Raziel   Archangel
associated with Chokmah and
with the Sphere of the Zodiac.
**AWRYAL**   Uriel   Archangel
associated with North and Earth.
**BMDBR**   Bamidbar   In the
Wilderness; Hebrew title of the
book of Numbers.
**ABRHM** (M=40)   Abraham
Abraham.
**RChM** (M=40)   Racham   Vulture.

# 249

**ARZYAL**   Araziel   Angel of
Taurus.
**GMWR**   Gamori   Goetic demon
by night of 2nd decanate of Libra.

# 250

**NR** Ner Lamp; prosperity; instruction.
**DRWM** (M=40) Darom South.
**RN** (N=50) Ron Shout, rejoicing.

# 251 p

**RYYAL** Reyayel Angel of 5th quinance of Sagittarius; angel by day of the 10 of Wands.
**ARN** (N=50) Aron Ark (of the covenant).

# 252

**NBR** Naberius Goetic demon by day of 3rd decanate of Scorpio.

# 253

Mystic number of 22nd Path (between Geburah and Tiphareth; Lamed; Libra).

**MTRD** Matred Mother of Mehetabel, wife of Hadar, a King of Edom.

# 254

**ZWRYAL** Zuriel Archangel of Libra.
**GRWDYAL** Gerodiel Angel of 3rd decanate of Aquarius.
**ALHY YTzChQ** Elohi Itzchaq The God of Isaac.

# 255

**MZRCh** Mizrach East.
**ANDR** Andras Goetic demon by night of 3rd decanate of Sagittarius.
**NHR** Naher River.
**HRN** (N=50) Haran Haran.

# 256 $16^2$

**AHRN** (N=50) Aaron Brother of Moses.
**DBRYM** (M=40) Devarim Words; Hebrew title of Deuteronomy.

# 257 p

**AWRYM** (M=40) Urim Urim.
**ChRTM** (M=40) Chartom Magician.

## 259

**RAWBN** (N=50)   Reuben   A tribe of Israel, associated with Aquarius.

## 260

Magic sum of the magic square of Mercury.

**TYRYAL**   Tiriel   The Intelligence of Mercury.
**SR**   Sar   Ill-humored.

## 261

**LRAYK** (K=20)   Leraje   Goetic demon by day of 2nd decanate of Leo.

## 263 p

**BRKYAL**   Barkiel   Archangel of Scorpio.
**GMTRYA**   Gematria   Hebrew numerology.
**ABDRWN** (N=50)   Abdaron Angel of 2nd decanate of Aquarius.
**AWRWN** (N=50)   Avron   Angel of 2nd decanate of Pisces.

## 264

**NChWR**   Nahor   Nahor.
**YRDN** (N=50)   Yordan   Jordan.

## 265

**YRMYH**   Yirmyah   Jeremiah.

## 267

**MRKBH**   Merkabah   Chariot.
**WRKYAL**   Verkiel   Archangel of Leo.

## 269 p

**SMNGLWP** (P=80)   Semangeloph One of the three angels invoked against Lilith.

## 270

**RO**   Ra   Evil.
         Rea   Friend.
**OR**   Ar   Enemy.

## 271 p

**WHRYN** (N=50)   Vehrin   Angel of 2nd decanate of Sagittarius.

# 272

**RYNWW** Ronové Goetic demon by day of 3rd decanate of Sagittarius.
**ORB** Arab To exchange, pawn; to grow dark; poplar, willow; Arabia.
    Areb Sweet, pleasant.
    Ereb Evening.
    Oreb Raven, crow.
**OBR** Eber Eber.

# 275

**ROH** Raah Evil.
**RHO** Reha 39th name of Shem Hamphorash, associated with 3rd quinance of Aquarius.

# 276

Mystic number of 23rd Path (between Geburah and Hod; Mem; Water).

**KRWKL** Crocell Goetic demon by night of 1st decanate of Leo.
**ROW** Reu Reu.
**AChWDRAWN** (N=50) Achodraon Lord of Triplicity by Night for Libra.
**ARYTWN** (N=50) Ariton Demon King of Water and the West.

# 277 p

**SHYBR** Sahiber Angel of 3rd decanate of Leo.
**KYMAWR** Kimaris Goetic demon by night of 3rd decanate of Capricorn.

# 278

**BOWR** Beor Father of Bela, a King of Edom.
**ARBOH** Arbaah Four.
**ORWB** Arov Wild Beasts; the 4th of the 10 plagues of Egypt.
**OZRA** Ezra Ezra.
**KRWBYM** (M=40) Kerubim Angelic Choir associated with Yesod and with the Sphere of the Moon.

# 280

**ORY** Eri 46th name of Shem Hamphorash, associated with 4th quinance of Pisces.
**PR** Par Bull; victim; offering.
**SNDLPWN** (N=50) Sandalphon Archangel associated with Malkuth.
**DGDGYRWN** (N=50) Dagdagiron The Snakey Ones; Qlippoth of Capricorn.

# 282

**OBRY**  Ibri  Hebrew.
**BOYR**  Beir  Beast, cattle.
**ARALYM** (M=40)  Aralim
Angelic Choir associated with
Binah and with the Sphere of
Saturn.

# 284

**AMBRYAL**  Ambriel  Archangel
of Gemini.
**OYRD**  Irad  Irad.

# 286

**MWRM** (M=40)  Murmus  Goetic
demon by night of 3rd decanate
of Virgo.

# 287

**MWRYAL**  Muriel  Archangel of
Cancer.
**WPAR**  Vepar  Goetic demon by
night of 3rd decanate of Taurus.
**YWBB BN ZRCh** (N=50)  Jobab
ben Zerah  Jobab, son of Zerah;
a King of Edom, associated with
Chesed.

# 288

**ZPAR**  Zepar  Goetic demon by
day of 1st decanate of Virgo.
**ChRP** (P=80)  Choreph  Winter.

# 290

**TzR**  Tzar  Persecutor, enemy;
distress, danger; stone.
**MRYM** (M=40)  Miriam  Sister of
Moses; Mary.
**RTz** (Tz=90)  Ratz  Piece.
**AMRYM** (M=40)  Emorim
Amorites.

# 291

**TzKMQYAL**  Tzakmiqiel  Angel
of Aquarius.
**ARTz** (Tz=90)  Eretz  Earth; one
of the four elements; one of the
seven earths, corresponding to the
three Supernal Sephiroth.

# 294

**NMRD**  Nimrod  Nimrod.
**ALHY ABRHM** (M=40)  Elohi
Abraham  The God of Abraham.

# 295

**MNRH**  Menorah   Candlestick.

# 297

**KWRSYA**  Korsia   Throne; a title of Binah.
**BTzRH**  Bozrah   A city of Edom; city of King Jobab.
**ALHYM GBWR** (M=40)   Elohim Gibor   Almighty God; divine name associated with Geburah.

# 298

**OKBWR**  Achbor   Father of Baal-Hanan, a King of Edom.
**BYPRW**  Bifrons   Goetic demon by night of 1st decanate of Cancer.

# 299

**RHDTz** (Tz=90)   Rahadetz Angel of 2nd decanate of Cancer.

# 300

Mystic number of 24th Path (between Tiphareth and Netzach; Nun; Scorpio).

**Sh**  Shin   21st letter of Hebrew alphabet.
**QR**  Qar   Cold; quiet.
**RQ**  Raq   Thin; only.
  Roq   Saliva.
**MTzPTz** (Tz=90)   Matz-Patz   A name of God by Temurah.
**RWCh ALHYM** (M=40)   Ruach Elohim   The Spirit of God.

# 301

**ASh**  Esh   Fire.
**ShA**  Sho   Destruction.

# 302

**SRAYAL**  Sarayel   Angel of Gemini.
**ARQA**  Arqa   Earth; one of the seven earths, corresponding to Hod.
**BQR**  Boqer   Morning.

# 303

**ShBA**  Sheba   Sheba.

# 304

**KAMBRYAL**  Kambriel   Archangel of Aquarius.
**ShD**  Shad   Teat.
  Shed   Demon; idol.

Shod    Violence, ruin.

# 305

**ORLH**    Arlah    Foreskin.
**ShH**    Seh    Sheep, goat.
**HQMMNO**    Haqamamna    The
25th through 30th letters of the
42-letter name of God, associated
with Netzach.

# 306

**AShH**    Ishah    Woman.
**ShAH**    Shaah    To lay waste,
devastate; 28th name of Shem
Hamphorash, associated with 4th
quinance of Sagittarius.
    Shah    Calamity,
devastation, ruin.
**RHOAL**    Rehael    Angel of 3rd
quinance of Aquarius; angel by
day of the 6 of Swords.
**PWRK** (K=20)    Furcas    Goetic
demon by night of 2nd decanate
of Leo.

# 307 p

**RBQH**    Ribeqah    Rebekah.
**ROWAL**    Reuel    Moses' father-in-
law.
**WRYATz** (Tz=90)    Oriax    Goetic
demon by night of 2nd decanate
of Scorpio.

# 308

**ShCh**    Seach    Thought,
meditation.
    Shach    Depressed.

# 309

**ShT**    Set    Transgression.

# 310

**YSh**    Yesh    Existence; there
is/are.
**ShY**    Shai    Gift, tribute.

# 311 p

**AYSh**    Ish    Man; a title of
Tiphareth.
**RPAL**    Raphael    1. Archangel
associated with Tiphareth, with
the Sun, with the East, and with
Air; 2. Angel ruling Mercury and
Wednesday.
**TzPQYAL**    Tzaphqiel    Archangel
associated with Binah and Saturn.
**ORYAL**    Ariel    Angel of 4th
quinance of Pisces; angel by night
of the 9 of Cups.
**ShBT**    Shevet    The 5th Hebrew
month.

# 312

**MORB**   Maarab   West.
**ChDSh**   Chodesh   Month.
**WShW**   Voso   Goetic demon by night of 3rd decanate of Libra.

# 313 p

**HChSh**   Hachash   51st name of Shem Hamphorash, associated with 3rd quinance of Aries.
**ANNAWRH**   Ananaurah   Angel of 1st decanate of Virgo.

# 314

**ShDY**   Shaddai   The Almighty.
**MTTRWN** (N=50)   Metatron Archangel associated with Kether.

# 315

**YTzYRH**   Yetzirah   Formation; the Angelic or Formative World.
**OMRH**   Amorah   Gomorah.
**MNChRAY**   Minacharai   Angel of 2nd decanate of Taurus.

# 316

**WShAGW**   Vassago   Goetic demon by day of 3rd decanate of Aries.

# 317 p

**YBShH**   Yabbashah   Dry Land; one of the seven earths, corresponding to Netzach.
**WALPR**   Valefor   Goetic demon by day of 3rd decanate of Taurus.
**WYQRA**   Wayiqra   And he called; Hebrew title of Leviticus.

# 319

**SRTN** (N=50)   Sarton   Crab; Cancer.

# 320

The number of children of Harim who returned from exile (Ezra II:32).

**SRYTYAL**   Saritiel   Angel of Sagittarius.
**OYRM** (M=40)   Eram   A Duke of Edom, associated with Malkuth.
**ShK** (K=20)   Sek   Thorn; enclosure.

# 321

**LSLRA**   Laslara   Lord of Triplicity by Day for Virgo.
**ALYNKYR**   Alinkir   Angel of 3rd decanate of Cancer.
**ShAHYH**   Sahiah   Angel of 4th

quinance of Sagittarius; angel by
night of the 9 of Wands.
**ADYMYRWN** (N=50)  Adimiron
The Bloody Ones; Qlippoth of
Taurus.
**DBRY HYMYM** (M=40)  Debere
ha-yamim  Events of the Days;
Hebrew title of Chronicles.

# 322
**OBRYM** (M=40)  Ibrim
Hebrews.
**LBRMYM** (M=40)  Lebarmim
Lord of Triplicity by Night for
Sagittarius.

# 323
The number of children of Bezai who
returned from exile (Ezra II:17).

**STNDR**  Satander  Angel of 3rd
decanate of Aries.
**BHYMYRWN** (N=50)  Bahimiron
The Bestial Ones; Qlippoth of
Aquarius.

# 325
Sum of all the numbers (1 to 25) of
the magic square of Mars.
Mystic number of 25th Path
(between Tiphareth and Yesod;
Samekh; Sagittarius).

**GRAPYAL**  Graphiel  The
Intelligence of Mars.
**BRTzBAL**  Bartzabel  The Spirit
of Mars.
**NYNDWHR**  Nundohar  Angel of
2nd decanate of Scorpio.

# 326
**KWSh**  Kush  Cush.

# 327
**BWTYSh**  Botis  Goetic demon
by day of 2nd decanate of Virgo.

# 328
**HChShYH**  Hechashiah  Angel of
3rd quinance of Aries; angel by
day of the 3 of Wands.
**ChShK** (K=20)  Choshek
Darkness; the 9th of the 10
plagues of Egypt.

# 329
**TRSNY**  Tarasni  Angel of 1st
decanate of Libra.

# 330

**MTzR** Metzar Distress; isthmus. Metzer Boundary; 60th name of Shem Hamphorash, associated with 6th quinance of Taurus.

**ShL** Shal Transgression, fault, crime.

# 332

**MBTzR** Mibzar A Duke of Edom, associated (with Magdiel) with Yesod.

**ANDRWMAL** Andromalius Goetic demon by night of 3rd decanate of Pisces.

**APRAYM** (M=40) Ephraim A tribe of Israel, associated with Taurus.

**MARATz** (Tz=90) Marax Goetic demon by day of 3rd decanate of Libra.

# 333

**AYQ BKR** Aiq Bekar The cabala of the nine chambers.

**GLSh** Galash To lie down.

**ShGL** Shagal To be sexually excited; to lie with.
Shegal Royal paramour.

**ShLG** Shaleg To snow.
Sheleg Snow.

# 335

**HR SYNY** Har Sinai Mount Sinai.

# 337 p

**ShAWL** Sheol Depth of the Earth; the 7th and lowest hell, corresponding to the three Supernal Sephiroth.
Saul A King of Edom, associated with Hod; Saul of the New Testament.

**PWRLAK** (K=20) Phorlakh Angel of Earth.

**PRZYM** (M=40) Perizzim Perizzites.

# 338

**ShLCh** Shelah Salah.

# 340

**YSGDYBRWDYAL**
Yasgedibarodiel Angel of 3rd decanate of Capricorn.

**SPR** Sepher Book.

**ShM** (M=40) Sham There, then.
Shem Sign; name; son of Noah.

# 341

Sum of the three mother letters (A, M, and Sh).

# 342

**ShBYL** Shevil Path.
**PWKLWR** Focalor Goetic demon by night of 2nd decanate of Taurus.
**KWRSWN** (N=50) Korson Demon King of the West (Goetia).

# 345

The number of children of Jericho who returned from exile (Ezra II:34).

**AL ShDY** El Shaddai God Almighty.
**MShH** Mosheh Moses.
**MHSh** Mahash 5th name of Shem Hamphorash, associated with 5th quinance of Leo.
**HShM** (M=40) Husham A King of Edom, associated with Geburah.
Ha-Shem The Name; Tetragrammaton.

# 346

**RTzWN** (N=50) Ratzon Delight, favor.

# 350

**ALYGWSh** Eligos Goetic demon by day of 3rd decanate of Leo.
**ShN** (N=50) Shen Tooth.

# 351

Mystic number of 26th Path (between Tiphareth and Hod; Ayin; Capricorn).

**LWSNHR** Losanahar Angel of 1st decanate of Leo.
**AShYM** (M=40) Eshim Flames; Angelic Choir associated with Malkuth.

# 353 p

**ChMShH** Chamishah Five.

# 354

**ShDYM** (M=40) Shedim Demons.

# 355

**PROH** Pharaoh Pharaoh.
**SPYRH** Sephira Sphere; number; emanation.
**ShNH** Shanah Year.
Senah Sleep.

# 356

**AShMDAY**   Asmodai   (A variant spelling.)

# 357

**ANWSh**   Enosh   Enos; son of Seth; father of Kenan.

**KGDYKSh**   Kegadikesh   The 13th through 18th letters of the 42-letter name of God, associated with Geburah.

# 358

**NChSh**   Nachash   Snake, serpent.
**MShYCh**   Mashiach   Messiah.
**ChShN** (N=50)   Chassan   Angel of Air.

Choshen   Breastplate of the High Priest.

# 359 p

**ShTN** (N=50)   Satan   Adversary, accuser; arch-demon corresponding (with Moloch) to Kether.
**STRYP** (P=80)   Satrip   Angel of 3rd decanate of Pisces.

# 360

**OPYR**   Ophir   Earth.
**MHShYH**   Mahashiah   Angel of 5th quinance of Leo; angel by day of the 7 of Wands.

**ShYN** (N=50)   Shin   Tooth; 21st letter of Hebrew alphabet.

# 361   $19^2$

The number of points on a Go board.

**MTzRAL**   Mitzrael   Angel of 6th quinance of Taurus; angel by night of the 7 of Pentacles.
**ADNY HARTz** (Tz=90)   Adonai ha-Eretz   Lord of the Earth; divine name associated with Malkuth, with Earth, and with the North.

# 362

**ARYK APYM** (K=20; M=40)   Arik Apim   Long of Face; a title of Kether.

# 363

**ShDY AL ChY**   Shaddai El Chai   Almighty Living God; divine name associated with Yesod, with Air, and with the East.

# 364

**AWR MWPLA**   Or Mopla   The Hidden Light; a title of Kether.
**OWLM HBRYAH** (M=40)   Olam ha-Briah   The World of Creation.
**ChShWN** (N=50)   Cheshvan   The 2nd Hebrew month.

# 365

The number of years Enoch lived (Gen. V:23).

**NShYH**  Neshiah  Oblivion; one of the seven earths, corresponding to Tiphareth.

# 366

**ANDRALP** (P=80)  Andrealphus Goetic demon by night of 2nd decanate of Capricorn.

# 368

**ShChYN** (N=50)  Shechin  Boils; the 6th of the 10 plagues of Egypt.

# 369

Magic sum of the magic square of the Moon.

**ChShMWDAY**  Chashmodai  The Spirit of the Moon.
**ShHDNY**  Shehadani  Angel of 2nd decanate of Gemini.

# 370

**ShLM** (M=40)  Shalom  Peace.

# 372

The number of children of

Shephatiah who returned from exile (Ezra II:4).

**OQRB**  Akrab  Scorpion; Scorpio.
**YHWH ShMW**  Yahweh Shemo Yahweh is His Name.

# 373 ₽

**GOSh**  Gash  Quaking.
**ALHY HOBRYM** (M=40)  Elohi ha-Ibrim  God of the Hebrews.

# 375

**ShLMH**  Shelomoh  Solomon.
**TzPRH**  Tzipporah  Zipporah, wife of Moses.
**ShMLH**  Samlah  A King of Edom, associated with Netzach.
**ShOH**  Shaah  Hour.

# 376

**OShW**  Esau  Esau.
**ShLWM** (M=40)  Shalom  Peace.

# 377

**ShBOH**  Shivah  Seven.
**ShMWAL**  Shemuel  Samuel.

# 378

Mystic number of 27th Path (between Netzach and Hod; Pe; Mars).

**ShBWO**  Shavua  Week.

**ShBNWK** (K=20)  Sabnock
Goetic demon by night of 1st
decanate of Gemini.

# 380

**RQYO**  Raqia  Firmament; the
2nd Heaven, corresponding to
Hod.

**OYSh**  Ayish  Ursa Major.

**PSh**  Pash  Folly.

**MShLY**  Mishle  Proverbs.

**MTzRYM** (M=40)  Mitzraim
Egypt.

# 381

**HWShO**  Hoshea  Hosea.

# 385

**OShYH**  Assiah  Action; the
Material World.

**ShKYNH**  Shekinah  Divine
Presence; a title of Malkuth.

# 387

**ShBYL HChLB**  Shevil ha-Chalav
Milky Way.

# 389 p

**ShPT**  Shephet  Judgment.

# 390

**ShMYM** (M=40)  Shamaim
Heaven, firmament, sky.

**ShTz** (Tz=90)  Shax  Goetic
demon by night of 2nd decanate
of Gemini.

# 391

**YHWShO**  Yehoshua  Joshua;
Jesus.

# 392

The number of Nethinims and
children of Solomon's servants
who returned from exile (Ezra
II:43-58).

**ShBYLYM** (M=40)  Shevilim
Paths.

# 395

**MNShH**  Manasseh  A tribe of
Israel, associated with Gemini.

**NShMH**  Neshamah  Highest part
of the soul.

**ShMNH**  Shemonah  Eight.

**YShOYH**  Yeshayah  Isaiah.

# 396

**YPWSh**  Ipos  Goetic demon by
day of 1st decanate of Scorpio.

# 397 p

**AWR PNYMY**   Or Penimi   The Internal Light; a title of Kether.

# 398

**STROTN** (N=50)   Sateraton Lord of Triplicity by Day for Aries.
**ChMShYM** (M=40)   Chamisham Fifty.

# 400 20²

**Th**   Taw   22nd letter of Hebrew alphabet.
**OShL**   Ashel   47th name of Shem Hamphorash, associated with 5th quinance of Pisces.
**QSh**   Qash   Straw, chaff.
**ShQ**   Saq   Sack.
**NShYM** (M=40)   Nashim Women, wives.
**ShNYM** (M=40)   Shenaim   Two.

# 401 p

**ATh**   Eth   Word used to indicate direct object; in Golden Dawn usage, essence or Spirit.
**ARR**   Arar   To curse.
**ThA**   Ta   Room.

# 402

**BTh**   Bath   Daughter.

# 403

**GTh**   Gath   Wine press.

# 404

**QDSh**   Qadesh   Holiness.
**DTh**   Dath   Royal command, law.

# 405

**SHRNTz** (Tz=90)   Saharnatz Angel of 2nd decanate of Libra.

# 406

Mystic number of 28th Path (between Netzach and Yesod; Sadhe; Aquarius or Aries).

**ThW**   Taw   Tau cross; 22nd letter of Hebrew alphabet.

# 407

**ThBH**   Tebah   Ark (Noah's).

**ARWR**  Arur  Cursed.

# 408

**ChTh**  Chath  Broken; terrified.

# 409 p

**AChTh**  Achath  One (feminine).

# 410

**QDWSh**  Qadosh  Holy.
**ShQY**  Sheqi  The penultimate three letters of the 42-letter name of God, associated with Yesod.
**MShKN** (N=50)  Mishkan Tabernacle.

# 411

**ThHW**  Tohu  Desolation; "without form."
**TBTh**  Tevet  The 4th Hebrew month.
**HYKL RTzWN** (N=50)  Hekel Ratzon  Palace of Delight; Heavenly Mansion corresponding to Tiphareth.

# 412

**BYTh**  Beth  House; 2nd letter of Hebrew alphabet.

# 414

**AYN-SWP AWR** (N=50; P=80)  Ain-Soph Or  The Limitless Light.

# 415

**AChWTh**  Achoth  Sister.
**OShLYH**  Asaliah  Angel of 5th quinance of Pisces; angel by day of the 10 of Cups.
**ZAWYR ANPYN** (N=50)  Zauir Anpin  The Lesser Countenance; a title of Tiphareth.

# 416

**QPTzPWNY**  Qaftzaphoni  Prince and King of Heaven, husband of Mehetabel, father of Lilith the Younger.

# 417

**ShKANWM** (M=40)  Shakanom A title of Tiphareth.

# 418

**ChYTh**   Cheth   Fence, enclosure; 8th letter of Hebrew alphabet.
**ABRAHADABRA**   Abrahadabra   Crowley's spelling of Abracadabra.
**RA HWWR**   Ra-Hoor   Ra-Horus, an Egyptian god.

# 419 p

**TYTh**   Teth   Serpent; 9th letter of Hebrew alphabet.

# 420

**ThK** (K=20)   Tok   Oppression.

# 421 p

**PShYAL**   Pasiel   Angel of 12th astrological house.
**ChGYTh**   Haggith   A wife of David, mother of Adonijah.   Hagith   Olympic Planetary Spirit of Venus.

# 422

**ARYK ANPYN** (K=20; N=50)   Arik Anpin   The Vast Countenance; a title of Kether.
**ShBOYM** (M=40)   Shivim   Seventy.

# 424

**ChYWTh**   Chayoth   Living Creatures.
**TWTTh**   Totath   Lord of Triplicity by Night for Taurus.

# 425

**KHTh**   Kahath   8th name of Shem Hamphorash, associated with 2nd quinance of Virgo.
**SDM WOMRH** (M=40)   Sodom we-Amorah   Sodom and Gomorah.

# 428

**GOShKLH**   Gasheklah   The Smiters, the Disturbers of All Things, the Breakers in Pieces; Qlippoth of Chesed.
**ChShMLYM** (M=40)   Chashmalim   Angelic Choir associated with Chesed and with the Sphere of Jupiter.

# 430

**NPSh**   Nephesh   Lowest part of the tripartite soul.
**ROMSS**   Rameses   Rameses.
**ThL**   Tel   Mound.
**TzDYQ-YSWD-OWLM** (M=40)   Tzadiq-Yesod-Olam   The Righteous Is the Foundation of the World; a title of Yesod.

# 431 p

**NWTRYQWN** (N=50)    Notariqon
The cabalistic theory of
acronymns.

# 432

**ThBL**    Tebhel    World; one of the
seven earths, corresponding (with
Cheled) to Yesod and Malkuth.
**BLO BN BOWR** (N=50)    Bela ben
Beor    Bela, son of Beor; a King
of Edom, associated with Daath.
**BN OYSh** (N=50)    Ben Ayish
Son of Ayish; Ursa Minor.

# 433 p

**ZKWTh**    Zakoth    Merit, privilege,
right.
**BLATh**    Beleth    Goetic demon
by day of 1st decanate of Leo.

# 434

**DLTh**    Daleth    Door; 4th letter
of Hebrew alphabet.

# 435

Mystic number of 29th Path
(between Netzach and Malkuth;

Qoph; Pisces).
The number of camels brought out
of exile (Ezra II:67).

# 439 p

**OWGRMON** (N=50)    Ogarman
Lord of Triplicity by Night for
Gemini.
**ShPTYM** (M=40)    Shophetim
Judges.

# 440

**ThLY**    Theli    Dragon; Satan.
**MTh**    Meth    Dead.
**ThHLH**    Tehillah    Psalm.
**ShMNYM** (M=40)    Shemonim
Eighty.
**ThM** (M=40)    Tam    Whole, com-
plete; simple, pious, innocent,
sincere, mild, perfect.
    Tom    Wholeness;
simplicity, piety, innocence,

sincerity, mildness, perfection.

## 441  21²

**RMRA**   Ramara   Lord of
Triplicity by Day for Pisces.
**AMTh**   Emeth   Truth

## 443 p

**BThWLH**   Betulah   Virgo; Virgin;
a title of Malkuth.
**BYTh-AL**   Bethel   House of God.

## 444

**DMShQ**   Damesq   Damascus.
**TzPRDO**   Tzephardea   Frogs; the
2nd of the 10 plagues of Egypt.

## 445

**MKShPH**   Mekshepah   Sorceror.

## 446

**MWTh**   Maveth   Death.
**PYShWN** (N=50)   Pison   A river
of Eden, associated with Fire.

## 450

**ThN** (N=50)   Tan   Jackal; the
great dragon.

## 451

**YShMOAL**   Ishmael   Ishmael.
**ShNANYM** (M=40)   Shinanim
Angelic Choir sometimes
associated with Tiphareth and the
Sphere of the Sun.
**ThHWM** (M=40)   Tehom
Abyss; "deep."

## 453

**BHMWTh**   Behemoth   The great
land-monster of Hebrew
mythology.
**ThMWZ**   Tammuz   The 10th
Hebrew month.

## 454

The number of children of Adin who
returned from exile (Ezra II:15).

**ZHRARYAL**   Zaharariel   A title
of Tiphareth.

## 455

**NThH** Nethah 25th name of Shem Hamphorash, associated with 1st quinance of Sagittarius.

## 456

**KHThAL** Kehethel Angel of 2nd quinance of Virgo; angel by night of the 8 of Pentacles.

## 458

**ShChQYM** (M=40) Shechaqim Clouds; the 3rd Heaven, corresponding to Netzach.

**ChThYM** (M=40) Chittim Hittites.

## 460

**QDSh LYHWH** Qadesh la-Yahweh Holy to the Lord.

**YHWH AYSh MLChMH** Yahweh Ish Milchamah The Lord is a man of war.

**NYTh** Nith 54th name of Shem Hamphorash, associated with 6th quinance of Aries.

## 461 p

**OWLM HYTzYRH** (M=40) Olam ha-Yetzirah The World of Formation.

## 463 p

**BAThYN** (N=50) Bathin Goetic demon by day of 3rd decanate of Virgo.

## 465

Mystic number of 30th Path (between Hod and Yesod; Resh; Sun).

**KShNYOYH** Kashenyayah Angel of 10th astrological house.

## 466

**GLGLTh** Gelgoleth Golgoltha; skull, head.

**SThW** Sethav Autumn.

**NWYTh** Nuit Egyptian sky goddess.

**ShMOWN** (N=50) Simeon A tribe of Israel, associated with Pisces.

# 468

**BYThWN** (N=50)    Bethon    Angel
of 3rd decanate of Gemini.

# 470

**NThHYH**    Nithahiah    Angel of
1st quinance of Sagittarius; angel
by day of the 8 of Wands.

# 474

**DOTh**    Daath    Knowledge; the
pseudo-Sephira.
**ODTh**    Edeth    Testimony.
**RODR**    Raadar    Lord of
Triplicity by Day for Cancer.

# 475

**KHNTh**    Koheneth    Priestess.

# 476

**BYThChWN** (N=50)    Bethchon
Lord of Triplicity by Day for
Scorpio.
**TzLYLYMYRWN** (N=50)
Tzelilimiron    The Clangers;
Qlippoth of Gemini.

# 478

**MChLTh**    Mahalath    Daughter of
Ishmael; wife of Esau; later

considered a major demon,
mother of Agrath.

# 480

The number of years from the
Exodus to the building of the
Temple (I Kings VI:1).

**LYLYTh**    Lilith    Queen of the
Night, Queen of Demons, wife of
Samael, wife of Asmodai, first
wife of Adam; arch-demon
corresponding to Yesod.
**ThLMWD**    Talmud    Teaching.
**OYTh**    Ayeth    The last three
letters of the 42-letter name of
God, associated with Malkuth.
**PTh**    Path    Bit, morsel.
        Poth    Opening; pudenda.
**ThP** (P=80)    Toph    Hand-drum;
bezel.

# 481

**ADYRYRWN** (N=50)    Adiryaron
"The Mighty One sings"; a title
of Tiphareth.

# 483

**MZLWTh**    Mazloth    Constella-
tions; the Sphere of the Zodiac.
**LA ThChMD**    Lo tha-chemod
Thou shalt not covet.

# 485

**ThHLYM** (M=40)    Tehillim
Psalms.

# 486

**OWYTh**    Avith    A city of Edom;
city of King Hadad.
**LA ThGNB**    Lo thi-genov    Thou
shalt not steal.

# 488

**ThAWMYAL**    Thaumiel    Twins
of God; Qlippoth of Kether.

# 490

The number of times one should for-
give his brother's sins (Matt.
XVIII:22).

**YPTh**    Yapheth    Japheth, son of
Noah.
**ThMYM** (M=40)    Thummim
Thummim.
**ThTz** (Tz=90)    Thetz    The third
two letters of the 42-letter name
of God, associated with Binah.

# 491 p

**NYThAL**    Nithael    Angel of 6th
quinance of Aries; angel by night
of the 4 of Wands.

# 496 Perfect

Mystic number of 31st Path
(between Hod and Malkuth; Shin;
Fire).

**MLKWTh**    Malkuth    Kingdom;
the 10th Sephira.
**LWYThN** (N=50)    Leviathan
The great sea-monster of Hebrew
mythology.

# 497

**ThAWMYM** (M=40)    Teomim
Twins; Gemini.

# 498

**HYKL ZKWTh**    Hekel Zakoth
Palace of Merit; Heavenly Mansion
corresponding to Geburah.
**YPThCh**    Yephthach    Jephthah,
the eighth judge of Israel.

# 500

**K** (as final)    Kaph    11th letter of Hebrew alphabet.
**ShR**    Sar    Master, prince, head, chief.
    Shor    Navel.
**ThYMN** (N=50)    Teman    A Duke of Edom, associated with Hod.

# 501

**AShR**    Asher    A tribe of Israel, associated with Libra.
**AK**    Ak    But, only, surely, indeed.
**ShAR**    Seere    Goetic demon by night of 1st decanate of Pisces.
**DTzK ODSh BAChB** (K=20) Detzak Adhash Beachav    The 10 plagues of Egypt (taking the first letter of each).

# 502

**DK**    Dak    Oppressed.

# 505

**ShRH**    Sarah    Wife of Abraham.

# 506

**ShWR**    Shor    Ox, bull; Taurus.
**AShRH**    Asherah    Phoenician goddess of prosperity.
**WShR**    Vesher    32nd name of Shem Hamphorash, associated with 2nd quinance of Capricorn.
**ThWLO**    Tola    The sixth judge of Israel.

# 507

**AShWR**    Ashur    Assyria.
**ZK**    Zak    Pure, clear, transparent, innocent.

# 508

**ShChR**    Shachar    Dawn.
**ChK**    Chek    Palate.

# 509 ק

**ShRWG**    Serug    Serug.

# 510

**RYSh**    Resh    Head; 20th letter of Hebrew alphabet.
**ShRY**    Sarai    Wife of Abram.
**ThYMNY**    Temani    The land of King Husham of Edom.

## 511

**RYShA**   Risha   Head; a title of
Kether.
**OThYAL**   Athiel   "Uncertainty";
Qlippoth of Ain Soph Or.

## 512  8³

**ShChDR**   Shachdar   Angel of 3rd
decanate of Libra.

## 514

**ShChWR**   Shachor   Black.

## 516

**ThMWO**   Timnah   A Duke of
Edom, associated with Daath.

## 519

**BRBTWSh**   Barbatos   Goetic
demon by day of 2nd decanate of
Gemini.

## 520

**ONTh**   Anath   A Semitic goddess
similar to Astarte.

## 521 p

**WShRYH**   Veshriah   Angel of
2nd quinance of Capricorn; angel
by night of the 2 of Pentacles.

## 523 p

**KHNTh HGDWL**   Koheneth ha-
Gadhol   High Priestess.

## 525

**YHWH TzBAWTh**   Yahweh
Tzabaoth   Lord of Hosts; divine
name associated with Netzach,
with Fire, and with the South.

## 526

**ABRAKALA**   Abrakala   The
original form of Abracadabra.

## 527

**MTBOWTh**   Matbeoth   Coins.

## 528

Mystic number of 32nd Path
(between Yesod and Malkuth;

Taw; Saturn).

**HOGNTh** Haagenti Goetic demon by night of 3rd decanate of Cancer.

# 537

**ATzYLWTh** Atziluth Nobility; the Divine or Archetypal world.
**ALWK** Alloces Goetic demon by night of 1st decanate of Virgo.

# 529 $23^2$

**ShYTRY** Sitri Goetic demon by day of 3rd decanate of Cancer.

# 541  פ

**YShRAL** Israel Israel.

# 531

**OWLM HOShYH** (M=40) Olam ha-Assiah The World of Action; the Material World.

# 543

**AHYH AShR AHYH** Ehyeh Asher Ehyeh Existence of Existences; "I AM WHAT AM"; a title of Kether.
**ShMGR** Shamgar The third judge of Israel.

# 533

**TBL WYLWN ShMYM** (N=50; M=40) Tebel Wilon Shamaim Veil of the Firmament; the 1st Heaven, corresponding to Yesod and Malkuth.

# 546

**RYShA DLA** Risha Dela The Head Which Is Not; a title of Kether.
**ShRHYAL** Sharhiel Angel of Aries.

# 535

**QHLTh** Qoheleth Preacher; Ecclesiastes.

# 548

**YHWH ALWH WDOTh** Yahweh Eloah wa-Daath Lord God of Knowledge; divine name associated with Tiphareth.

**BOYRYRWN** (N=50)   Beiriron
The Herd; Qlippoth of Aries.

**OBYRYRWN** (N=50)   Abiriron
The Clayish Ones; Qlippoth of
Libra.

# 550

**ShRTYAL**   Sharatiel   Angel of
Leo.

**NShR**   Nesher   Eagle, bird of
prey.

**MYK**   Mik   42nd name of Shem
Hamphorash, associated with 6th
quinance of Aquarius.

# 551

**AMDWK**   Amdukias   Goetic
demon by night of 1st decanate of
Aquarius.

# 554

**MRChWSh**   Marchosias   Goetic
demon by day of 2nd decanate of
Pisces.

# 556

**GRGShYM** (M=40)   Girgasim
Girgashites.

# 557 p

**SPR HZHR**   Sepher ha-Zohar
Book of Splendor.

# 559

**NQDH PShWTh**   Neqedah
Peshutah   The Simple Point; a
title of Kether.

# 560

**MKShR**   Mekeshar   Sorceress.

**SK**   Sak   Crowd.

**BOL ChNN BN OKBWR** (both final
N's=50)   Baal-Hanan ben Achbor
Baal-Hanan, son of Achbor; a
King of Edom, associated with
Yesod.

# 561

The sum of 1 through 33.

**OThNYAL**   Athniel   Othniel, the
first judge of Israel.

# 562

**LA ThNAP** (P=80)   Lo thi-ne'aph
Thou shalt not commit adultery.

# 563 P
**SGRSh** Sagarash Angel of 1st decanate of Gemini.

# 564
**ChNWK** Chanok Enoch.
**ChLM YSWDWTh** (M=40) Cholam Yesodoth The Breaker of Foundations; the Sphere of the Elements; the part of the material world corresponding to Malkuth.

# 566
**TzLMWTh** Tzal-Maweth Shadow of Death; the 2nd hell, corresponding to Hod.

# 570
**MLK** Melek King; a title of Tiphareth; one of the Melekim.
Moloch Arch-demon corresponding (with Satan) to Kether.
**NPThLY** Naphtali A tribe of Israel, associated with Virgo.
**ShOR** Shar Gate; a title of Malkuth.
**KSPYTh** Kaspith Mercury, the metal of the planet Mercury.
**LMK** Lamek Lamech.

# 571 P
**MLAK** Malak Angel.

# 572
**PWRPWR** Furfur Goetic demon by day of 1st decanate of Pisces.

# 575
**OShRH** Asarah Ten.

# 576 24²
**MQLWTh** Maqqeloth Wands.

# 579
**ORB ZRQ** Oreb Zaraq Raven of Dispersion; Qlippoth of Netzach.

# 580
**PK** Pak Flask, bottle.
**ShOYR** Sair Hairy one; he-goat; demon; hairy.
**GYA-TzLMWTh** Gey-Tzalmaweth Valley of the Shadow of Death.
**NLK** Nelak 21st name of Shem Hamphorash, associated with 3rd quinance of Scorpio.
**ShRP** (P=80) Seraph Ruler of Fire; one of the Seraphim.

# 581

**OThYQA** Atiqa The Ancient
One; a title of Kether.
**AWR KShDYM** (M=40) Ur
Kasdim Ur of the Chaldees.

# 583

**ABYMLK** Abimelech A King of
the Philistines.
**AChD-OShR** Achad-Asar Eleven.
**TMYRA DTMYRYN** (N=50)
Temira de-Temirin The
Concealed of the Concealed; a
title of Kether.

# 585

**ALHYM TzBAWTH** (M=40)
Elohim Tzabaoth God of Hosts;
divine name associated with Hod,
with Water, and with the West.

# 586

**PWK** Puk Antimony.
**PRWSh** Parush Hermit.

# 587 p

**PWRASh** Foras Goetic demon
by day of 1st decanate of
Aquarius.

# 592

**PWRShWN** (N=50) Purson
Goetic demon by day of 2nd
decanate of Libra.

# 598

**ThWBL QYN** (N=50) Tubal-Qayin
Tubal-Cain.

# 600

Noah's age at the Deluge (Gen.
VII:6).

**M** (as final) Mem 13th letter of
Hebrew alphabet.
**SMK** Samekh Prop, support;
15th letter of Hebrew alphabet.
**ShSh** Shesh White marble.

# 601 p

**AM** Em Mother.

# 602

**AWR PShWT** Or Pashot The
Simple Light; a title of Kether.

# 603

**ThGR**  Tiger  To haggle.
**GM**  Gam  Together; also.
**ShLHBYRWN** (N=50)  Shalhebiron
The Flaming Ones; Qlippoth of
Leo.

# 604

**DM**  Dam  Blood; the 1st of the
10 plagues of Egypt.
**AGRTh**  Agrath  A Queen of
Demons.

# 605

**ADM**  Adam  Adam; Man; a title
of Tiphareth.
  Adhom  Red.
**ARPKShD**  Arphaxad  Arphaxad.
**ShShH**  Shishah  Six.
**HM**  Hem  They.

# 606

**RWTh**  Ruth  Ruth.

# 607 P

**AWM**  Aum  30th name of Shem
Hamphorash, associated with 6th
quinance of Sagittarius.

# 608

**ChM**  Cham  Ham, son of Noah;
father-in-law; warm, hot; warmth,
heat.
**ThRCh**  Terah  Father of
Abraham.

# 610

**YM**  Yam  Sea.
**YRTh**  Yereth  27th name of
Shem Hamphorash, associated
with 3rd quinance of Sagittarius.

# 611

**ADWM**  Edom  Edom.
**ThWRH**  Torah  Law.
**AYM**  Aim  Goetic demon by
day of 2nd decanate of Scorpio.

# 612

**BRYTh**  Berith  Covenant;
Goetic demon by day of 1st
decanate of Capricorn.
**YBM**  Yabam  Brother-in-law.
  Yebem  70th name of
Shem Hamphorash, associated
with 4th quinance of Cancer.
**BYM**  Bimé  Goetic demon by
day of 2nd decanate of Sagittarius.

# 616

**YWM** Yom Day.
**YThRW** Yithero Jethro.
**ChRBWTh** Charavoth Swords.
**OThYK YWMYN** (K=20; N=50)
Atik Yomin The Ancient of
Days; a title of Kether.

# 617 p

**DGYM** Dagim Fishes; Pisces.
**RHBYTh** Rehoboth A city of
Edom; city of King Saul.

# 618

**BYThWR** Bethor Olympic
Planetary Spirit of Jupiter.

# 620

**KThR** Kether Crown; the 1st
Sephira.
**MShPR** Mishpar Angel of 3rd
decanate of Virgo.
**OShRYM** (M=40) Esrim
Twenty.

# 621

The number of children of Ramah
and Gaba who returned from exile
(Ezra II:26).

# 623

The number of children of Bebai
who returned from exile (Ezra
II:11).

# 624

**NChShYRWN** (N=50)
Nachashiron The Snakey Ones;
Qlippoth of Sagittarius.
**ChWYM** Chivim Hivites.

# 626

**QLYPWTh** Qlippoth Shells,
demons.

# 628

**ChYYM** Chayim Life.

# 630

The sum of 1 through 35.

**SORSh** Sarash Lord of
Triplicity by Day for Gemini.
**ShRPYM** (M=40) Seraphim
Angelic Choir associated with

Geburah and with the Sphere of Mars.

**ShOYRYM** (M=40)    Sheirim
Hairy ones; he-goats; demons.

# 632

**OWLM YSWDWTh** (M=40)    Olam Yesodoth    The World of Foundations; the Sphere of the Elements; the part of the material world corresponding to Malkuth.

# 635

**ShLShH**    Shelshah    Three.
**HYLL BN ShChR** (N=50)    Heylel ben Shachar    Morning Star, Son of the Dawn; Lucifer.

# 636

**TzPRYRWN** (N=50)    Tzaphiriron
The Scratchers; Qlippoth of Virgo.

# 637

**ShALWSh**    Sallos    Goetic demon by day of 1st decanate of Libra.
**PWRNASh**    Forneus    Goetic demon by day of 3rd decanate of Capricorn.

# 639

**OTz HDOTh** (Tz=90)    Etz ha-Daath
Tree of Knowledge.
**OShRYM WAChD** (M=40)    Esrim we-Echad    Twenty-one.

# 640

**ShMSh**    Shemesh    The Sun.

# 64I פ

**YRThAL**    Yerathel    Angel of 3rd quinance of Sagittarius; angel by day of the 9 of Wands.

# 642

The number of children of Bani who returned from exile (Ezra II:10).

# 645

**MShRQH**    Masrekah    A city of Edom; city of King Samlah.

# 646

**ALHYM**    Elohim    A name of God; Angelic Choir associated with Netzach and with the Sphere of Venus. (This is not the usual enumeration, which is with the final M counted as 40.)

**MWM** Mum Blemish; 72nd name of Shem Hamphorash, associated with 6th quinance of Cancer.

**LWYM** Levim Levites; the priest tribe.

# 650

**MYM** Mem Water; 13th letter of Hebrew alphabet.
Maim Water.

**DWMM** Domem Silent.

**ShShYM** (M=40) Shishim Sixty.

# 651

**ThMWRH** Temurah Permutation; Hebrew cryptology.

**ShTWLWSh** Stolas Goetic demon by day of 3rd decanate of Pisces.

# 652

The number of children of Pelaiah, Tobiah, and Nekuda who returned from exile (Ezra II:60).

# 653 ף

**ANKY YHWH ALHYK** Anoki Yahweh Eloheka I am the Lord thy God.

**ThGRN** (N=50) Tageran Haggler.

# 654

**MDYM** Madim Mars.

**ZLBRHYTh** Zalbarhith Lord of Triplicity by Night for Leo.

# 655

**SPR YTzYRH** Sepher Yetzirah Book of Formation.

**HQDWSh BRWK HWA** (K=20) Ha-Qadosh Baruk Hu The Holy One, blessed be He.

**HYKL OTzM ShMYM** (both final M's=40) Hekel Etzem Shamaim Palace of the Body of Heaven; Heavenly Mansion corresponding to Netzach.

# 657

**WThRWDYAL** Uthrodiel Angel of 3rd decanate of Scorpio.

# 660

**SM**  Sam  Spice; drug; poison.

# 66I ק

**ASThR**  Esther  Esther.
**ThRGBWN** (N=50)  Thergebon
Lord of Triplicity by Day for
Libra.

# 662

**MLAK HALHYM** (M=40)  Malak
ha-Elohim  Angel of God.

# 664

**SDM**  Sodom  Sodom.
**NChWM**  Nacham  Nahum.

# 666

The number of the Beast of The
Revelation (XIII:18).
The number of talents of gold that
Solomon received in one year
(I Kings X:14).
The number of children of
Adonikam who returned from
exile (Ezra II:13).
The sum of all the numbers (1 to
36) on the magic square of the
Sun.

**SWRTh**  Sorath  The Spirit of the
Sun.
**NShYMYRWN** (N=50)
Nashimiron  Malignant Women;
Qlippoth of Pisces.

# 670

**OM**  Am  Nation, populace.
  Em  With, by, near.

# 67I

**ThROA**  Throa  Gate; a title of
Malkuth.

# 672

**YHWH ALHYM**  Yahweh Elohim
The Lord God; divine name associated with Binah.

# 674

**GYHNWM**  Ge-Hinnom  Gehenna;
hell; specifically, the 1st hell,
corresponding to Yesod and
Malkuth.

# 676 $26^2$

**OThWR**  Athor  Lord of

Triplicity by Day for Aquarius.

# 678

**ADM BLYAL**   Adam Belial
Arch-demon corresponding
(according to Waite) to Chokmah.
**ORBWTh**   Arabhoth   Plains; the
7th Heaven, corresponding to the
three Supernal Sephiroth.
**ChOM**   Cham   38th name of
Shem Hamphorash, associated
with 2nd quinance of Aquarius.

# 680

**PRTh**   Phrath   Euphrates; a river
of Eden, associated with Earth.
**KNYM**   Kinnim   Vermin; the 3rd
of the 10 plagues of Egypt.
**ShLShYM** (M=40)   Shelshim
Thirty.

# 683 P

**OWLM ATzYLWTh** (M=40)   Olam
Atziluth   The World of Nobility;
the Divine or Archetypal World.

# 688

**YBWSYM**   Yebusim   Jebusites.

# 690

**SLM**   Sellam   Ladder.
**NMM**   Nemem   57th name of
Shem Hamphorash, associated
with 3rd quinance of Taurus.

# 696

**ShMShWN**   Shimshon   Samson,
the twelfth judge of Israel.
**LA YHYH-LK ALHYM AChRYM
OL-PNY** (K=20; M=40)
Lo yiheyeh-leka Elohim acherim
al-pana   Thou shalt have no
other gods before me.

# 700

**N** (as final)   Nun   14th letter of
Hebrew alphabet.
**MLKYM**   Melekim   Kings;
Angelic Choir associated with
Tiphareth and with the Sphere of
the Sun; book of the Bible.
**OLM**   Alem   4th name of Shem
Hamphorash, associated with
4th quinance of Leo.
**RK**   Rok   Softness.
**ShTh**   Seth   Son of Adam.
Shath   Pillar; prince.
Sheth   Buttocks; noise.

# 701 ᵖ

**OWLM**   Olam   World.
**AN**   An   Where?
**ARK**   Erech   Uruk, city of
ancient Mesopotamia.
**WHNH ShLShH**   We-hineh shelshah
"And behold, three . . ."; the first
words of Gen. XVIII:2, describing
Abraham's confrontation with
three men representing God.
**ALW MYKAL GBRYAL WRPAL**
Elu Michael Gabriel we-Raphael
"These are Michael, Gabriel, and
Raphael." This tells who the three
men were (see above). This is *the*
classic example of gematria.

# 702

**BN**   Ben   Son; a title of
Tiphareth; secret name of the
World of Action.
**BLOM**   Balaam   Balaam.
**BOLM**   Balam   Goetic demon by
night of 3rd decanate of Leo.
**BRK**   Barak   To kneel, bless.
     Berek   Knee, lap.
**RBK**   Ravak   To be mixed,
mingled.
**ShBTh**   Sabbath   Day of rest.

# 703

The sum of 1 through 37.

**GN**   Gan   Garden.

**SAThARYAL**   Satariel   The
Concealers; Qlippoth of Binah.

# 704

**DN**   Dan   A tribe of Israel, associated with Scorpio.
**QDM**   Qedem   Before; the east;
ancient things.

# 705

**HQM**   Haqem   16th name of
Shem Hamphorash, associated
with 4th quinance of Libra.
**HN**   Hen   Lo!; whether, if.

# 707

**AWN**   Avnas   Goetic demon by
night of 1st decanate of Scorpio.
     On   Strength; wealth;
sorrow.
**ZN**   Zan   Species, kind.

# 708

**BNY ALHYM**   Beni Elohim
Sons of the Gods; Angelic Choir
associated with Hod and with the
Sphere of Mercury.
**MAZNYM**   Moznaim   Scales;
Libra.

**BRWK**  Baruk  Blessed.
**ChN**  Chen  Grace, charm.

# 710

**NSThR**  Nisetar  Hidden, secret.
**OMM**  Amem  52nd name of
Shem Hamphorash, associated
with 4th quinance of Aries.
Amam  To darken, dim.

# 711

**AYN**  Ain  Nothing.
**ZAGN**  Zagan  Goetic demon by
night of 1st decanate of
Sagittarius.

# 713

**ShBThAY**  Shabbathai  Saturn.
**ABDWN**  Abaddon  Destruction; ;
The angel of the bottomless pit;
the 6th hell, corresponding to
Chesed.
**DGWN**  Dagon  Philistine fish
god.

# 714

**DYN**  Din  Justice; a title of
Geburah.

# 715

**SNHM**  Sanahem  Lord of
Triplicity by Day for Leo.

# 720

**NOM**  Naam  To be lovely,
pleasant.
**KN**  Ken  Honest; so, thus, just
so, such, so much.

# 721

**NQDH RAShWNH**  Neqedah
Rishonah  The Primordial Point;
a title of Kether.

# 724

**GYHWN**  Gihon  A river of Eden,
associated with Water.

# 725

The number of children of Lod,
Hadid, and Ono who returned
from exile (Ezra II:33).

**KHN**  Kohen  Priest.

**HDD BN BDD**   Hadad ben Bedad
Hadad, son of Bedad; a King of
Edom, associated with Tiphareth.

# 733 p

**RYShA HWWRH**   Risha Havurah
The White Head; a title of Kether.

# 726

**WYThRYOL**   VITRIOL
Acronym for the alchemical
formula *Visita interiora terrae
rectificando invenies occultum
lapidem* ("Visit the interior of the
earth; by rectification, you shall
find the hidden stone").

# 729 27²

**YAChYN**   Jachin   One of the
pillars in the Temple of Solomon.
**LA ThRTzCh**   Lo thi-retzach
Thou shalt not kill.

# 730

The number of shekels of gold used
in the construction of the Tabernacle in the Wilderness.

**KSYLYM**   Kesilim   Fools; Orion.

# 731

**KAYN**   Camio   Goetic demon by
night of 2nd decanate of Virgo.

# 735

**BMRTzThG**   Bamratztag   The
19th through 24th letters of the
42-letter name of God, associated
with Tiphareth.

# 736

The number of horses brought out of
exile (Ezra II:66).

**ARWN HODTh** (N=50)   Aron
ha-Edeth   Ark of the Testimony.

# 737

**ShLHBTh**   Shalhebeth   Flame.
**ALWN**   Elon   The tenth judge of
Israel.

# 740

**MN**   Man   Manna.
Men   Portion.

# 741

The sum of 1 through 38.

**AMN** Amen Firm, faithful; so be it!; a title of Kether.

**LRAYK** Leraje Goetic demon by day of 2nd decanate of Leo.

# 742

**MLAK HALHYM** (K=20) Malak ha-Elohim Angel of God.

# 743 p

The number of children of Kirjatharim, Chephirah, and Beeroth who returned from exile (Ezra II:25).

# 745

**ZBWLN** Zebulun A tribe of Israel, associated with Capricorn.

# 746

**ShMWTh** Shemoth Names; the Hebrew title of Exodus.

# 747

**AWPNYM** Ophanim Wheels; Angelic Choir associated with Chokmah and with the Sphere of the Zodiac.

**AMWN** Amon Goetic demon by day of 1st decanate of Gemini; chief god of the Egyptians.

# 749

**TYTHYWN** Tit-ha-yawen Mire of Mud; the 4th hell, corresponding to Tiphareth.

# 751 p

**NThDWRYNAL** Nathdorinel Lord of Triplicity by Night for Pisces.

# 752

**WYLWN** Wilon Veil; the 1st Heaven, corresponding to Yesod and Malkuth.

# 754

**MDYN** Midian Midian.

# 756

**NYN**  Nun  Fish; 14th letter of Hebrew alphabet; father of Joshua.
**SPYRWTh**  Sephiroth  Spheres; numbers; emanations.

# 757 פ

**AWNN**  Onan  Onan.

# 758

**NChShTh**  Nechsheth  Copper, brass; the metal of Venus.
**MShChYTh**  Mashchith  The Destroyer (Ex. XII:23).

# 760

The number of children of Zaccai who returned from exile (Ezra II:9).

**OTzM**  Etzem  Bone, substance, body.
**QROShMN** (N=50)  Qerashamen The 7th through 12th letters of the 42-letter name of God, associated with Chesed.

# 766

**HMYGYN**  Gamigin  Goetic demon by day of 1st decanate of Taurus.
**MKWN**  Makhon  Emplacement; the 6th Heaven, corresponding to Chesed.

# 767

**MZYQYM**  Meziqim  Demons; injurers.

# 768

**NChShThY**  Necheshethi Coppery, brassy.

# 770

**NPLYM**  Nephilim  "Giants" (Gen. VI:4).

# 771

**ShLThYAL**  Shelathiel  Angel of Virgo.
**ShOYR ANPYN** (N=50)  Seir Anpin  The Bearded Countenance; a title of Tiphareth.

# 773 P

**KHN HGDWL**   Kohen ha-Gadhol
High Priest.

# 774

**ODN**   Eden   Eden.

# 775

The number of children of Arah who
returned from exile (Ezra II:5).

**ThShOH**   Tishah   Nine.

# 776

**SYWN**   Sivan   The 9th Hebrew
month.

# 777

The number of years that Lamech
lived (Gen. V:31).

**OWLM HQLYPWTh**   Olam
ha-Qlippoth   The World of
Shells or Demons.
**MThWShAL**   Methusael
Methusael.
**AChTh RWCh ALHYM ChYYM**
(M=40)   Achath Ruach Elohim

Chayyim   One is the Spirit of
the Living God.

# 780

The sum of 1 through 39.

**OYN**   Ayin   Eye; 16th letter of
Hebrew alphabet.
**SPLYM**   Sephalim   Cups.
**PN**   Pen   Lest.

# 782

**ALHY ABRHM ALHY YTzChQ
WALHY YOQB**   Elohi Abraham
Elohi Itzchaq we-Elohi Yaaqob
The God of Abraham, the God of
Isaac, and the God of Jacob.
**OBDWN**   Abdon   The eleventh
judge of Israel.

# 783

**GDOWN**   Gideon   The fifth judge
of Israel.

# 784 28²

**MThWShLCh**   Methushelach
Methuselah.
**ShYChRYRWN** (N=50)
Shichiriron   The Black Ones;

Qlippoth of Cancer.

# 785

**GWSYWN**    Gusion    Goetic demon by day of 2nd decanate of Cancer.

# 786

**PWRK**    Furcas    Goetic demon by night of 2nd decanate of Leo.

# 787   p

**AWPN**    Ophan    Wheel; one of the Ophanim.

# 788

**ChKMH NSThRH**    Chokmah Nisetarah    Secret Wisdom.

# 790

**TzN**    Tzen    Thorn.

# 793

**ABTzN**    Ibtzan    Ibzan, the ninth judge of Israel.
**OTz HChYYM** (Tz=90)    Etz ha-Chayim    Tree of Life.

# 798

**AMAYMWN**    Amaimon    Demon King of the North and Earth; Demon King of the East (Goetia).

# 800

**P** (as final)    Pe    17th letter of Hebrew alphabet.
**QShTh**    Qasshat    Bow; Sagittarius.
**SSPM**    Saspam    Angel of 1st decanate of Aquarius.
**QN**    Qen    Nest.
**RM**    Ram    Ram (Job XXXII:2).
**ShK**    Sek    Thorn; enclosure.
**KNONYM**    Kanaanim    Canaanites.

# 801

**AP**    Aph    Also.

# 803

**ABRM**    Abram    Abram.

**GP** Gaph Back, top; body, person.

**GWAP** Göap Demon King of the South (Goetia).

# 806

**ShWThQ** Shotheq Silent.
**TzYWN** Tzion Zion.

# 807

**RAWM** Räum Goetic demon by night of 1st decanate of Taurus.

# 808

**ChShK** Choshek Darkness; the 9th of the 10 plagues of Egypt.
**ABRHM** Abraham Abraham.
**ChP** Chaph Pure, innocent.
**RChM** Racham Vulture.

# 809 p

**TP** Taph Children.

# 810

**DRWM** Darom South.
**QYN** Qayin Cain.
**YThTh** Jetheth A Duke of Edom, associated with Daath.

# 813

**ARARYThA** Ararita A name of God; acronym for Echad Rosh Achdotho Rosh Ichudo Temurahzo Echad, "One is His beginning, one is His individuality, His permutation is one."

# 815

**ShThYQH** Shethiqah Silence.

# 816

**OLYWN** Elyon The Most High; a name of God and title of Kether.
**DBRYM** Devarim Words; Hebrew title of Deuteronomy.
**MOWN** Maon Residence; the 5th Heaven, corresponding to Geburah.

# 817

**PWRLAK** Phorlakh Angel of Earth.
**AWRYM** Urim Urim.
**ChRTM** Chartom Magician.

**ASYMWN**　Asimon　Old coin; telephone token; some sort of infernal being associated with the northwest.

# 820

The sum of 1 through 40.

**KP**　Kaph　Palm of hand; 11th letter of Hebrew alphabet.
**NYSN**　Nisan　The 7th Hebrew month.
**ThShOYM** (M=40)　Tishim Ninety.

# 821 p

**PLAYN**　Polayan　Lord of Triplicity by Night for Aquarius.

# 827 p

**GN ODN** (N in GN=50)　Gan Eden Garden of Eden.

# 830

**YShShKR**　Issachar　A tribe of Israel, associated with Cancer.

# 831

**ALP**　Aleph　Ox; 1st letter of Hebrew alphabet.
Elep　Thousand.

# 832

**YHWH AYSh MLChMH YHWH ShMW**　Yahweh Ish Milchamah Yahweh Shemo　The Lord is a man of war; Yahweh is His Name. (Ex. XV:3).

# 833

**ChYWTh HQDSh**　Chayoth ha-Qadosh　Holy Living Creatures; Angelic Choir associated with Kether.

# 836

**HALP**　Halphas　Goetic demon by night of 2nd decanate of Aries.

# 837

**ThTh ZL**　Tath Zal　The Profuse Giver; a title of Kether.
**ALWP**　Alup　Chief, "duke."
**PAYMWN**　Paimon　Demon King of Fire; Goetic demon by day of

3rd decanate of Gemini.

# 838

**KRWBYM**   Kerubim   Angelic
Choir associated with Yesod and
with the Sphere of the Moon.

# 840

**PYNN**   Pinon   A Duke of Edom,
associated with Tiphareth.
**PNYN**   Panin   Pearl; a title of
Malkuth.
**KNON**   Kanaan   Canaan.
**MP**   Moph   Memphis (Egypt).

# 842

**ARALYM**   Aralim   Angelic Choir
associated with Binah and with
the Sphere of Saturn.

# 846

**MWRM**   Murmus   Goetic demon
by night of 3rd decanate of Virgo.

# 848

**ARBOH-OShR**   Arbaah-Asar
Fourteen.

# 849

**MLAK HMShChYTh** (K=20)
Malak ha-Mashchith   The Angel
of Destruction.

# 850

**MRYM**   Miriam   Sister of Moses;
Mary.
**NP**   Noph   Memphis (Egypt).
**ThKLTh**   Tekheleth   Purple.

# 853 p

**NGP**   Negep   Plague.

# 854

**ALHY ABRHM**   Elohi Abraham.
The God of Abraham.

# 857 p

**ALHYM GBWR**   Elohim Gibor
Almighty God; divine name
associated with Geburah.

# 858

**ShBNWK**   Sabnock   Goetic

demon by night of 1st decanate of
Gemini.

**AThH GBWR LOWLM ADNY**
(M=40)    Ateh Gibor le-Olam
Adonai    Thou art mighty
forever, O Lord; usually abbrevi-
ated Agla and used as a name of
God.

**ARAThRWN** (N=50)    Arathron
Olympic Planetary Spirit of
Saturn.

# 869

**ThGRYRWN** (N=50)    Tageriron
The Hagglers; Qlippoth of
Tiphareth.

# 871

**MALP**    Malphas    Goetic demon
by night of 3rd decanate of Aries.

# 860

**BOL ChNN**    Baal-Hanan    A King
of Edom, associated with Yesod;
arch-demon corresponding
(according to Waite) to Netzach.
**MSNYN**    Misnin    Angel of 1st
decanate of Capricorn.
**QYNN**    Cainan    Kenan.
**SP**    Saph    Threshold, entrance.
**RWCh ALHYM**    Ruach Elohim
The Spirit of God.

# 873

**GOP**    Gaap    Goetic demon by
day of 3rd decanate of Aquarius.

# 876

**TzPWN**    Tzaphon    North.
**YSWP**    Yoseph    Joseph.

# 864

**QDWSh QDShYM** (M=40)    Qadosh
Qadeshim    Holy of Holies.
**ASh Th ZNWNYM** (M=40)    Isheth
Zenunim    Woman of
Whoredom; Demon of Prostitu-
tion; arch-demon corresponding
(according to Crowley) to
Chokmah.

# 878

**ThWOBTh**    Thoabath    Abomination.

# 880

**KSP**    Kesep    Silver, the metal of
the Moon.
**OYRM**    Eram    A Duke of Edom,

associated with Malkuth.

# 881 p

**DBRY HYMYM**    Debere ha-yamim
Events of the clays; Hebrew title
of Chronicles.

# 882

**OBRYM**    Ibrim    Hebrews.
**LBRMYM**    Lebarmim    Lord of
Triplicity by Night for Sagittarius.

# 883 p

**ARBOYM**    Arbaim    Forty.

# 888

The number of Christ in Gnosticism.

**ChPP**    Chapap    To cover, protect.

# 892

**APRAYM**    Ephraim    A tribe of
Israel, associated with Taurus.

# 895

The number of years Mahaleel lived
(Gen. V:17).

**ADM QDMWN** (M=40)    Adam
Qadmon    The archetypal man.

# 897

**PRZYM**    Perizzim    Perizzites.

# 900  $30^2$

**Tz** (final)    Sadhe    18th letter of
Hebrew alphabet.
**RN**    Ron    Shout, rejoicing.
**ShM**    Sham    There, then.
         Shem    Sign; name; son of
Noah.
**ThK**    Tok    Oppression.

# 901

**ARN**    Aron    Ark (of the
covenant).

# 902

**HYKL LBNTh HSPYR**    Hekel
Lebanath ha-Saphir    Palace of
the Pavement of Sapphire Stone;
Heavenly Mansion corresponding

to Yesod and Malkuth.
**BTz**   Botz   Mud.

# 905

The number of years Enos lived
(Gen. V:11).

**HShM**   Husham   A King of
Edom, associated with Geburah.
Ha-Shem   The Name;
Tetragrammaton.
**HRN**   Haran   Haran.

# 906

**QWP**   Qoph   Back of Head; 19th
letter of Hebrew alphabet.
**AHRN**   Aaron   Brother of Moses.

# 908

**ChTz**   Chetz   Arrow; lightning;
punishment; wound.

# 909

**RAWBN**   Reuben   A tribe of
Israel, associated with Aquarius.

# 910

The number of years Cainan lived
(Gen. V:14).

**ThShRY**   Tishri   The 1st Hebrew
month.

# 911 p

**AShYM**   Eshim   Flames; Angelic
Choir associated with Malkuth.
**RAShYTh**   Rashith   Beginning.
**BARShChTh**   Bar Shacharth; the 5th
hell, corresponding to Geburah.

# 912

The number of years Seth lived (Gen.
V:8).
**BThShYR**   Bath Shir   Song-maiden;
muse.

# 913

**ABDRWN**   Abdaron   Angel of
2nd decanate of Aquarius.
**AWRWN**   Avron   Angel of 2nd
decanate of Pisces.
**BRAShYTh** (B=2)   Bereshith   In
the beginning; Hebrew title of
Genesis.

# 914

**YRDN**   Yordan   Jordan.
**ShDYM**   Shedim   Demons.

# 918

**BYThWN** Bethon Angel of 3rd decanate of Gemini.

# 921

**WHRYN** Vehrin Angel of 2nd decanate of Sagittarius.

# 922

**ARYK APYM** (K=20) Arik Apim Long of Face; a title of Kether.

# 923

**ChMShH-OShR** Chamishah-Asar Fifteen.

# 924

**OWLM HBRYAH** Olam ha-Briah The World of Creation.

# 926

**AChWDRAWN** Achodraon Lord of Triplicity by Night for Libra.
**ARYTWN** Ariton Demon King

of Water and the West.

# 927

**AYN-SWP** (N=50) Ain-Soph Infinity.

# 928

**KBD ATh-ABYK WATh-AMK** (K=20) Kabed eth-abika we-eth-immeka Honor thy father and thy mother.

# 929 p

**HYKL QDWSh QDShYM** (M=40) Hekel Qadesh Qadeshim Palace of the Holy of Holies; Heavenly Mansion corresponding to the three Supernal Sephiroth.

# 930

The number of years Adam lived (Gen. V:5).

**SNDLPWN** Sandalphon Archangel associated with Malkuth.
**DGDGYRWN** Dagdagiron The Fishy Ones; Qlippoth of Capricorn.
**LTz** Letz Mocker.

# 932

**OTz HDOTh TWB WRO** (Tz=90)
Etz ha-Daath Tob wa-Ra    Tree
of the Knowledge of Good and
Evil.

# 933

**ALHY HOBRYM**    Elohi ha-Ibrim
God of the Hebrews.

# 936

**ShLWM**    Shalom    Peace.

# 937 ש

**YWBB BN ZRCh**    Jobab ben
Zerah    Jobab, son of Zerah; a
King of Edom, associated with
Chesed.

# 939

**ChBRH ZRCh BQR AWR**    Chevrah
Zerach Boqer Or    "Society of
the Shining Light of Dawn"; offi-
cial Hebrew name of the Hermetic
Order of the Golden Dawn.

# 940

**MTzRYM**    Mitzraim    Egypt.
**MTz**    Motz    Chaff.

# 941 ש

**MShRATh**    Mishrath    Angel of
1st decanate of Sagittarius.

# 945

The number of children of Zattu
who returned from exile (**Ezra**
II:8).

# 947 ש

**MThRAWSh**    Mathravash    Angel
of 1st decanate of Cancer.
**ShBOH-OShR**    Shivah-Asar
Seventeen.

# 950

**ShMYM**    Shamaim    Heaven,
firmament, sky.
**NTz**    Netz    Flower; hawk.

# 951

**RWM MOLH**   Rom Maalah   The Inscrutable Height; a title of Kether.

# 952

**ShBYLYM**   Shevilim   Paths.

# 956

**SPR HThWRH**   Sepher ha-Torah Book of the Law.

# 958

**ChMShYM**   Chamishim   Fifty.

# 960

**NShYM**   Nashim   Women, wives.
**ShNYM**   Shenaim   Two.

# 962

The number of years Jared lived (Gen. V:20).

# 964

**MTTRWN**   Metatron   Archangel associated with Kether.

# 965

**ShMNH-OShR**   Shemonah-Asar Eighteen.
**ShM HMPRSh** (M=40)   Shem Hamphorash   The Name of God; Tetragrammaton; the 72-fold name of God.

# 966

**KMWTz**   Kamotz   Angel of 1st decanate of Scorpio.

# 969

The number of years Methuselah lived (Gen. V:27).

**SRTN**   Sarton   Crab; Cancer.

# 970

**ThRShYS**   Tharsis   Ruler of Water.
**OTz**   Etz   Tree.
**ShNYM-OShR** (M=40)   Shenaim-Asar   Twelve.

# 971 ‪ף‬

**ADYMYRWN**  Adimiron  The Bloody Ones; Qlippoth of Taurus.

# 973

The number of children of Jedaiah who returned from exile (Ezra II:36).

**BHYMYRWN**  Bahimiron  The Bestial Ones; Qlippoth of Aquarius.

# 977 ‪ף‬

**ShKANWM**  Shakanom  A title of Tiphareth.

# 981

**DTzK ODSh BAChB**  Detzak Adhash Beachav  The 10 plagues of Egypt (taking the first letter of each).

# 982

**ShBOYM**  Shivim  Seventy.

# 985

**SDM WOMRH**  Sodom we-Amorah Sodom and Gomorah.

# 988

**ChShMLYM**  Chashmalim Angelic Choir associated with Chesed and with the Sphere of Jupiter.

# 989

**SMNGLWP**  Semangeloph  One of the three angels invoked against Lilith.

# 990

The sum of 1 through 44.

**TzDYQ-YSWD-OWLM**  Tzadiq-Yesod-Olam  The Righteous Is the Foundation of the World; a title of Yesod.

# 992

**KWRSWN**  Korson  Demon King of the West (Goetia).

# 996

**OThYQA QDYShA** Atiqa Qadisha The Most Holy Ancient One; a title of Kether.
**RTzWN** Ratzon Delight, favor.

# 999

**ShPTYM** Shephetim Judges.

# 1000 10³

**ShMNYM** Shemonim Eighty.
**QTz** Qetz End.
**ShN** Shen Tooth.
**ThM** Tam Whole, complete; simple, pious, innocent, sincere, mild, perfect.
Tom Wholeness; simplicity, piety, innocence, sincerity. mildness, perfection.

# 1006

**QWTz** Qotz Thorn.

# 1008

**ChShN** Chassan Angel of Air. Choshen Breastplate of the High Priest.
**ChRP** Choreph Winter.

# 1009 p

**ShTN** Satan Adversary, accuser; arch-demon corresponding to Kether.

# 1010

**ShYN** Shin Tooth; 21st letter of Hebrew alphabet.
**QYTz** Qayitz Summer.

# 1011

**ShNANYM** Shinanim Angelic Choir sometimes associated with Tiphareth and the Sphere of the Sun.
**ThHWM** Tehom Abyss; "deep."

# 1014

**ChShWN** Cheshvan The 2nd Hebrew month.

# 1017

The number of children of Harim who returned from exile (Ezra II:39).

# 1018

**ShChQYM**  Shechaqim  Clouds; the 3rd Heaven, corresponding to Netzach.
**ShChYN**  Shechin  Boils; the 6th of the 10 plagues of Egypt.
**ChThYM**  Chittim  Hittites.

# 1021

**OWLM HYTzYRH**  Olam ha-Yetzirah  The World of Formation.

# 1024  $32^2$

**NChShThYRWN** (N=50)  Nechesh-thiron  The Brazen Ones; Qlippoth of Scorpio.

# 1026

**OShRYM WShNYM** (both final M's= 40)  Esrimu-Shenaim  Twenty-two.
**LA ThOShH-LK PSL** (K=20)  Lo tha'aseh-leka pesel  Thou shalt not make unto thee any graven image.
**ShORYMWTh**  Shaare-Maweth  Gates of Death; the 3rd hell, corresponding to Netzach.

# 1031  p

**PANTz**  Phenex  Goetic demon by night of 1st decanate of Aries.

# 1032

**RAShYTh HGLGLYM** (M=40)  Rashith ha-Gilgalim  The Beginning of Revolvings; the Primum Mobile.

# 1045

**ThHLYM**  Tehillim  Psalms.

# 1048

**STROTN**  Sateraton  Lord of Triplicity by Day for Aries.

# 1049  p

**YKSGNWTz**  Yakasaganotz  Angel of 3rd decanate of Taurus.

# 1050

**ThMYM**   Thummim   Thummim.

# 1052

The number of children of Immer
who returned from exile (Ezra
II:37).

# 1057

**ThAWMYM**   Teomim   Twins;
Gemini.

# 1060

**MShKN**   Mishkan   Tabernacle.

# 1061 p

**HYKL RTzWN**   Hekel Ratzon
Palace of Delight; Heavenly
Mansion corresponding to
Tiphareth.

# 1065

**ZAWYR ANPYN**   Zauir Anpin
The Lesser Countenance; a title of
Tiphareth.

# 1072

**ARYK ANPYN** (K=20)   Arik
Anpin   The Vast Countenance; a
title of Kether.

# 1075

**ShYR HShYRYM** (M=40)   Shir
Ha-shirim   The Song of Songs.

# 1079

**STRYP**   Satrip   Angel of 3rd
decanate of Pisces.

# 1081

The sum of 1 through 46.

**ThPARTh**   Tiphareth   Beauty;
the 6th Sephira.
**NWTRYQWN**   Notariqon   The
cabalistic theory of acronyms.

# 1082

**BLO BN BOWR**   Bela ben Beor
Bela, son of Beor; a King of
Edom, associated with Daath.
**BN OYSh**   Ben Ayish   Son of
Ayish; Ursa Minor.

# 1086

**ANDRALP** Andrealphus Goetic demon by night of 2nd decanate of Capricorn.

# 1089 $33^2$

**OWGRMON** Ogarman Lord of Triplicity by Night for Gemini.

# 1091 p

**OWLM HOShYH** Olam ha-Assiah The World of Action; the Material World.

# 1093 p

**TBL WYLWN ShMYM** (N=50) Tebel Wilon Shamaim Veil of the Firmament; the 1st Heaven, corresponding to Yesod and Malkuth.

# 1094

**MKTh BKWRWTh** Makath be-Khoroth The Slaying of the Firstborn; the 10th of the 10 plagues of Egypt.

# 1096

**PYShWN** Pison A river of Eden, associated with Fire.

# 1100

**RTz** Ratz Piece.
**ThN** Tan Jackal.

# 1101

**ARTz** Eretz Earth, one of the four elements; one of the seven earths, corresponding to the three Supernal Sephiroth.

# 1109 p

**RHDTz** Rahadetz Angel of 2nd decanate of Cancer.

# 1110

**MTzPTz** Matz-Patz A name of God by Temurah.

# 1113

**BAThYN** Bathin Goetic demon by day of 3rd decanate of Virgo.

## 1116

**ShMOWN**   Simeon   A tribe of Israel, associated with Pisces.
**GRGShYM**   Girgasim   Girgashites.

## 1117 p

**WRYATz**   Oriax   Goetic demon by night of 2nd decanate of Scorpio.

## 1124

**ChLM YSWDWTh**   Cholam Yesodoth   The Breaker of Foundations; the Sphere of the Elements; the part of the material world corresponding to Malkuth.

## 1126

**BYThChWN**   Bethchon   Lord of Triplicity by Day for Scorpio.
**TzLYLYMYRWN**   Tzelilimiron The Clangers; Qlippoth of Gemini.

## 1131

**ADYRYRWN**   Adiryaron   "The Mighty One Sings"; a title of Tiphareth.

## 1134

**AYN-SWP AWR** (N=50)   Ain-Soph Or   The Limitless Light.

## 1135

**HQDWSh BRWK HWA**   Ha-qadosh Baruk Hu   The Holy One, blessed be He.

## 1141

**AWR KShDYM**   Ur Kasdim   Ur of the Chaldees.

## 1142

**MARATz**   Marax   Goetic demon by day of 3rd decanate of Libra.

## 1145

**ALHYM TzBAWTh**   Elohim Tzabaoth   God of Hosts; divine name associated with Hod, with Water, and with the West.

## 1146

**LWYThN**   Leviathan   The great

sea-monster of Hebrew mythology.

# 1150

**ThYMN**  Teman  A Duke of
Edom, associated with Hod.

# 1171 p

**ADNY HARTz**  Adonai ha-Eretz
Lord of the Earth; divine name
associated with Malkuth, with
Earth, and with the North.

# 1175

**ShShH-OShR**  Shishah-Asar
Sixteen.

# 1180

**OShRYM**  Esrim  Twenty.

# 1190

**ShRPYM**  Seraphim  Angelic
Choir associated with Geburah
and with the Sphere of Mars.
**ShOYRYM**  Seirim  Hairy
Ones; he-goats; demons.

# 1192

**OWLM YSWDWTh**  Olam
Yesodoth  The World of
Foundations; the Sphere of the
Elements; the part of the material
world corresponding to Malkuth.

# 1198

**BOYRYRWN**  Beiriron  The
Herd; Qlippoth of Aries.
**OBYRYRWN**  Abiriron  The
Clayish Ones; Qlippoth of Libra.

# 1199

**OShRYM WAChD**  Esrim ha-Echad
Twenty-one.

# 1200

**ShTz**  Shax  Goetic demon by
night of 2nd decanate of Gemini.
**ThP**  Toph  Hand-drum; bezel.

# 1205

**ShLShH-OShR**  Shelshah-Asar
Thirteen.

# 1210

**ShShYM** Shishim Sixty.

**ThRShYSh** Tarshish Tarsis, a city in Spain; chrysolite; precious stone.

**BOL ChNN BN OKBWR** (N in BN= 50) Baal-Hanan ben Achbor Baal-Hanan, son of Achbor; a King of Edom, associated with Yesod.

# 1215

**SHRNTz** Saharnatz Angel of 2nd decanate of Libra.

**HYKL OTzM ShMYM** (M in OTzM= 40) Hekel Etzem Shamaim Palace of the Body of Heaven; Heavenly Mansion corresponding to Netzach.

# 1222

The number of children of Azgad who returned from exile (Ezra II:12).

**MLAK HALHYM** Malak ha-Elohim Angel of God.

# 1225 $35^2$

Sum of all the numbers (1 to 49) on the magic square of Venus.

# 1210

**OThYQA DOThYQYN** (N=50) Atiqa de-Atiqin The Ancient of the Ancient Ones; a title of Kether.

# 1231

**OShRTh HDBRYM** (M=40) Asereth ha-davarim Ten Commandments.

# 1233

**TMYRA DTMYRYN** Temira de-Temirin The Concealed of the Concealed; a title of Kether.

# 1240

**ShLShYM** Shelshim Thirty.

# 1243

**OWLM ATzYLWTh** Olam Atziluth The World of Nobility; the Divine or Archetypal World.

# 1247

The number of children of Pashur who returned from exile (Ezra

II:38).

title of Kether.

## 1248

**ThWBL QYN**   Tubal-Qayin
Tubal-Cain.

## 1253

**ShLHBYRWN**   Shalhebiron   The
Flaming Ones; Qlippoth of Leo.

## 1254

The number of children of Elam who
returned from exile (Ezra II:7).
The number of children of "the
other Elam" who returned from
exile (Ezra II:31).

## 1260

**ThRShYShYM** (M=40)   Tarshishim
Chrysolites; Angelic Choir sometimes associated with Netzach and
the Sphere of Venus.

## 1266

**OThYK YWMYN** (K=20)   Atik
Yomin   The Ancient of Days; a

## 1274

**NChShYRWN**   Nachashiron   The
Snakey Ones; Qlippoth of Sagittarius.

## 1282

**LA ThNAP**   Lo thi-ne'aph   Thou
shalt not commit adultery.

## 1285

**HYLL BN ShChR**   Heylel ben
Shachar   Morning Star, Son of
the Dawn; Lucifer.

## 1286

**TzPRYRWN**   Tzaphiriron   The
Scratchers; Qlippoth of Virgo.

## 1292

**PWRShWN**   Purson   Goetic
demon by day of 2nd decanate of
Libra.

# 1300

**ShRP** Seraph Ruler of Fire; one of the Seraphim.

# 1303 p

**ThGRN** Tageran Haggler.

# 1307 p

**AShThRWTh** Ashtaroth Archdemon corresponding to Chesed (Mathers and Waite) or to Geburah (Crowley); Goetic demon by day of 2nd decanate of Capricorn.

# 1311

**ThRGBWN** Thergebon Lord of Triplicity by Day for Libra.

# 1316

**NShYMYRWN** Nashimiron Malignant Women; Qlippoth of Pisces.

# 1329

**MLAK HMShChYTh** Malak ha-Mashchith Angel of Destruction.

# 1337

**OWLM HQLYPWTh** Olam ha-Qlippoth The World of Shells or Demons.

**AChTh RWCh ALHYM ChYYM** Achath Ruach Elohim Chayyim One is the Spirit of the Living God.

# 1342

**ALHY ABRHM ALHY YTzChQ WALHY YOQB** Elohi Abraham Elohi Itzchaq we-Elohi Yaaqob The God of Abraham, the God of Isaac, and the God of Jacob.

# 1345

**ThShOH-OShR** Tishah-Asar Nineteen.

# 1346

**ShMShWN** Shimshon Samson, the twelfth judge of Israel.

# 1370

OShThRTh    Ashtoreth    Astarte,
a Phoenician goddess.

# 1378

The sum of 1 through 52.

# 1380

ThShOYM    Tishim    Ninety.

# 1386

ARWN HODTh    Aran ha-Edeth
Ark of the Testimony.

# 1402

ARYK APYM    Arik Apim    Long
of Face; a title of Kether.

# 1418

AThH GBWR LOWLM ADNY
Ateh Gibor le-Olam Adonai
Thou art mighty forever, O Lord;
usually abbreviated Agla and used
as a name of God.

# 1421

ShOYR ANPYN    Seir Anpin    The
Bearded Countenance; a title of
Tiphareth.

# 1424

QDWSh QDShYM    Qadosh
Qadeshim    Holy of Holies.
AShTh ZNWNYM    Isheth Zenunim
Woman of Whoredom; Demon of
Prostitution; arch-demon corre-
sponding (according to Crowley)
to Chokmah.

# 1434

ShYChRYRWN    Shichiriron    The
Black Ones; Qlippoth of Cancer.

# 1449

OTz HDOTh    Etz ha-Daath    Tree
of Knowledge.

# 1455

ADM QDMWN    Adam Qadmon
The archetypal man.

# 1477

**GN ODN**  Gan Eden  Garden of Eden.

# 1484

**AGRTh BTh MChLTh**  Agrath bath Mahalath  Agrath, daughter of Mahalath; a queen of demons; one of the three wives of Samael.

# 1489 P

**HYKL QDWSh QDShYM**  Hekel Qadosh Qadeshim  Palace of the Holy of Holies; Heavenly Mansion corresponding to the three Supernal Sephiroth.

# 1495

The sum of all the letters of the Hebrew alphabet.

# 1506

**LA ThOShH-LK PSL**  La tha'aseh-leka pesel  Thou shalt not make unto thee any graven image.

# 1508

**ARAThRWN**  Arathron  Olympic Planetary Spirit of Saturn.

# 1519

**ThGRYRWN**  Tageriron  The Hagglers; Qlippoth of Tiphareth.

# 1522

**LA-ThONH BROK OD ShQR** (K=20) Lo-tha'aneh be-re'aka ed shaqer Thou shalt not bear false witness against thy neighbor.

# 1525

**ShM HMPRSh**  Shem Hamphorash  The Name of God; Tetragrammaton; the 72-fold name of God.

# 1530

**ShNYM-OShR**  Shenaim-Asar  Twelve.

# 1552

**ARYK ANPYN**   Arik Anpin   The Vast Countenance; a title of Kether.

# 1577

**AYN-SWP**   Ain-Soph   Infinity.

# 1586

**OShRYM WShNYM** (M in OShRYM =40)   Esrum u-Shenaim   Twenty-two.

# 1592

**RAShYTh HGLGLYM**   Rashith ha-Gilgalim   The Beginning of Revolvings; the Primum Mobile.

# 1603

**OTz HChYYM**   Etz ha-Chayim   Tree of Life.

# 1635

**ShYR HShYRYM**   Shir Ha-Shirim   Song of Songs.

# 1656

The year (after Creation) of the Deluge.

# 1674

**NChShThYRWN**   Necheshthiron   The Brazen Ones; Qlippoth of Scorpio.

# 1742

**OTz HDOTh TWB WRO**   Etz ha-Daath Tob wa-Ra   Tree of the Knowledge of Good and Evil.

# 1743

**TBL WYLWN ShMYM**   Tebel Wilon Shamaim   Veil of the Firmament; the 1st Heaven, corresponding to Yesod and Malkuth.

# 1746

**OThYK YWMYN**   Atik Yomin   The Ancient of Days; a title of Kether.

# 1775

The number of shekels of silver used in the construction of the Tabernacle in the Wilderness.

HYKL OTzM ShMYM   Hekel Etzem Shamaim   Palace of the Body of Heaven; Heavenly Mansion corresponding to Netzach.

# 1784

AYN-SWP AWR   Ain-Soph Or The Limitless Light.

# 1791

OShRTh HDBRYM   Asereth ha-davarim   The Ten Commandments.

# 1820

ThRShYShYM   Tarshishim Chrysolites; Angelic Choir sometimes associated with Netzach and the Sphere of Venus.

# 1837

ZKWR ATh-YWM HShBTh LQDShW

(M=40)   Zakhor eth-yom ha-shabath le-qadesho   Remember the sabbath day, to keep it holy.

# 1860

BOL ChNN BN OKBWR   Baal-Hanan ben Achbor   Baal-Hanan, son of Achbor; a King of Edom, associated with Yesod.

# 1875

OThYQA DOThYQYN   Atiqa de-Atiqin   The Ancient of the Ancient Ones; a title of Kether.

# 1888

KBD ATh-ABYK WATh-AMK Kabed eth-abika we-eth-immeka Honor thy father and thy mother.

# 1902

LA ThShA ATh-ShM-YHWH ALHYK LShWA (M=40; K=20)   Lo thisa eth-shem-Yahweh Eloheka lashawe   Thou shalt not take the name of the Lord thy God in vain.

## 2002

**LA-ThONH BROK OD ShQR**   La-tha'aneh be-re'aka ed shaqer
Thou shalt not bear false witness against thy neighbor.

## 2056

The number of children of Bigvai who returned after the exile (Ezra II:14).

## 2080

The sum of all the numbers (1 to 64) on the magic square of Mercury.

**ThPThRThRTh**   Taphthartharath
The Spirit of Mercury.

## 2146

**OShRYM WShNYM**   Esim u-Shenaim   Twenty-two.

## 2151

**AChD RASh AChDWThW RASh YChWDW ThMWRHZW AChD**
Echad Rosh Achdotho Rosh Ichudo Temurahzo Echad   One is His beginning, one is His individuality, His permutation is one; usually abbreviated *Ararita* and used as a name of God.

## 2172

The number of children of Parosh who returned after the exile (Ezra II:3).

## 2296

**LA YHYH-LK ALHYM AChRYM OL-PNY**   Lo yiheyeh-leka elohim acherim al-pana   Thou shalt have no other gods before me.

## 2397

**ZKWR ATh-YWM HShBTh LQDShW**
Zakhor eth-yom ha-shabath le-qadesho   Remember the sabbath day, to keep it holy.

## 2812

The number of children of Pahathmoab who returned from exile (Ezra II:6).

## 2911

**BRAShYTh** (B=2000)  Bereshith
In the beginning; Hebrew title of
Genesis.

## 2942

**LA ThShA ATh-ShM-YHWH
ALHYK LShWA**  Lo thisa
eth-shem-Yahweh Eloheka
lashawe  Thou shalt not take the
name of the Lord thy God in vain.

## 3321

The sum of all the numbers (1 to 81)
on the magic square of the Moon.

**MLKA BThRShYShYM WOD BRWH
ShHQYM** (final M in ShHQYM=
700)  Malka be-Tarshishim
we-ad be-Ruah Shehaqim  The
Intelligence of the Intelligences of
the Moon.
**MLKA BThRShYSYM WOD
RWChWTh ShChLYM**  Malka
be-Tarshisim we-ad Ruachoth
Shechalim  A different version
of the preceding.
**ShD BRShMOTh HShRThThN**
Shed Barshemath ha-Sharthathan
The Spirit of the Spirits of the
Moon.
**ShDBRShHMOTh ShRThThN**
Shed Barshehmath Sharthathan
A different version of the

preceding.

## 3630

The number of children of Senaah
who returned from exile (Ezra II:
35).

## 3783

**ABGYThTzQROShMNKGDYKSh-
BMRTzThGHQMMNOYGLPZQ-
ShQYOYTh**  Ab-gi-thetz-
qerashamen-kegadikesh-bamratz-
tag-haqamamna-yaglepzeq-sheqi-
ayeth  The name of God of 42
letters.

## 6720

The number of asses brought out of
exile (Ezra II:67).

## 7337

The number of servants and maids
who returned from exile (Ezra
II:65).

# 9623 ק

The sum of the names of Shem
Hamphorash, not counting the
finals as such.

# 10171

The sum of the letters of the Ten
Commandments, not counting
finals as such.

# 14583

The sum of the names of Shem
Hamphorash.

# 16011

The sum of the letters of the Ten
Commandments.

# 20303

The sum of the verses of Shem
Hamphorash.

# 42360

The number who returned from exile
(Ezra II:64).

# APPENDICES

APPENDICES

# APPENDIX

# A

# THE DECANATES OF THE ZODIAC

## RULING PLANET

| Sign and Decanate | Golden Dawn | Traditional Astrology | Tarot Card |
|---|---|---|---|
| Aries (Taleh) | | | |
| 1 | Mars | Mars | 2 of Wands |
| 2 | Sun | Sun | 3 of Wands |
| 3 | Venus | Jupiter | 4 of Wands |
| Taurus (Shor) | | | |
| 1 | Mercury | Venus | 5 of Pentacles |
| 2 | Moon | Mercury | 6 of Pentacles |
| 3 | Saturn | Saturn | 7 of Pentacles |
| Gemini (Teomim) | | | |
| 1 | Jupiter | Mercury | 8 of Swords |
| 2 | Mars | Venus | 9 of Swords |
| 3 | Sun | Saturn* | 10 of Swords |
| Cancer (Sarton) | | | |
| 1 | Venus | Moon | 2 of Cups |
| 2 | Mercury | Mars** | 3 of Cups |
| 3 | Moon | Jupiter*** | 4 of Cups |
| Leo (Ari) | | | |
| 1 | Saturn | Sun | 5 of Wands |
| 2 | Jupiter | Jupiter | 6 of Wands |
| 3 | Mars | Mars | 7 of Wands |
| Virgo (Betulah) | | | |
| 1 | Sun | Mercury | 8 of Pentacles |
| 2 | Venus | Saturn | 9 of Pentacles |
| 3 | Mercury | Venus | 10 of Pentacles |

## RULING PLANET

| Sign and Decanate | Golden Dawn | Traditional Astrology | Tarot Card |
|---|---|---|---|
| Libra (Moznaim) | | | |
| 1 | Moon | Venus | 2 of Swords |
| 2 | Saturn | Saturn* | 3 of Swords |
| 3 | Jupiter | Mercury | 4 of Swords |
| Scorpio (Akrab) | | | |
| 1 | Mars | Mars** | 5 of Cups |
| 2 | Sun | Jupiter*** | 6 of Cups |
| 3 | Venus | Moon | 7 of Cups |
| Sagittarius (Qasshat) | | | |
| 1 | Mercury | Jupiter | 8 of Wands |
| 2 | Moon | Mars | 9 of Wands |
| 3 | Saturn | Sun | 10 of Wands |
| Capricorn (Gedi) | | | |
| 1 | Jupiter | Saturn | 2 of Pentacles |
| 2 | Mars | Venus | 3 of Pentacles |
| 3 | Sun | Mercury | 4 of Pentacles |
| Aquarius (Deli) | | | |
| 1 | Venus | Saturn* | 5 of Swords |
| 2 | Mercury | Mercury | 6 of Swords |
| 3 | Moon | Venus | 7 of Swords |
| Pisces (Dagim) | | | |
| 1 | Saturn | Jupiter** | 8 of Cups |
| 2 | Jupiter | Moon | 9 of Cups |
| 3 | Mars | Mars*** | 10 of Cups |

*Or Uranus
**Or Pluto
***Or Neptune

# APPENDIX

# B

# THE TAROT

In this dictionary, I have used the Tarot terminology of the so-called Rider pack of A. E. Waite and Pamela Coleman Smith, primarily because this has been until recently the most widely available deck. It is not necessarily the best deck. From the standpoint of artistic execution and aesthetic design, the pack designed by Aleister Crowley and Frieda Harris, distributed by Llewellyn, is immeasurably superior. For convenience, I am including the following table showing the differences in terminology among some of the currently available Tarot packs.

| Tarot of Marseilles | Waite/Smith | Crowley/Harris |
|---|---|---|
| Clubs | Wands | Wands |
| Cups | Cups | Cups |
| Swords | Swords | Swords |
| Money | Pentacles | Disks |
| King | King | Knight |
| Queen | Queen | Queen |
| Knight | Knight | Prince |
| Knave | Page | Princess |
| The Fool | 0. The Fool | 0. The Fool |
| I. The Magician | I. The Magician | I. The Magus |
| II. The High Priestess | II. The High Priestess | II. The Priestess |
| III. The Empress | III. The Empress | III. The Empress |
| IV. The Emperor | IV. The Emperor | IV. The Emperor |
| V. The Pope | V. The Hierophant | V. The Hierophant |
| VI. The Lovers | VI. The Lovers | VI. The Lovers |
| VII. The Chariot | VII. The Chariot | VII. The Chariot |
| VIII. Justice | XI. Justice | VIII. Adjustment |
| IX. The Hermit | IX. The Hermit | IX. The Hermit |

| Tarot of Marseilles | Waite/Smith | Crowley/Harris |
|---|---|---|
| X. The Wheel of Fortune | X. The Wheel of Fortune | X. Fortune |
| XI. Force | VIII. Strength | XI. Lust |
| XII. The Hanged Man | XII. The Hanged Man | XII. The Hanged Man |
| XIII. Death | XIII. Death | XIII. Death |
| XIV. Temperance | XIV. Temperance | XIV. Art |
| XV. The Devil | XV. The Devil | XV. The Devil |
| XVI. The Tower of Destruction | XVI. The Tower | XVI. The Tower |
| XVII. The Star | XVII. The Star | XVII. The Star |
| XVIII. The Moon | XVIII. The Moon | XVIII. The Moon |
| XIX. The Sun | XIX. The Sun | XIX. The Sun |
| XX. Judgment | XX. Judgment | XX. The Aeon |
| XXI. The World | XXI. The World | XXI. The Universe |

# APPENDIX

# C

# THE CABALA OF THE BIBLE

The information in this section of the appendix was added too late for inclusion in Parts I through III but, except for the census figures, is included in Part IV, the numerological section.

### The Judges of Israel

The twelve judges (shophetim, ShPYTM, 439 or 999) of Israel, who governed between Joshua and Saul and who can presumably be attributed to the twelve tribes, were as follows:

| | | |
|---|---|---|
| 1. Othniel | OThNYAL | 561 |
| 2. Ehud | AHWD | 16 |
| 3. Shamgar | ShMGR | 543 |
| 4. Deborah | DBWRH | 217 |
| 5. Gideon | GDOWN | 783 or 133 |
| 6. Tola | ThWLO | 506 |
| 7. Jair | YAYR | 221 |
| 8. Jephthah | YPThCh | 498 |
| 9. Ibzan | ABTzN | 793 or 143 |
| 10. Elon | ALWN | 737 or 87 |
| 11. Abdon | OBDWN | 782 or 132 |
| 12. Samson | ShMShWN | 1346 or 696 |

### The Nations of Canaan

The nations of Canaan who held the Promised Land were seven in number, as follows:

| | | | |
|---|---|---|---|
| 1. Canaanites | Kenaanim | KNONYM | 800 or 240 |
| 2. Hittites | Hittim | ChThYM | 1018 or 458 |
| 3. Hivites | Chivvim | ChWYM | 624 or 64 |
| 4. Perizzites | Perizzim | PRZYM | 897 or 337 |
| 5. Girgashites | Girgasim | GRGShYM | 1116 or 556 |

| 6. Amorites | Emorim | AMRYM | 850 or 290 |
| 7. Jebusites | Yebusim | YBWSYM | 688 or 128 |

## The Ten Commandments

The Ten Commandments (asereth ha-davarim, OShRTh HDBRYM, 1231 or 1791) are as follows:

1. Thou shalt have no other gods before me.    2296
   Lo yiheyeh-leka elohim acherim al-pana:    696
   LA YHYH-LK ALHYM AChRYM OL-PNY:
2. Thou shalt not make unto thee any graven image.    1506
   La tha'aseh-leka pesel    1026
   LA ThOShH-LK PSL
3. Thou shalt not take the name of the Lord thy God in vain. 2942
   Lo thisa eth-shem-Yahweh Eloheka lashawe    1902
   LA ThShA ATh-ShM-YHWH ALHYK LShWA
4. Remember the sabbath day, to keep it holy.    2397
   Zakhor eth-yom ha-shabath le-qadesho:    1837
   ZKWR ATh-YWM HShBTh LQDShW:
5. Honor thy father and thy mother.    1888
   Kabed eth-abika we-eth-immeka    928
   KBD ATh-ABYK WATh-AMK
6. Thou shalt not kill.    729
   Lo thi-retzach:
   LA ThRTzCh
7. Thou shalt not commit adultery.    1282
   Lo thi-ne'aph:    562
   LA ThNAP:
8. Thou shalt not steal.    486
   La thi-genov
   LA ThGNB
9. Thou shalt not bear false witness against thy neighbor.    2002
   Lo-tha'aneh be-re'aka ed shaqer:    1522
   LA-ThONH BROK OD ShQR:
10. Thou shalt not covet.    483
    Lo tha-chemod
    LA ThChMD

All ten add to 10,171 or 16,011. They contain 128 letters and therefore could conceivably have been written on two eight-by-eight tablets. The verses containing the commandments (Ex. XX:2-14) contain 620 letters and add to 79,935 or 48,405.

## The Books of the Bible

There are thirty-nine books in the Jewish scriptures, and they correspond one for one with the books of the Old Testament in the King James Bible. The order, however, is different. Roman Catholics recognize seven additional books. The following table gives the English and Hebrew names and enumerations for the books of Jewish scripture. Roman Catholic titles, if different, are included in parentheses.

| Genesis | Bereshith ("In the beginning") | BRAShYTH | 2911 |
|---|---|---|---|
| Exodus | Shemoth ("Names") | ShMWTh | 746 |
| Leviticus | Wayiqra ("And he called") | WYQRA | 317 |
| Numbers | Bamidbar ("In the wilderness") | BMDBR | 248 |
| Deuteronomy | Eleh ha-devarim ("These be the words") | ALH HDBRYM | 857 |
| | | | 297 |
| Joshua (Josue) | Yehoshua | YHWShO | 391 |
| Judges | Shophetim | ShPTYM | 439 |
| | | | 999 |
| Samuel (I & II) (Kings I & II) | Shemuel (I & II) | ShMWAL | 377 |
| Kings (I & II) (Kings III & IV) | Melekim (I & II) | MLKYM | 570 |
| | | | 90 |
| Isaiah (Isaias) | Yeshayah | YShOYH | 395 |
| Jeremiah (Jeremias) | Yirmyah | YRMYH | 265 |
| Ezekiel (Ezechiel) | Yechezqel | YChZQAL | 156 |
| Hosea (Osee) | Hosea | HWShO | 381 |
| Joel | Yoel | YWAL | 47 |
| Amos | Amos | OMWS | 176 |
| Obadiah (Abdias) | Obadyah | OBDYH | 91 |
| Jonah (Jonas) | Yonah | YWNH | 71 |
| Micah (Micheas) | Mikah | MYKH | 75 |
| Nahum | Nachum | NChWM | 664 |
| | | | 104 |
| Habakkuk (Habacuc) | Chabaqquq | ChBQWQ | 216 |
| Zephaniah (Sophonias) | Tzephanyah | TzPNYH | 235 |
| Haggai (Aggeus) | Chaggai | ChGY | 21 |
| Zechariah (Zacharius) | Zekaryah | ZKRYH | 242 |
| Malachi (Malachias) | Maleaki | MLAKY | 101 |
| Psalms | Tehillim | ThHLYM | 1045 |
| | | | 485 |

| Job | Iyyob | AYWB | 19 |
|---|---|---|---|
| Proverbs | Mishle | MShLY | 380 |
| Ruth | Ruth | RWTh | 606 |
| The Song of | Shir Hashirim | ShYR | 1635 |
| Solomon (Canti- | ("Song of Songs") | HShYRYM | 1075 |
| cle of Canticles) | | | |
| Ecclesiastes | Qohelleth ("Preacher") | QHLTh | 535 |
| Lamentations | Ekah ("How") | AYKH | 36 |
| Esther | Esther | ASThR | 661 |
| Daniel | Daniel | DNYAL | 95 |
| Ezra (I Esdras) | Ezra | OZRA | 278 |
| Nehemiah | Nechemyah | NChMYH | 113 |
| (II Esdras) | | | |
| Chronicles (I & II) | Debere hayamim ("Events of | DBRY HYMYM | 881 |
| (Paralipomenon | the Days") (I & II) | | 321 |
| I & II) | | | |

## The Census in the Wilderness

Although this dictionary contains several references to numbers specifically mentioned in the Bible, it makes no pretense at being a numerical concordance. Such information is available elsewhere, and much of it is of doubtful value to the student of the cabala. The census of men over twenty years of age who were fit to go to war, in Numbers I and XXVI (the latter having been taken after a plague), illustrates this point rather well. The numbers are so large that whole chapters, even books, would have to be added to approach them, and then the likelihood of their coming out to even hundreds is rather small.

| Tribe | Numbers I | Numbers XXVI |
|---|---|---|
| Reuben | 46,500 | 43,370 |
| Simeon | 59,300 | 22,200 |
| Gad | 45,650 | 40,500 |
| Judah | 74,600 | 76,500 |
| Issachar | 54,400 | 64,300 |
| Zebulun | 57,400 | 60,500 |
| Ephraim | 40,500 | 32,500 |
| Manasseh | 32,200 | 52,700 |
| Benjamin | 35,400 | 45,600 |
| Dan | 62,700 | 64,400 |

| | | |
|---|---|---|
| Asher | 41,500 | 53,400 |
| Naphtali | 53,400 | 45,400 |
| TOTALS | 603,550 | 601,730 |

Other figures, such as the ages of the patriarchs and the numbers of the returning exiles following the decree of Cyrus, are included as being of some interest. In general, however, I have avoided such things as the dimensions of Noah's ark or Solomon's Temple, most of which are good round numbers of little interest and doubtful significance.

# APPENDIX

# D

# PRONUNCIATION

This section of the appendix consists of a general guide for the pronunciation of Hebrew. However, in using this guide, the following points should be borne in mind.

(1). Scarcely any rule can be set forth that does not have *some* exception.

(2). There are variations in pronunciation among Sephardic, Ashkenazic, medieval, and ancient Hebrew, not to mention local variations or Yiddish, which is in fact a different language. Thus the *ai* in *Adonai* may be pronounced like the *oi* in *oil*, like the *i* in *light*, or as *ah-ee*. The latter is probably closest to the original.

(3). Traditional transliterations, which I have used in this dictionary when their usage has been so widespread as to be unavoidable, are not standardized and are not always as literal as modern practices would dictate. For example, *Michael* should properly be transliterated as *Mikha'el* (to distinguish *kaph* from *cheth*) and pronounced mee-chah-*ail*, with a glottal stop between the last two syllables (which may be ignored for all practical purposes) and the *kaph* pronounced like the soft German *ch* in *ich*. The present form comes from the Greek, wherein the *kaph* was transliterated as *chi*.

(4). Inasmuch as vowel points were not introduced until the seventh century A.D., there is some doubt as to whether the traditional pronunciations are equivalent to those of the ancient Hebrew.

(5). The anglicized spellings and pronunciations in the King James Bible often bear only a minimal relationship to the original; for example, *Isaac* and *Itzchaq*.

(6). In my own transliterations, I have tended to disregard schwas when they receive exceptionally little stress, and I have not made use of ' and ' to designate the presence of *aleph* and *ayin* as is done in strict transliteration. These consonants may be regarded as silent, hence there seems little need to indicate them in a work of this nature in which the Hebrew spellings are also given.

In general, Hebrew words are accented on the last syllable, with secondary accents falling on every other syllable before the ultimate. There are exceptions.

Here, then, are the pronunciations of transliterated Hebrew, insofar as any rules can be given:

| Transliterated letter | Usually transliteration of | Pronunciation |
|---|---|---|
| a | vowel point | a as in *father* or a as in *cat* |
| b | beth | b |
| c | kaph | k |
| ch | cheth; kaph* | ch in German *nacht*; ch in German *ich* |
| d | daleth | d |
| dh | daleth | th in *the* (hard th) |
| e | vowel point | e as in *met* or e as in *grey*; as a schwa, a as in *sofa, abut* |
| f | pe | f |
| g | gimel | g as in *gamble* (never like *j*) or Semitic gh |
| h | he; cheth** | h; ch in German *nacht* |
| i | vowel point; yod | i as in *fin* or i as in *gasoline*; as a consonant, y |
| j | yod | y |
| k | kaph | k |
| kh | kaph | ch in German *ich* |
| l | lamed | l |
| m | mem | m |
| n | nun | n |
| o | vowel point; waw | o as in *not* or o as in *obey* (as waw, always the latter) |
| p | pe | p |
| ph | pe | f |
| q | qoph | k |
| r | resh | r |
| s | samekh; shin | s |
| sh | shin | sh |
| t | teth; tau | t |

---

*I have generally tried to avoid *ch* as a transliteration of *kaph,* although there are some cases (such as *Michael*) where it has proved unavoidable.

**I have avoided transliterating *cheth* as *h.*

| Transliterated letter | Usually transliteration of | Pronunciation |
|---|---|---|
| th | taw | th as in *thin* (soft th) |
| ts | tzaddi | ts as in *tsar, cats* |
| tz | tzaddi | ts as in *tsar, cats* |
| u | vowel point; waw | u as in *cut* or u as in *glue* (as waw, always the latter) |
| v | beth; waw | v; w |
| w | waw | w |
| x | — | not used |
| y | yod | y |
| z | zayin | z |

This table is not altogether complete, as I have not included all possible peculiarities of transliteration. Practices which I have tried to avoid include the transliteration of *tzaddi* as *s* or *t* and the use of *gh* or *a'a* for *ayin*, although *a'a* is sometimes justified by the vowel points. In Ashkenazic, *taw* becomes *s*.

In biblical Hebrew and in some modern pronunciations, a definite distinction is made between the *t* of *tau* and the emphatic *t* of *teth*, between the *s* of *shin* (or *sin*) and the emphatic *s* of *samekh*, and between the *k* of *kaph* and the emphatic *k* of *qoph*. These distinctions are rarely noticeable, however, and may safely be ignored.

In reference to the pronunciation of the names of the Goetic demons, it should be remembered that these names in their present form are from a French manuscript. Their Hebrew forms, if any, have been altered beyond recognition in most cases, although they aren't quite French, either. Personally, I prefer to pronounce them as if they were Latin—except for the accented vowels, which I give the French pronunciation. I would most certainly *not* recommend that anyone try his or her hand at summoning any of these entities, however, regardless of how their names are pronounced. At least one popular book on witchcraft has given detailed instructions for such a summoning. Although I believe in the free dissemination of information, I cannot but regard such instructions as irresponsible. Anyone with less expertise than an adept is asking for serious trouble if he or she dabbles with demons. I must emphasize that this statement is true even if demons are regarded as subjective, interior psychic forces and not as independent, objective entities. To project an autonomous part of the unconscious mind, perhaps an archetype, into complete awareness is to court neurosis or worse. No amount of circles, amulets, sigils, talismans, or lesser rituals of the pentagram prepared or carried out by an amateur will protect him from schizophrenia. Even the summoning of angels or the invocation of a god has its dangers, although not so drastic. For all practical purposes, I think one may assume that demons do have an objective existence and are fully capable of possessing or rending the would-be magus.

For magical purposes generally, it is my opinion that one should bear in mind the general rules of Hebrew pronunciation but use the pronunciation that seems most natural to the tongue or that seems to carry the most power or psychic weight. It could just as well be argued, however, that only the true names truly pronounced have any real power. In any case, I think it is safe to assume that many names and words of power no longer have quite the force they once did when they were spoken only in secret by the few. It is said that the power of a word is dissipated by overuse, and this is certainly true subjectively, psychologically. *Yahweh*, when it occurs in Scripture, is still invariably read aloud as *Adonai*. It was once supposed that the proper pronunciation of YHWH would shake the foundations of the universe. I don't suppose many people suppose that anymore.

# APPENDIX

# E

# NOTES TO THE SECOND EDITION

**Agrath** is also spelled, in various places, *Igereth* or *Igrath*. She seems to be another version of Lilith. No mention of anyone named AGRTh occurs in the Bible, although the word *iggereth* (AGRTh) is used severeal times. It means "letter" or "message." Agrath is said to be *bath Mahalath*, the daughter of Mahalath. The Bible mentions two women of this name, one the daughter of Ishmael and wife of Esau, the other a granddaughter of David and wife of Rehoboam. In neither case is any mention made of her having a demon-daughter or writing any letters.

**Alchemical Elements**—The three elements of alchemy:

| Sulfur | *Gaphrith* | GPRYTh | 693 |
|--------|-----------|--------|-----|
| Mercury | *Kaspith* | KSPYTh | 570 |
| Salt | *Melach* | MLCh | 78 |

**ALH**—As well as being *Elah*, "goddess," *Aleph-Lamed-He* is also *Eleh*, "these" or "those"; hence *Eleh ha-Devarim*, "These are the words."

**Aph**—As well as "also," *aph* means both "nose" and "wrath"; hence *Arik Apim*, "long of nose," meaning slow to anger or merciful.

**Arabic**—Inasmuch as most of the organized cabala was transmitted to (and altered by?) Jewish sources in Moorish Spain from Arabic originals, a few key Arabic words might be of interest: *Allah*, God, is ALLH, 66, according to the Arabic numerological system—the double consonant is indicated, as in Hebrew, by a diacritical mark, but such consonants are counted twice in the Arabic system; *Muhammad* the prophet is MHMMD, 132, the same enumeration as *Qalb*, QLB, heart, center. *Khidr*, KhDR, "green" is 804, and *Al Khidr*, the green one, the mysterious guide of men who instructed Moses, is AL KhDR, 835. *Salaam*, SLAM, "peace," is 131. Arabic "gematria" is a field that deserves its own separate study. That the Hebrew system is derivative, although perhaps at a date far earlier than the Middle Ages, may be indicated by the fact that the Arabic alphabet contains 28 characters—exactly enough to indicate hundreds through 900—plus one character (*ghayn*) for 1,000—without the somewhat awkward device of using secondary forms of letters such as the "finals" of Hebrew.

**Aleister Crowley**—"Frater Perdurabo" was a brilliant, charismatic man with a great deal of influence on many aspects of modern life as well as occultism. For example, according to Francis King, he probably introduced Aldous Huxley to mescalin and thus indirectly provided impetus to the entire hippie/drug movement of the '60s. Much of the material he originated has been used with and without acknowledgement by many organizations and mystery schools. His attraction lies largely in the facts that (1) he often applied a needed dose of common sense in areas where emotionalism and delusion abound (although he himself was certainly not immune from delusion), and (2) he became heavily involved, sometimes courageously, in practicing and experimenting with what others (e.g., E. A. Waite) only studied academically or contemplated abstractly. *However*, it should also be pointed out that he was without doubt a pompous ass, drug-addicted, obsessional, possibly sociopathic, and at least severely neurotic if not "quite mad." Unfortunately, he found at the end of his life that all of the energy he had expended in his attempts to follow the Path (and to promulgate *The Book of the Law* and usher in the new aeon) had ended in nothing.

**Eloi, Eloi, Lama Sabachthani**—"My God, my God, why hast Thou forsaken me?"—Words spoken by Jesus on the cross. This is the English rendition of the Greek rendition of the Hebrew/Aramaic *Elochai Elochai lamah sabaqthani* (ALChY ALChY LMH ShBQThNY, although *Lama* is also legitimately spelled LMA). The enumeration is 1035 (or 1031), which has no listed correspondences herein or in 777. It is, however, the sum of the numbers 1 through 45, and 45 is ADM, Adam. Thus 1035 can be said to represent "the sum of man," inasmuch as "Adam" means "man." According to some theologians, this statement made by Jesus on the cross epitomizes the extremity of his humanity as opposed to his divinity and thus is "the sum of man." It may also be observed that the summation of mankind may be that he ultimately feels forsaken by God, when in fact he is guided and cherished. (All this may be one example of the results of "cabalistic contemplation" as described in the Preface.) Jesus is also said to be "the second Adam." In any event, once you understand that *Eloi* is *Elochai* and *Elijah* in Hebrew is *Eliyahu*, it becomes more comprehensible why one hearer thought that Jesus was calling upon Elijah (Elias).

**Emeth**—Emeth is a Hebrew word (AMTh, 441) meaning "Truth." I include it here because (a) I do not wish it to be said that Truth is absent from this encyclopedia and because (b) the word is interesting if for no other reason than because of its connection with the *golem*, the artificial man of Jewish folklore. The word *Emeth* was inscribed on the forehead of the golem. When the *Aleph* was erased, leaving only MTh (*Mem-Taw*), *Meth*, "dead," the golem ceased to be animated.

**Ezah** and **Ezal**—"A giant" or "The name of a giant" as a definition for either of these two entities fails to relate their somewhat interesting background. Ezah and Ezal, it is stated, are giants chained to *Arqa*, one of the Seven Earths— the one that contains the Seven Hells. Another account has it that they were angels sent to earth to tempt mankind as a test. The two were, however, condemned for being overcome by their love for a mortal woman. Common variant spellings for the pair are Uzza and Azael—the latter being the same name (with the same Hebrew spelling, OZAL) given to the demon prince of Water. Their names are preserved in pagan, pre-Islamic Arabian religion wherein Uzza is a god and Azael an angel.

**"The first number . . . and . . . the last"**—Aleister Crowley considered it legitimate to take 135 as a number of Saturn (see Preface) because it is the product of "the first number of Saturn," 3, the number of the associated Sephira, and "the last," 45, which is the sum of the numbers 1 through 9 ($3^2$) that appear on the magic square of Saturn. By this same method, we can arrive at similar numbers for the other planets: Jupiter, 543; Mars, 1625; Sun, 3996; Venus, 8575; Mercury, 16,640; and the Moon, 29,889. As a well-known television personality might say, "I pity the fool who encounters a spirit whose name adds to 29,889." By the time the name were summed, it would be too late, one way or the other.

**Handwriting on the Wall**—The handwriting on the wall in the 5th chapter of the book of Daniel, foretelling the doom of Belshazzar, was *Mene Mene Tekel Upharsin*, meaning "Numbered, numbered, weighed, and divisions." In Hebrew, this is *Menah Menah Teqel Upharsin*, MNH MNH ThQL WPRSYN, 1126 or 1776. *Menah* can also be spelled MNA, *Mena*, in which case the phrase adds to 1118 or 1768. (MNH = 95; MNA = 91; ThQL = 530; and WPRSYN = 1056 or 406).

**Hell**—I have stated in the Introduction that "Kether itself has the same numerical value as the lowest hell." That's true only if you accept the citations of Francis Barrett in *The Magus* (c. 1801). His listing of the seven hells was followed in this book (see *Gehenna*), but it is probably (as I now perceive) a botched job. Aleister Crowley's list of the seven hells is undoubtedly more nearly accurate and at least has the virtue of being intelligible Hebrew, which Barrett's list is not. Crowley's list is as follows:

| Hell | Associated Sephira | Name and Meaning | Numerical Value |
|------|--------------------|------------------|-----------------|
| 7th | Supernals | Sheol (ShAWL)—Abyss, Hell | 337 |
| 6th | Chesed | Abaddon (ABDWN)—Destruction | 713/63 |
| 5th | Geburah | Beer Shachath (BAR ShChTh)—Pit of Destruction (Psalms LV:23) | 911 |
| 4th | Tiphareth | Tit Ha-yawen (TYT HYWN)—Miry Clay (Psalms XL:2) | 749/99 |
| 3rd | Netzach | Shaare Maweth (ShORY MWTh)—Gates of Death (Psalms IX:13) | 1026 |
| 2nd | Hod | Tzal-Maweth (TzLMWTh)—Shadow of Death (Psalms XXIII:4) | 566 |
| 1st | Yesod & Malkuth | Ge-Hinnom (GYHNWM)—Valley of Hinnom | 674/114 |

The Valley of Hinnom outside Jerusalem was the garbage dump and crematorium for the poor and for condemned criminals—hence, the name came to be applied to an other-worldly hell. It is noteworthy, however, that warnings about ending up in Ge-Hinnom once were not intended to refer to any situation in the afterlife, but were equivalent to the slightly more modern "You'll end up at the end of the hangman's rope."

In view of Crowley's list, it is probably safe to ignore Barrett's probable misprints "Gihebem," "Retzeltoth," "Yadash-chom," "Badshechath," and "Aboz," to give my anglicized versions, or, in Barrett's Hebrew, GYHBM (620/60), RTzLTWTh (435), YDOShChWM (998/438), BADShChTh (715), and ABWZ (16).

**Kings**—The ancient kings of Israel and Judah, as recorded in the Bible, are certainly of no less importance than the judges or indigenous Palestinian tribes. After the monarchies of Saul, David, and Solomon, the kingdom split into Judah, under Solomon's son, Rehoboam, and Israel, under the leader of the rebellious ten tribes, Jeroboam. They are listed on the following page.

## JUDAH

## ISRAEL

| Judah | | | Israel | | |
|---|---|---|---|---|---|
| Rehoboam | RChBOM | 830/320 | Jeroboam | YRBOM | 882/322 |
| Abijam | ABYM | 615/53 | Nadab | NDB | 56 |
| a.k.a. Abijah | ABYH | 18 | Baasha | BOShA | 373 |
| Asa | ASA | 62 | Elah | ALH or | 36 |
| Jehoshaphat | YHWShPT | 410 | | ALA | 32 |
| Joram | YRM or | 810/250 | Zimri | ZMRY | 257 |
| | YWRM | 816/256 | Omri | OMRY | 320 |
| a.k.a. Jehoram | YHWRM | 821/261 | Ahab | AChAB | 12 |
| Jehoahz | YWAChZ | 32 | Ahaziah | AChZYHW | 37 |
| | YHWAChZ | 37 | | or AChZYH | 31 |
| a.k.a. Azariah | OZRYH | 292 | Joram | YRM or | 810/250 |
| a.k.a. Ahaziah | AChZYH or | 31 | | YWRM | 816/256 |
| | AChZYHW | 37 | a.k.a. Jehoram | YHWRM | 821/261 |
| Joash | YASh or | 311 | Jehu | YHWA | 22 |
| | YWASh | 317 | Jehoahaz | YWAChZ or | 32 |
| a.k.a. Jehoash | YHWASh | 322 | | YHWAChZ | 37 |
| Amaziah | AMTzYHW | 152 | Athaliah | OThLYH or | 515 |
| | or AMTzYH | 146 | | OThLYHW | 521 |
| Azariah | OZRYH | 292 | Joash | YASh or | 311 |
| Jotham | YWThM | 1016/456 | | YWASh | 317 |
| Ahaz | AChZ | 16 | a.k.a. Jehoash | YHWASh | 322 |
| Hezekiah | ChZQYHW | 136 | Jeroboam II | YRBOM | 882/322 |
| | orChZQYH | 130 | Zacariah | ZKRYHW | 248 |
| Manesseh | MNShY | 400 | | or ZKRYH | 242 |
| | or MNShH | 395 | Shallum | ShLWM | 936/376 |
| Amon | AMWN | 747/97 | | or ShLM | 930/370 |
| | or AMN | 741/91 | Menahem | MNChM | 698/138 |
| Josiah | YAShYH or | 326 | Pekahiah | PQChYH | 203 |
| | YAShYHW | 332 | Pekah | PQCh | 188 |
| Jehoahaz | YWAChZ or | 32 | Hoshea | HWShO | 381 |
| | YHWAChZ | 37 | | | |
| a.k.a. Shallum | ShLWM | 936/376 | | | |
| | or ShLM | 930/370 | | | |
| Jehoiakim | YHWQYM | 731/171 | | | |
| a.k.a. Eliakim | ALYQYM | 751/191 | | | |
| Jehoiachin | YWYKYN or | 756/106 | | | |
| | YHWYKYN | 761/111 | | | |

Also of importance in any consideration of the kings of Israel is the infamous Jezebel (Hebrew: *Izebel*), daughter of the Zidonian king Ethbaal, wife of Ahab and then of Joram. The Hebrew spelling is AYZBL, 50.

It will be noted that most of the names ending in "iah," YH, - *yah*, also appear with a final *Waw*. The Bible uses these names in both spellings (for example, Josiah vs. Josiahu) in a seemingly random fashion. Both spellings and enumerations are legitimate.

**Malka be-Tarshishim we-Ad be-Ruah Shehaqim** and **Shed Barshemath ha-Sharthathan**—As pointed out in the definitions of these two phrases, translation is difficult if not impossible. They were constructed—possibly by Francis Barrett in 1801—to add up to 3321, the sum of all numbers from 1 to 81; that is, of all the numbers appearing on the 9 by 9 magic square associated with the Moon. The names of the intelligences (or daemons) and spirits of each planet add up to the sum of all the numbers on the magic square associated with each planet. In the case of Saturn with its 3 by 3 magic square, the matter is fairly simple; the number called for is only 45. Thus, we get Agiel (AGYAL) and Zazel (ZAZL). A number like 3321 is not so simple, however. Some elaborate title or lengthy name is required. And so we have Barrett giving the puzzling combinations MLKA BThRShYShYM WOD BRWH ShH-QYM, which misses the mark by 100 unless the final *Mem* is unaccountably counted as 700 instead of 600, and ShD BRShMOTh HShRThThN, both "improved on" or "restored" by Israel Regardie to MLKA BThRShYSYM WOD RWChWTh ShChLYM and ShD BRShHMOTh ShRThThN and by Aleister Crowley to MLKA BThRShYShYM WOD BRWH ShHRYM and ShDBRShHMOTh ShRThThN, the latter the same as Regardie's version. In any case, the "translations" of "Spirit of the Spirits of the Moon" and "Intelligence of the Intelligences of the Moon" are a bit misleading. The Hebrew translation of *these* two phrases would be *Ruach ha-Ruachoth ha-Levanah* (RWCh HRWChWTh HLBNH), which only adds to 931, and perhaps *Shed ha-Shedim ha-Levanah* (ShD HShDYM HLBNH), which only adds to 1318. As the "names" stand, possible trans-lations might be, for Regardie's *Malka* etc., "Queen with the Chrysolites and Eternity-Spirits of the Lions" and, for *Shed* etc., "Demon, son of Shimeath, the Servant-Jackal." In the Bible, Shimeath (ShMOTh) was an Ammonitess, the mother of Jozachar (YWZKR, 243) and Zabad (ZBD, 13), who collaborated in the slaying of King Joash (YWASh, 317, or YASh, 311) of Judah. One difficulty with *Tarshishim*, "chrysolites" or "berels," is that it is the name of an angelic choir usually associated with *Netzach* and Venus, not with *Yesod* or the Moon. If we accept the above translation for *Shed* etc., the proper configuration of the letters would be ShD BR ShMOTh HShRTh ThN, *Shed Bar Shimeath ha-Sharath Tan.* We may also attempt to "re-store" *Malka* etc. by taking it as MLKH HThRShYShYM WHRWChWTh HShChQYM, *Malkah ha-Tarshishim we-ha-Ruachoth ha-Shechaqim,* "Queen of the Chrysolites and of the Spirits of the Clouds," but the enumeration overshoots the mark at 3574. If the object is simply to construct an intelligible name or phrase that adds to 3321, it is not that big a problem. For example, one obvious possibility is MLKH HThRShYShYM WHRWChWTh NPLYM, *Malkah Ha-Tarshishim we-ha-Ruachoth Nephilim,* "Queen of the Chrysolites and of the Spirits of the Giants," or (if we wish to become facetious) HYLL BN ShChR BHShMYM BYHLWM BShLWM, *Heylel ben Shachar be-ha-Shamaim be-Yahalomim be-Shalom,* "Lucifer in the Sky with Diamonds, in Peace." Perhaps, however, the best solution is to accept the bizarre traditional phrases as proper names, no more capable of translation than "Bill Jones" or "Aleister Crowley."

**Muses**—A 15th-century neo-Platonic document assigns Apollo to Kether and the nine muses of Greek mythology to the other nine heavenly spheres (i.e., to the Sephiroth). I have supplied probable Hebrew spellings and their enumerations:

| Sephira | Muse | Area of Influence | Hebrew | Enumeration |
|---------|------|-------------------|--------|-------------|
| Chokmah | Urania | Astronomy | WRANYH | 272 |
| Binah | Polyhymnia | Sacred Lyric | PLYHMNYH | 230 |
| Chesed | Euterpe | Music | WThRP | 686/1406 |
| Geburah | Erato | Lyric and Love Poetry | ARThW | 607 |
| Tiphareth | Melpomene | Tragedy | MLPWMN | 246/896 |
| Netzach | Terpsichore | Dancing and Choral Song | ThRPShKWR | 1206 |
| Hod | Calliope | Eloquence and Heroic Poetry | KLYWP | 146/866 |
| Yesod | Clio | History | KLYW | 66 |
| Malkuth | Thalia | Comedy and Pastoral Poetry | ThALYH | 446 |

The Hebrew term for "muse" is *Bath Shir* (BTh ShYr), song maiden, the enumeration of which is 912. The plural, "muses," is *Banoth Shir*, BNWTh ShYR, 968. "The Nine Muses" would be *Ha-Tishah Banoth Shir*, HThShOH BNWTh ShYR, 1748.

**Plutarch**—The Greek biographer of the 1st century B.C. came up with a series of numbers associated with the planets that bear no relationship to later tradition or cabalism, but which may be of some interest: Antichthon (a hypothetical counter-earth), 3; the Earth, 9; the Moon, 27; Mercury, 81; Venus, 243; and the Sun, 729, a number also said to be of importance to Pythagoras. The solar number, 729, is 365 + 364—the number of days plus the number of nights in a year. It is also the square of 27, the number of days in the lunar period with respect to the stars. (The geocentric lunar period is closer to 29½ days. Evidently the Pythagoreans were able to distinguish the sidereal period as well.) By extending the method of deriving these numbers, we get Mars, 2187; Jupiter, 6561; and Saturn, 19,683 (and fixed stars, 59,049; primum mobile, 177,147?). it will be observed that these are progressive powers of 3.

**Prefixes**—A good deal of manipulation in gematria can be achieved by the use of Hebrew prefixes—one-letter conjunctions, articles, and prepositions. The letter in question is simply "tacked on" to the beginning of any noun.

| | | | |
|---|---|---|---|
| *Beth* | B | *be, ba, bi* | in, by, at, with |
| *He* | H | *ha, he* | the |
| *Waw* | W | *we, wa, wi* | and, but |
| *Kaph* | K | *ke, ki, ka* | as, like, almost |
| *Lamed* | L | *le, la, li* | to, into; for, at |
| *Mem* | M | *mi, me* | from, of; since |
| *Shin* | Sh | *she* | who, which, that; because |

Thus it becomes a simple matter to convert "peace," ShLWM, 936, into "the peace," HShLWM, 941; "and peace," WShLWM, 942; "and the peace," WHShLWM, 947; "in peace," BShLWM, 938, etc.

**Senoy, Sansenoy, Semangeloph**—These are the three angels invoked against the demon-queen of the night, Lilith. The formula is *"Senoy, Sansenoy, Semangeloph! Adam we-Chavvah! Chotz Lilith!"* ("Senoy, Sansenoy, Semangeloph! Adam and Eve! Out, Lilith.") The invocation may be a case of gematriatic misfire, inasmuch as, disappointingly, the names of the three angels enumerate as 631 but *Adam we-Chavvah* as only 630 (the same, surprisingly, as *Gog we-Magog*). *Chotz Lilith* is 578, 584, 1388, or 1394, depending on whether the final *Sadhe* is taken as 90 or 900 and upon whether *Chotz* is spelled ChTz or ChWTz, either being a legitimate Biblical form of the word. Therefore the whole invocation enumerates as 1839, 1845, 2649, or 2655.

**Shem Hamphorash** is the form usually given in magical textbooks, but the proper Hebrew form is closer to *Shem Ha-Mephorash*, meaning literally "name of extension."

**Tarot**—According to Idries Shah (*The Sufis*, Anchor Books, 1971), all Western versions of the Tarot are hopelessly distorted from the Arabic original. The word "Tarot," he says, is derived from the Arabic *turuq*, "four ways," and the deck was originally a Sufi teaching tool. The distortions involve warping the meanings to fit cabalistic theory, transpositions of meanings, mistranslations of the titles from Arabic, and substituting pictures. In light of these facts, the efforts of Waite and Crowley to restore the deck to its original form appear pitiful. Those seriously interested in the inner meaning of the Tarot would be well advised to peruse the Arabic deck and the material from which it was derived. Nevertheless, the deck as it is remains useful for divination, and, after all, Shah's statements are only the assertions of an undoubted Master of The Divine Science.

**Teachers**—It ought to go without saying, and certainly ought to be strongly emphasized, that carrying out any sort of "spiritual exercises," including some of those described in this volume and even including meditation, without the guidance of a qualified teacher is tantamount to playing Russian roulette with your mind. Only by chance can they be of any benefit, and they are far more likely to be destructive to your inner development. Who is a qualified teacher? Since the entire field abounds with no end of charlatans, megalomaniacs, and sincere but misguided souls, the search for a teacher is not always an easy task. Nor is everyone qualified, because of hidden prejudices and conditioning that prevent learning, to be a student. Some say that, if you are ready, the teacher will find *you*. In any case, beware of personality cults and organizations that cater to your desire for attention and excitement, and do not flit from one thing to another, for you will only pollute your mind with all manner of "systems," which, if all taken seriously, will drive you mad. Nor can you pick and choose what you like from a variety of approaches, for you are not qualified to do so. All this advice is simply repeated from the sayings and writings of those who should know. Good luck.

**Titles of Kether**—Any student of Biblical Hebrew is likely to be puzzled if not appalled by the Hebrew spellings of some of the "titles" (appellations) of the Sephiroth—indeed, by some of the words themselves. *Tath Zal*, "the profuse giver," for example, has no equivalent in Biblical (or modern) Hebrew. Inasmuch as textbooks on medieval Hebrew are hard to come by in English—if they exist at all—I confess to a certain amount of ignorance on the subject. Are these medieval Sephardic spellings? Did the author of the *Zohar* take unconscionable liberties with the language for the sake of numerical considerations? Are the spellings simply regrettable mistakes of Samuel Mathers, translator of von Rosenroth's *Kabbala Denudata*? Are they mistakes on the part of von Rosenroth? Other examples: In the Bible, "long" is ARK, *arok*. ARYK, *arik*, does not occur. In fact, in *Sepher Sephiroth*, Crowley spells *Arik Apim* without the *Yod* in ARYK, thus giving an enumeration of 352 instead of 362. Yet he retains the *Yod* in the similar expression, *Arik Anpin*. "Internal" is PNYMY, not PNMY, as in *Or Penimi*. Hebrew in general is mostly lacking in terminal *Alephs*, yet they abound in these "titles": MWPLA, RYShA, OThYQA (vs. the Biblical OThYQ), QDYShA, etc. Perhaps this is a grammatical device of which I am unaware.

## NUMERICAL INDEX TO NOTES

**12**—AChAB, Ahab, 7th king of Israel
**16**—AChZ, *Ahaz*, 11th king of Judah
**18**—ABYH, *Abijah*, 2nd king of Judah. He is called Abijam in *Kings*, but Abijah in *Chronicles*
**22**—YHWA, *Jehu*, 10th king of Israel
**31**—AChZYH, *Ahaziah*, (1) 6th king of Judah, better known as Jehoahaz; (2) 8th king of Israel
**32**—ALA, *Elah*, 4th king of Israel
—YWAChZ, *Jehoahaz*, (1) 6th king of Judah; (2) 16th king of Judah; (3) 11th king of Israel
**36**—ALH, *Elah*, 4th king of Israel

**37**—AChZYHW, *Ahaziahu*, (1) 6th king of Judah, better known as Jehoahaz; (2) 8th king of Israel

—YHWAChZ, *Jehoahaz* (1) 6th king of Judah; (2) 16th king of Judah; (3) 11th king of Israel

**50**—AYZBL, *Jezebel*, the infamous lady who dabbled in Israeli politics

**52**—ALYHW, *Eliyahu*, the prophet Elijah

**53**—ABYM, *Abijam*, 2nd king of Judah

**62**—ASA, *Asa*, 3rd king of Judah

**56**—NDB, *Nadab*, 2nd king of Israel

**63**—ABDWN (N = 50), *Abaddon*, Destruction, the 6th hell

**66**—ALLH (Arabic), *Allah*, God

—KLYW, *Clio*, Muse of History

**78**—MLCh, *Melach*, Salt

**91**—AMN (N = 50), *Amon*, 14th king of Judah

—MNA, *Mena*, Numbered

**95**—MNH, *Menah*, Numbered

**97**—AMWN (N = 50), *Amon*, 14th king of Judah

**99**—TYT HYWN (N = 50), *Tit Ha-yawen*, Miry Clay, the 4th hell

**106**—YWYKYN (N = 50), *Jehoiachin*, 18th and last king of Judah, a puppet of the Persian king

**111**—YHWYKYN (N = 50), *Jehoiachin*, 18th and last king of Judah, a puppet of the Persian king

**114**—GYHNWM (M = 40), *Ge-Hinnom*, Valley of Hinnom, Gehenna, the 1st hell

**130**—ChZQYH, *Hezekiah*, 12th king of Judah

**131**—SLAM (Arabic), *Salaam*, Peace

**132**—MHMMD (Arabic), *Muhammad*, the prophet of Islam

—QLB (Arabic), *Qalb*, heart

**136**—ChZQYHW, *Hezekiahu*, 12th king of Judah

**138**—MNChM (M = 40), *Menahem*, 17th ruler of Israel

**146**—AMTYzYH, *Amaziah*, 8th king of Judah

**146**—KLYWP (P = 80), *Calliope*, Muse of Eloquence and Heroic Poetry

**152**—AMTzYHW, *Amaziahu*, 8th king of Judah

**171**—YHWQYM (M = 40), *Jehoiakim*, 17th king of Judah, a puppet of Pharaoh-Necho

**188**—PQCh, *Pekah*, 19th ruler of Israel

**191**—ALYQYM (M = 40), *Eliakim*, original name of Jehoiakim

**203**—PQChYH, *Pekahiah*, 18th ruler of Israel

**230**—PLYHMNYH, *Polyhymnia*, Muse of Sacred Lyric

**246**—MLPWN (N = 50), *Melpomene*, Muse of Tragedy

**250**—YRM (M = 40), *Joram*, (1) 5th king of Judah; (2) 9th king of Israel

**256**—YWRM (M = 40), *Joram*, (1) 5th king of Judah; (2) 9th king of Israel

**257**—ZMRY, *Zimri*, 5th king of Israel

**261**—YHWRM (M = 40), *Jehoram*, (1) 5th king of Judah; (2) 9th king of Israel

**272**—WRANYH, *Urania*, Muse of Astronomy

**292**—OZRYH, *Azariah*, (1) 6th king of Judah, better known as Jehoahaz; (2) 9th king of Judah

**311**—YASh, *Joash*, (1) 7th king of Judah; (2) 13th ruler of Israel

**317**—YWASh, (1) 7th king of Judah; (2) 13th ruler of Israel

**320**—RChBOM (M = 40), *Rehoboam*, son of Solomon and 1st king of Judah

—OMRY, *Omri*, 6th king of Israel

**322**—YRBOM (M = 40), *Jeroboam*, (1) 1st king of Israel; (2) 14th ruler of Israel, Jeroboam II

—YHWASh, *Jehoash*, (1) 7th king of Judah; (2) 13th ruler of Israel

**326**—YAShYH, *Josiah*, 15th king of Judah

**332**—YAShYHW, *Josiahu*, 15th king of Judah

**337**—ShAWL, *Sheol*, Abyss, the 7th hell

**370**—ShLM (M = 40), *Shallum*, (1) 16th king of Judah, better known as Jehoahaz; (2) 16th ruler of Israel

**373**—BOShA, *Baasha*, 3rd king of Israel

**376**—ShLWM, *Shallum*, (1) 16th king of Judah, better known as Jehoahaz; (2) 16th ruler of Israel

**381**—HWShO, *Hoshea*, 20th and last king of Israel

**395**—MNShH, *Manasseh*, 13th king of Judah

**400**—MNShY, *Manasseh*, 13th king of Judah

**406**—WPRSYN (N = 50), *Upharsin*, Divisions

**410**—YHWShPT, *Jehoshaphat*, 4th king of Judah

**411**—ALYShO, *Elisha*, the Hebrew prophet, successor to Elijah

**441**—AMTh, *Emeth*, Truth

**446**—ThALYH, *Thalia*, Muse of Comedy and Pastoral Poetry

**456**—YWThM (M = 40), *Jotham*, 10th king of Judah

**515**—OThLYH, *Athaliah*, Queen and 12th ruler of Israel

**521**—OThLYHW, *Athaliahu*, Queen and 12th ruler of Israel

**530**—ThQL, *Teqel*, Weighed

**566**—TzLMWTh, *Tzal-Maweth*, Shadow of Death, the 2nd hell

**578**—ChTz LYLYTh (Tz = 90), *Chotz Lilith*, Out, Lilith!

**584**—ChWTz LYLYTH (Tz = 90), *Chotz Lilith*, Out, Lilith! (alternate spelling of above)

**607**—ARThW, *Erato*, Muse of Lyric and Love Poetry

**615**—ABYM, *Abijam*, 2nd king of Judah

**630**—ADM WChWH, *Adam we-Chavvah*, Adam and Eve

**631**—SNWY SNSNWY SMNGLWP (P = 80), *Senoy, Sansenoy, Semangeloph*, The three angels invoked against Lilith

**674**—GYHNWH, *Ge-Hinnom*, Valley of Hinnom, Gehenna, the 1st hell

**686**—WThRP (P = 80), *Euterpe*, Muse of Music

**693**—GPRYTh, *Gaphrith*, Sulfur, brimstone

**698**—MNChM, *Menahem*, 17th ruler of Israel

**713**—ABDWN, *Abaddon*, Destruction, the 6th hell

**731**—YHWQYM, *Jehoiakim*, 17th king of Judah, a puppet of Pharaoh-Necho

**741**—AMN, *Amon*, 14th king of Judah

**747**—AMWN, *Amon*, 14th king of Judah

**751**—ALYQYM, *Eliakim*, Original name of Jehoiakim

**749**—TYT HYWN, Tit Ha-yawen, Miry Clay, the 4th hell

**756**—YWYKYN, *Jehoiachin*, 18th and last king of Judah, a puppet of the Persian king

**761**—YHWYKYN, *Jehoiachin*, 18th and last king of Judah, a puppet of the Persian king

**804**—KhDR (Arabic), *Khidr*, Green

**810**—YRM, *Joram*, (1) 5th king of Judah; (2) 9th king of Israel

**816**—YWRM, *Joram*, (1) 5th king of Judah; (2) 9th king of Israel

**821**—YHWRM, *Jehoram*, (1) 5th king of Judah; (2) 9th king of Israel

**830**—RChBOM, *Rehoboam*, Son of Solomon and 1st king of Judah

**835**—AL KhDR (Arabic), *Al Khidr*, The Green One, the Guide of Men

**866**—KLYWP, *Calliope*, Muse of Eloquence and Heroic Poetry

**882**—YRBOM, *Jeroboam*, (1) 1st king of Israel; (2) 13th ruler of Israel, Jeroboam II

**896**—MLPWN, *Melpomene*, Muse of Tragedy

**911**—BAR ShChTh, *Beer Shachath*, Pit of Destruction, the 5th hell

**912**—BTh ShYR, *Bath Shir*, Song maiden, muse

**930**—ShLM, *Shallum*, (1) 16th king of Judah, better known as Jehoahaz; (2) 16th ruler of Israel

**936**—ShLWM, *Shallum*, (1) 16th king of Judah, better known as Jehoahaz; (2) 16th ruler of Israel

**968**—BNWTh ShYR, *Banoth Shir*, Song maidens, muses

**1016**—YWThM, *Jotham*, 10th king of Judah

**1026**—ShORY MWTh, *Shaare Maweth*, Gates of Death, the 3rd hell

**1031**—ALChY ALChY LMA ShBQThNY, *Elochai Elochai Lama Sabqthani*, "My God, my God, why hast Thou forsaken me?" *Lama* is given the Aramaic spelling of LMA.

**1035**—ALChY ALChY LMH ShBQThNY, *Elochai Elochai Lamah Sabaqthani*, "My God, my God, why hast Thou forsaken me?" *Lamah* is given the Hebrew, as opposed to Aramaic, spelling; that is, LMH instead of LMA.

**1056**—WPRSYN, *Upharsin*, Divisions

**1118**—MNA MNA ThQL WPRSYN (N = 50), *Mena Mena Teqel Upharsin*, Numbered, numbered, weighed, and divisions; the Handwriting on the Wall

**1126**—MNH MNH ThQL WPRSYN (N = 50), *Menah Menah Teqel Upharsin*, An alternate spelling for the above

**1206**—ThRPShKWR, *Terpsichore*, Muse of Dancing and Choral Song

**1388**—ChTz LYLYTh, *Chotz Lilith*, Out, Lilith!

**1394**—ChWTz LYLYTh, *Chotz Lilith*, Out, Lilith! (an alternate spelling for the above)

**1406**—WThRP, *Euterpe*, Muse of Music

**1748**—HThShOH BNWTh ShYR, *Ha-Tishah Banoth Shir*, The Nine Muses

**1768**—MNA MNA ThQL WPRSYN, *Mena Mena Teqel Upharsin*, Numbered, numbered, weighed, and divisions; the Handwriting on the Wall

**1776**—MNH MNH ThQL WPRSYN, *Menah Menah Teqel Upharsin*, an alternate spelling for the above

**1839**—SNWY SNSNWY SMNGLWP ADM WChWH ChTz LYLYTh (Tz = 90), *Senoy, Sansenoy, Semangeloph! Adam we-Chavvah! Chotz Lilith!*, Senoy, Sansenoy, Semangeloph! Adam and Eve! Out, Lilith!—An invocation against the night-demon Lilith

**1845**—SNWY SNSNWY SMNGLWP ADM WChWH ChWTz LYLYTh (Tz = 90)—Same as the above, but with *Chotz* spelled with a *Waw*.

**2649**—SNWY SNSNWY SMNGLWP ADM WChWH ChTz LY-

LYTh—See no. 1839; here *Sadhe* is given its full value of 900.

**2655**—SNWY SNSNWY SMNGLWP ADM WChWH ChWTz LY-LYTh—See no. 1845; here *Sadhe* is given its full value of 900.

# APPENDIX

# F

# BIBLIOGRAPHY

Anon.: *The Lesser Key of Solomon: Goetia: The Book of Evil Spirits*. L. W. de Laurence, ed. De Laurence, Scott & Co. (Chicago), 1916.

Anon.: *Sepher Yetzirah: The Book of Formation*. The Arx Foundation (Austin, TX), 1970.

Achad, Frater (i.e., Charles Stansfeld Jones): *Q.B.L. or The Bride's Reception*. Samuel Weiser, Inc. (New York), 1969.

Barrett, Francis: *The Magus*. The Citadel Press (Secaucus, NJ), 1967.

Ben-Yehuda, Ehud; and Weinstein, David: *Ben-Yehuda's Pocket English-Hebrew Hebrew-English Dictionary*. Washington Square Press (New York), 1971.

Campbell, Joseph: *The Masks of God: Creative Mythology*. Penguin Books (Harmondsworth, Middlesex, U.K.), 1968.

Case, Paul Foster: *The Tarot: A Key to the Wisdom of the Ages*. Macoy Publishing Co. (Richmond, VA), 1947.

Crowley, Aleister: *777 and Other Qabalistic Writings*. Israel Regardie, ed. Samuel Weiser, Inc. (York Beach, ME), 1977.

Crowley, Aleister: *The Confessions of Aleister Crowley: An Autobiography*. John Symonds and Kenneth Grant, eds. Hill and Wang (New York), 1969.

Crowley, Aleister: *The Law Is for All*. Israel Regardie, ed. Falcon Press (Phoenix, AZ), 1986.

Crowley, Aleister: *Magick in Theory and Practice*. Dover Publications, Inc. (New York), 1976.

Davidson, Gustav: *A Dictionary of Angels*. The Free Press (New York), 1967.

Feyerabend, Karl: *Langenscheidt's Pocket Hebrew Dictionary to the Old Testament*. Barnes & Noble, Inc. (New York), 1961.

Gardner, Martin: "Mathematical Games: Dr. Matrix finds numerological wonders in the King James Bible." *Scientific American* CCXXXIII:3 (Sept. 1975), pp. 174ff.

King, Francis: *The Rites of Modern Occult Magic*. The Macmillan Co. (New York), 1970.

Kittle, Rudolph (ed.): *Biblia Hebraica*. Wurttembergische Bibelanstalt (Stuttgart), 1973.

Knight, Gareth: *A Practical Guide to Qabalistic Symbolism*. Helios Book Service (Publications) Ltd. (Cheltenham, Glos., U.K.), 1969.

Magil, Joseph: *Magil's Linear School Bible: The Five Books of Moses*. Hebrew Publishing Co. (New York), 1905.

The Master Therion (i.e., Aleister Crowley), *The Book of Thoth*. Samuel Weiser, Inc. (York Beach, ME), 1974.

Mathers, S. L. MacGregor: *The Kabbalah Unveiled*. Samuel Weiser, Inc. (York Beach, ME), 1983.

Patai, Raphael: *The Hebrew Goddess*. Ktav Publishing House, Inc., 1967.

Regardie, Israel: *The Tree of Life: A Study in Magic*. Samuel Weiser, Inc. (New York), 1969.

Regardie, Israel: *The Golden Dawn*. Llewellyn Publications (St. Paul, MN), 1987.

Regardie, Israel: *The Eye in the Triangle*. Llewellyn Publications (St. Paul, MN), 1970.

Shah, Idries: *The Sufis:* Anchor Books (Garden City, NY), 1971.

Waite, Arthur Edward: *The Book of Ceremonial Magic*. The Citadel Press (Secaucus, NJ), 1961.

Waite, A. E.: *The Holy Kabbalah*. University Books (New Hyde Park, NY), 1960.

Yates, Kyle M.: *The Essentials of Biblical Hebrew*. Harper & Row (New York), no date.

Young, Robert: *Analytical Concordance to the Bible*. Wm. B. Eerdmans Publishing Co. (Grand Rapids, MI), 1970.

# SEPHER SEPHIROTH

# PREFACE

CAN any good thing come out of Palestine? is the broader anti-Semiti
retort to the sneer cast by the Jews themselves against the harmless an
natural Nazarene; one more example of the poetic justice of History. And n
doubt such opponents of the modern Jew will acclaim this volume as a
admirable disproof of that thesis which it purports to uphold.

The dissimilarities, amounting in some cases to sheer contradiction, which
mark many numbers, will appear proof positive that there is nothing in th
numerical Qabalah, especially as we may presume that by filling up th
dictionary from the ordinary Hebrew Lexicon one would arrive at a me
hotch-pot.

Apart from this, there is a deeper-lying objection to the Qabalah; viz., tha
the theory is an example of the fallacy Post hoc propter hoc.

Are we to believe, asks the sceptic, that a number of learned men deliberatel
sat down and chose words for the sake of their numerical value? Language
a living thing, with many sources and diverse; can it be moulded in any suc
arbitrary fashion?

The only reply seems to be a mere assertion that to some extent it certainl
is so. Examples of a word being spelt deliberately wrong do occur; and such
jugglery as the changing of the names Abram and Sarai to Abraham and Sara
can hardly be purposeless. Once admit the end of such a wedge, and it
difficult to say whether it may not be driven home so far as to split asunder th
Tree of Knowledge, if not the Tree of Life.

Another line of argument is the historical. We do not here refer to th
alleged forgery of the Qabalah by Rabbi Moses ben Leon—was it not?—but
the general position of the ethnologist that the Jews were an entirely barbarou
race, incapable of any spiritual pursuit. That they were polytheists is clear fro
the very first verse of Genesis; that Adonai Melekh is identical with "Moloch
is known to every Hebraist. The "Old Testament" is mainly the history of th
struggle of the phallic Jehovah against the rest of the Elohim, and that h
sacrifices were of blood, and human blood at that, is indisputable.

# PREFACE

Human sacrifices are to-day still practised by the Jews of Eastern Europe, as is set forth at length by the late Sir Richard Burton in the MS. which the wealthy Jews of England have compassed heaven and earth to suppress, and evidenced by the ever-recurring Pogroms against which so senseless an outcry is made by those who live among those degenerate Jews who are at least not cannibals.

Is it to such people, indeed, that we are to look for the highest and subtlest spiritual knowledge?

To this criticism there are but two answers. The first, that an esoteric tradition of great purity may co-exist with the most crass exoteric practice. Witness the Upanishads in the land of Jagganath, hook-swinging, and the stupidest forms of Hatha-Yoga.

Witness the Tipitaka (with such perfections as the Dhammapada) in the midst of peoples whose science of torture would seem to have sprung from no merely human imagination. The descriptions in the Tipitaka itself of the Buddhist Hells are merely descriptions of the actual tortures inflicted by the Buddhists on their enemies.

The second, that after all is said, I find it work very well. I do not care whether $\sqrt{-1}$ is an impossible, an unimaginable thing, or whether de Moivre really invented it, and if so, whether de Moivre was an immoral man, and wore whiskers. It helps me to make certain calculations; and so long as that is so, it is useful, and I stick to it.

Other criticisms of the methods of the Qabalah itself have been made and disposed of in the article on the subject in "The Temple of Solomon the King" (Equinox V) and no further reference need be made to them in this place. It is only necessary to say that that article should be studied most thoroughly, and also the article "A Note on Genesis" in the second number of The Equinox.

With these two weapons, and the Sword of the Spirit, the Practicus, fully armed, may adventure himself in the great battle wherein victory is Truth.

PERDURABO.

# EDITORIAL NOTE

T HIS dictionary was begun by Allan Bennett (Fra ∴ Iehi Aour, now Bhikkhu Ananda Metteya) in the last decade of the nineteenth century since ψ-J.C. It was bequeathed to the present Editor, with many other magica MSS., on I.A.'s departure for Ceylon in 1899.

Frater Perdurabo used it, and largely added to it, in the course of hi Qabalistic workings. With George Cecil Jones (Fra ∴ Volo Noscere) he further added to it by making it a complete cross-correspondence to the Book DCCLXXVII

It was further revised and checked, re-copied by a Jewish scribe, and again checked through, in the year V of the present Era.

The mathematical additions were continued by Fra ∴ P. and Fra ∴ Lampada Tradam; and the MS. finally copied on a specially constructed typewriter by Gerald Rae Fraser (Fra ∴ ψ) who added yet further mathematical data.

This copy has again been checked by Fra ∴ P. and Soror ∴ N.N. and the proofs further by three separate scholars.

The method of employing the dictionary has been fully indicated in The Temple of Solomon the King [Equinox V].

None of the editors claim to possess even the smallest degree of scholarship The method of compilation has been to include all words given in Von Rosen roth's Qabalistic Dictionary, those specially commented on in S.D., I.R.Q., and I.Z.Q., those given in 777, and those found by Fratres I.A. and P. Some of them are found in texts of the Hebrew Scriptures which appeared to those adepts to be of magical importance. Owing to their carelessness, the meaning of some few words has been lost, and cannot now be traced.

# TABLE OF FACTORS

| | | | | | | | | | |
|---|---|---|---|---|---|---|---|---|---|
| $\boxed{1}$ | P. | 83 | P. | 171 | — | 259 | 7 | 347 | P. |
| 2 | P. | 87 | — | 173 | P. | 261 | — | 349 | P. |
| 3 | P. | 89 | P. | 177 | — | 263 | P. | 351 | — |
| 5 | P. | 91 | 7 | 179 | P. | 267 | — | 353 | P. |
| 7 | P. | 93 | — | 181 | P. | 269 | P. | 357 | — |
| $\boxed{9}$ | $3^2$ | 97 | P. | 183 | — | 271 | P. | 359 | P. |
| 11 | P. | 99 | — | 187 | 11 | 273 | — | $\boxed{361}$ | $19^2$ |
| 13 | P. | 101 | P. | 189 | — | 277 | P. | 363 | — |
| 17 | P. | 103 | P. | 191 | P. | 279 | — | 367 | P. |
| 19 | P. | 107 | P. | 193 | P. | 281 | P. | 369 | — |
| 21 | — | 109 | P. | 197 | P. | 283 | P. | 371 | 7 |
| 23 | P. | 111 | — | 199 | P. | 287 | 7 | 373 | P. |
| 27 | $3^3$ | 113 | P. | 201 | — | $\boxed{289}$ | $17^2$ | 377 | 13 |
| 29 | P. | 117 | — | 203 | 7 | 291 | — | 379 | P. |
| 31 | P. | 119 | 7 | 207 | — | 293 | P. | 381 | — |
| 33 | — | $\boxed{121}$ | $11^2$ | 209 | 11 | 297 | — | 383 | P. |
| 37 | P. | 123 | — | 211 | P. | 299 | 13 | 387 | — |
| 39 | — | 127 | P. | 213 | — | 301 | 7 | 389 | P. |
| 41 | P. | 129 | — | 217 | 7 | 303 | — | 391 | 17 |
| 43 | P. | 131 | P. | 219 | — | 307 | P. | 393 | — |
| 47 | P. | 133 | 7 | 221 | 13 | 309 | — | 397 | P. |
| $\boxed{49}$ | $7^2$ | 137 | P. | 223 | P. | 311 | P. | 399 | — |
| 51 | — | 139 | P. | 227 | P. | 313 | P. | 401 | P. |
| 53 | P. | 141 | — | 229 | P. | 317 | P. | 403 | 13 |
| 57 | — | 143 | 11 | 231 | — | 319 | 11 | 407 | 11 |
| 59 | P. | 147 | — | 233 | P. | 321 | — | 409 | P. |
| 61 | P. | 149 | P. | 237 | — | 323 | 17 | 411 | — |
| 63 | — | 151 | P. | 239 | P. | 327 | — | 413 | 7 |
| 67 | P. | 153 | — | 241 | P. | 329 | 7 | 417 | — |
| 69 | — | 157 | P. | 243 | $3^5$ | 331 | P. | 419 | P. |
| 71 | P. | 159 | — | 247 | 13 | 333 | — | 421 | P. |
| 73 | P. | 161 | 7 | 249 | — | 337 | P. | 423 | — |
| 77 | 7 | 163 | P. | 251 | P. | 339 | — | 427 | 7 |
| 79 | P. | 167 | P. | 253 | 11 | 341 | 11 | 429 | — |
| $\boxed{81}$ | $3^4 = 9^2$ | $\boxed{169}$ | $13^2$ | 257 | P. | 343 | 7 | 431 | P. |

# ABBREVIATIONS, SIGNS, AND FIGURES

K.D. L.C.K. p.— = KABBALA DENUDATA cuius Pars Prima continet Loci  
                Communes Kabbalisticos.

| | |
|---|---|
| Dec. | = Decan. |
| S.P.M. | = Sphere of the Primum Mobile. |
| S.S.F. | = Sphere of the Fixed Stars. |
| L.T.N. | = Lesser Angel governing Triplicity by Night. |
| L.T.D. | = Lesser Angel governing Triplicity by Day. |
| K.Ch.B. | = Kether—Chokmah—Binah. |
| (Ch.) | = Chaldee. |
| S.D. | = Siphra Dtzenioutha. |
| I.R.Q. | = Idra Rabba Qadisha. |
| Tet. | = Tetragrammaton. |
| L.A. Angel | = Lesser Assistant Angel. |
| I.Z.Q. | = Idra Zuta Qadisha. |
| M.T. | = Magister Templi. |
| 𝒲 | = Shemhamphorasch. |
| W. | = Wands. |
| C. | = Cups. |
| S. | = Swords. |
| P. | = Pentacles. |
| K. of S. | = Key of Solomon. |
| O.P.A.A. | = Oriens—Paimon—Ariton—Amaimon. |

| | | | | | |
|---|---|---|---|---|---|
| ♈ | = | Aries. | ♄ | = | Saturn. |
| ♉ | = | Taurus. | ☉ | = | Sun. |
| ♊ | = | Gemini. | ☽ | = | Moon. |
| ♋ | = | Cancer. | ♂ | = | Mars. |
| ♌ | = | Leo. | ☿ | = | Mercury. |
| ♍ | = | Virgo. | ♃ | = | Jupiter. |
| ♎ | = | Libra. | ♀ | = | Venus. |
| ♏ | = | Scorpio. | | | |
| ♐ | = | Sagittarius. | | | |
| ♑ | = | Capricornus. | | | |
| ♒ | = | Aquarius. | | | |
| ♓ | = | Pisces. | | | |

| | | | | | | |
|---|---|---|---|---|---|---|
| ▭ | enclosing | a number shows that the number is | | | | a perfect square. |
| $\sqrt[4]{\phantom{x}}$ | before | ,, | ,, | ,, | | a squared square. |
| ✿ | above | ,, | ,, | ,, | | a perfect number. |
| ⌊ | about | ,, | ,, | ,, | | a factorial.* |
| ‖⌊ | about | ,, | ,, | ,, | | a sub-factorial. |
| R(n) | before | ,, | ,, | ,, | | a reciprocal (or 'amicable number. |

Σ (1—k) is an abbreviation for "the sum of the first k natural numbers."

\* See special table following.

| | | | | | | | | | |
|---|---|---|---|---|---|---|---|---|---|
| 433 | P. | 529 | $23^2$ | 623 | 7 | 719 | P. | 813 | — |
| 437 | 19 | 531 | — | 627 | — | 721 | 7 | 817 | 19 |
| 439 | P. | 533 | 13 | 629 | 17 | 723 | — | 819 | — |
| 441 | $-21^2$ | 537 | — | 631 | P. | 727 | P. | 821 | P. |
| 443 | P. | 539 | 7 | 633 | — | 729 | $3^6=9^3=27^2$ | 823 | P. |
| 447 | — | 541 | P. | 637 | 7 | 731 | 17 | 827 | P. |
| 449 | P. | 543 | — | 639 | — | 733 | P. | 829 | P. |
| 451 | 11 | 547 | P. | 641 | P. | 737 | 11 | 831 | — |
| 453 | — | 549 | — | 643 | P. | 739 | P. | 833 | 7 |
| 457 | P. | 551 | 19 | 647 | P. | 741 | — | 837 | — |
| 459 | — | 553 | 7 | 649 | 11 | 743 | P. | 839 | P. |
| 461 | P. | 557 | — | 651 | — | 747 | — | 841 | $29^2$ |
| 463 | P. | 559 | 13 | 653 | P. | 749 | 7 | 843 | — |
| 467 | P. | 561 | — | 657 | — | 751 | P. | 847 | 7 |
| 469 | 7 | 563 | P. | 659 | P. | 753 | — | 849 | — |
| 471 | — | 567 | — | 661 | P. | 757 | P. | 851 | 23 |
| 473 | 11 | 569 | P. | 663 | — | 759 | — | 853 | P. |
| 477 | — | 571 | P. | 667 | 23 | 761 | P. | 857 | P. |
| 479 | P. | 573 | — | 669 | — | 763 | 7 | 859 | P. |
| 481 | 13 | 577 | P. | 671 | 11 | 767 | 13 | 861 | — |
| 483 | — | 579 | — | 673 | P. | 769 | P. | 863 | P. |
| 487 | P. | 581 | 7 | 677 | P. | 771 | — | 867 | — |
| 489 | — | 583 | 11 | 679 | 7 | 773 | P. | 869 | 11 |
| 491 | P. | 587 | P. | 681 | — | 777 | — | 871 | 13 |
| 493 | 17 | 589 | 17 | 683 | P. | 779 | 19 | 873 | — |
| 497 | 7 | 591 | — | 687 | — | 781 | 11 | 877 | P. |
| 499 | P. | 593 | P. | 689 | 13 | 783 | — | 879 | — |
| 501 | — | 597 | — | 691 | P. | 787 | P. | 881 | P. |
| 503 | P. | 599 | P. | 693 | — | 789 | — | 883 | P. |
| 507 | — | 601 | P. | 697 | 17 | 791 | 7 | 887 | P. |
| 509 | P. | 603 | — | 699 | — | 793 | 13 | 889 | 7 |
| 511 | 7 | 607 | P. | 701 | P. | 797 | P. | 891 | — |
| 513 | — | 609 | — | 703 | 19 | 799 | 17 | 893 | 19 |
| 517 | 11 | 611 | 13 | 707 | 7 | 801 | — | 897 | — |
| 519 | — | 613 | P. | 709 | P. | 803 | 11 | 899 | 29 |
| 521 | P. | 617 | P. | 711 | — | 807 | — | 901 | 17 |
| 523 | P. | 619 | P. | 713 | 23 | 809 | 9 | 903 | — |
| 527 | 17 | 621 | — | 717 | — | 811 | P. | 907 | P. |

| | | | | | | | | | |
|---|---|---|---|---|---|---|---|---|---|
| 909 | — | 1003 | 17 | 1099 | 7 | 1193 | P. | 1289 | P. |
| 911 | P. | 1007 | 19 | 1101 | — | 1197 | — | 1291 | P. |
| 913 | 11 | 1009 | P. | 1103 | P. | 1199 | 11 | 1293 | — |
| 917 | 7 | 1011 | — | 1107 | — | 1201 | P. | 1297 | P. |
| 919 | P. | 1013 | P. | 1109 | P. | 1203 | — | 1299 | — |
| 921 | — | 1017 | — | 1111 | 11 | 1207 | 17 | 1301 | P. |
| 923 | 13 | 1019 | P. | 1113 | — | 1209 | — | 1303 | P. |
| 927 | — | 1021 | P. | 1117 | P. | 1211 | 7 | 1307 | P. |
| 929 | P. | 1023 | — | 1119 | — | 1213 | P. | 1309 | 7 |
| 931 | 7 | 1027 | 13 | 1121 | 19 | 1217 | P. | 1311 | — |
| 933 | — | 1029 | — | 1123 | P. | 1219 | 23 | 1313 | 13 |
| 937 | P. | 1031 | P. | 1127 | 7 | 1221 | — | 1317 | — |
| 939 | — | 1033 | P. | 1129 | P. | 1223 | P. | 1319 | P. |
| 941 | P. | 1037 | 17 | 1131 | — | 1227 | — | 1321 | P. |
| 943 | 23 | 1039 | P. | 1133 | 11 | 1229 | P. | 1323 | — |
| 947 | P. | 1041 | — | 1137 | — | 1231 | P. | 1327 | P. |
| 949 | 13 | 1043 | 7 | 1139 | 17 | 1233 | — | 1329 | — |
| 951 | — | 1047 | — | 1141 | 7 | 1237 | P. | 1331 | 11 |
| 953 | P. | 1049 | P. | 1143 | — | 1239 | — | 1333 | 31 |
| 957 | — | 1051 | P. | 1147 | 31 | 1241 | 17 | 1337 | 7 |
| 959 | 7 | 1053 | — | 1149 | — | 1243 | 11 | 1339 | 13 |
| 961 | $31^2$ | 1057 | 7 | 1151 | P. | 1247 | 29 | 1341 | — |
| 963 | — | 1059 | — | 1153 | P. | 1249 | P. | 1343 | 17 |
| 967 | P. | 1061 | P. | 1157 | 13 | 1251 | — | 1347 | — |
| 969 | — | 1063 | P. | 1159 | 19 | 1253 | 7 | 1349 | 19 |
| 971 | P. | 1067 | 11 | 1161 | — | 1257 | — | 1351 | 7 |
| 973 | 7 | 1069 | P. | 1163 | P. | 1259 | P. | 1353 | — |
| 977 | P. | 1071 | — | 1167 | — | 1261 | 13 | 1357 | 23 |
| 979 | 11 | 1073 | 29 | 1169 | 7 | 1263 | — | 1359 | — |
| 981 | — | 1077 | — | 1171 | P. | 1267 | 7 | 1361 | P. |
| 983 | P. | 1079 | 13 | 1173 | — | 1269 | — | 1363 | 29 |
| 987 | — | 1081 | 23 | 1177 | 11 | 1271 | 31 | 1367 | P. |
| 989 | 23 | 1083 | — | 1179 | — | 1273 | 19 | 1369 | $37^2$ |
| 991 | P. | 1087 | P. | 1181 | P. | 1277 | P. | 1371 | — |
| 993 | — | 1089 | $-33^2$ | 1183 | 7 | 1279 | P. | 1373 | P. |
| 997 | P. | 1091 | P. | 1187 | P. | 1281 | — | 1377 | — |
| 999 | — | 1093 | P. | 1189 | 29 | 1283 | P. | 1379 | 7 |
| 1001 | 7 | 1097 | P. | 1191 | — | 1287 | — | 1381 | P. |

| | | | | | | | | | |
|---|---|---|---|---|---|---|---|---|---|
| 383 | — | 1479 | — | 1573 | 11 | 1669 | P. | 1763 | 41 |
| 387 | 19 | 1481 | P. | 1577 | 19 | 1671 | — | 1767 | — |
| 389 | — | 1483 | P. | 1579 | P. | 1673 | 7 | 1769 | 29 |
| 391 | 13 | 1487 | P. | 1581 | — | 1677 | — | 1771 | 7 |
| 393 | 7 | 1489 | P. | 1583 | P. | 1679 | 23 | 1773 | — |
| 397 | 11 | 1491 | — | 1587 | — | 1681 | 41² | 1777 | P. |
| 399 | P. | 1493 | P. | 1589 | 7 | 1683 | — | 1779 | — |
| 401 | — | 1497 | — | 1591 | 37 | 1687 | 7 | 1781 | 13 |
| 403 | 23 | 1499 | P. | 1593 | — | 1689 | — | 1783 | P. |
| 407 | — | 1501 | 19 | 1597 | P. | 1691 | 19 | 1787 | P. |
| 409 | P. | 1503 | — | 1599 | — | 1693 | P. | 1789 | P. |
| 411 | 17 | 1507 | 11 | 1601 | P. | 1697 | P. | 1791 | — |
| 413 | — | 1509 | — | 1603 | 7 | 1699 | P. | 1793 | 11 |
| 417 | 13 | 1511 | P. | 1607 | P. | 1701 | — | 1797 | — |
| 419 | — | 1513 | 17 | 1609 | P. | 1703 | 13 | 1799 | 7 |
| 421 | 7 | 1517 | 37 | 1611 | — | 1707 | — | 1801 | P. |
| 423 | P. | 1519 | 7 | 1613 | P. | 1709 | P. | 1803 | — |
| 427 | P. | 1521 | -39² | 1617 | — | 1711 | 29 | 1807 | 13 |
| 429 | P. | 1523 | P. | 1619 | P. | 1713 | — | 1809 | — |
| 431 | — | 1527 | — | 1621 | P. | 1717 | 17 | 1811 | P. |
| 433 | P. | 1529 | 11 | 1623 | — | 1719 | — | 1813 | 7 |
| 437 | — | 1531 | P. | 1627 | P. | 1721 | P. | 1817 | 23 |
| 439 | P. | 1533 | — | 1629 | — | 1723 | P. | 1819 | 17 |
| 441 | 11 | 1537 | 29 | 1631 | 7 | 1727 | 11 | 1821 | — |
| 443 | — | 1539 | — | 1633 | 23 | 1729 | 7 | 1823 | P. |
| 447 | P. | 1541 | 23 | 1637 | P. | 1731 | — | 1827 | — |
| 449 | — | 1543 | P. | 1639 | 11 | 1733 | P. | 1829 | 31 |
| 451 | P. | 1547 | 7 | 1641 | — | 1737 | — | 1831 | P. |
| 453 | P. | 1549 | P. | 1643 | 31 | 1739 | 37 | 1833 | — |
| 457 | 31 | 1551 | — | 1647 | — | 1741 | P. | 1837 | 11 |
| 459 | P. | 1553 | P. | 1649 | 17 | 1743 | — | 1839 | — |
| 461 | — | 1557 | — | 1651 | 13 | 1747 | P. | 1841 | 7 |
| 463 | 7 | 1559 | P. | 1653 | — | 1749 | — | 1843 | 19 |
| 467 | — | 1561 | 7 | 1657 | P. | 1751 | 17 | 1847 | P. |
| 469 | 13 | 1563 | — | 1659 | — | 1753 | P. | 1849 | 43² |
| 471 | P. | 1567 | P. | 1661 | 11 | 1757 | 7 | 1851 | — |
| 473 | — | 1569 | — | 1663 | P. | 1759 | P. | 1853 | 17 |
| 477 | 7 | 1571 | P. | 1667 | P. | 1761 | — | 1857 | — |

# SEPHER SEPHIROTH

| | | | | | | | | | |
|---|---|---|---|---|---|---|---|---|---|
| 1859 | 11 | 1953 | — | 2049 | — | 2143 | P. | 2239 | P. |
| 1861 | P. | 1957 | 19 | 2051 | 7 | 2147 | 19 | 2241 | — |
| 1863 | — | 1959 | — | 2053 | P. | 2149 | 7 | 2243 | P. |
| 1867 | P. | 1961 | 37 | 2057 | 11 | 2151 | — | 2247 | — |
| 1869 | — | 1963 | 13 | 2059 | 29 | 2153 | P. | 2249 | 13 |
| 1871 | P. | 1967 | 7 | 2061 | — | 2157 | — | 2251 | P. |
| 1873 | P. | 1969 | 11 | 2063 | P. | 2159 | 17 | 2253 | — |
| 1877 | P. | 1971 | — | 2067 | — | 2161 | P. | 2257 | 37 |
| 1879 | P. | 1973 | P. | 2069 | P. | 2163 | — | 2259 | — |
| 1881 | — | 1977 | — | 2071 | 19 | 2167 | 11 | 2261 | 7 |
| 1883 | 7 | 1979 | P. | 2073 | — | 2169 | — | 2263 | 31 |
| 1887 | — | 1981 | 7 | 2077 | 31 | 2171 | 13 | 2267 | P. |
| 1889 | P. | 1983 | — | 2079 | — | 2173 | 41 | 2269 | P. |
| 1891 | 31 | 1987 | P. | 2081 | P. | 2177 | 7 | 2271 | — |
| 1893 | — | 1989 | — | 2083 | P. | 2179 | P. | 2273 | P. |
| 1897 | 7 | 1991 | 11 | 2087 | P. | 2181 | — | 2277 | — |
| 1899 | — | 1993 | P. | 2089 | P. | 2183 | 37 | 2279 | 43 |
| 1901 | P. | 1997 | P. | 2091 | — | 2187 | $3^7$ | 2281 | P. |
| 1903 | 11 | 1999 | P. | 2093 | 7 | 2189 | 11 | 2283 | — |
| 1907 | P. | 2001 | — | 2097 | — | 2191 | 7 | 2287 | P. |
| 1909 | 23 | 2003 | P. | 2099 | P. | 2193 | — | 2289 | — |
| 1911 | — | 2007 | — | 2101 | 11 | 2197 | 13 | 2291 | 29 |
| 1913 | P. | 2009 | 7 | 2103 | — | 2199 | — | 2293 | P. |
| 1917 | — | 2011 | P. | 2107 | 7 | 2201 | 31 | 2297 | P. |
| 1919 | 19 | 2013 | — | 2109 | — | 2203 | P. | 2299 | 11 |
| 1921 | 17 | 2017 | P. | 2111 | P. | 2207 | P. | 2301 | — |
| 1923 | — | 2019 | — | 2113 | P. | 2209 | $47^2$ | 2303 | 7 |
| 1927 | 41 | 2021 | 43 | 2117 | 29 | 2211 | — | 2307 | — |
| 1929 | — | 2023 | 7 | 2119 | 13 | 2213 | P. | 2309 | P. |
| 1931 | P. | 2027 | P. | 2121 | — | 2217 | — | 2311 | P. |
| 1933 | P. | 2029 | P. | 2123 | 11 | 2219 | 7 | 2313 | — |
| 1937 | 13 | 2031 | — | 2127 | — | 2221 | P. | 2317 | 7 |
| 1939 | 7 | 2033 | 19 | 2129 | P. | 2223 | — | 2319 | — |
| 1941 | — | 2037 | — | 2131 | P. | 2227 | 17 | 2321 | 11 |
| 1943 | 29 | 2039 | P. | 2133 | — | 2229 | — | 2323 | 23 |
| 1947 | — | 2041 | 13 | 2137 | P. | 2231 | 23 | 2327 | 13 |
| 1949 | P. | 2043 | — | 2139 | — | 2233 | 11 | 2329 | 17 |
| 1951 | P. | 2047 | 23 | 2141 | P. | 2237 | P. | 2331 | — |

| | | | | | | | | | |
|---|---|---|---|---|---|---|---|---|---|
| 2333 | P. | 2429 | 7 | 2523 | — | 2619 | — | 2713 | P. |
| 2337 | — | 2431 | 11 | 2527 | 7 | 2621 | P. | 2717 | 11 |
| 2339 | P. | 2433 | — | 2529 | — | 2623 | 43 | 2719 | P. |
| 2341 | P. | 2437 | P. | 2531 | P. | 2627 | 37 | 2721 | — |
| 2343 | — | 2439 | — | 2533 | 17 | 2629 | 11 | 2723 | 7 |
| 2347 | P. | 2441 | P. | 2537 | 43 | 2631 | — | 2727 | — |
| 2349 | — | 2443 | 7 | 2539 | P. | 2633 | P. | 2729 | P. |
| 2351 | P. | 2447 | P. | 2541 | — | 2637 | — | 2731 | P. |
| 2353 | 13 | 2449 | 31 | 2543 | P. | 2639 | 7 | 2733 | — |
| 2357 | P. | 2451 | — | 2547 | — | 2641 | 19 | 2737 | 7 |
| 2359 | 7 | 2453 | 11 | 2549 | P. | 2643 | — | 2739 | — |
| 2361 | — | 2457 | — | 2551 | P. | 2647 | P. | 2741 | P. |
| 2363 | 17 | 2459 | P. | 2553 | — | 2649 | — | 2743 | 13 |
| 2367 | — | 2461 | 23 | 2557 | P. | 2651 | 11 | 2747 | 41 |
| 2369 | 23 | 2463 | — | 2559 | — | 2653 | 7 | 2749 | P. |
| 2371 | P. | 2467 | P. | 2561 | 13 | 2657 | P. | 2751 | — |
| 2373 | — | 2469 | — | 2563 | 11 | 2659 | P. | 2753 | P. |
| 2377 | P. | 2471 | 7 | 2567 | 17 | 2661 | — | 2757 | — |
| 2379 | — | 2473 | P. | 2569 | 7 | 2663 | P. | 2759 | 31 |
| 2381 | P. | 2477 | P. | 2571 | — | 2667 | — | 2761 | 11 |
| 2383 | P. | 2479 | 37 | 2573 | 31 | 2669 | 17 | 2763 | — |
| 2387 | 7 | 2481 | — | 2577 | — | 2671 | P. | 2767 | P. |
| 2389 | P. | 2483 | 13 | 2579 | P. | 2673 | — | 2769 | — |
| 2391 | — | 2487 | — | 2581 | 29 | 2677 | P. | 2771 | 17 |
| 2393 | P. | 2489 | 19 | 2583 | — | 2679 | — | 2773 | 47 |
| 2397 | — | 2491 | 47 | 2587 | 13 | 2681 | 7 | 2777 | P. |
| 2399 | P. | 2493 | — | 2589 | — | 2683 | P. | 2779 | 7 |
| $\boxed{2401}$ | $7^4 = 49^2$ | 2497 | 11 | 2591 | P. | 2687 | P. | 2781 | — |
| 2403 | — | 2499 | — | 2593 | P. | 2689 | P. | 2783 | 11 |
| 2407 | 29 | 2501 | 41 | 2597 | 7 | 2691 | — | 2787 | — |
| 2409 | — | 2503 | P. | 2599 | 23 | 2693 | P. | 2789 | P. |
| 2411 | P. | 2507 | 23 | $\boxed{2601}$ | $-51^2$ | 2697 | — | 2791 | P. |
| 2413 | 19 | 2509 | 13 | 2603 | 19 | 2699 | P. | 2793 | — |
| 2417 | P. | 2511 | — | 2607 | — | 2701 | 37 | 2797 | P. |
| 2419 | 41 | 2513 | 7 | 2609 | P. | 2703 | — | 2799 | — |
| 2421 | — | 2517 | — | 2611 | 7 | 2707 | P. | 2801 | P. |
| 2423 | P. | 2519 | 11 | 2613 | — | 2709 | — | 2803 | P. |
| 2427 | — | 2521 | P. | 2617 | P. | 2711 | P. | 2807 | 7 |

# SEPHER SEPHIROTH

| | | | | | | | | | |
|---|---|---|---|---|---|---|---|---|---|
| 2809 | 53² | 2903 | P. | 2999 | P. | 3093 | — | 3189 | — |
| 2811 | — | 2907 | — | 3001 | P. | 3097 | 19 | 3191 | P. |
| 2813 | 29 | 2909 | P. | 3003 | — | 3099 | — | 3193 | 31 |
| 2817 | — | 2911 | 41 | 3007 | 31 | 3101 | 7 | 3197 | 23 |
| 2819 | P. | 2913 | — | 3009 | — | 3103 | 29 | 3199 | 7 |
| 2821 | 7 | 2917 | P. | 3011 | P. | 3107 | 13 | 3201 | — |
| 2823 | — | 2919 | — | 3013 | 23 | 3109 | P. | 3203 | P. |
| 2827 | 11 | 2921 | 23 | 3017 | 7 | 3111 | — | 3207 | — |
| 2829 | — | 2923 | 37 | 3019 | P. | 3113 | 11 | 3209 | P. |
| 2831 | 19 | 2927 | P. | 3021 | — | 3117 | — | 3211 | 13 |
| 2833 | P. | 2929 | 29 | 3023 | P. | 3119 | P. | 3213 | — |
| 2837 | P. | 2931 | — | 3027 | — | 3121 | P. | 3217 | P. |
| 2839 | 17 | 2933 | 7 | 3029 | 13 | 3123 | — | 3219 | — |
| 2841 | — | 2937 | — | 3031 | 7 | 3127 | 53 | 3221 | P. |
| 2843 | P. | 2939 | P. | 3033 | — | 3129 | — | 3223 | 11 |
| 2847 | — | 2941 | 17 | 3037 | P. | 3131 | 31 | 3227 | 7 |
| 2849 | 7 | 2943 | — | 3039 | — | 3133 | 13 | 3229 | P. |
| 2851 | P. | 2947 | 7 | 3041 | P. | 3137 | P. | 3231 | — |
| 2853 | — | 2949 | — | 3043 | 17 | 3139 | 43 | 3233 | 53 |
| 2857 | P. | 2951 | 13 | 3047 | 11 | 3141 | — | 3237 | — |
| 2859 | — | 2953 | P. | 3049 | P. | 3143 | 7 | 3239 | 41 |
| 2861 | P. | 2957 | P. | 3051 | — | 3147 | — | 3241 | 7 |
| 2863 | 7 | 2959 | 11 | 3053 | 43 | 3149 | 47 | 3243 | — |
| 2867 | 47 | 2961 | — | 3057 | — | 3151 | 23 | 3247 | 17 |
| 2869 | 19 | 2963 | P. | 3059 | 7 | 3153 | — | 3249 | −57² |
| 2871 | — | 2967 | — | 3061 | P. | 3157 | 7 | 3251 | P. |
| 2873 | 13 | 2969 | P. | 3063 | — | 3159 | — | 3253 | P. |
| 2877 | — | 2971 | P. | 3067 | P. | 3161 | 29 | 3257 | P. |
| 2879 | P. | 2973 | — | 3069 | — | 3163 | P. | 3259 | P. |
| 2881 | 43 | 2977 | 13 | 3071 | 37 | 3167 | P. | 3261 | — |
| 2883 | — | 2979 | — | 3073 | 7 | 3169 | P. | 3263 | 13 |
| 2887 | P. | 2981 | 11 | 3077 | 17 | 3171 | — | 3267 | — |
| 2889 | — | 2983 | 19 | 3079 | P. | 3173 | 19 | 3269 | 7 |
| 2891 | 7 | 2987 | 29 | 3081 | — | 3177 | — | 3271 | P. |
| 2893 | 11 | 2989 | 7 | 3083 | P. | 3179 | 11 | 3273 | — |
| 2897 | P. | 2991 | — | 3087 | — | 3181 | P. | 3277 | 29 |
| 2899 | 13 | 2993 | 41 | 3089 | P. | 3183 | — | 3279 | — |
| 2901 | — | 2997 | — | 3091 | 11 | 3187 | P. | 3281 | 17 |

# SEPHER SEPHIROTH

| | | | | | | | | |
|---|---|---|---|---|---|---|---|---|
| 3283 | 7 | 3293 | 37 | 3301 | P. | 3309 | — | 3317 | 31 |
| 3287 | 19 | 3297 | — | 3303 | — | 3311 | 7 | 3319 | P. |
| 3289 | 11 | 3299 | P. | 3307 | P. | 3313 | P. | 3321 | — |
| 3291 | — | | | | | | | | |

*The first dozen factorials, and sub-factorials; and the ratios they bear to one another; note that* $\lfloor n / \lVert n = e$

| N | $\lfloor N$ | $\lVert N$ | $\lfloor N \div \lVert N$ | $\lVert N \div \lfloor N$ |
|---|---|---|---|---|
| 1 | 1 | 0 | ∞ | 0·000000 |
| 2 | 2 | 1 | 2·000000 | 0·500000 |
| 3 | 6 | 2 | 3·000000 | 0·333333 |
| 4 | 24 | 9 | 2·666666 | 0·375000 |
| 5 | 120 | 44 | 2·727272 | 0·366666 |
| 6 | 720 | 265 | 2·716981 | 0·368055 |
| 7 | 5040 | 1854 | 2·718446 | 0·367857 |
| 8 | 40320 | 14833 | 2·718262 | 0·367881 |
| 9 | 362880 | 133496 | 2·718283 | 0·367879 |
| 10 | 3628800 | 1334961 | 2·718281 | 0·367879 |
| 11 | 39916800 | 14684570 | 2·718281 | 0·367879 |
| 12 | 479001600 | 176214841 | 2·718281 | 0·367879 |

Factorial $n$, or $\lfloor n$, is the continued product of all the whole numbers from 1 to $n$ inclusive and is e number of ways in which $n$ different things can be arranged.

Sub-factorial $n$, or $\lVert n$, is the nearest whole number to $\lfloor n \div e$, and is the number of ways in which a row n elements may be so deranged, that no element may have its original position.

Thus
$$\lfloor n = 1 \times 2 \times 3 \times \ldots \times n,$$

d
$$\lVert n = \frac{1 \times 2 \times 3 \times \ldots \times n}{2\cdot71828188\ldots} \pm h,$$

here $h$ is the smaller decimal fraction less than unity by which the fraction $\dfrac{1 \times 2 \times \ldots \times n}{2\cdot718281\ldots}$ differs from a hole number, and is to be added or subtracted as the case may be.—The most useful expression for $n$ is:

$$\lVert n \equiv \lfloor n - \frac{n}{1} \lfloor n-1 + \frac{n(n-1)}{1.2} \lfloor n-2 - \frac{n(n-1)(n-2)}{1.2.3} \lfloor n-3 + \text{etc.}$$

$(n+1)$ terms.

$$e \equiv 1 + \frac{1}{\lfloor 1} + \frac{1}{\lfloor 2} + \frac{1}{\lfloor 3} + \ldots \text{ to } \infty$$

$$\equiv 2\cdot71828188\ldots.$$

# SEPHER SEPHIROTH

| Names of the letters | Figures of the letters | Value of the letters | | English equivalents of the letters |
|---|---|---|---|---|
| (M) Aleph | א | 1 | | A |
| (D) Beth | ב | 2 | | B |
| (D) Gimel | ג | 3 | | G |
| (D) Daleth | ד | 4 | | D |
| (S) Heh | ה | 5 | | H (E) |
| (S) Vau | ו | 6 | | V (U) |
| (S) Zayin | ז | 7 | | Z |
| (S) Kheth (Cheth) | ח | 8 | | Ch |
| (S) Teth | ט | 9 | | T |
| (S) Yodh | י | 10 | | Y (I or J) |
| (D) Kaph | כ ך | 20 | 500 | K |
| (S) Lamed | ל | 30 | | L |
| (M) Mem | מ ם | 40 | 600 | M |
| (S) Nun | נ ן | 50 | 700 | N |
| (S) Samekh | ס | 60 | | S |
| (S) Ayin | ע | 70 | | O (A'a or Ng) |
| (D) Peh | פ ף | 80 | 800 | P |
| (S) Tzaddi | צ ץ | 90 | 900 | Tz |
| (S) Qoph | ק | 100 | | ꞌQ |
| (D) Resh | ר | 200 | | R |
| (M) Shin | ש | 300 | | S Sh |
| (D) Tau | ת | 400 | | T Th |

When written large, the Value of a Hebrew letter is increased to one thousand times its ordinary value. A large Aleph is counted 1000: a large Beth, 2000: and so on.

Note that A, I, O, U, H, are really consonants, mere bases for the vowels. The vowels are not here given, as they have no importance in Gematria.

M, D, and S before the names of the letters shews their division into Mother, Double and Single letters, referred respectively to active Elements, Air, Water, Fire, Planets, and Signs. But ש and ת also serve to signify the Elements of Spirit and of Earth. See Liber 777.

The Mystic Number π√1
of Kether. S. P. M.

|2. ||3. S. S. F. π2

Abbreviation for 422, אא:א
אריך אנפין, q.v.]

Σ(1—2). ♄. The Mystic π3
Number of Chokmah

ather אב

come, go בא

The Number of Abra-Melin √4
Princes. ♃. 2²

ather אבא

ollow; a vein בב

oud גא

♂ π5

ist, vapour אד

ck בג

Σ(1—3). |3. ☉. The Mystic 6
Number of Binah

gather, collect גבא

g, the giant whose partner is גג
Magog

bear דב

window הא

♀ π7

st, ruined אבד

name of GOD attributed to אהא
Venus. Initials of Adonai
ha-Aretz

esire; either, or או

---

Gad, a Tribe of Israel; good גד
fortune

Was weary דאב

Riches, power דבא

Fish דג

2³. The Number of Abra-Melin ³√8
Sub-Princes, and of the Servitors of Oriens. ☿

To will, intend אבה

Desired, beloved אהב

אוא

Then אז

The entrance, threshold באה

To be anxious, grieve דאג

Love; beloved, breast; pleasures דד
of love

Nqn. Zauir Anpin 478 q.v. אז

||4. 3². ♄. ☽ √9

Ventriloquus: the special 'fire' אוב
of black magic, whence Obi,
Obeah. Cf. 11 and 207

He kindled אזא

Brother אח

A garment בגד

Became powerful, grew high גאה

Middle גו

Splendour; cf. 15 הד

Σ(1—4). The Mystic Number of 10
Chesed. Elementorum Sphaera.
The Number of Abra-Melin Servi-
tors of Amaimon and Ariton

Enchanter אט

[Vide K.D. L.C.K. p. 185] בגה

Elevated, exalted, high — גבה
Flew, soared — דאה
Two — דו
Window — הה
A wolf — זאב
A hidden place; bosom — חב

π 11

Ahah — אהה
Firebrand, volcanic fire: the special 'fire' or 'light' of the Sacred Magic of Light, Life, and Love; hence "Odic Force" &c. Cf. 9 and 207 — אוד
Where — אי
When — בבוא
To tear, cut, attack — גדר
Gold (Ch.) — דהב
Proud, haughty — זד
To conceal — חבא
A circularity of form or motion; a feast — חג

12

He longed for, missed — אוה
He departed, went forth — אזר
A little book, pamphlet, letter; tools — גט
To multiply — דגה
A city of Edom — הבה
HE. [ה is referred to Mater, ו to Pater, א to Corona] — הוא
Vau; hook, nail, pin — וו
This, that — זה
To penetrate, be sharp; (Ch.) one — חד

π 13

A small bundle, bunch — אגדה
Beloved; Love — אהבה

Unity — אחד
Hated — איב
Emptiness — בהו
Raised up — גהה
Chokmah, 42-fold Name in Yetzirah. (See 777) — גי
Anxiety — דאגה
A fisher — דוג
Thunder; to meditate; he removed — הגה
A city of Edom — הדר
Here; this — זו
A locust — חגב
He shall come — יבא

I

Rhamnus; a thorn, spine — אטד
Rising ground; Earth of Geburah. (See 777) — גיא
Sacrifice v. & s. (Ch.). (?) — דבח
Love, beloved; David • — דוד
Give, give! [Vide no. 17, יהב] — הב הב
To grind, direct, stretch out — הדה
Gold — זהב
Hand — יד

Σ (1—5). Σ {1—(3 × 3)} ÷ 3. The Mystic Number of Geburah. The Number of Abra-Melin Servitors of Asmodee and Magot, and of Paimon — I

Angel of 3rd Dec. ♐ — אבוהא
The month of Exodus and Passover — אביב
Steam, vapour — איד
Pride; a carrying out; exaltation — גאוה

| | | | |
|---|---|---|---|
| endour, the Eighth Sephira | הוד | Living | חי |
| erflowing, abounding | זוב | Notariqon of Yehi Aur, etc. | יאוא |
| who impels; to force | זח | | π 19 |
| hide | חבה | Angel L.T.D. of ♐ | אהה |
| e Monogram of the Eternal | יה | An enemy | אויב |
| The Number of Abra-Melin √ ∛ 16 | | Job | איוב |
| Servitors of Asmodee | | Was black | דיה |
| ssopus | אזוב | Chavvah; to manifest, shew forth; Eve | חוה |
| seized, cleaved to | אחז | | |
| vated, exalted, high | גבוה | The Number of Abra-Melin 20 | |
| erb. subst.) Injury, war, lust; ell | הוה | Servitors of Amaimon | |
| | היא | Fraternity | אחוה |
| s!—Woe | יי | Black liquid | דיו |
| e, equal to | זוג | It was | היה |
| | π 17 | The breast; a vision; a prophet; to gaze | חזה |
| ts | אגוז | Jobab, an Edomite King | יובב |
| !—Alas! | אוי | The hand | יוד |
| ricornus | גדי | Σ (1—6). The Mystic Number 21 of Tiphareth | |
| ve, sinew. [Gen. xxxii. 5 & 32] | גיד | Existence, Being, the Kether-name of GOD | אהיה |
| rative, subtle discourse | הגדה | But, yet, certainly | אך |
| ). L.C.K. p. 267 | ההוא | Deep meditation | הגיג |
| dream, rave | הזה | Ah!—Alas! | הוי |
| ly | זבוב | Purity, innocence | זהו |
| rificed | זבח | Vide Sepher Yetzirah | יהו |
| seethe, boil | זוד | The Number of Abra-Melin 22 | |
| brighten, make joyful | חדה | Servitors of Ariton | |
| ircle, orbit | חוג | With his hand; Night Demon of 1st Dec. ♋ | בידו |
| d | טוב | By Yodh | ביוד |
| give, place | יהב | Hearer in secret; Angel of 8 W. | האאיה |
| | 18 | The state of puberty | זוג |
| favourite, my beloved | אהבי | A magical vision (Ch.) | חזוא |
| red | איבה | | |
| antique Serpent | חמא | | |

3

| | |
|---|---|
| Wheat | חטה |
| Good | טובה |
| Notariqon of "Tet. Elohim Tet. Achad." | יאא |
| Unity | יחד |

π 23

| | |
|---|---|
| Parted, removed, separated | זחח |
| Joy | חדוה |
| A thread | חוט |
| Life | חיה |

|4. The Number of the 'Elders' in the Apocalypse    24

| | |
|---|---|
| He whom I love | אהובי |
| He who loves me | אוהבי |
| A Mercurial GOD. His essence is אז, 8 | אזבוגה |
| Substance; a body | גויה |
| A pauper | דך |
| Angel of 2 C. | הבביה |
| Abundance | זיז |
| A water-pot, a large earthen-ware vessel | כד |

5²                          √ 25

| | |
|---|---|
| To break | דכא |
| The Beast | חיוא |
| Jehewid, GOD of Geburah of Binah | יהוד |
| Let there be | יהי |
| Will be separated | יזח |
| Thus | כה |

The Numbers of the Sephiroth of the Middle Pillar; 1 + 6 + 9 + 10    26

| | |
|---|---|
| [Vide K.D. L.C.K. p. 273] | הויה |
| Seeing, looking at | חוזה |

| | |
|---|---|
| Sight, vision | חזוה |
| TETRAGRAMMATON, "Jehovah," the Unutterable Name, the Lost Word | יהוה |
| Kebad, husband of the impure Lilith. [K.D. L.C.K. 464] | כבד |

3³                          ∛

| | |
|---|---|
| Wept, mourned | בכה |
| Purity | זך |
| A parable, enigma, riddle | חידה |

Σ (1—7).  The Mystic Number of Netzach    2

| | |
|---|---|
| Clay | טיט |
| Union, unity | יחוד |
| Power | כח |

π

| | |
|---|---|
| Is broken.  [Ps. x. 10] | דכה |
| To break down, overturn | הדך |

| | |
|---|---|
| A party to an action at law; defendant, plaintiff.  [Note ל = 30 = �)= 'Justice'] | חייב |
| Judah | יהודה |
| It will be | יהיה |

π

| | |
|---|---|
| How? | אין |
| GOD of Chesed, and of Kether of Briah | אל |
| To go | הוך |
| A beating, striking, collision | הכאה |
| And there was.  [Vide S.D.I. par. 31] | ויהי |
| K. of S. Fig. 31 | ייא |
| Not | לא |

4

2⁵. The Number of Abramelin $\sqrt{}$ 32
Servitors of Astarot

|alescence of אהיה and אהיהוה
יהוה Macroprosopus and
Microprosopus. This is
symbolized by the Hexa-
gram. Suppose the 3 ה's
conceal the 3 Mothers
א, מ & ש and we get
358 q.v.

|rd     בל

|gel of 5 W.     והויה

|pula Maritalis     זיווג

|s pure     זכה

|-zag, fork-lightning     חזיז

|ity K.D. L.C.K. p. 432     יחיד

|ory     כבוד

|nd, heart     לב

33

|row; wept, mourned     אבל

|y Demon of 1ˢᵗ Dec. ♈     באל

| destroy (Ch.); (?) a King     בלא
of Edom

|ing, fountain     גל

$\Sigma \{1—(4 \times 4)\} \div 4.$ ♃     34

|OD the Father," divine     אל אב
name attributed to Jupiter

ransom, avenge, pollute     גאל

| reveal     גלא

|pauper     דל

|common person; un-     הדיוט
educated, ignorant

|gel of 7 C.     ההויה

---

35

Agla, a name of GOD; אגלא
notariqon of Ateh Gibor
le-Olahm Adonai

Boundary, limit     גבל

He will go     יהך

$6^2 = \Sigma (1—8)$. ⊙. The Mystic $\sqrt{}$ 36
Number of Hod

Tabernaculum     אהל

How? (Vide Lamentations) איכה

Duke of Geburah in Edom; אלה
to curse; name of GOD
attributed to ☿

To remove, cast away     הלא

Confession     וידוי

Leah     לאה

Perhaps, possibly; would that! לו

π 37

Angel of 8 P.     אכאיה

GOD (Ch.)     אלהא

Behold!     אלו

Perished, grew old     בלה

To grow great     גדל

Banner     דגל

Tenuity, breath, vanity; in vain; הבל
Abel. [I.Z.Q., "the Super-
nal Breathers."]

Night Demon of 2ⁿᵈ Dec. ♐     ואל

Profession     זל

Jechidah, the Atma of Hindu יחידה
philosophy

Flame     להב

(?) Devotion of force     לז

| | | 38 |
|---|---|---|
| Night Demon of 2nd Dec. ♋ | אואל | |
| He departed | אזל | |
| Gehazi, servant of Elisha | גיחזי | |
| A City in the Mountains of Judah | גלה | |
| Innocent | זכאי | |
| The palate | חיך | |
| To make a hole, hollow; to violate | חל | |
| Green | לח | |

| | | 39 |
|---|---|---|
| To abide, dwell | זבל | |
| Dew | טל | |
| The Eternal is One | יהוה אחד | |
| Angel of 3 P. | יחויה | |
| Metathesis of יהוה | כוזו | |
| He cursed | לט | |

| | | 40 |
|---|---|---|
| Bildad | בלדד | |
| Liberator; a title of Jesod | גואל | |
| To cut off | גזל | |
| A rope; ruin; to bind | חבל | |
| Milk | חלב | |
| The Hand of the Eternal | יד יהוה | |
| To me, to mine | לי | |

| | | π 41 |
|---|---|---|
| Fecundity | אחלב | |
| Ram; force; hence = a hero | איל | |
| Night Demon of 1st Dec. ♍ | אלוד | |
| My GOD | אלי | |
| Mother | אם | |
| To fail, cease | בטל | |

| Divine Majesty | גאואל |
|---|---|
| Terminus | גבול |
| To burn | גחל |
| Terror | הול |
| To go round in a circle | חגל |
| [Vide Ps. cxviii. & I.R.Q. 778] | יה יהוה |
| The Number of the letters of a great name of GOD terrible and strong, and of the Assessors of the Dead | |
| Angel of ♈ | איאל |
| Eloah, a name of GOD | אלוה |
| The Supernal Mother, unfertilized; see 52 | אמא |
| Terror, calamity | בלהה |
| Loss, destruction | בלי |
| To cease | חדל |
| The World, Earth of Malkuth | חלד |
| My glory | כבודי |

| | | π 4 |
|---|---|---|
| Great | גדול | |
| To rejoice | גיל | |
| Challah; to make faint. [Vide K.D. L.C.K. p. 346] | חלה | |
| [Vide K.D. L.C.K. p. 151; see no. 340] | לביא | |
| Hazel, almond | לוז | |

‖5. 220 ÷ 5

| Drops | אגלי |
|---|---|
| A pool, pond; sorrow | אגם |
| Captive, captivity | גולה |
| Angel ruling Ⅱ | גיאל |

# SEPHER SEPHIROTH

uarius דלי

od דם

id : also horror. See חול
Scorpion Pantacle in K. of S.
and 10th Aethyr

am; ♈ טלה

t. in ? World. יוד הא וו הא
Vide K.D. L.C.K. p. 251]

me להט

Σ (1—9). The Mystic Number    45
    of Jesod

elligence of ♄ אניאל

am אדם

e Fool אמר

demption, liberation גאולה

grow warm הם

aven of Tiphareth זבול

sitated. [Vide no. 405] זחל

rit of ♄ זואל

who ruins חבלה

t. in Yetzirah יוד הא ואו הא

atly, strongly מאד

zirah's 'Secret Nature' מה
Vide I.R.Q. xxxiv.]

ame of GOD    46   אלהי

emale slave; cubitus אמה

, the metal of ♃ בדיל

dividing, sundering, הבדלה
eparation

gel of 7 S. ההאל

uiner חובל

gel ruling ♉ טואל

---

Levi, Levite לוי

π 47

Foolish, silly. (Stultus) אויל

A weeping בכייה

Cloud; high place; waves; במה
fortress

Angel ruling ♍ יואל

To clutch, hold חלט

48

Mercy גדולה

Angel of 2 W. והואל

A woman [vide K.D. L.C.K. חיל
p. 320]; strength; an army

To grow warm; heat, fire; black; חם
Ham, the son of Noah

Jubilee יובל

A star, planet; Sphere of ☿ כוכב

[Vide Ps. xciii. & Prov. viii. 22] מאז

  The Number of Abra-Melin    √49
  Servitors of Beelzebub. 7². ♀

The Living GOD אל חי

Qliphoth of Geburah גולהב

Resembled; meditated; דמה
silent

Intelligence of ♀ הגיאל

Drooping, being sick חולה

Strength חילא

Heat, fury (Ch.) חמא

A bringing forth, birth, nativity לידה

A measuring, measure מדה

Solve. [Vide no. 103] מוג

The Rod of Aaron מט

**50**

Red earth, the soil; Earth of אדמה
Chesed

Closed, shut up אטם

Angel of 9 P. אלדיה

Jonah's Whale דג גדול

To ferment המה

Pains, sorrows חבלי

Unclean, impure טמא

58th ש ייל

2nd ש ילי

The sea ים

All, every כל

To thee לך

What?—Which? מי

**51**

Edom אדום

Terrible; Day Demon of 2nd אים
Dec. ♏

Ate; devoured אכל

Pain אן

Tumultuously (vide no. 451); הום
to harass, perturb

Angel of 8 S. [Vide K. of S., יההאל
fig. 52]

Failure נא

**52**

Father and Mother אבא ואמא

Supernal Mother אימא

Elihu = Eli Hua, "He is my אליהו
GOD," who is the Holy
Guardian Angel of Job in
the Allegory

[Vide K.D. L.C.K. p. 134] אנא

A mare; brute animal, beast בהמה

Day Demon of 2nd Dec. ♐ בים

From all, among all בכל

The Son: Assiah's "Secret בן
Nature"

Meditation, imagination, sin זמה

A desirable one; to desire חמד

A husband's brother יבם

Angel of Kether of Binah, יהואל
and of Jesod of Binah

Tet. in Assiah יוד הה וו הה

A dog כלב

Angel of 4 C., and of 10 P. לאויה

The Number of Abra-Melin Servitors π
of Astarot and Asmodee

The stone that slew Goliath; אבן
a stone, rock

Elihu. (Vide 52) אליהוא

The garden גן

Angel of 9 P. הזיאל

To defend, hide; a wall; the חמה
sun; fury

The spleen טחול

A lover מאהבה

A basin, bowl, vessel. אגן
[Ex. xxiv. 6]

Rest דמי

A Tribe of Israel; to judge, rule. דן
[Vide K.D. L.C.K. p. 37]

Pertaining to summer חום

8

| | |
|---|---|
| flame; enchantments | להטי |
| bed; stick, rod | מטה |
| remove | נד |
| 1 – 10). The Mystic Number of 55 Malkuth | |
| ief; stole | גנב |
| bbery, pillage | גזילה |
| ence. [For name of Angels, see Sohar Sch. V. Cap. 18] | דומה |
| footstool | הדום |
| swell, heave. [Vide no. 51] | הים |
| walk | הלך |
| uckle; member, limb | חוליא |
| e bride | כלה |
| on; midday | נגב |
| nament | נה |
| 56 | |
| ead, terror | אימה |
| suffered | אנה |
| gel of 4 C. | הייאל |
| y | יום |
| autiful | נאה |
| 57 | |
| m | אבדן |
| nsuming | אוכל |
| ealth, an age, Time; Night Demon of 1st Dec. ♏ | און |
| rmidable, terrible | איום |
| e | אנו |
| breaking down, subversion, destruction | ביטול |

| | |
|---|---|
| Built | בנה |
| ♓. [Fish (pl.); vide 7] | דגים |
| Angel of 8 C. | וליה |
| Angel of 5 C. | לוויה |
| Altar | מזבח |
| The laying-by, making secret | מחבוא |
| | 58 |
| [Vide no. 499] | אהבים |
| [Vide K.D. L.C.K. p. 69.] An ear | אזן |
| Night Demon of 1st Dec. ♐ | דאגן |
| My strength, power, might | חילי |
| Love, kindness, grace; notariqon of Chokmah Nesethrah, the Secret Wisdom | חן |
| Ruler of Water | טליהד |
| Angel of 6 S. | ייזאל |
| Angel of 3 P. | להחיה |
| [Vide K.D. L.C.K. p. 69] | נח |
| | π 59 |
| Brethren. [Referred to Lilith & Samael—K.D. L.C.K. p. 54] | אחים |
| Heathen | גוים |
| A wall | חומה |
| Menstruata | נדה |
| | 60 |
| Tried by fire; a watch-tower | בחן |
| Excellence, sublimity, glory, pride | גאון |
| Constitution, tradition | הלכה |
| To behold | הנה |
| A basket | טנא |
| Angel of 8 C. | ילהיה |

9

B

| | |
|---|---|
| Vision | מחזה |
| The Southern district | נגבה |

**π 61**

| | |
|---|---|
| Master, Lord, Adon | אדון |
| The Negative, non-existent; not | אין |
| Towards, to thee | אליך |
| I, myself | אני |
| The belly | בטן |
| Angel of 10 S. | דמביה |
| Wealth | הון |
| Angel of 6 C. | יייאל |
| Habitaculum | נוה |

**62**

| | |
|---|---|
| Healing | אסא |
| Angel of 2nd Dec. ♈ | בההמי |
| The sons | בני |
| To commit; healing | זנה |

**63**

| | |
|---|---|
| Abaddon, the Hell of Chesed | אבדון |
| Dregs, roll; faeces (globular); dung | גלל |
| Fed | זון |
| The nose | חוטם |
| Fervour | חימה |
| Tet. in Briah | יוד הי ואו הי |
| Briah's "Secret Nature" | סג |

$$8^2 = 4^3 = 2^6. \quad ☿ \quad \sqrt{} \quad \sqrt[3]{} \quad \sqrt[6]{} \quad 64$$

| | |
|---|---|
| A sigh, groan, deep breath | אנחה |
| Justice | דין |
| (Din and Doni are twin Mercurial Intelligences in Gemini) | דני |

---

| | |
|---|---|
| The golden waters | מי זהב |
| [I.R.Q. xl. 996] | מיזהב |
| Prophecy | נבואה |
| Sphere of ♀ | נוגה |
| Noach | נוח |

$\Sigma \{1 - (5 \times 5)\} \div 5.$ The Number of 6... Abra-Melin Servitors of Magot and Kore

| | |
|---|---|
| Adonai | אדני |
| Weasels and other terrible animals | אוחים |
| The Palace | היכל |
| Shone, gloried, praised | הלל |
| To keep silence | הם |
| Defective. [Vide K.D. L.C.K. p. 339] | חזן |
| 6th ש | ללה |
| A door post | מזוזה |
| A beating, striking | מכה |
| [Vide K.D. L.C.K. p. 563] | נהי |

The Mystic Number of the Qliphoth, and of the Great Work.
$$\Sigma (1—11)$$

| | |
|---|---|
| Food, victuals | אכילה |
| The Lord thy GOD (is a consuming Fire). [Deut. iv. 24] | אלהיך |
| A ship | אניה |
| A trial, an experiment | בחון |
| A wheel. [Called "Cognomen Schechinae"] | גלגל |
| A City of Edom | דנהבה |

π67

| de K.D. L.C.K. p. 57] | אוני |
| e Understanding | בינה |
| ht Demon of 3rd Dec. ♏ | וינא |
| in | זין |
| based | זלל |
| embalm | חנט |
| gel of 3 C. | יבמיה |

68

| se.—Intelliget ista? | ויבן |
| be wise | חכם |
| ptiness | חלל |
| pity | חם |
| mus Tabernacularis | לולב |

69

| anger, stable; an enclosure | אבום |
| rtle | הדם |
| A. Angel of ♓ | וכביאל |

70

| proper name) | אדניה |
| sh, be silent | הסה |
| ne | יין |
| ht | ליל |
| de Ps. xxv. 14.] The Secret | סוד |

π71

| y terror | אימך |
| thing; an apparition, image | אליל |
| nce; silent | אלם |
| ht Demon of 1st Dec. ♒ | אמרוך |
| ad, the metal of Saturn; a plummet-line, level, water-level | אנך |

| Vision | חזון |
| A dove, pigeon | יונה |
| A dove | ינוה |
| Plenitude, fullness | מלא |

72

[72 × 3 = 216, אריה; vide K.D. L.C.K. p. 151.] There are 72 quinaries (spaces of 5°) in the Zodiac. The Shemhamphorasch or 'divided name' of GOD consists of 72 triliteral names, which by adding יה or אל give 72 angels. Vide Lib. DCCLXXVII

| Adonai, transliterated as by Lemegeton, etc. | אדונאי |
| Geomantic Intelligence of ♐ | אדוכיאל |
| In, so, thus, then | בכן |
| In the secret | בסוד |
| And they are excellent, finished | ויכלו |
| Kindness, mercy | חסד |
| Tet. in Atziluth | יוד הי ויו הי |
| Maccabee | מכבי |
| Atziluth's "Secret Nature"— thickness, cloud; Aub | עב |

π73

| Demon-King of Hod, and Night Demon of 2nd Dec. ♒ | בריאל |
| Gimel | גמל |
| The Wise One | חכמה |
| To trust in, shelter in | חסה |
| A day of feast | יום טוב |

74

| A leader, chief, judge | דיין |

| | |
|---|---|
| Worn-out (¿shameless) Beggars | דכים |
| Ox-goad | למד |
| A circuit; roundabout | סביב |
| All the way, constantly | עד |

**75**

| | |
|---|---|
| Hues, colours, complexions | גווני |
| Lucifer, the Herald Star | הילל |
| [Vide K. of S., fig. 53] | יכדיאל |
| A lamenting, wailing | יללה |
| The Pleiades | כימה |
| Night; by night | לילה |
| NUIT, THE STAR GODDESS | נויט |

**76**

| | |
|---|---|
| Secret, put away; a hiding-place | חביון |
| Rest, peace | ניחח |
| Slave, servant | עבד |

**77**

| | |
|---|---|
| Prayed | בעה |
| The river Gihon. [Gen. ii. 13] | גיחון |
| Overflowing. [Ps. cxxiv. 5] | זידון |
| Towers, citadels | מגדל |
| The Influence from Kether | מזל |
| Strength; a he-goat | עז |

There are 78 cards in the Tarot. Σ(1—12). The Mystic Number of Kether as Hua. The sum of the Key-Numbers of the Supernal Beard **78**

| | |
|---|---|
| Angel of 10 W. | אומאל |
| Angel of Ra Hoor Khuit | איואם |
| Briatic Palace of Chesed | היכל אהבה |
| Angel of ♂ | זמאל |

| | |
|---|---|
| The breaker, dream | חלם |
| To pity | חמל |
| To initiate | חנך |
| Angel of 2 S. | יזלאל |
| Angel of 1st Dec. ♉ | כדמרי |
| Bread (Ps. lxxviii. 25)=חלם, by metathesis. [K.D. L.C.K. p. 500] | לחם |
| Angel of 2 S. | מבהאל |
| The Influence from Kether | מזלא |
| Salt | מלח |
| The name of a Giant | עזא |

π

| | |
|---|---|
| Boaz, one of the Pillars of the Temple of Solomon | בעז |
| Die | גוע |
| Angel of 8 S. | ומבאל |
| Jachin, one of the Pillars of the Temple of Solomon | יאחין |
| 3rd ש | סיט |
| Conjunction, meeting, union | עדה |

| | |
|---|---|
| Union; an assembling | ועד |
| GOD of Jesod-Malkuth of Briah | יה אדני |
| Foundation | יסוד |
| Universal, general | כלל |
| Throne. [Exod. xvii. 16] | כס |
| | מם |

$9^2=3^4$. ☽

| | |
|---|---|
| GODS | אלים |
| I. [Ex. xxiii. 20] | אנכי |
| Anger, wrath; also nose | אף |

| | |
|---|---|
| earer of Cries; Angel of 6 P., and of 5 W. | יילאל |
| ight Demon of 2nd Dec. ♍ | כאין |
| rone | כסא |
| ere, hither | פא |

**82**

| | |
|---|---|
| ngel of ♀ | אנאל |
| prayer (Ch.) | בעי |
| iatic Palace of Hod | היכל גוגה |
| indly, righteous, holy | חסיד |
| ban; white | לבן |
| e beloved thing; res grata | ניחוח |

**π 83**

| | |
|---|---|
| breviatura quatuor systematum | אביע |
| e drops of dew. [Job xxxviii. 28] | אגלי טל |
| najahu, son of Jehoiada | בנייהו |
| e 73 | גימל |
| flowing, wave | גלים |
| rson, self; (Ch.) wing | גף |
| nsecration; dedicated | חנכה |
| gel of 2 P. | לכבאל |
| flee, put one's things in safety. [Jerem. vi. 1] | זוע |

**84**

| | |
|---|---|
| × 12; or (2² + 3)(2² × 3)—hence esteemed by some | |
| wing (army), squadron; a chosen troop | אגף |
| Z.Q. 699] | אהחע |
| ide K.D. L.C.K. p. 71] | אהחע |
| as silent | דמם |

| | |
|---|---|
| A dream | חלום |
| Enoch | חנוך |
| Knew | ידע |

**85**

| | |
|---|---|
| Boaz (is referred to Hod) | בועז |
| A flower, cup | גביע |
| Put in motion, routed | המם |
| Circumcision | מילה |
| The mouth; the letter פ | פה |

**86**

| | |
|---|---|
| A name of GOD, asserting the identity of Kether and Malkuth | אהיה אדני |
| Elohim. [Note masc. pl. of fem. sing.] | אלהים |
| Hallelu-Jah | הללויה |
| A rustling of wings | המולה |
| Geomantic Intelligence of ♈ | הנאל |
| [Vide I.R.Q. 778] | יה יהוה אדם |
| A cup: hence Pudendum Muliebre | כוס |
| A blemish, spot, stain | מום |
| Angel of 10 C. | מיהאל |
| Plenitude | מלוי |

**87**

| | |
|---|---|
| [Vide K.D. L.C.K. p. 114] | אלון |
| A cup | אסוך |
| Angel of 1st Dec. ♓ | בהלמי |
| Blasphemed | גדף |
| Standards, military ensigns | דגלים |
| Determined | זמם |

13

| | | | |
|---|---|---|---|
| White Storks | חסידה | Archangel of Geburah | כמאל |
| Whiteness; frankincense; Sphere of ☽ | לבנה | Food, fare | מאכל |
| | | Angel | מלאך |
| | | Daughter, virgin, bride, Kore | מלכא |
| **88** | | Manna | מנא |
| Redness; sparkling | חכלל | A hut, tent | סוכה |
| To be hot | חמם | Pekht, 'extension' | פאהה |
| Darkness | חסך | | |
| A duke of Edom | מגדיאל | | |
| Roaring, seething; burning | נחל | Angel of 5 S. | אניאל |
| | | Mud | בץ |
| **π 89** | | (Deut. xxviii. 58.) [Vide no. 572] | יהוה אלהיך |
| Shut up | גוף | | |
| Body | גוף | Terror, a name of Geburah | פחד |
| Silence | דממה | | |
| Angel of 9 S. | מחיאל | | |
| | | A duke of Edom. [Vide also Ezekiel xxiii.] | אהליבמה |
| **90** | | The sons of (the merciful) GOD | בני אל |
| Very silent | דומם | | |
| The Pillar, Jachin | יכין | Incense | לבונה |
| Water | מים | A disc, round shield | מגן |
| Kings | מלך | Possession | נחלה |
| Wicker-basket | סל | Arduous, busy; an army | צבא |
| Night Demon of 2nd Dec. ♌ | פור | | |

Σ(1—13). The Mystic Number of **91** Kether as Achad. The Number of Paths in the Supernal Beard; according to the number of the Letters, כ = 11, etc.

| | |
|---|---|
| A tree | אילן |
| Amen. [Cf. 741] | אמן |
| The Ephod | אפוד |
| The "יהוה אדני", inter-laced | יאהדונהי |
| Angel of 4 S. | כליאל |

Corpse — גופה
The valley of vision — גיחזיון
To extinguish — דעך
Destruction. [Ps. l. 20] — דפי
A shore — חוף
A window — חלון
A drop — מפה
Children — ילדים

| | |
|---|---|
| **95** | |
| e great Stone | אבן גדלה |
| gel of 2 W.—Daniel | דניאל |
| gel of 10 P. | ההעיה |
| e waters | המים |
| ltitude, abundance; Haman | המן |
| ulon | זבלון |
| gel of 2nd Dec. ♌ | זחעי |
| | מאדים |
| rney | מהלך |
| een | מלכה |
| ah. [Ps. xxxii. 5, 6, etc.] | סלה |
| **96** | |
| name of GOD | אל אדני |
| aldee form of אלהים | אלהין |
| day | יומם |
| iseworthy; Angel of 7 W. | ללהאל |
| rk | מלאכה |
| e secret (counsel) of the Lord. [Ps. xxv. 14] | סוד יהוה |
| **π 97** | |
| eeder, rearer; Day Demon of 1st Dec. ♊ | אומן |
| angeless, constant; the GOD Amon | אמן |
| e Son of Man | בן אדם |
| changel of Netzach | האניאל |
| e appointed time | זמן |
| seize suddenly (rapere) | חטף |
| hand-breadth, palm. [1 Kings vii. 26—Ex. xxv. 25] | טפה |
| brick, tile | לבינה |

| | |
|---|---|
| A building; an architect | מבנה |
| Aquae EL Boni. [" Quicksilver," K.D. L.C.K. p. 442] | מי אל הטב |
| **98** | |
| A name of GOD | הוא אלהים |
| Temporary dwelling. [Ex. xxxiii. 11] | זמנא |
| Image; hid, concealed—pertains to Sol and the Lingam-Yoni | חמן |
| To consume, eat | חסל |
| White | צח |
| **99** | |
| The pangs of childbirth | חבלי לידה |
| The Vault of Heaven; an inner chamber; wedlock, nuptial | חופה |
| Clay of Death, Infernal Abode of Geburah | טיטהיון |
| Cognition, knowledge | ידיעה |
| $10^2$   $\sqrt{100}$ | |
| A day; the seas; the times. [Vide no. 1100] | ימים |
| Vases, vessels | כלים |
| The palm; the letter Kaph | כף |
| An effort, exertion. [I.R.Q. 995] | מדון |
| Mitigation of the one by the other | מחי טבאל |
| **π 101** | |
| Swallowed, destroyed | אלע |
| A storehouse | אסם |
| [Vide K.D. L.C.K. p. 147] | אק |
| Angel of 4 C. | מומיה |

Archangel of ☉ and △; **מיכאל**
Angel of 7 S.; Angel of
Malkuth of Briah, etc.

Kingdom; a virgin princess; **מלוכה**
esp. THE Virgin Princess,
i.e. Ecclesia

Gut; gut-string **נימא**

102

A white goose **אווז לבן**

Trust, truth, faith **אמונה**

Bela, a King of Edom; to **בעל**
possess; lands, government

Concupiscibilis **נחמד**

Grace, pride, fame, glory; a **צבי**
wild goat

π 103

Dust **אבק**

To guard, protect **גנן**

Loathed **געל**

Food, meat (Ch.) **מזון**

Oblation **מנחה**

Prophets **נבאים**

A calf **עגל**

104

Father of the mob, or of **אב המון**
the multitude

Quarrel, dispute **מדין**

Personal (belongings), small **סגולה**
private property

Sodom **סדם**

Giving up, presenting, re- **סולה**
mitting

Trade; a fish-hook **צדי**

Σ (1—14)    10

To subvert, ruin, change **הפך**

Desert land: Earth of Netzach **ציה**

10

Attained **דבק**

Angel of 7 C. **מלהאל**

Fish; the letter Nun **נון**

Angel of 9 C. **סאליה**

Stibium **פוך**

Line, string, linen thread **קו**

π 10

An egg **ביצה**

Angel of Netzach of Briah **וסיאל**

Angel ruling ♌ **עואל**

$2^2 \times 3^3$: hence used as the number of 1
beads on a rosary by some sects

The ears **אזנים**

The fruit of a deep valley **באבי הנחל**

Hell of Jesod-Malkuth **גיהנם**

A wall **חיץ**

To force, do wrong to **חמס**

To love very much **חנן**

To shut up, obstruct **חסם**

The middle **חצי**

To measure out; a decree; **חק**
tall. (Masc. gender.) Cf. 113

Angel L.T.D. of ♌ **סגהם**

A Giant: "the lust of GOD" **עזאל**

π 1

Day-demon of 2nd Dec. ♒ **אסכוזדאי**

Lightning **בזק**

| | |
|---|---|
| iet | מנוחה |
| usic | נגון |
| gel of ♃ | סחיאל |
| rcle, sphere | עגול |
| | צדידא |

110

| | |
|---|---|
| ther of Faith | אב האמונה |
| ctum coeli fabrilis sub quo desponsationes con- iugum fiunt | גג החופה |
| esemblance, likeness | דמיון |
| erubic Signs—♏ replaced by ♈ | ומהץ |
| embrace | חבק |
| the end of the days; the right hand | ימין |
| sign, flag, standard | נס |
| ngel of 6 W. | סימאל |
| insman | עם |

he Number of Abra-Melin Servitors 111
f O.P.A.A. Σ{1—(6×6)}÷6. ☉

| | |
|---|---|
| ed. [Vide Gen. xxv. 25] | אדמונא |
| name of GOD | אחד הוא אלהים |
| thousand; Aleph | אלף |
| uin, destruction, sudden death | אסן |
| UM | אעם |
| hick darkness | אפל |
| asswords of ...... | יוד יהוה אדני |
| ad | מהולל |
| ngel of ☉ | נכיאל |
| ommon holocaust; an ascent | עולה |
| Duke of Edom | עלוה |

| | |
|---|---|
| Title of Kether. (Mirum occultum) | פלא |

112

| | |
|---|---|
| Angel of 2 C. | איעאל |
| A structure; mode of building | בנין |
| Was angry | בנם |
| Sharpness | חדק |
| Jabok. [Gen. xxxii. 22.] Note 112 = 4 × 28 | יבק |
| The Lord GOD | יהוה אלהים |
| Ebal | עיבל |

π 113

| | |
|---|---|
| Likewise; the same. (Fem. gender.) Cf. 108 | חקה |
| A giving away, remitting | סליחה |
| A stream, brook | פלג |

114

| | |
|---|---|
| Qliphoth of Jesod | גמליאל |
| Tear (weeping) | דמע |
| Gracious, obliging, indulgent | חנון |
| Science | מדע |
| Brains | מוחון |

115

| | |
|---|---|
| Geomantic Intelligence of ♍ | דמליאל |
| Here am I | הנני |
| The heat of the day | חום היום |
| To make strong; vehement, eager | חזק |

116

| | |
|---|---|
| Doves | יונים |
| Heaven of Chesed | מכון |
| The munificent ones | נדיבים |

# SEPHER SEPHIROTH

| | |
|---|---|
| Primordial | עילאה |

**117**

| | |
|---|---|
| Fog, darkness | אופל |
| Guide; Duke | אלוף |

**118**

| | |
|---|---|
| To pass, renew, change | חלף |
| To ferment | חמע |
| Strength; Chassan, Ruler of Air | חסן |
| The High Priest | כהן גדול |

**119**

| | |
|---|---|
| Lydian-stone | אבן בוחן |
| Beelzebub, the Fly-GOD | בעלזבוב |
| Weeping (subst.) | דמעה |
| Night Demon of 2nd Dec. ♐ | חאלף |
| Abominable | פגול |

$\underline{5} = \Sigma\,(1{-}15){:}{-}$ ה being the **120**
5th Path

| | |
|---|---|
| Master | בעל |
| Foundation, basis | מוסדי |
| The time of the decree | מועד |
| Strengthening | מכין |
| Prophetic sayings, or decrees: "His days shall be";—hence Abra-Melin | מלים |
| Velum | מסך |
| Prop; the letter Samekh | סמך |
| A name of GOD | עז |

$11^2$ $\sqrt{}$ **121**

| | |
|---|---|
| Vain idols | אלילים |
| ?Termination of Abr-amelim? | אמילם |
| An end, extremity | אפם |

| | |
|---|---|
| Emanated from | אצל |
| Of whirling motions | הגלגלים |
| Nocturnal vision | חזוה די ליליא |
| Angel ruling ♋ | כעאל |
| It is filled | נמלא |
| Angel L.T.N. of ♋ | עכאל |

**12**

| | |
|---|---|
| Vi compressa | אנוסה |
| Revolutiones (Animarum) | גלגולים |

**12**

| | |
|---|---|
| A name of GOD, implying Kether—Chokmah—Binah, 3, 4, & 5 letters | אהה יהוה אלהים |
| War | מלחמה |
| A blow, plague | נגע |
| Pleasure, delight | ענג |
| Laesio aliqualis, violatio | פגם |

**12**

| | |
|---|---|
| An oak; hardness | חוסן |
| Pleasure, delight; Eden | עדן |
| Qliphoth of Chokmah | עיגיאל |

$5^3$ $^3/$ **12**

| | |
|---|---|
| Night Demon of 2nd Dec. ♓ | הנמאל |
| [Vide S.D. v. 16] | כפכה |
| Angel of 4 P. | מנדאל |

**12**

| | |
|---|---|
| A widow | אלמנה |
| Darkness | אפילה |
| Day Demon of 1st Dec. ♉ | גימינין |
| A name of GOD | יהוה אדני אגלא |
| Hospitality | מלון |

| | |
|---|---|
| rse | סום |
| , a name of GOD [see 120], penalty of iniquity; "being aken away" | עון |

**π 127**

| | |
|---|---|
| terial | מוטבע |
| gel of 5 P. | פויאל |

**2⁷**    **√ 128**

| | |
|---|---|
| phaz | אליפז |
| gel ruling ≈ | אנמואל |
| deliver, loose | חלץ |
| bustus gratià. [Vide K.D. ..C.K. p. 399] | חסין |
| D, the Eternal One | יהוה אלהינו |

**129**

| | |
|---|---|
| asure [Gen. xviii. 12] | עדנה |
| light, pleasure | עונג |

**130**

| | |
|---|---|
| liverance | הצלה |
| e Angel of re-demption | מלאך הגאל |
| crees, prophetic sayings | מלין |
| ; the letter Ayin | עין |
| e Pillars | עמודי |
| stitute | עני |
| taircase, ladder | סלם |
| gel of 5 C. | פהליה |

**π 131**

| | |
|---|---|
| was angry | אנף |
| se | אפים |
| rn, roll | אפן |
| le of Kether | מכוסה |

| | |
|---|---|
| Angel of 6 C. | נלכאל |
| Samael; Qliphoth of Hod | סמאל |
| Angel L.T.N. of ♍ | ססיא |
| Humility | ענוה |

**132**

| | |
|---|---|
| To make waste | בלק |
| Angel of 4 W. | ננאאל |
| To receive | קבל |

**133**

| | |
|---|---|
| [Vide I.Z.Q. 699] | גיבק |
| Vine | גפן |
| Angel of 5 S. | חעמיה |
| The salt sea | ים המלח |

**134**

| | |
|---|---|
| Burning | דלק |

**135**

| | |
|---|---|
| Day Demon of 2nd Dec. ♋ | גוסיין |
| Geomantic Intelligence of ♈ | מלכדיאל |
| A destitute female | עניה |
| The congregation. [Vide no. 161] | קהל |
| [Vide K.D. L.C.K. p. 673] | קלה |

**Σ (1—16). ♃**    **136**

| | |
|---|---|
| Spirit of ♃ | הסמאל |
| Intelligence of ♃ | יהפיאל |
| The Avenging Angel | מלאך הגואל |
| Fines, penalties | ממון |
| A voice | קול |

**π 137**

| | |
|---|---|
| A wheel | אופן |

19

The belly, gullet. אסטומכא
[? Hebrew: vide K.D.
L.C.K. p. 138]

An image, a statue. מצבה
[Gen. xxviii. 22]

A receiving; the Qabalah קבלה

**138**

The Son of GOD בן אלהים

To smoothe, divide חלק

To leaven, ferment חמץ

To pollute חנף

Libanon. [Cant. iv. 11, 15] לבנון

He shall smite מחץ

Forehead מצח

**π 139**

Hiddekel, the eastern river הדקל
of Eden

**140**

Kings; Angels of Tiphareth מלכים
of Assiah, and of Netzach
of Briah

**141**

Robust; oaken אמיץ

Gathered, collected אסף

Angel of 4 P. כוקיה

Precept מצוה

Trusty, steady נאמן

L.A. Angel of ♋ פכיאל

Prima קמא

**142**

Geomantic Intelligence אסמודאל
of ♉

Wickedness, destruction בליעל

A stranger; Balaam בלעם

Night Demon of 3rd Dec. ♌ בעלם

Delights (△ & ▽) מחמרים

**I**

The unshoeing חליצה

Running waters. [Cant. iv. 15] נוזלים

**12²** √ **I**

A sandal סנדל

Anterius; the East; days first קדם
of the first

The numerical value of the 13 Paths **I**
of the Beard of Microprosopus

The Staff of GOD. מטה האלהים
[Ex. xvii. 9]

Inscrutable מעלה

Angel of 6 P. נממיה

A feast סעודה

**I**

The First Gate. [Vide בבא קמא
K.D. L.C.K. p. 184]

Limit, end; boundless סוף

The world; an adult עולם

The Four Names in the Lesser **I**
Ritual of the Pentagram;

viz.: יהוה אדני אהיה אגלא

**I**

A name of אהיה יה יהוה אלהים
GOD

Angels of Hod in Assiah בני אלהים
and Briah

Glutton and drunkard. זולל וסובא
[Deut. xxi. 20]

To withdraw, retire חמק

| | |
|---|---|
| ales; ♎ | מאזנים |
| ctory | נצח |
| our, meal | קמח |
| | π 149 |
| e living GODS. [Cf. 154] | אלים חיים |
| beating of the breast; a noisy striking | המספד |
| | 150 |
| iolus. [K.D. L.C.K. p. 53] | ידעוני |
| walking shoe | נעל |
| ine eye. [Vide I.R.Q. 652] | עינך |
| est | קן |
| | π 151 |
| אה spelt in full | אלף הה יוד הה |
| TETRAGRAMMATON of the GODS is One TETRAGRAMMATON" | יהוה אלהים יהוה אחד |
| ght Demon of 3rd Dec. ♈ | מאלף |
| e Fountain of Living Waters. [Jer. xvii. 13] | מקוה |
| standing upright, stature | קומה |
| alous | קנא |
| | 152 |
| njamin | בנימן |
| e Bringing-forth One | המוציא |
| esidence, station | נציב |
| Σ (1—17) | 153 |
| A. Angel of ♎ | חדקיאל |
| | 154 |
| ohim of Lives. [Cf. 149] | אלהים חיים |

| | |
|---|---|
| | 155 |
| Adonai the King | אדני מלך |
| The faithful friend | דוד נאמן |
| The beard (correct). [S.D. ii. 1, et seq.] | דקנא |
| Letters of the Cherubic signs | ו:נ:ט:צ |
| Angel of 2nd Dec. ♑ | יסיסיה |
| "The Concealed and Saving"; Angel of 6 W. | עלמיה |
| A seed | קנה |
| 12 × 13, the number of letters in each 'tablet of Enoch' | 156 |
| The Tabernacle of the congregation. [Lev. i. 1] | אהל מועד |
| A viper | אפעה |
| BABALON, THE VICTORIOUS QUEEN. [Vide XXX Aethyrs: Liber CDXVIII] | באבאלען |
| Angel of Hod of Briah | הסניאל |
| Joseph [referred to Jesod] | יוסף |
| Angel of 1st Dec. ♏ | כמוץ נעול |
| A bird | עוף |
| "Crying aloud"; the name of a King of Edom | פעו |
| Zion | ציון |
| Limpid blood | צלול |
| | π 157 |
| The setting of the Sun | דמרומי חמה |
| Was angry, enraged; anger | זעף |

Lingam ... זקן

The beard. [Vide S.D. ii. 467, and no. 22] ... זקן

Occult ... מופלא

Female; Yoni ... נקבה

Angel of 9 S. ... ענואל

A Duke of Edom ... קנז

158

Arrows ... חיצים

To suffocate ... חנק

Balances. [Ch.] ... מאזנין

159

Surpassing Whiteness. [Vide 934] ... בוצינא

Point ... נקדה

[Vide I.R.Q. 652] 160

Angel of 3 S. ... הקמיה

Silver ... כסף

Fell down. Decidit ... נפל

A rock, stone ... סלע

A tree ... עץ

A Duke of Edom ... פינן

Lay, fell. [Ez. iii. 8] ... פניך

Image ... צלם

Cain ... קין

161

The heavenly man; lit. the 'primordial' or 'exalted' man ... אדם עילאה

The Congregation of the Eternal ... קהל יהוה

קינא

---

Nine Paths of the Inferior Beard;
$14 + 15 + \dots + 22 =$ ... 16

Son of the Right Hand; pr. n. of Benjamin ... בנימין

Day Demon of 1st Dec. ♐ ... גלאסלבול

Angel ruling ♏ ... סוסול

π 16

[Vide no. 361, a numerical Temurah of 163] ... הוא אלהים אדני

Woman, wife ... נוקבה

16

רצע

Ye shall cleave ... הדבקים

Outer; civil, as opposed to sacred. [Vide K.D. L.C.K. p. 342] ... חיצון

The Pillars ... עמדים

Strength. [Ez. iii. 8] ... חזקים

"To make them know." [Ps. xxv. 14] ... להודיעם

Nehema ... נעמה

NEMO. [Name of M.T.] Angel of 3 W. ... עממיה

An assembly ... עצה

A King of Edom ... בעלחנו

Reus mulctae. [Vide K.D. L.C.K. p. 498] ... חייב ממן

Heaven of Geburah ... מעון

Night Demon of 3rd Dec. ♏ ... נפול

Native land of Job ... עוץ

The Most High ... עליון

π 167

Unnameable One [a demon] — אסימון

...ers. [Job xxxvi. 8] — זיקים

168

...entes Superni — אבא ואמא עילאה

13²  √ 169

...accentuator — טעמים

170

Wand; (David's) Staff — מקל

...d — ענן

Σ (1—18)  171

...cipium emittens — מאציל

...anating from — נאצל

...el L.T.N. of ≈ — פלאין

..."e Face of God"; name — פניאל
... an angel

172

..., divided — בקע

...affected. [Not written] — יעצב

...ters; grapes — ענבים

...heel, the end. [Mic. vii. 20] — עקב
...cob

π 173

...ten mine eyes — גל עיני
Demon of 3rd Dec. ≈ — גצף

174

...ches — לפידים

...ndor ei per cir-itum — נוגה לו סביב

Σ {1 − (7 × 7)} ÷ 7.  ♀  175

...ion — יניקה

...licity — מכפלה

...ipping, falling — נפילה

---

Spirit of ♀ — קדמאל

176

An advisor, counselling — יועץ
To eternity — לעולם
Illegitimate — פסול

177

Dominus Domino-rum — אדון האדונים

The Garden of Eden — גן עדן
To cry out for help — זעק
Angel L.T.D. of ♈ — סגדלעי
Plenitude of plenitudes — מלוי המלוי

178

The lower part, the loins — חלצים

Good pleasure, choice, decision, will — חפץ

Quicksilver — כסף חי

π 179

Ligatio — עקדה

180

A spring, fountain. [Cant. iv. 15] — מעיין

The front part — פנים

π 181

Vicious, faulty — פסולה

182

Deus Zelotes — אל קנא
Outcry, clamour — זעקה
Layer of snares, supplanter; Jacob — יעקב
King of the Gods — מלאך האלהים
Passive [as opposed to מחקבל = active] — מקביל

23

183

184

Ancient time; eastward נקדל

185

186

A stone of stumbling; a rock to fall over. [Is. viii. 14] אבן נגף

An increase מוסף

Praefecti ממונים

A place מקום

Back of the Head; an ape; the letter Qoph קוף

187

Angels of Chokmah, and of Chokmah of Briah אופנים

Lifted up זקף

[K. of S., Fig. 52] סופיאל

188

Jaacob. [Vide K.D. L.C.K. p. 443] יעקוב

The Master of the Nose כעל החוטם

189

Fons obseratus. [Cant. iv. 11] גל נעול

The Ancient among the ancient סבא דסבין

Σ (1—19)

Ubi perrexit Angelus ויסע ויבא ויט

Internal פנימי

Corona florida prominens ציץ

The side or flank; rib צלע

First devil. V. Porta Coelorum Fig. XVI קמטיאל

The end, appointed time. [Dan. xii. 13.] [Vide no. 305] קץ

190

Countenance אנפין

[Vide K.D. L.C.K. p. 143] אפסים

Night Demon of 1st Dec. ♍ פאבץ

A box, chest; a repository קופה

Poisonous wind, Simoon זלעפה

Ye shall cleave in TETRAGRAMMATON. [Vide no. 220] חדבקים ביהוה

Righteousness, equity, justice: the Sphere of ♃. [Vide K.D. L.C.K. p. 656] צדק

A flock מקנה

Visitation פקודה

$14^2$

Mare Soph. [Vide K.D. L.C.K. p. 435] ים סוף

The crown, summit, point קוץ

El Supernus אל עליון

[Vide K.D. L.C.K. p. 71] אנא חטא עם הזה

Victories נצחים

A giving freely; Ἐλεημοσύνη צדקה

Alae. [Vide K.D. L.C.K. p. 483] כנפים

A branch ענף

| | |
|---|---|
| bone | עצם |
| ‑chetypal | קדמון |
| ‑longing to the Spring | קיץ |
| sling; a casting-net | קלע |
| ‑vination | קסם |

201

| | |
|---|---|
| ght (Ch.) | אר |

202

| | |
|---|---|
| ‑ make empty | בקק |
| ‑re; a field; son | בר |
| ‑evatio | זקיפה |
| ‑ertures | נקבים |
| A. Angel of ♏ | סאיציאל |
| ‑any, much | רב |

203

| | |
|---|---|
| ‑itials of the Trinity: | אבר |
| אב:בן:רוח | |
| ‑ssed away, perished; feather, wing; (it. membrum et quid. genitale) | אבר |
| ‑ lie in wait | ארב |
| ‑well, spring | באר |
| ‑eated | ברא |
| ‑otic, foreign | גר |

204

| | |
|---|---|
| ‑mmencement of the name Abra-Melin | אברא |
| ‑reign resident; race S.; an ‑ge (Ch.) | דר |
| ‑e righteous | צדיק |

205

| | |
|---|---|
| ‑y Demon of 2nd Dec. ♈ | אנאר |
| ‑endrous | אדר |

| | |
|---|---|
| Mighty; hero | גבר |
| Mountain | הר |

206

| | |
|---|---|
| Assembly; area | אדרא |
| Hail | ברד |
| Spake; word; cloud | דבר |
| They of the World | ימי עולם |

207

| | |
|---|---|
| ♏, a scorpion | אגראב |
| Lord of the Universe | אדון עולם |
| Light. Cf. 9 and 11. Aur is the balanced Light of open day | אור |
| Limitless | אין סוף |
| Ate | ברה |
| Walled, fenced | גדר |
| That which cuts. [Vide no. 607] | הבר |
| The Elders. [Deut. xxi. 19] | זקנים |
| Melt, fuse | זקק |
| The Crown of the Ark | זר |
| Grow great | רבה |

208

| | |
|---|---|
| Feather | אברה |
| A cistern | בור |
| Bowed | גהר |
| To make strife, contend | גרה |
| Hagar | הגר |
| To kill | הרג |
| Abominable | זרא |
| Jizchak. [Vide K.D. L.C.K. p. 266] | יצחק |
| Multitude | רוב |

25

D

**209**

| | |
|---|---|
| Chief Seer or Prophet (hence Abra-Melin) | אבראה |
| Reward, profit, prize | אגרה |
| To delay, tarry; behind (prep.) | אחר |
| Way | ארח |
| 10th Spirit of Goetia. | בואר |
| Dispersed | בזר |
| Sojourned, dwelt | גור |
| Honour; a King of Edom; the Supernal Benignity | הדר |
| Oppressed | זרב |

Σ (1—20)    **210**

| | |
|---|---|
| Adam Primus. [Vide no. 607] | אדהר |
| Day Demon of 1st Dec. ♋ | בזאר |
| Choice | בחר |
| Pass on, fly | ברח |
| To decide, determine | גזר |
| To dwell; circle, cycle; generation | דור |
| To conceive | הרה |
| A joining of words; incantations; to conjoin; a brother | חבר |
| A sword | חרב |
| Angel of 1st Dec. ♑ | מסנין |
| Naaman | נעמן |
| [Vide ΘΕΛΗΜΑ] | נ:ע:ץ |
| Punctata | נקודים |

π 211

| | |
|---|---|
| [Worthy] | אבחר |
| A lion | ארי |
| Strong | גבור |
| A flash; lightning | האַרה |

| | |
|---|---|
| A girdle | חגר |
| A flood; Jeor | יאר |
| "Fear," the fear of the יהוה (i.e. wonderment) | ירא |

**21**

| | |
|---|---|
| Great Voice | דבור |
| Night Demon of 1st Dec. ♑ | האור |
| Splendour; to enlighten | זהר |
| To spread out; harlot; golden | זרה |
| To enclose; secret chamber | חדר |

**21**

| | |
|---|---|
| Strong, powerful, mighty | אביר |
| Calx | גיר |
| [I.R.Q. 234 (?)] | הדדר |
| Slaughter | הרגה |
| Loaded | וזר |
| To be strange; a stranger | זור |
| The Supernal Mercy of GOD | חסד עלאה דאל |
| Nubes Magna | ענן גדול |

**21**

| | |
|---|---|
| A girdle | אזור |
| Angel of 1st Dec. ♈ | זזר |
| Whiteness | חור |
| Came down | ירד |
| Air; Spirit; wind; Mind | רוח |

**21**

| | |
|---|---|
| Eminent; a Prince. [Ps. viii. 1] | אדיר |
| A path, narrow way | אורח |
| Posterior; the reversed part | אחור |
| A rising; to rise "as the Sun," give light | זרח |

| | |
|---|---|
| encompass. [Vide K.D. | חזר |
| L.C.K. p. 340] | |

6⁸     ∛216

| | |
|---|---|
| ght Demon of 1ˢᵗ Dec. ♎ | אוראת |
| on | אריה |
| e middle Gate. | בבא מציעא |
| Vide K.D. L.C.K. | |
| p. 184] | |
| urage | גבורה |
| acle | דביר |
| ood of grapes | דם ענבים |
| ead, fear | יראה |
| ofound. [Ps. xcii. 6] | עומק |
| ger, wrath | רוגז |
| titude | רוחב |

217

| | |
|---|---|
| e air | אויר |
| mple, palace | בירה |
| od | בריה |
| bee | דבורה |
| e navel | טבור |
| gel ruling ♐ | מויעסאל |
| gel L.T.N. of ♏ | סהקנב |
| ntroversia Domini | ריבה |

218

| | |
|---|---|
| ner. [Vide K.D. L.C.K. | אורא |
| p. 55] | |
| e Creative World | בריאה |
| e benignity of Time | • חסד עולם |
| e Moon | ירח |
| ltitude | רבוי |
| cana | רזיא |

| | |
|---|---|
| Odour, a smell | ריח |

219

| | |
|---|---|
| Mundatio, mundities | טהרה |
| The Number of Verses in Liber | R 220 |
| Legis | |
| The Elect | בחיר |
| Heroina; Augusta; Domina | גבירה |
| Ye shall cleave | הדבקים ליהוה |
| unto TETRAGRAMMATON. | |
| [*Not* written] | |
| Clean, elegant | טהור |
| Giants. [Fully written only | נפילים |
| in Num. xiii. 33] | |
| Left-handed Svastika, drawn on the | 221 |
| square of ♂ given by Agrippa. | |
| Cf. 231 | |
| Long | ארך |
| Angel of 10 S. | מנקאל |

222

| | |
|---|---|
| Urias | אוריה |
| " Unto the Place." | אל המקום |
| [Ex. xxiii. 20] | |
| Whiteness | הורה |
| Goodly mountain. | הר טוב |
| [Ex. iii. 25] | |
| Now, already; K'bar, "the | כבר |
| river Khebar"; Day Demon | |
| of 3ʳᵈ Dec. | |
| I will chase | ראויה |

π 223

224

| | |
|---|---|
| Male (Ch.) | דכר |
| Walk, journey; The PATH | דרך |
| Principia emanandi | חוקקי |

| | |
|---|---|
| Effigurata | חקוקי |
| Union | יחור |

**15²** √ 225

[Vide K.D. L.C.K. p. 234] — גזרדיא

226

Profound, hidden; the North. — צפון
[Vide K.D. L.C.K. p. 666]

π 227

| | |
|---|---|
| Long, tall | ארוך |
| A piscine, pond; [Blessing, Prov. x. 22] | ברכה |
| Remember; male (sacred Phallus—Vide S.D. ii. p. 467) | זכר |
| Damna. [Vide K.D. L.C.K. p. 569] | נזיקין |

228

| | |
|---|---|
| First-born | בכור |
| Blessed! | ברוך |
| Ruler of Earth | כרוב |
| The Tree of Life | עץ חיים |

π 229

230

| | |
|---|---|
| Astonishment | הכרה |
| [Vide K.D. L.C.K. p. 153] | מקיף |
| Fasciata | עקורים |
| Angel of 2nd Dec. ♍ | ראידיה |
| Hod, 42-fold Name in Yetzirah. [Vide Liber 777, Col. xc. p. 18] | יגלפזק |

Σ (1—21). Right-handed Svastika, 231 drawn on Sq. of ♂

| | |
|---|---|
| Prolonged; grew long | אריך |
| Male | דכורא |

Sum of the Four Ways of spelling 2 TETRAGRAMMATON in the Four Worlds

| | |
|---|---|
| Geomantic Intelligence of ♒ | אמניציאל |
| Ruler of Fire | אראל |
| Equivalent to יהי אור, Fiat Lux. [Vide K.D. L.C.K. p. 55] | יה אויר |
| Let there be Light! The Mystic Name of Allan Bennett, a Brother of the Cross and Rose, who began this Dictionary. | יהי אור |

π 2

| | |
|---|---|
| Memento | זכור |
| The Tree of Life. [Vide no. 228] | עץ החיים |

| | |
|---|---|
| Night Demon of 3rd Dec. ♒ | דכאוראב |
| Archangel of Chesed, and Angel of Chesed of Briah | צדקיאל |
| Angel L.T.N. of ♈ | ספעטאוי |
| A handful | קומץ |
| Angel of 3 C. | ראהאל |
| Dominus Mirabilium | אדון הנפלאוה |
| Rachel | רחל |

π 2

| | |
|---|---|
| Azrael, the Angel of Death | אזראל |
| Iron | ברזל |
| The lot | גורל |

| | |
|---|---|
| ngel of 3rd Dec. ♉ | יכסגנוץ |

240

| | |
|---|---|
| yrrh | מר |
| lagae Filiorum Hominum. [I.e. Succubae, K.D. L.C.K. p. 562] | נגעי בני אדם |
| rima Germina | נצנים |
| ngel of 1st Dec. ♒ | ססמם |
| ash; counted out, paid down | פקודים |
| igh, lofty | רם |

π 241

| | |
|---|---|
| .A. Angel of ♑ | סמקיאל |

242

| | |
|---|---|
| riel, Angel of Air | אריאל |
| ecollection | זכירה |

243

| | |
|---|---|
| bram. [Vide 248] | אברם |
| reated (he them). [Gen. v. 2] | בראם |
| earned, complete. To finish, bring to pass (Ch.) | גמר |
| bone; to destroy | גרם |

244

| | |
|---|---|
| ngel of 7 P. | הרחאל |
| o be insensible; in deep sleep, in trance. [Vide no. 649] | רדם |

245

| | |
|---|---|
| dam Qadmon | אדם קדמון |
| all, bile | מרה |
| pirit of God | רוח אל |

246

| | |
|---|---|
| ngel of 3 S. | הריאל |
| yrrh | מור |

| | |
|---|---|
| Vision, aspect | מראה |
| | מרגג |
| Angel L.T.D. of ♉ | ראידאל |
| Height, altitude | רום |

247

| | |
|---|---|
| Angel L.T.N. of ♑ | אלויר |
| To overwhelm (Ps. lxxvii. 18); a flood | זרם |
| A light | מאור |
| Night Demon of 1st Dec. ♉ | ראום |
| Sensus symbolicus | רמז |

248

| | |
|---|---|
| Abraham. [Vide 243 and 505, 510. Discussed at length in Zohar] | אברהם |
| The Three that bear witness, above and beneath, respectively. אדם the Spirit, the Water, and the Blood; א being Air (Spiritus), ד standing for דם Blood, and מ being both Water and the initial of מים, water. For ברא see 203 | אדם + ברא |
| Uriel or Auriel, archangel of Earth, and angel of Netzach; = "The light of God" | אוריאל |
| In vision. [Vide K.D. L.C.K. p. 553] | במראה |
| Gematria | גמרה |
| Wine; bitumen; an ass (from "to disturb") | חמר |
| Mercy; womb | רחם |
| A lance | רמח |

# SEPHER SEPHIROTH

249

L.A. Angel of ♉    ארזיאל

Night Demon of 2nd Dec. ♎   גמור

Fear, terror    מגור

250

The living GOD of אלהי העולמים
the Worlds; or,
of the Ages

[The South.] Midday    דרום

Habit, action (Ch.)    מדור

π 251

Fir, cedar    ארן

The angel Uriel: "Vrihl,"   וריהל
i.e. Magical Force. [Vide
Lytton's "Coming Race,"
and Abra-Melin—forehead
Lamen]

Angel of 10 W.    רייאל

252

Serpent's den    מאורה

Σ (1—22)    253

Proselytes    גרים

Matred; who symbolizes the מטרד
Elaborations on the side of
Severity

254

Angel of 3rd Dec. ♒    גרודיאל

Geomantic Intelligence of ♎ זוריאל

An ass    חמור

A mark, aim    מטרה

A solemn promise, vow    נדר

Spikenard. [Cant. iv. 14]    נרד

A spear    רומח

Merciful    רחום

25

Night Demon of 3rd Dec. ♐   אנדר

Burdensome; with difficulty   חומרא

The East    מזרח

A river, stream. [Gen. ii. 10]   נהר

Cantatio elata    רנה

$16^2 = 4^4 = 2^8 = 256$   √ ∜ ∛ 25

Aaron    אהרן

Tidings (Ps. lxviii. 12); a אמירה
saying, speech. [Vide
K.D. L.C.K. p. 128]

The Sons of the Righteous   בני צדק

[See no. 705] [Vide K.D. מפולמין
L.C.K. p. 20]

The Spirit of the Mother   רוח אמא

Aromatarius    רוכל

π 25

The Ark    ארון

A Magician    חרטם

"To His fearers."    ליראיו
[Ps. xxv. 14]

The White Wand    מקל לבנה

Terribilis Ipsa    נורא

2

The red light    אור אדום

Hiram (King of Tyre)    חירם

Mercy    רחמי

2

Throat    גרון

Nitre    נטר

Reuben    ראובן

30

Σ {1—(8 × 8)} ÷ 8.  ☿  260

elligence of ☿ — טיריאל

e Concealed — טמירא

.R. [Vide 270] — יׁנׁרׁיׁ:

altabitur — ירים

vineyard — כרם

ptos et profanos — לפסילים

. viii. 1] — מה אדיר

clined — סר

gather, draw together — צמצם

261

bound; an obligation, a prohibition — אסר

horrence, abomination. Is. lxvi. 24] — דראון

262

fty; Aaron — אהרון

erities — גבוראן

rrible — הנורא

nclavia — חדרים

e to eye. [I.R.Q. 645] — עין בעין

π 263

gel of 2nd Dec. ♒ — אבדרון

gel of 2nd Dec. ♓ — אורון

omantic Intelligence of ♏ — ברכיאל

matria — גמטריא

ned — גרם

264

anantia. [Vide K.D. L.C.K. p. 338] — חקוקים

den. [Vide K.D. L.C.K. p. 455] — ירדן

---

Footprints (foot's breadth). [Deut. ii. 5] — מדרך

A straight row. [Vide K.D. L.C.K. p. 455] — סדר

Channels, pipes — רהטים

‖6   265

Architect — אדריכל

Broke down — הרם

A cry of the heart; anguish, anxiety — צעקה

266

Chebron — חברון

Termination of Qliphoth of 12 Signs — ירון

Contraction — צמצום

267

Illicit, forbidden — אסור

Geomantic Intelligence of ♌ — ורכיאל

Currus; Vehiculum; Thronus — מרכבה

Nasiraeus — נזיר

268

Stones of the sling — אבני הקלע

π 269

By-ways — ארחין

Father—Spirit—Son — בן רוח אב

Angel of Binah of Briah — כרוביאל

270

Levers, bars — בריחים

I.N.R.I. Initials of: Jesus — יׁנׁרׁיׁ: Nazaraeus Rex Judaeorum; Igni Natura Renovata Integra; Intra Nobis Regnum deI; Isis Naturae Regina

Ineffabilis; and many other sentences. Vide Crowley Coll. Works Vol. I. Appendix

π 271

Earth (Ch.); whence = low, mean    ארע

Angel of 2nd Dec. ♐    והרין

[Vide no. 256, אמירה]    לאמר

272

Earth    ארעא

To consume, injure; brutish    בער

Percussione magna    מכה רבה

The evening: an 'Arab,' i.e. a person living in the West    ערב

Day Demon of 3rd Dec. ♐    רינוו

273

The stone which אבן מאסו הבונים the builders rejected [Ps. cxviii. 22]

The Hidden Light    אור גנוז

Four    ארבע

Rebuked    גער

Took away    גרע

274

Paths    דרכים

275

[Vide K.D. L.C.K. p. 72] אחוריים

Domicilium pulchrum. דירה נאה [Vide K.D. L.C.K. p. 395]

Fluvius Iudicii. [Vide יאר דין K.D. L.C.K. p. 117]

Qy. Sruti " scripture "    סרטו

---

ℤ (1—23)     2'

Angel L.T.N. of ♎. אחובראין [Vide Liber 777, p. 29]

A Cithara    כנור

Night Demon of 1st Dec. ♌ כרוכל

The Moon    סיהרא

π 2

To sow, propagate; seed, semen    זרע

[For multiplying.] [Not למרבה written. Vide K.D. L.C.K. pp. 157 and 837]

Angel of 3rd Dec. ♌    סהיבר

Gratia, benevolentia    רעוא

2

Angels of Jesod, and of כרובים Binah of Briah—Cherubim

Passing over    עובר

The Material World עולם המוטבע

2

Leprosy. [Vide K.D. סגירו L.C.K. p. 495]

[7 × 40, the Squares on the walls of 2 the Vault. See Equinox I. 3. p. 222]

Qliphoth of ♑    דגדגירון

A record (Ch.)    דכרון

Angel of the Wood of the יער World of Assiah

The Letters of Judg- כ:מ:נ:פ:צ: ment: the 5 letters having a final form

Archangel of Malkuth    סנדלפון

Citizenship    עיר

32

| | |
|---|---|
| ide S.D. 528] | פר |
| rror | רף |
| | π 281 |
| crown—Ashes | אפר |
| tire; adorned | פאר |
| | 282 |
| ngels of Briah, and of Malkuth of Briah | אראלים |
| irit of Lives | רוח חיים |
| | π 283 |
| rum inclusum | זהב סגור |
| moriale. [Vide no. 964] | זכרון |
| at goes on foot | רגלים |
| | 284 |
| omantic Intelligence of Π | אמבריאל |
| e small area of an en-closed gárden | ערוגה |
| | 285 |
| | 286 |
| gh, lofty | מרום |
| | 287 |
| rs Azymorum | אפיקומן |
| ght Demon of 3rd Dec. ♉ | ופאר |
| ttle | זעיר |
| omantic Intelligence of ♋ | מוריאל |
| | 288 |
| ndication | ביעור |
| y Demon of 1st Dec. ♍ | זאפר |
| eeding, bearing; offspring. [Vide K.D. L.C.K. p. 313] | עיבור |
| ide K.D. L.C.K. p. 571] | רפח |

| | |
|---|---|
| 17² | √ 289 |
| Apertio. [Vide no. 537] | פטר |
| Particulare | פרט |
| | 290 |
| Thine enemy | ערכ |
| | 291 |
| Torrentes Aquarum | אפיקי מים |
| (He) treasured | אצר |
| Earth: in particular, the Earth of Malkuth | ארץ |
| Qy. spotted? | נמרא |
| Adhaesio; adhaerens; princeps | סירכא |
| L.A. Angel of ♒ | צכמקיאל |
| | 292 |
| A young bird. [Deut. xxii. 6] | אפרוה |
| Gold | בצר |
| A medicine, drug | רפואה |
| | π 293 |
| Day Demon of 2nd Dec. ♉ | צארב |
| | 294 |
| Purple | ארגמן |
| Pertaining to Autumn | חורף |
| Melchizedec. [Gen. xiv. 18] | מלכיצדק |
| | 295 |
| Curtain, canopy; vault. [Ps. civ. 2] | יריעה |
| Eyelids | כנפי העין |
| [Vide K.D. L.C.K. p. 498] | פטור |
| | 296 |
| Of the Earth. [Vide no. 992] | הארץ |
| Incurvens se | כורע |

33

Rigorose procedere; fumarie; rock. [Vide K.D. L.C.K. pp. 459, 663] — צור

**297**

Thesaurus; gazophylacium; conservatorium — אוצר

A name of GOD attributed to Geburah — אלהים גבור

A secured house; a fortified castle — ארמון

A City of Edom — בצרה

The Thröne; a Name of Briah — כורסיא

Nuriel — נוריאל

The neck — צואר

**298**

Amen, our Light — אמן אור

Son of the GODS — בר אלהין

White — צחר

Pathetic appeals; commiserations — רחמים

**299**

Angel of 2nd Dec. ♋ — רהדץ

Σ (1—24) **300**

Khabs am Pekht — אור בפאהה

Vide Beth Elohim. Dissert. II. Cap. 1. A spelling of אלהים in full. — אלף למד הי יוד מם

Formation — יצר

Profundities — מעמקים

God of Chesed, and of Hod of Briah; Temura of יהוה — מצפצ

Incircumcisus — ערל

---

Separation — פירוד

The Spirit of GOD. [Vide Gen. i. 3] — רוח אלהים

**30**

"My Lord, the faithful King"; a name of GOD — אדני המלך נאמן

Fire — אש

A candlestick — מנורה

**30**

Earth of Hod — ארקא

To cut open, inquire into; Dawn — בקר

L.A. Angel of ♈ — סראיאל

Hath protected — קבר

To putrefy — רקב

**30**

Did evil; putrefaction — באש

**30**

A species of gold — חרוץ

Green — דש

Geomantic Intelligence of ♒ — כאמבריאל

White — קדר

**3**

Dazzling white light — אור צח

Tender herb. [Gen. i. 11] — דשא

Netzach, 42-fold Name in Yetzirah. [Vide Liber 777, col. xc.] — הקממנע

Yetzirah: "formation" — יצרה

A curving, bending — כריעה

E 2

e end of days, appointed קץ הימין
ime. [Dan. xii. 13]

amb שה
הש

**306**

her of Mercy אב הרחמים

rciful Father אב הרחמן

voman, wife; virago אשה

ney דבש

nina. [Vide K.D. מטרונא
.C.K. p. 528]

le K.D. L.C.K. p. 571] ניצוצין

dness; pertaining to Winter קור

gel of 6 S. רהעאל

o-Granatum רימון

**π 307**

ht Demon. of 2nd Dec. ♏ וריאץ

kah רבקה

**308**

break בוקר

rsor זרקא

estigation חקר

arsh, grating sound חרק

roaching, near קרוב
קרה

**309**

per. [Vide K.D. מוסגר
.C.K. p. 495]

el of 2nd Dec. ♉ מנחראי

pitus cordis, mussitatio, שאגה
surratio, rugitus

d, soil, land שדה

**310**

To trample on, conquer דוש

To govern, bind חבש

Formed. [I.R.Q. 227] ייצר

The Initials of Idra Rabba י:ר:ק:
Qadisha. [Each Letter
is half of each Letter of
כחר, Kether]

Is, are; essence, being יש

Leo iuvenis כפיר

Habitations מדורין

**π 311**

Man: but vide K.D. L.C.K. איש
p. 83

Angel of 9 C. עריאל

Archangel of Binah צפקיאל

Archangel of Air; Angel of רפאל
☿, and of Chokmah of
Briah, etc.

Rod. [Ps. xxiii. 4] שבט

26 × 12, the Twelve Banners **312**

Night Demon of 3rd Dec. ♎ ושו

To renew; hence = a new חדש
moon, a month

West. [Cf. 272] מערב

**π 313**

Angel of 1st Dec. ♍ אננאורה

**314**

[Vide K.D. L.C.K. p. 275] הלל גמור

Metatron, Archangel of מטטרון
Kether, and Angel of
Tiphareth of Briah.
[When spelt with י
after ט it denotes
Shekinah]

# SEPHER SEPHIROTH

| | |
|---|---|
| Out of the way, remote | רחוק |
| Shaddai: " The Almighty "; a name of GOD | שדי |

**315**

| | |
|---|---|
| Ice; crystal | גביש |
| Gullet | ושט |
| Formation | יצירה |
| Visio Splendoris | מראה הנוגה |
| Gomorrah | עמרה |

The Number of Servitors of Abra-Melin Sub-Princes  **316**

| | |
|---|---|
| Day Demon of 3rd Dec. ♈ | ושאגו |
| Ligatus | חבוש |
| Green | ירוק |
| JESU | ישו |
| A bundle, handful | עומר |
| Visitans iniquitatem | פוקד עון |
| Aporrhea | קוטרא |
| [Vide K.D. L.C.K. p. 54] | שאיה |
| To worship, bow down | שחח |

π **317**

| | |
|---|---|
| Day Demon of 3rd Dec. ♉ | ואלפר |
| [Vide Ps. xcvii. 11] | זרעם |
| Arida | יבשה |
| Iron (Ch.) | פרזל |
| Hoariness | שיבה |

**318**

| | |
|---|---|
| Labrum lavacri, et basio eius | כיור וכנו |
| A copse, bush | שיח |

| | |
|---|---|
| " Boy," Name of Enoch, and of Metatron | נער |
| A Duke of Edom. [Vide Liber 777, p. 22] | עירם |
| The friends | רעים |
| L.A. Angel of ♐ | סריטיאל |

| | |
|---|---|
| Angel of 3rd Dec. ♋ | אלינכיר |
| Angel L.T.D. of ♍ | לסלרא |
| Angel of 9 W. | שאהיה |
| Qliphoth of ♉ | אדימירון |

| | |
|---|---|
| Lamb | כבש |
| Angel L.T.N. of ♐ | לברמים |
| Linea media | קו האמצעי |

| | |
|---|---|
| Long-absent brother | אח רחוק |
| Qliphoth of ♒ | בהיסירון |
| Angel of 3rd Dec. ♈ | סטנדר |

18²  √3

| | |
|---|---|
| See no. 314; it denotes Shekinah | מיטטרון |

Σ (1—25). ♂

| | |
|---|---|
| Spirit of ♂ | ברצבאל |
| Intelligence of ♂ | גראפיאל |
| Angel of 2nd Dec. ♏ | נינדוהר |
| Need, indigence | צריכה |

| | |
|---|---|
| Jesus. [Note the letters of TETRAGRAMMATON completed by ש 300 q.v. the Spirit of GOD] | יהשוה |

| | |
|---|---|
| sion שאיה | |

**327**

y Demon of 2nd Dec. ♍ בוטיש

ide K.D. L.C.K. p. 461] ישיבה

ght Demon of 3rd Dec. ♑ כיצאור

**328** 4 Princes + 8 Sub-Princes + 316 servient to Spirits

gel of 3 W. החשיה

steam; darkness. [Vide חשך K.D. L.C.K. p. 280]

**329**

gel of 1st Dec. ♎ טרסני

**330**

undary, terminus; crosspath מצר

volution; hurricane, tempest סער

ror: fault של

**♈ 331**

hraim אפרים

bor magna. [Gen. xxi. 33] אשל

changel of Chokmah רציאל

**332**

x Ardoris אור היקוד

ght Demon of 3rd Dec. ♓ אנדרומאל

Duke of Edom. [Vide מבצר Liber 777, p. 22]

cus vacuus. [Vide מקום פנוי K.D. L.C.K. p. 551]

**333**

balah of the Nine Chambers איק בכר

oronzon. [Vide Dr Dee, חורונזון & Lib. 418, 10th Aire]

ow שלג

---

**334** A still, small Voice. קול דממה דקה [1 Kings, xix. 12]

**335** Dies Mali ימי רעה

The KING מלך מלכי המלכים above the King of Kings. [Vide K.D. L.C.K. p. 537]

Ordering, disposition מערכה

**336** An attack; a request, petition שאלה

Night Demon of 1st Dec. ♊ שבכיד

**♈ 337** Ruler of Earth פורלאך

Hell of Supernals; a City of שאול Edom; the Place of Askings. [Vide Liber 777, p. 23]

**338** To cast down חלש

He hath pardoned (or, subjected) יכבוש

A garment; clothing לבוש

To send forth שלח

**339**

**340** Angel of 3rd Dec. ♐ יסגדיברודיאל

"Ferocious" lion ליש

Uncus focarius—fire-shovel מגרופיא

Book ספר

Pares; a word written on the wall at Belshazzar's feast. פרס [Vide Dan. v. 28]

There; The Name שם

The sum of the 3 Mother letters; 341
א, מ, and ש

Yesterday    אמש

Guilty, damned    אשם

A red cow    פרה אדומה

Expansum; sepimentum;    פרסא
diaphragma

The Name (Ch.)    שמא

342

Coctio    בישל

Perfume    בשם

Night Demon of 2nd Dec. ♉ פוכלור

A blaze, flame    שלהבה

$7^3$    $\sqrt[3]{}$ 343

"And GOD said."    ויאמר אלהים
[Gen. i. 3]

A sweet smell    זפרון

344

A plantation, garden.    פרדם
[Cant. iv. 13]

345

Di Alieni    אלהים אחרים

GOD Almighty    אל שדי

"In that also"—referred to    בשגם
Daath

*The* NAME    השם

Lioness. [Vide K.D. L.C.K. לישה
p. 501]

5th ש    מהש

Moses. [See 543, numerical משה
Temurah of 345]

Dominator    שולט

Shiloh    שילה

He was appeased. [Esther, שככה
vii. 10]

34

A spring; spring water    מקור

A water-pipe; channel    צנור

Good pleasure; the Will-power רצון

π 34

Palanquin (Cant. iii. 9); אפריון
Bridal bed; nuptial chariot.
["thalamus seu coelum fab-
rile sub quo copulantur nu-
bentes"]

34

Five; to set in array    חמש

Third King of Edom    חשם

π 34

35

Day Demon of 3rd Dec. ♌ אריגוש

A sapphire (Ex. xxviii. 18). ספיר
[Vide K.D. L.C.K. p. 19]

Ophir; a young mule; dust עפר
of the Earth

The Horn; head    קרן

Vacuum    ריקם

Intellectus    שכל

Σ (1—26)    35

Man    אנש

Angels of Malkuth; burnt or אשים
incense offering; "The
flames"

Hiram-Abif, a cunning    חירם אביף
artificer at the Temple
of Solomon; the hero

ɔf a famous allegory prophetical of FRATER PERDURABO

in ♌. Angel ruling 1st Dec. ♌, that was rising at the birth of FRATER PER-ᴅURABO      לוסנהר

ɔses the Initiator      מושה

evatus      נשא

**352**

e Exalted Light      אור מעלה

ng of Nose; i.e. Merciful; a title of the upreme GOD      ארך אפים

htning      ברקים

approach      קרבן

π **353**

shen      גשן

e fifth      חמשה

e Secret of TETRAGRAMMATON is ɔ His fearers. [Ps. xxv. 14]      סוד יהוה ליראיו

light, joy      שמחה

**354**

ɘw fat; anointed      דשן

ptaeteris intermissoria      שמטה

**355**

ɔught; idea      מחשבה

ar      שנה

**356**

e Cedars of Lebanon      ארזי לבנון

piationes. [Vide K.D. ᴸ.C.K. p. 612]      כפורים

---

A young mule      עופר

Ophra, mother of Goliath      עורף

Spirits of the living      רוחין דחיין

**357**

42-fold Name, Geburah in Yetzirah      כגד יכש

Iniquity      נושא

**358**

Shame      גשנה

Shiloh shall come      יבא שילה

*Messiach*, the Messiah      משיח

Nechesh, the Serpent that initiated Eve      נחש

(Taking the three ה's in אהיהוה as concealing the Mothers, we get I. A. Ω. &)      אשיאום

π **359**

Angel of 3rd Dec. ♓      סטריף

The Sacred Wind      שטים

Satan. [Vide K.D. L.C.K. p. 235]      שטן

**360**

The Messiah      המשיה

[Vide K.D. L.C.K. p. 235]      הנשה

[Vide K.D. L.C.K. p. 235]      השנה

Angels of Jesod of Binah      ישים

Seeking safety; Angel of 7 W.      מהשיה

Tonitrus      רעמים

*Shin*; a tooth      שין

Two      שני

$19^2.$ $\begin{matrix} 3 \\ 6 \\ 1 \end{matrix}$ ⋰ $\sqrt{361}$

| | |
|---|---|
| God of Malkuth | אדני הארץ |
| "Men"; "impurities" | אנשי |
| Foundations. [Ch.] | אשין |
| The Mountain Zion | הר ציון |
| Ruler of ♄ | כשיאל |
| Angel of 7 P. | מצראל |

362

363

| | |
|---|---|
| The Almighty and Ever-living GOD | שדי אל חי |

364

| | |
|---|---|
| Lux Occulta | אור מופלא |
| Satan | השטן |
| Demons | שדין |
| Opposition; resistance | שטנה |

365

| | |
|---|---|
| Earth of Tiphareth | נשיה |
| An uncovering, exposing | פריעה |

366

| | |
|---|---|
| Night Demon of 2nd Dec. ♑ | אנדראלף |

π367

| | |
|---|---|
| Black [scil. of eye-pupil]: middle: homunculus | אישון |
| Day Demon of 3rd Dec. ♊ | פאיכורן |

368

| | |
|---|---|
| The Spirit of the GODS of the Living | רוח אלהים חיים |

Σ {1—(9 × 9)} ÷ 9. ☾        369

| | |
|---|---|
| Spirit of ☽. [Vide Liber 777, p. 19] | חשמודאי |

| | |
|---|---|
| The World of Briah | עולם הבריאה |
| Angel of 2nd Dec. ♊ | שהדני |

3

| | |
|---|---|
| A foundation, basis | עקר |
| Creation | עש |
| Salices rivi. [Lev. xxiii. 40] | ערבי נחל |
| Zopher | צפר |
| White lead, tin | קסטרא |
| To rend, cut, blame, curse | קרע |
| Green. [Vide S.D. p. 104] | רענן |
| Salem | שלם |

3

| | |
|---|---|
| Sinistrum | שמאל |

3

| | |
|---|---|
| Aqua spherica | אספירכא |
| Agni | כבשים |
| An oven, furnace | כבשן |
| ♏ | עקרב |
| Herbage, grass | עשב |
| Seven | שבע |

π3

3

3

| | |
|---|---|
| Generally and specially | כלל ופרט |
| Solomon | שלמה |
| A City of Edom | שמלה |

3

| | |
|---|---|
| Dominator | מושל |

40

au, father of the men of Edom. עשו
(Ad-om, Adlantes*)

bird צפור

ace. [Refers to Kether] שלום

377

ervus luxatus; Vena גיד הנשה
Ischiatica. [Gen. xxxii. 32]

ven שבעה

Σ (1—27) 378

n peace' בשלום

una ignita; Chaschmal חשמל

ramentum. [K.D. L.C.K. שבוע
p. 695]

π 379

ɔschalom אבשלום

he sum of the letters of TETRA- 380
GRAMMATON multiplied
severally by those of Adonai;
$[(י × א)+(ה × ד)+(ו × נ)+(ה × י)]$
$= י:כ:ש:ן:$

ifficulty, narrowness מצרים

in, trouble, misery עצב עצבון

hick darkness, fog ערפל

ide no. 370] קסטירא

eaven of Hod רקיע

381

amour, prayer שועה

382

ay Demon of 3rd Dec. ≏ צאראץ

π 383

Iuramentum. [Vide K.D. שבועה
L.C.K. pp. 67, 695]

384

385

Angel of 2nd Dec. ≏ מהרנץ

Assiah, the World of Matter עשיה

Gloria cohabitans [vide K.D. שכינה
L.C.K. p. 711]; the Glory
of God

Lip שפה

386

Jesus ישוע

Tongues לשון

Tziruph, a table of Temurah צירוף

387

388

The hardest rock. חלמיש
[Ps. cxiv. 8]

To search out diligently חפש

Table; bread שלחן

π 389

390

Gen. v. 2 זכר ונקבה

Retrorsum מפרע

Alens, pascens פרנס

Heaven שמים

Oil שמן

Night Demon of 2nd Dec. II שץ

* Refers to a theory that the 'Kings of Edom' who perished before the creation of Adam were a
evious race inhabiting 'Atlantis.'

| | | |
|---|---|---|
| | | **391** |
| Salvation, help | ישועה | |
| The Inscrutable Height. רום מעלה [Kether] | | |
| | | **392** |
| Aromata | בשמים | |
| Habitaculum | משבן | |
| | | **393** |
| | | **394** |
| Table. [Vide no. 388] | שולחן | |
| | | **395** |
| Robustus (virilitas) Iacob אביר יעקב | | |
| The Heavens | השמים | |
| Oil | השמן | |
| Manasseh | מנשה | |
| Second | משבה | |
| Judge | שופט | |
| | | **396** |
| Day Demon of 1st Dec. ♏ | יפרש | |
| | | π **397** |
| Lux Interna. (Title of אור פנימי Kether) | | |
| | | **398** |
| Fifty | חמשים | |
| Book | חפשי | |
| Angel L.T.D. of ♈ | סטרעטן | |
| Pride; esp. of gait | שחץ | |
| | | **399** |
| | שגופי | |
| 20³ | √ **400** |
| To use Magic, witchcraft | כשף | |
| Erudiens, a title of Yesod | משכיל | |

---

| | | |
|---|---|---|
| Sensus literalis. [Vide K.D. פשוטה L.C.K. p. 12] | | |
| (He had) Karnaim (in his hand) | קרנים | |
| Angels of Chesed of Briah | שיככים | |
| Sack | שק | |
| | | π 4( |
| Cursing | ארר | |
| Essence; "the" | את | |
| | | 4( |
| Sought into, or after | בקש | |
| Tested, purified | ברר | |
| Filia | בת | |
| A spider | עכביש | |
| Paths | שבילין | |
| | | 4( |
| The Stone; Sapphire | אבן ספיר | |
| | | 4( |
| Law, edict | דת | |
| Almond; to watch, be awake; שקד to hasten | | |
| | | 4( |
| Fearful things, serpents of זחלי עפר the dust. [Job] | | |
| [Cf. no. 227, זכר.] Phallus; שפכה urethra. [Vide Deut. xxiii. 2] | | |
| | Σ (1—28) | 4( |
| THOU: a name of GOD | אתה | |
| Vulgar, common; plebeian עם הארץ | | |
| Leg | שוק | |
| Alterations | שנוים | |
| The letter Tau | תו | |

407

num אות

e Precious Oil שמן טוב

408

pis sapphirinus אבן הספיר

ec זאת

de Deut. x. 10, 15] חשק

π 409

riarchs אבהתא

hers אבות

e (fem.) אחת

-Qadesh; Holy Ones הקדש

410

erty; a swallow דרור

ions, imaginations. [Dan. דרהר
v. 2]

tzareph מצרף

Tabernacle משכן

red; Saint קדוש

ly קודש

heareth שמע

d, 42-fold Name in Yetzirah שקי

411

ha אלישע

atic Palace of היכל רצון
iphareth

damenta Terrae מוסדי ארץ

bitaculum משכנא

o temporum סדר זמנים

olation, emptiness. (Ex- תהו
resses first root of all good)

412

letter Beth בית

---

New. (Ch.) חדת

Jesus GOD יהשוה אלהים

White whorl צמר לבן

Celsitudo superna· רום עליון

A longing for תאוה

413

414

Azoth, the fluid. A+Z (Lat.) אזות
+ Ω (Grk.) + ת (Heb.). Initial and final in 3 tongues

The Limitless Light אין סוף אור

Meditation. [Ps. xlv. 4] הגות

Going forth. [Vide no. 770] משוטטים

415

The Voice of the Chief אבראה דבר
Seer

Sister אחות

The Holy One; Sodomite הקדוש

Work מעשה

Angel of 10 C. עשליה

416

Thought, meditation הרהור

A pledge משכון

417

Olive זית

Arca. (Noah's Ark) תיבה

(Note 4 + 1 + 8 = 13) 418

Boleskine בולשכין

Peccatum. (Est femina חטאת
Lilith impia)

Kheth, a fence חית

Servans misericordiam נוצר חסד

"The Word of the מאכאשאנה
Aeon." [Vide Liber 418]

אברא ההא דראברא

418=חית=הא בית, the House of Hé: because of I.Z.Q. 694; for ה formeth כ, but ה formeth יוד: each = 20. Thus is Abrahadabra a Key of the Pentagram.

Also, by Aiq Bkr, it = 22 : and 418 = 19 × 22. 19 = Manifestation; it therefore manifests the 22 Keys of R.O.T.A.

The first meaning is ABRAH DBR, = The Voice of the Chief Seer.

It resolves into Pentagram and Hexagram as follows :

1st *method.*

$$R \overset{A}{\underset{A}{\diagup}} B$$

A✡A forms 12 and 406, הוא
DH
B\_ /R
\A/

and אתה [406 = תו], where AThH = Microprosopus, and HVA = Macroprosopus. The Arcanum is therefore that of the Great Work.

2nd *method.*

A✡A   R✡H   Here BHR = 207
A A   B D
      R

= אין סוף אור, etc., and DBR = Voice ("The Vision and the Voice"); thus showing, by Yetziratic attribution, the Three Wands—Caduceus : Phoenix : Lotus. Note always אבר are the three Supernals.

3rd *method.*

A✡A   B✡A   give 205 + 213;
R B   H R D

both mean "Mighty," whence Abrahadabra is "The Word of Double Power." AAB show AB : AIMA : BN, viz., Amoun : Thoth : Mout. By Yetziratic Method, H:D:R: are Isis : Horus : Osiris. (Also, for H:D:R:, vide I.R.Q. 992.)

Dividing as 3 and 8, we get △ of Horus dominating the Stooping Dragon, ארר יאו; also—

from   R△B   we get
A—B        A—H
A—D        R—A

8 = דד, Love, and 207 = אור, Light; 8 × 207 = 18, which is equivalent to חי, Living; further, 297 = 23 × 9 = חיה, Life : hence, Licht : Liebe : Leben.

Again, 418 = את. + יאו, = 21 + 397, q.v. דבר and 678 = 6 + 7 + 8 = 21. 2 × ב + 2 × ר + ד = 32. The Five different letters represent Amoun : Thoth : Isis : Horus : Osiris. They (A + B + R + H + D) add to 212 (q.v.).

Finally, א is the Crown, ב the Wand, ד the Cup, ה the Sword, ר the R.C.

See Equinox, V and VII, for further details.

| | | π 4 |
|---|---|---|
| Serpent : the letter Teth | טית | |
| Sodom and Gomorrah | סדם + עמרה | |
| | | 4 |
| It was | היתה | |
| Dolium, vas | חבית | |
| Vapour, smoke | עשן | |
| Pacifica | שלמים | |
| | רצפים | |
| | | π |
| Angel ruling ♑ | כשויעיה | |
| Angel ruling ♓ | פשיאל | |

**422**

e Vast Countenance אריך אנפין

nea Flava (quae circumdat קו ירוק
Mundum)

**423**

x. xxvii. 10, 11.] לוי העמורים
[Vide K.D. L.C.K. p. 420]

**424**

gel L.T.N. of ♉ טוטת

**425**

ide no. 1175] הגזית

ide K.D. L.C.K. p. 208] נעשה

ditus שמיעה

**426**

rvator; salvator מושיע

edium תוך

**427**

**428**

e Breakers-in-pieces; גערשכלה
he Qliphoth of Chesed

e Brilliant Ones; Angels חשמלים
of Chesed, and of Tiphareth
of Briah

averunt נשבעו

**429**

ion's whelp. גור אריה
Gen. xl. 9]

gment, equity משפט

שגעון

**430**

phesch, the animal soul of נפש
Man

vered with mist; darkness, נשף
wilight

---

Membra פרקים

Full Title of Ninth צדיק יסוד עולם
Sephirah. "The Righteous
is the Foundation of the
world"

Concealed שפן

Tohu v-Bohu; see Gen. i. תהו ובהו

Dew תל

**π 431**

Notariqon נוטריקון

**432**

Eventide shadows צללי ערב

Earth of Jesod תבל

**π 433**

Day Demon of 1st Dec. ♌ בלאת

Merit זכות

**434**

The Lord of War. איש מלחמה
[Ex. xv. 3]

The letter Daleth; door דלת

Σ (1—29) **435**

Deceived התל

[Vide K.D. L.C.K. p. 156] משפטו

**436**

Tutor, curator; prae- אפטרופס
fectus; administrator

Angel L.T.D. of ♏ ביתחוי

Hoschanah הושענה

"Σαταναs." [Vide K.D. שטן עז
L.C.K. p. 505]

[Vide K.D. L.C.K. p. 505; שעטנז
723 & 701, nos. 9, 10;
also at שבירה]

| | | |
|---|---|---|
| Balm; the balsam tree | אפרסמון | 437 |
| The whole (perfect) stone. [Deut. xxvii. 6] | אבן שלימה | 438 |
| Exilium | גלות | π 439 |
| Angel L.T.N. of ♊ | עוגרמען | |
| Collaudatio. [Vide K.D. L.C.K. pp. 90, 729] | תהלה | 440 |
| The Great Dragon; means "curls." [I.R.Q. 834; vide 510] | תלי | |
| Irreproachable; perfect | תם | |
| Cerva | אילת | $21^2$ √441 |
| Truth; Temurah of אדם, by Aiq Bekar | אמת | |
| A live coal | גחלת | |
| Day Demon of 2nd Dec. ♌ | לריאר | |
| Angel L.T.D. of ♓ | רמרא | |
| Termini Terrae | אפסי ארץ | 442 |
| A virgin; a city. ♍ | בתולה | π 443 |
| Goliath | גלית | |
| The Sanctuary | מקדש | 444 |
| Damascus | דמשק | |
| The total value of the Single Letters; ק, and ה, ו, ז, ח, ט, י, ל, נ, ס, ע, צ, | | 445 |
| Number of Stars in the Northern hemisphere | | 446 |
| Destruction; death | מות | |

| | | |
|---|---|---|
| Pison | פישון | |
| Tali pedum | קרסולים | |
| Initials of the Three Above and the Three Beneath. [Vide 248] | רמר רבא | 44 |
| Excelsa | במות | 44 |
| Lux fulgentissima | אור מצוחצח | π 44 |
| Cloak | טלית | |
| Tabulae | לוחות | 4: |
| [Vide K.D. L.C.K. p. 508] | מדות | |
| The Fruit of the Tree | פרי עץ | |
| Transgression | פשע | |
| Beneplacitum termino carens; Arbitrum illimitatum | רצון באין גבול | |
| Inhabitans Aeternitatem | שוכן עד | |
| Craftiness, cunning | שעלים | |
| The Dragon | תן | |
| The Essence of Man | את האדם | 4! |
| Mortis | מיתא | |
| Angels of Tiphareth | שנאנים | |
| The Abyss | תהום | |
| [Vide no. 552] | חמדת | 4: |
| The crop; the maw | קרקבן | |
| Behemoth | בהמות | 4 |

Animal Soul, in its
...llness; i.e. including
...e Creative Entity or
...go, Chiah    נפש חיה

454    ...lum    חותם

"Holy Ones"; Con-
...crated catamites kept
...y the Priesthood    קדשים

455

456    ...mido maxima    אימתה

...Mountain of Myrrh.    הר המור
...ant. iv. 6]

...es    כותל

...ra    שוקים

...Fig-tree and fruit    תאנה

π 457    ...es    זתים

458    ...ovenant; an engagement;    חתן
betrothed

...tusores; cloudy heavens;    שחקים
...eaven of Netzach

459

460    ...le K.D. L.C.K. p. 371]    טנתא

...hoth of ח    צללד מירון

...oly unto TETRA-    קדש ליהוה
...RAMMATON."
...x. xxxix. 30]

π 461    ...le K.D. L.C.K. p. 539]    אדנות

...ustus, validus, asper,    איתן
...orridus, rigidus

---

462    Terra Superna (est Binah)    ארץ עליונה

A path    ניתב

Profundum Celsitudinis    עומק רום

π 463    Day Demon of 3rd Dec. מ    באתין

Pillar of Mildness—paths, ג,    גסת
ס, and ת

Crystal, glass    זכוכית

A rod of almond    מטה השקד

The Special Intelligence.    תבונה
[I.Z.Q. 264, et seq.]

Caps, crowns, diadems    תגין

Precatio    תחנה

464

Σ (1—30)    465

A kiss; a little (or, sweet)    נשיקה
mouth

466    Skull    גלגלת

Renes    כליות

The World of    עולם היצירה
Formation

Simeon    שמעון

π 467    [Vide S.D. 33]    גלגלתא

468    Angel of 3rd Dec. ח    ביתון

469    Trabeationes ligaturae    חשוקיהם
illarum

**470**

| | |
|---|---|
| Eternity. (Literally, a cycle of cycles) | דור דורים |
| Angel of 8 S. | נתהיה |
| Pure Wool | עמר נקי |
| Period of time ; Time | עת |
| Solum ; fundus | קרקע |

**471**

| | |
|---|---|
| Palatia | היכלות |
| Mount Moriah. [2 Chron. iii. 1] | המוריה הר |

**472**

| | |
|---|---|
| Was terrified | בעת |

**473**

| | |
|---|---|
| The Three Persons. [ATH: HVA: ANI coalesced] | אתהואני |
| Skull | גולגלתא |
| Molitrices | טחנות |

**474**

| | |
|---|---|
| Knowledge. [Vide K.D. L.C.K. p. 252, et seq.] | דעת |
| (Plural)—Wisdom | חכמות |
| The Testimony within the Ark | עדת |
| A ram, he-goat ; a prepared sacrifice | עתד |
| Angel L.T.D. of ♋ | רעדר |

**475**

| | |
|---|---|
| [Vide no. 473.] In Golgotha | בגולגלתא |

**476**

| | |
|---|---|
| Domus Iudicii ; Curia ; Consistorium iudiciale | בית דין |

**4**

| | |
|---|---|
| Cranium, calvaria | גולגלת |
| The Lesser Countenance, Microprosopus | זעיר אנפין |
| Hagiographa | כתובים |

**π 4**

| | |
|---|---|
| Molentes | טוחנות |

**4**

| | |
|---|---|
| Lapides inanitatis | אבני תוהו |
| [Vide K.D. L.C.K. p. 252] | דעות |
| Lilith, Qliphoth of Malkuth | לילית |
| [Vide K.D. L.C.K. p. 252] | עדות |
| Malkuth, 42-fold Name in Yetzirah | עית |

**4**

| | |
|---|---|
| | בעונת |
| Hills | גבעות |
| Reus mortis | חייב מיתא |
| Annulus | טבעת |

**4**

| | |
|---|---|
| A looking-glass, mirror | אספקלריא |

**4**

| | |
|---|---|
| Ferens iniquitatem | נושא עון |

**22²**

√ 4

**4**

| | |
|---|---|
| Filia scaturiginum. [Is. x. 30, " Daughter of Gallim "] | בת גלים |
| Mockeries [Job xvii. 2. Vide 435] | התלים |

**4**

| | |
|---|---|
| A name of GOD | יהוה בחכפה ימר ארץ |

| | |
|---|---|
| undations | יסודות |
| ymum fractum | מצה פרוסה |
| King of Edom | עוית |
| gel of 8 P. | נהתאל |

π 487

488

| | |
|---|---|
| nua, ostium | פתח |
| photh of Kether | תאומיאל |
| shall worship | תעבודו |

tribuens; rependens    משלם גמול    489
retributionem

490

| | |
|---|---|
| e giving. [Vide no. 1106] | מתן |
| ne flour, meal | סלת |
| fect | תמים |
| nah, 42-fold Name in Yetzirah | תץ |

π 491

| | |
|---|---|
| trix | אמנת |
| gel of 4 W. | ניתאל |

492

493

| | |
|---|---|
| e Name given in Deut. xxviii. 58; without את=92, q.v. | את יהוה אלהיך |

494

| | |
|---|---|
| dea salutis | כובע הישועה |
| apple | תפוח |

495

| | |
|---|---|
| nilitudo hominis | דמות אדם |
| t | מתנה |

---

Σ (1—31)    496

| | |
|---|---|
| Leviathan | לויתן |
| Malkuth | מלכות |
| A small bundle | צרור |

497

| | |
|---|---|
| Nutrix | אומנת |
| Gemini; ♊ | תאומים |

498

| | |
|---|---|
| Briatic Palace of Geburah | היכל זכות |

π 499

| | |
|---|---|
| Cerva amorum. [Prov. v. 19, "a loving hind"] | אילת אהבים |
| Busy, arduous; an army; 'hosts' | צבאות |

500

| | |
|---|---|
| The humerus | כתף |
| Kimelium aureum | מכתם |
| Princeps | שר |
| A Duke of Edom | תימן |

501

| | |
|---|---|
| Asher; blessedness | אשר |
| Fortis; fortia, robusta | אתנים |
| The head | ראש |
| Flesh; Night Demon of 1st Dec. ♓ | שאר |
| Schechinah Superior | שכינה עילאה |
| Likeness, similitude | תמונה |

502

| | |
|---|---|
| To tell glad tidings; flesh, body | בשר |
| To cut | בתק |

| | |
|---|---|
| | $8^8 = 2^9$ |

**503** (π 503)

☖ The Cup of the Stolistes — π 503

Expelled, cast forth — גרש

**504**

Sought for — דרש

**505**

Sarah; Principissa. [Vide 510 שרה & cf. 243 & 248]

**506**

אבגיתץ

[Vide no. 1196] — כפות

Bovis aᵉ sinistra; an ox; Taurus. [Vide K.D. L.C.K. p. 99.]—ℵ — שור

**507**

That which causes ferment; yeast — שאור

**508**

Daybreak; black — שחר

**π 509**

Bridge — גשור

**510**

Sensus allegoricus. [Vide K.D. L.C.K. p. 12] — דרוש

Rectitudo, aequitas recta; rectilineum — ישר

The head — ריש

Song — שיר

Sarai. [Vide 505] — שרי

Draco; see 440 — תנין

**511**

עתיאל

*The* HEAD — רישא

[Vide K.D. L.C.K. p. 463] — שורה

---

Adhaesio, cohaesio — דבקות

Angel of 3ʳᵈ Dec. ♎ — שחדר

**51**

**51**

[Vide K.D. L.C.K. p. 213] — חקות

**51**

Possessio sine angustiis — נחלה בלי מצרים

Minister iudicii — שוטר

Phylacterium — תפלה

**51**

Lucus. [Vide K.D. L.C.K. p. 168] — אשירה

Personae — פרצופין

**51**

Qliphoth of ♉. [Vide no. 321, & Liber 777] — ארימירון

The good gift, i.e. Malkuth — מתנה טובה

Occultae. [Vide 417] — פלאות

Confractio. [Vide K.D. L.C.K. p. 698, et seq.] — שבירה

**5**

**5**

Day Demon of 2ⁿᵈ Dec. ♊ — ברבטוש

**52**

Tears — דמעות

Legitium — כשר

**π 5**

Ignis descendens — אש יורד

Angel of 2 P. — ושריה

Nudatio candoris — מחשוף הלבן

G 2

| | | |
|---|---|---|
| | 522 | |
| | π 523 | |
| | 524 | |
| | 525 | |

e LORD of Hosts,  יהוה צבאות
. name of GOD re-
erred to Netzach

526

erliminare  משקוף

527

Σ (1—32)  528

23²  √529

atura ollaris cum  ציקי קדירה
usculo dulci

y Demon of 3rd Dec. ♋  שיטרי

530

e Rose  חבצלת

ces  קלת

el, a word of the 'writing  תקל
n the wall' at Belshazzar's
abled feast

531

532

533

aven of Jesod  טבל וילון שמים
of Malkuth

g of Terrors  מלך בלהות

534

ertain Name of GOD  קלדשק

535

536

white cloak  טלית לבנה

ere of the fixed stars  מסלות

---

The World of Assiah,  עולם העשיה
the 'material' world

537

Emanatio; Atziluth, the  אצילות
Archetypal World

Medulla spinalis  חוט השדרה

Apertio uteri  פטר רחם

538

Daughter of the Voice.—  בת קול
Echo.  [The Bath Qol
is a particular and very
sacred method of divi-
nation]

539

540

Lumbi; the upper part  מתנים

π 541

Israel  ישראל

542

543

"Existence is  אהיה אשר אהיה
Existence," the
NAME of the
Highest GOD

544

Apples.  [Cant. ii. 5]  תפוחים

545

Aper de Sylva  חזיר מיער

546

Sweet  מתוק

P's; a watchman  שומר

Custodi  שמור

L.A. Angel of ♈  שרהיאל

π 547

548

Qliphoth of ♈    בעירירון

Night Demon of 3rd Dec. ♋ הצגנת

A Name of GOD, יהוה אלוה ודעת
referred to Tiphareth

Qliphoth of ♎    עבירירון

549

Moral    מורגש

Ventus turbinis    רוח סערה

550

Aquila; decidua. [Vide K.D. נשר
L.C.K. p. 600; connect with
no. 496, Malkuth]

A rod of iron. [Ps. ii.]    שבט ברזל

L.A. Angel of ♌    שרטיאל

Principes    שרים

Dragons. (Restricted.)    תנינם
[Ps. lxxiv. 13]

551

552

Desiderium dierum    חמדת ימים

553

Draco magnus    תנין גדול

554

Day Demon of 2nd Dec. ♓    מרחוש

555

Obscurity    עפתה

556

Mark, vestige, footstep    רשימו

Sharon. [Cant. ii. 1]    שרון

π 557

The First    ראשון

---

דרושים

Waters of quiet    מי מנוחות

Puncta    נקודת

A Duke of Edom    תמנע

Dragons    תנינים

Σ (1—33)

Cain    אתקין

Concealed Mystery    דצניותא

Primordial    ראשונה

π 5

Lotio manuum    נטילת ידים

Angel of 1st Dec. ♊    סגרש

Lapis capitalis    אבן הראשה

[I.R.Q. 941.] ויהי האדם לנפש חיה
"And the Adam was formed
into a living Nephesh"

Sphere of Malkuth    חלם יסודות

Parvitatio    קטנות

Praetoriani    שוטרים

A valley; a plain    ישרון

Puncta    נקודות

[SMK + VV + DLTh, SVD ס:ו:ד:
= a secret, spelt in full]

The Shadow of Death; Hell צלמות
of Netzach

edintegratio, configuratio, depositio, conformatio, restoratio, restitutio — תיקון

567 — rstborn — ראשוני

568

π 569 — ngers — אצבעות

570 — aphtali — נפתלי

ectus — ערש

en — עשר

eads — רישין

oncussion, earthquake — רעש

ide K.D. L.C.K. p. 691] — רשע

ate; the Door — שער

π 571 — e mountains of Zion — הררי ציון

dance — מתקלא

572 — chastening GOD. [Deut. xxviii. 58.] [ך counted as final] — יהוה אלהיך

schurun — ישורון

e was touched. [I.R.Q. 1117] — יתעצב

tive — מתקבל

y Demon of 1st Dec. )( — פורפור

573

574

aldee. [Hath a general meaning of movement. S.D. p. 87] — ירחשן

575 — Beerschebha, Fons Septenarii. [2 Sam. xxiv. 7 —Gen. xxi. 31.] [Vide K.D. L.C.K. p. 183] — באר שבע

"And the GODS said, Let there be LIGHT" — ויאמר אלהים יהי אור

$24^2$ √576 — Wands — מקלות

The tenth — עשור

π 577 — The Concealed of the Concealed; a name of GOD most High — טמירה דטמרין

578

579 — Media nox — חצות לילה

Qliphoth of Netzach — ערב זרק

Sons of Adam — תענוגים

580 — Rich — עשיר

Ancient — עתיק

"Le bouc émissaire"; shaggy, hairy. [Levit. xvi. 22] — שעיר

Angel of Fire — שרף

581 — The Ancient One — עתיקא

Barley — שעורה

582

583

584

585
The GODS of Battle אלהים צבאות
(lit. of Hosts); the
Divine Name of
Hod
[Vide K.D. L.C.K. p. 386] תקיעה

586
War-trumpet שופר

587
Day Demon of 1st Dec. ≋ פוראש

588

589
Viror. [Vide K.D. אב לשון ענף
L.C.K. p. 15]

590
Rib. [Gen. ii. 22] צלעת

591

592

π 593

594
The Stone of Israel. אבן ישראל
[Gen. xlix. 24]

Σ (1—34) 595

596
Jeruschalim ירושלים

597

598
Our iniquities עונותינו
π 599

600
Mirabilia, vel occulta פליאות חכמה
sapientiae
Peniculamentum, fimbria ציצת
peniculata

---

A knot, ligature קשר
Red שרק
Six; marble שש

π 60

60
Lux simplicissima אור פשוט
Brightness; splendores צחצחות
Extremitates קצוות

60
Qliphoth of ♌ שלהבירון

60
Congeries; epistola אגרת
Israel Senex ישראל סבא

60
Magnificentia אדרת
[Vide K.D. L.C.K. p. 226] גברת

60
Let them bring forth ישרצו
Ipseitas, seu ipsa essentia. עצמות
[Vide K.D. L.C.K. pp. 571,
631]
Nexus, ligature קשור
Ruth רות
A turtle-dove תור

π 60
Adam Primus אדם הראשון
The mountains of spices. הרי בשמים
[Cant. viii. 14]
A span, palm. [Lit. "the זרת
little finger"]

60
The last Gate. [Vide בבא בתרא
K.D. L.C.K. p. 184]

# SEPHER SEPHIROTH

de K.D. L.C.K. p. 640]　חתר

609

610

mulus argenteus　אגורת

rus, malum citrum ; (lust　אתרוג
nd desire). [Vide K.D.
.C.K. p. 178]

ıth　מעשר

611

he Fear" of the LORD.　יראת
Ps. cxi. 10]

e Law. (Occasional　תורה
pelling)

612

e covenant)—Day Demon　ברית
f 1st Dec. ♑. [Ps. xxv. 14]

number of the Divine Precepts　π 613

Quintessence of Light　את האור

ses, our Rabbi　משה רבינו

de K.D. L.C.K. p. 179]　תריג

614

615

616

photh of ♓　שמירון

Five Books of Moses ; the　תירן
aw on Sinai. Cf. Tarot

π 617

ighty acts." (Plur. of　גבורות
Strength.") [Ps. cvi. 2]

umnae Nubis　עמודי האש והענן
Ignis

ing of Edom　רהבית

618

tentiones　ריבות

---

π 619

Novissimum　אחרית

620

Chokmah, Binah,　חכמה בינה ודעת
Daath ; the first
descending triad

The Crown : Kether　כתר

Angel of 3rd Dec. ♍　משפר

[Vide Ps. xxxi. 20]　צפנת

The Doors　שערים

[Temurah of בבל]　ששך

621

Mucro gladii　אבחת חרב

By-paths. [Vide no. 1357]　אורחות

[Vide I.R.Q. 234]　622

Blessings　ברכת

Profunda Maris. [Samael　מצולות ים
et Uxor Eius]

Latitudines ; Rechoboth　רחובות

623

Barietha ; Doctrina ex-　ברייתא
tranea ; conclusio extra
Jeruschalem facta

624

His Covenant. [Ps. xxv. 14]　ובריתו

Liberty　חירות

Qliphoth of ♐　נחשירון

$25^2 = 5^4$　√ ∜ 625

The Mountain of Ararat　הרי אררט

626

The tenth portion　עשרון

627

55

628

Light. [Spelt in full, with אור:ו:א
[אוֹ as ו]

Blessings ברכות

629

The great trumpet שופר גדול

630

Angel L.T.D. of ♊ סערש

The Holy Spirit רוחא קדישא
שליש

Angels of Geburah, and of שרפים
Kether of Briah

π 631

Concealed Mystery דצניעותא

632

633

Light. [Spelt in full, when אור:ו:א
[וו = ו]

[Gen. v. 2] זכר ונקבה בראם

634

635

636

Qliphoth of ♍ צפרירון

637

Day Demon of 3rd Dec. ♑ פורנאש

Day Demon of 1st Dec. ♎ שאלוש

638

639

The Tree of Knowledge עץ הדעת

640

The Cup of Con- כוס תנחומים
solations

Third. [Vide K.D. L.C.K. שליש
p. 719]

Sun; Sphere of ☉ שמש

Palm of the hand; palm-tree תמר

π 6

Dema purpureum אמרת

Angel of 9 W. ירתאל

" Lights "; defective. מארת
[S.D. 142]

6

Day Demon of 2nd Dec. ♏ פורשון

π 6

Light. [Spelt in full, אור:ו:א
when ו = יו]

Severities of TETRA- גבורות יהוה
GRAMMATON

The Cup of Bene- כוס של ברכה
dictions

$(12 \times 13 \times 4) + 20 =$ number of letters 6
in the five tablets of Enoch.
[Vide Equinox VII]

6

A King of Edom משרקה

6

Elohim. [ם counted as Final] אלהים

Licitum מותר

Rejoicing משוש

π 6

Lights מארות

6

6

Trance, deep sleep. [Vide תרדמה
no. 244]

6

Nitre נתר

| | |
|---|---|
| **651** | |
| 'emurah | תמורה |
| **652** | |
| π **653** | |
| **654** | |
| **655** | |
| **656** | |
| rose, lily. [Vide no. 706] | שושן |
| delight, joy | ששון |
| furnace | תנור |
| **657** | |
| angel of 3rd Dec. ♏ | ותרודיאל |
| elbarachith; ♌ | זלברחית |
| **658** | |
| π **659** | |
| **660** | |
| scintillae | ניצוצת |
| ones; members | קשרין |
| | תינר |
| π **661** | |
| sther | אסתר |
| ay Demon of 3rd Dec. ♓ | ישטולוש |
| rinorrhodon (vide K.D. L.C.K. p. 708); a rose | שושנה |
| angel L.T.D. of ♎ | תרגבן |
| **662** | |
| orona Dei | אכתריאל |
| **663** | |
| apides marmoris. [Vide Zohar, pt. I. fol. 34. col. 134] | אבני שש |

| | |
|---|---|
| Cantio | זמירות |
| **664** | |
| **665** | |
| The womb | בית הרחם |
| Σ (1—36). ☉. The Number of THE BEAST | **666**[1] |
| Aleister E. Crowley | אלהיסטהר ה כרעולהי |
| Aleister Crowley [Rabbi Battiscombe Gunn's v.l.] | אליסטיר קרולי |
| The number 5, which is 6 (ה א), on the Grand Scale | הא × אלף |
| Qliphoth of ♓ | נשימירן |
| Spirit of ☉ | סורת |
| Ommo Satan, the 'Evil Triad' of Satan-Typhon, Apophras, and Besz | עממו סתן |
| The Name Jesus | שם יהשוה |
| **667** | |
| The oil for lighting | שמן למאור |
| **668** | |
| Negotiatrix | סחרת |
| **669** | |
| **670** | |
| | ערת |
| Deprecatus | עתר |
| **671** | |
| Ferens fructum | עושה פרי |
| The Law | תעְרא |
| The Gate | תרעא |

[1] See Equinox, V & VII, for further details.

H

Adonai. [Spelt in full] **אֲדֹנָי׃**

672

π 673

674

[Vide K.D. L.C.K. p. 395] **סוחרת**

675

Briatic Palace of **היכל עצשׁמים**
Netzach

26²  √676

Artificial. [ם final] **גלגלים**

Angel L.T.D. of ♒ **עתור**

π 677

678

Planities coeli; Assiatic **ערבות**
Heaven of 1st palace

679

The chrysolite stone. **אבן מעולפת**
[Cant. v. 14]

680

Phrath, one of the four rivers **פרת**
of Eden

681

Joyful noise; battle-cry; the **תרועה**
sound (of a trumpet)

682

Of the evening; of the West **ערבית**

π 683

684

685

686

687

688

689

---

69

The candlestick **מנרת**
Palm-trees **תמרים**

π 69

69

The fourth portion **רביעית**

69

Sulphur **גפרית**

69

69

The Moral World **עולם מורגש**

69

69

Castella munita; domus **ארמנות**
munitae

69

69

70

The Mercy Seat **כפרת**
The Veil of the Holy **פרכת**
Seth **שת**

π 7

[Deut. xxiii. 1] **אשת**

"And lo! three men." **והנה שלשה**
[These be Michael,
Gabriel and Raphael,

**[אלו־מיכאל־גבריאל־ורפאל—**

Prolapsus in faciem **נפילת אפים**

7

Sabbathum quies **שבת**

Σ(1—37)  7

Taenia **מסגרת**
Qliphoth of Binah **סאתאריאל**

58

H 2

704 ‏אַרבעתאל‎ "batel." [The *Arbatel* of Magic, by Pietro di Abano]

‏נתדוריגאל‎ el L.T.N. of ♓.

705 ‏אבנים מפולמות‎ stones of dampness. [Job xxviii. 3]

706 ‏כפורת‎ pitiatorium

‏שושנים‎ lies" (I.R.Q. 878), or Roses" (von Rosenroth)

707

708 ‏מלאך הברית‎ Angel of the Covenant

‏שחת‎ dition

π 709 The Seven Double Letters
‏ב, ג, ד, כ, פ, ר, ת‎

710 ‏מערת‎ unca

‏שית‎ (Ch.)

711

712

713 ‏שבתאי‎ ere of ♄

‏תשובה‎ versio

714

715 ‏נסתרה‎ ret

‏קטורת‎ fumed, fumigated

716 ‏ושתי‎ chti. [Est. i. 9]

---

Matrona ‏מטרוניתא‎

717

718

π 719

720 |6

‏חשבתי‎

Thy Navel. [Cant. vii. 3] ‏שררך‎

721 The Primordial Point ‏נקדה ראשונה‎

722 The voice of the trumpet ‏קול שופר‎

723

724 The end of the days ‏אחרית הימים‎

725

726

π 727

728 [Vide K.D. L.C.K. p. 506] ‏תשכח‎

$27^2 = 9^3 = 3^6$  $\sqrt{\ }\ \sqrt[3]{\ }\ \sqrt[9]{\ }$ 729

[Vide K.D. L.C.K. p. 505] ‏קרע שטן‎

730

731

732

π 733 The white head: a title of GOD most High ‏רישא הוורה‎

734 To bring forth ‏שתלד‎

735 Tiphareth, 42-fold Name in Yetzirah ‏במרצתג‎

59

**736**

Tortuosae עקלקלות

**737**

(Live coal)—Blaze, flame שלהבת
שת הבל

**738**

π **739**

**740**

Σ (1—38) **741**

(ן counted as Final) Amen: אמן
see 91

The four letters of the elements; hence a concealed אמתש
יהוה

**742**

The Ark of the Testimony. [Lit. "of tremblings," scil. "vibrations"] ארון העדות

π **743**

**744**

**745**

**746**

The Names שמות

**747**

The voice of the turtledove. [Cant. ii. 12] קול התור

**748**

The oil of Anointment שמן המשחה

**749**

**750**

Conclave לשכת

Lead עפרת

π **751**

Vir integer איש תם

---

Satan שאתאן

Abraham and Sarah. [Either spelling. Vide 243, 248, 505, & 510]

Emanations: numbers ספירות

Years שנות

Netzach and Hod אשכלות

Perdition משחית

Copper ore; bronze נחשת

Pulvis aromatarii אבקת רוכל

"Both Active and Passive"; said in the Qabalah concerning the Sephiroth מקביל ומתקבל

Confinement, detention עצרת

Yesod, 42-fold Name in Yetzirah קרעשמן

| | |
|---|---|
| | π 769 |
| | 770 |
| ing forth. [Said of the Eyes of TETRA-GRAMMATON] | משוטטות |
| nfruitful, barren | עקרת |
| | 771 |
| A. Angel of ♍ | שלתיאל |
| | 772 |
| ptennium | שבע שנים |
| | π 773 |
| pis, seu canalis lapideus Potationis | אבן השתיה |
| | 774 |
| ia Septenarii | בת שבע |
| | 775 |
| ide no. 934] | דקרדינותא |
| | 776 |
| | 777 |
| e *Flaming Sword*, if the path from Binah to Chesed be taken as = 3. For ג connects Arikh Anpin with Zauir Anpin | |
| e is the Ruach of the Elohim of Lives | אחת רוח אלהים חיים |
| e World of Shells | עולם הקליפות |
| | 778 |
| | 779 |
| | 780 |
| dwell, have dwelt. (*Not* written.) [I.R.Q. 1122; Prov. viii. 12] | שכנתי |
| ore, bank | שפת |

| | |
|---|---|
| | 781 |
| | 782 |
| | 783 |
| Qliphoth of ♋    28² | √784  שיחרירון |
| | 785 |
| Smooth | 786  פשות |
| | π 787 |
| The Secret Wisdom: חכמה נסתרה i.e., The Qabalah. [Vide 58] | 788 |
| | 789 |
| My presence. [I.R.Q. 1122; Prov. xii.] | 790  שיכנתי |
| | 791 |
| [Vide K.D. L.C.K. p. 460, and Ps. xviii. 51] | 792  ישועות |
| | 793 |
| | 794 |
| | 795 |
| Calix horroris | 796  כום התרעלה |
| | π 797 |
| Mount Gaerisim and mount Ebal. [Deut. xi. 29] | 798  הר גריזים והר עיבל |
| Consisting of Seven | שביעיות |
| | 799 |

61

800

A bow; ♐. The three Paths קשת
leading from Malkuth; hence
much symbolism of the Rain-
bow of Promise

801

401 × 2 = The Reflection of 401, 802
which is את, α and ω

Consessus vel ישיבה של מעלה
Schola vel Academia Superna.
[Refers to A∴A∴, the three
grades which are above the
Abyss. Vide K.D. L.C.K.
p. 461]

Vindicta foederis נקם ברית

An ark, as of Noah or of Moses תבת

803

804

805

806

807

808

"A piece of brass"—the נחשתן
Brazen Serpent

π 809

810

A Duke of Edom יתת

Octava שמינית

π 811

812

813

Signa אותות

---

Ararita; a name of GOD אראריתא
which is a Notariqon of the
sentence אחד ראש :
אחדותו ראש ייחודותו:
תמורתו אחד. "One is
His Beginning; one is
His Individuality; His
Permutation One."

ויאמר אלהים יהי אור ויהי אור
[Genesis i. 3]

8ɪ

8ɪ

Ahasuerus אחשורש

8ɪ

8ɪ

8ɪ

8ɪ

Σ(1—40) 8ɪ

π 82

82

π 8ɪ

Lapis effigiei seu אבן משכית
figuratus. [Lev. xxvi. 1]

Litterae אותיות

8ɪ

8

8ɪ

π 8ɪ

8ɪ

π 8ɪ

8

Issachar יששכר

Three (? third) תלת

62

| | | |
|---|---|---|
| | | 831 |
| edo Crystalli | לבנת ספיר | 832 |
| ir of Angels in Kether | חיות הקדש | 833 |
| nsiens super prevaricatione | עובה על רפשע | |
| | | 834 |
| chia Mundi | זרועות עולם | 835 |
| | | 836 |
| profuse giver. [Cf. the Egyptian word Tat.] | תת זל | 837 |
| counted as Final. Vide 77. This *is* written] | למרבה | |
| | | 838 |
| | | π 839 |
| | | 840 |
| 29² | | √ 841 |
| des | תהלות | |
| | | 842 |
| | | 843 |
| | | 844 |
| | | 845 |
| | כב אותיות | |
| um influxus | שמן השפע | |
| | | 846 |
| | | 847 |
| | | 848 |
| | | 849 |
| tus Sabbathi | סוצאי שבת | |

| | | |
|---|---|---|
| | | 850 |
| Blue ; perfection | תכלת | |
| My perfect one. (*Not* written.) [Cant. v. 2.] Vide 857 | תמתי | |
| Souls. [I.R.Q. 1052 et seq.] | נשמתהון | 851 |
| Occellata Aurea ; Netzach and Hod receiving influence from Geburah | משבצות זהב | 852 |
| An orchard | שדה תפוחים | π 853 |
| | | 854 |
| | | 855 |
| | | 856 |
| Summitatis bifidae in Lulabh | תיומת | |
| My twin-sister. [*Is* written] | תאומתי | π 857 |
| "To Thee be Power unto the Ages, my Lord" [Vide 35 s.v. אגלא] | אתה גבור לעולם אדני | 858 |
| Iunctio, copula, phy-lacterium, ornamentumve manus. [Connect with נשר] | תפלה של יד | π 859 |
| | | 860 |
| Σ (1—41) | | 861 |
| | | 862 |
| | | π 863 |

| | | | | |
|---|---|---|---|---|
| | | 864 | | 8 |
| The Woman of Whoredom | אשת זנונים | | | 8 |
| ⊙ and ☽ | שמש וירח | | | π 8 |
| | | 865 | | 8 |
| | | 866 | | 8 |
| Latera aquilonis | ירכתי צפון | | | 8 |
| | | 867 | Spelunca duplex מערת המכפלה | 8 |
| | | 868 | | 8 |
| Semitae | נתיבות | | | 8 |
| Qliphoth of Tiphareth | תגרירון | 869 | Defectus cogitationis אפיסת הרעיון | 8 |
| Twelve | תריסר | 870 | | 8 |
| | | 871 | | 8 |
| | | 872 | | 8 |
| Septiduum | שבעת ימים | | | 8 |
| | | 873 | | 8 |
| | | 874 | | 8 |
| | | 875 | | 8 |
| | | 876 | $30^2$ √ 9 | |
| | | π 877 | | 9 |
| | | 878 | | 9 |
| | | 879 | Briatic Palace of היכל לבנת הספיר Jesod—Malkuth | |
| | | 880 | | |
| A King of Edom | השסההתימני | | Σ (1—42) | |
| | | π 881 | Secret name of Cagliostro אשאראת | |
| Os cranii, cranium | קרקפתא | | | |
| | | 882 | | 9 |
| Dilationes fleminis | רחובות הנהר | | | 9 |
| | | π 883 | | |
| Lux oriens | אור מתנוצץ | | Licentia. [Vide K.D. L.C.K. רשות p. 693] | |
| | | 884 | | |
| Domination | תועבות | | Vermis תולעת | |

π907

908

909

910

eginning.  [Vide I.Z.Q. רשית
547, et seq.]

π911

ell of Tiphareth בארשחת

eginning ראשית

emnant שארית

912

. of 506 שור q.v. שורות

913

rashith; "in the בראשית
Beginning."  [With *small* B.]
[Vide A Note on Genesis,
Equinox II 163–185, and 2911]

914

915

916

917

918

π919

920

921

kudoth; intuitus as- הסתכלות
pectus.  [Vide K.D.
L.C.K. p. 547]

922

923

924

925

926

---

927

928

π929

Gazophylacia Septen- אוצרות צפון
trionis

Briah, the Palace היכל קודש קדשים
of the Supernals
therein

930

931

932

The Tree of the עץ הדעת טוב ורע
Knowledge of
Good and Evil

933

Foedus nuditatis vel ברית המעור
Sabbathi vel arcus

934

Coruscatio בוצינא דקרדינותא
vehementissima; splendor
exactissime dimeticus

935

The Cause of causes סבת הסבות
[Vide Eccles. ii. 8, & תענוגות
S.D. v. 79]

936

Kether.  [Spelt in full] כ:ת:ר:

π937

938

939

940

π941

Angel of 1st Dec. ♐ משראת

942

943
944
945

The small point: a title נקרה פשות
of GOD most High

$\Sigma$ (1—43)   946

π 947

Angel of 1st Dec. ♋   מתראוש

948
949
950

[Vide no. 1204]   המתהפכת

951

The Book of the Law   ספר תורה

952

π 953

Vigiliae   אשמורות

954
955
956
957

Unguentum Magnificentiae   משחא רבות

958
959
960

Tubae argenteae   חצוצרות כסף

$31^2$   √961

962
963

Achad; unity. [Spelt fully]   א:ח:ד:
Garland, Crown; a little עטרת עטרה
wreath. [Vide K.D.
L.C.K. p. 614]

96

Memoriale iubilationis. זכרון תרועה
[Note Root זכר, 227 q.v.
showing phallic nature of
this 'memorial']

96
96
π96
96
96
97

Angel of Water   תרשים

π97

Shemhamphorasch,   שם המפורש
the 'Divided Name'
of GOD

9
9
9
π9
9
9
9
9
9
π9
9

Urbs Quaternionis   קרית ארבע

9

The Beginning of   ראשית חכמה
Wisdom (is The Wonderment
at TETRAGRAMMATON.
Psalms).

985

986

hementia; obiectio
rigorosa    התקפתא

987

988

edus pacis    ברית שלום

989

cens inter Lilia    רועה בשושנים

Σ (1—44)    990

π 991

992

e joy of the
whole Earth.
Vide no. 296]    משוש כל הארץ

993

994

995

996

e Most Holy
Ancient One    עתיקא קדישא

π 997

998

dus linguae    ברית לשון

999

$10^3$    $\sqrt[3]{}$ 1000

de no. 1100]    ששת

Qabalistic Method of
Exegesis; "spelling
Qabalistically back-
ward"    תשרק

1001

1002

e bank of a stream    שפת היאור

---

1003

1004

1005

1006

The law    תרות

1007

TAROT. [But vide 671]    תארות

1008

π 1009

1010

1011

1012

π 1013

1014

1015

1016

[Vide no. 1047]    יותרת

1017

Vasa vitrea, lagenae, phiale    אשישות

1018

π 1019

1020

π 1021

1022

1023

$32^2 = 4^5 = 2^{10}$    $\sqrt{}$ $\sqrt[5]{}$ $\sqrt[10]{}$ 1024

Qliphoth of ♍    נחשתירון

1025

Absconsiones
sapientiae    תעלומות חכמה

1026

1027

| | | | |
|---|---|---|---|
| | 1028 | | 10 |
| | 1029 | | 10 |
| | 1030 | The Tabernacle [N final] מׁשכן | |
| | π 1031 | | π 10 |
| | 1032 | אסתתר | |
| Sphere of Primum ראׁשית הגלגלים Mobile | | ויפח באפיו נׁשמת חיים [Vide I.R.Q. 939] | |
| | π 1033 | | 10 |
| | 1034 | | π 10 |
| Σ (1—45) | 1035 | | 10 |
| | 1036 | | 10 |
| | 1037 | | 10 |
| | 1038 | | 10 |
| | π 1039 | | 10 |
| | 1040 | | π 10 |
| | 1041 | | 10 |
| | 1042 | | 10 |
| | 1043 | | 10 |
| | 1044 | | 10 |
| | 1045 | | 10 |
| | 1046 | | 10 |
| | 1047 | | 10 |
| Diaphràgma supra hepar (vel hepatis) | | יותרת הכבד | 10 |
| | 1048 | | 10 |
| | π 1049 | | 10 |
| | 1050 | Σ (1—46) | 10 |
| | π 1051 | Tiphareth תפארת | |
| | 1052 | | 10 |
| | 1053 | | 10 |
| | 1054 | | 10 |
| | 1055 | | 1 |
| | 1056 | | 1 |
| The lily ׁשוׁשנת | | | π 10 |
| | 1057 | | 1 |
| | 1058 | 33² | √ 1 |

68

| | | |
|---|---|---|
| 1090 | | π 1123 |
| π 1091 | | 1124 |
| ie Rose of Sharon חבצלת השרון | | 1125 |
| 1092 | | 1126 |
| π 1093 | | 1127 |
| 1094 | Σ (1—47) | 1128 |
| 1095 | | π 1129 |
| 1096 | | 1130 |
| π 1097 | | 1131 |
| 1098 | | 1132 |
| 1099 | | 1133 |
| 1100 | | 1134 |
| xtiduum ששת ימים | | 1135 |
| 1101 | | 1136 |
| 1102 | | 1137 |
| π 1103 | | 1138 |
| 1104 | | 1139 |
| 1105 | | 1140 |
| 1106 | | 1141 |
| ie giving of the Law מתן התורה | | 1142 |
| 1107 | | 1143 |
| 1108 | | 1144 |
| π 1109 | | 1145 |
| 1110 | | 1146 |
| 1111 | Jars, globular vessels צנתרות | |
| 1112 | | 1147 |
| 1113 | Byssus contorta שש משזר | |
| 1114 | | 1148 |
| 1115 | | 1149 |
| 1116 | | 1150 |
| π 1117 | | π 1151 |
| 1118 | | 1152 |
| 1119 | | π 1153 |
| 1120 | | 1154 |
| 1121 | | 1155 |
| 1122 | 34² | √ 1156 |

# SEPHER SEPHIROTH

| | | | |
|---|---|---|---|
| | 1157 | | 118 |
| Specula turmarum מראות הצובאות | | | 119 |
| | 1158 | | 119 |
| | 1159 | | 119 |
| | 1160 | | π 119 |
| | 1161 | | 119 |
| | 1162 | | 119 |
| | π 1163 | | 119 |
| | 1164 | Fasciculi; rami pal- כפות תמרים | |
| | 1165 | marum | |
| | 1166 | | 11 |
| | 1167 | | 11 |
| | 1168 | | 11 |
| | 1169 | | 12 |
| | 1170 | | π 12 |
| | π 1171 | | 12 |
| | 1172 | | 12 |
| | 1173 | | 12 |
| [With ן counted as את יהוה אלהין Final] | | Flamma להט חרב המתהפכת gladii versatilis | |
| | 1174 | | 12 |
| | 1175 | | 12 |
| Conclave caesum לשכת הגזית | | The Holy Intelli- נשמתא קדישא gence | |
| Σ (1—48) | 1176 | | |
| | 1177 | A water-trough שקתות | |
| | 1178 | | 12 |
| | 1179 | | 12 |
| | 1180 | | 12 |
| | π 1181 | | 12 |
| | 1182 | Angel of Geburah of Briah תרשיש | |
| | 1183 | | 12 |
| | 1184 | | 12 |
| | 1185 | | π 12 |
| | 1186 | | 12 |
| | π 1187 | | 1: |
| | 1188 | | 12 |

70

| | | | |
|---|---|---|---|
| | π 1217 | | 1247 |
| | 1218 | | 1248 |
| | 1219 | | π 1249 |
| mator eius quod principiis | יוצר בראשית | | 1250 |
| | | | 1251 |
| | 1220 | | 1252 |
| of Hod | שעירמרת | | 1253 |
| beaten oil | שמן כתית | | 1254 |
| | 1221 | | 1255 |
| | 1222 | | 1256 |
| | π 1223 | | 1257 |
| | 1224 | | 1258 |
| Σ(1—49) = 35². ♀ √1225 | | | π 1259 |
| Ancient of the ncient Ones | עתיקא דעתיקין | | 1260 |
| | 1226 | Angels of Netzach and of Geburah of Briah | תרשישים |
| | 1227 | | 1261 |
| | 1228 | | 1262 |
| | π 1229 | | 1263 |
| | 1230 | | 1264 |
| | π 1231 | | 1265 |
| | 1232 | | 1266 |
| | 1233 | | 1267 |
| | 1234 | | 1268 |
| | 1235 | | 1269 |
| | 1236 | | 1270 |
| | π 1237 | | 1271 |
| | 1238 | | 1272 |
| | 1239 | | 1273 |
| | 1240 | | 1274 |
| | 1241 | Σ(1—50) | 1275 |
| | 1242 | | 1276 |
| | 1243 | | π 1277 |
| | 1244 | | 1278 |
| | 1245 | | π 1279 |
| | 1246 | Ignis sese reciprocans | אש מתלקחת |

| | | | |
|---|---|---|---|
| | 1280 | | 13 |
| | 1281 | | 13 |
| | 1282 | | 13 |
| | $\pi$ 1283 | | 13 |
| | 1284 | | 13 |
| | 1285 | | 13 |
| | 1286 | | 13 |
| | 1287 | | 13 |
| | 1288 | | $\pi$ 13 |
| | $\pi$ 1289 | | 13 |
| | 1290 | | $\pi$ 13 |
| | $\pi$ 1291 | The Lily of the Valleys | |
| | 1292 | | 13 |
| | 1293 | | 13 |
| | 1294 | | 13 |
| Chorda fili coccini תקות חוט השני | 1295 | $\Sigma\,(1\!-\!51)$ | 13 |
| $36^2 = 6^4$ $\sqrt{\ }\ \sqrt[4]{\ }$ 1296 | | | $\pi$ 13 |
| | $\pi$ 1297 | | 13 |
| | 1298 | | 13 |
| | 1299 | | 13 |
| | 1300 | $11^3$ | $\sqrt[3]{\ }$ 13 |
| | $\pi$ 1301 | | 13 |
| | 1302 | | 13 |
| | $\pi$ 1303 | | 13 |
| | 1304 | | 13 |
| | 1305 | | 13 |
| | 1306 | | 13 |
| | $\pi$ 1307 | | 13 |
| Angel L.T.D. of 2nd Dec. א, אשתרות and King-Demon of Geburah | | | 13 |
| | | | 13 |
| | | | 13 |
| | 1308 | | 13 |
| | 1309 | | 13 |
| | 1310 | | 13 |

| | | | |
|---|---|---|---|
| | 1345 | | 1376 |
| | 1346 | | 1377 |
| | 1347 | Σ (1—5²) | 1378 |
| | 1348 | | 1379 |
| | 1349 | | 1380 |
| he numerical value of the 9 Paths | 1350 | The lip of the liar שפת שקר | |
| of the Lesser Beard: viz. נ, ס, | | | π 1381 |
| ע, פ, צ, ק, ר, ש, and ת | | | 1382 |
| | 1351 | | 1383 |
| | 1352 | | 1384 |
| | 1353 | | 1385 |
| | 1354 | | 1386 |
| | 1355 | | 1387 |
| | 1356 | | 1388 |
| | 1357 | | 1389 |
| rooked by- אורחות עקלקלות | | | 1390 |
| paths. [Jud. v. 6] | | | 1391 |
| | 1358 | | 1392 |
| | 1359 | | 1393 |
| | 1360 | | 1394 |
| | π 1361 | | 1395 |
| | 1362 | | 1396 |
| | 1363 | | 1397 |
| | 1364 | | 1398 |
| | 1365 | | π 1399 |
| | 1366 | | 1400 |
| | π 1367 | Chaos, or = את, 401 q.v. את | |
| | 1368 | Tria Capita תלת רישין | |
| 37² | √ 1369 | | 1401 |
| | 1370 | | 1402 |
| | 1371 | | 1403 |
| | 1372 | | 1404 |
| | π 1373 | | 1405 |
| | 1374 | | 1406 |
| | 1375 | | 1407 |

| | | | |
|---|---|---|---|
| | 1408 | | 144 |
| | π 1409 | 38² | √ 144 |
| | 1410 | | 144 |
| | 1411 | The remnant of | לשאירית נחלתו |
| | 1412 | his heritage | |
| | 1413 | | 144 |
| | 1414 | | π 14 |
| | 1415 | | 144 |
| | 1416 | | 144 |
| | 1417 | | 145 |
| | 1418 | | π 145 |
| | 1419 | | 145 |
| | 1420 | | π 145 |
| | 1421 | | 145 |
| | 1422 | | 145 |
| | π 1423 | | 145 |
| | 1424 | | 145 |
| | 1425 | | 145 |
| | 1426 | | π 145 |
| | π 1427 | | 146 |
| | 1428 | Quies cessationis | שבת שבתון |
| | π 1429 | | 146 |
| | 1430 | | 146 |
| Σ (1—53) | 1431 | | 146 |
| | 1432 | | 146 |
| | π 1433 | | 146 |
| | 1434 | | 146 |
| | 1435 | | 146 |
| | 1436 | | 146 |
| | 1437 | | 146 |
| | 1438 | | 147 |
| | π 1439 | | π 147 |
| | 1440 | | 147 |
| | 1441 | | 147 |
| | 1442 | | 147 |

K 2

| | | | |
|---|---|---|---|
| | 1475 | | 1504 |
| | 1476 | | 1505 |
| | 1477 | | 1506 |
| | 1478 | | 1507 |
| | 1479 | | 1508 |
| | 1480 | | 1509 |
| tem heptaeterides שבע שבתות | | | 1510 |
| | π 1481 | | π 1511 |
| | 1482 | | 1512 |
| tunditates, seu גולות הכותרות | | | 1513 |
| asa rotunda capitellarum, | | | 1514 |
| eu capitella rotunda | | | 1515 |
| | π 1483 | | 1516 |
| | 1484 | | 1517 |
| (1—54) | 1485 | | 1518 |
| | 1486 | | 1519 |
| | π 1487 | | 1520 |
| | 1488 | | |
| | π 1489 | 39² | √‾1521 |
| | 1490 | | 1522 |
| | 1491 | | π 1523 |
| | 1492 | | 1524 |
| | π 1493 | | 1525 |
| | 1494 | | 1526 |
| total numerical value of the 1495 | | | 1527 |
| Paths of the Tree; i.e. of the | | | 1528 |
| Beards conjoined; i.e. of the | | | 1529 |
| whole Hebrew Alphabet | | | 1530 |
| | 1496 | | π 1531 |
| | 1497 | | 1532 |
| | 1498 | | 1533 |
| | π 1499 | | 1534 |
| | 1500 | | 1535 |
| | 1501 | | 1536 |
| | 1502 | | 1537 |
| | 1503 | | 1538 |

| | | |
|---|---|---|
| | 1539 | |
| Σ (1—55) | 1540 | |
| | 1541 | |
| | 1542 | |
| The Oil of the Anointing | שמן משחת קרש | |
| | π 1543 | |
| | 1544 | |
| | 1545 | |
| | 1546 | |
| | 1547 | |
| | 1548 | |
| | π 1549 | |
| | 1550 | |
| | 1551 | |
| | 1552 | |
| | π 1553 | |
| | 1554 | |
| | 1555 | |
| | 1556 | |
| | 1557 | |
| | 1558 | |
| | π 1559 | |
| | 1560 | |
| | 1561 | (1—56) |
| | 1562 | |
| | 1563 | |
| | 1564 | |
| | 1565 | $40^8$ |
| | 1566 | |
| | π 1567 | |
| | 1568 | |
| | 1569 | |
| | 1570 | |
| | π 1571 | |

| | | |
|---|---|---|
| π 1607 | | 1642 |
| 1608 | | 1643 |
| π 1609 | | 1644 |
| 1610 | | 1645 |
| 1611 | | 1646 |
| 1612 | | 1647 |
| π 1613 | | 1648 |
| 1614 | | 1649 |
| 1615 | | 1650 |
| 1616 | | 1651 |
| 1617 | | 1652 |
| 1618 | Σ (1—57) | 1653 |
| π 1619 | | 1654 |
| 1620 | | 1655 |
| π 1621 | | 1656 |
| 1622 | | π 1657 |
| 1623 | | 1658 |
| 1624 | | 1659 |
| 1625 | | 1660 |
| 1626 | | 1661 |
| π 1627 | | 1662 |
| 1628 | | π 1663 |
| 1629 | | 1664 |
| 1630 | The pure olive  שמן זית זך כתית | |
| 1631 | oil beaten out | |
| 1632 | | 1665 |
| 1633 | | 1666 |
| 1634 | | π 1667 |
| 1635 | | 1668 |
| 1636 | | π 1669 |
| π 1637 | | 1670 |
| 1638 | | 1671 |
| 1639 | | 1672 |
| 1640 | | 1673 |
| 1641 | | 1674 |

| | | | |
|---|---|---|---|
| | 1675 | | 171 |
| | 1676 | Σ(1—58) | 171 |
| | 1677 | | 171 |
| | 1678 | | 171 |
| | 1679 | | 171 |
| | 1680 | | 171 |
| $41^2$ | $\sqrt{\ }$ 1681 | | 171 |
| | 1682 | | 171 |
| | 1683 | | 171 |
| | 1684 | | 171 |
| | 1685 | | 172 |
| | 1686 | | π 172 |
| | 1687 | | 172 |
| | 1688 | | π 172 |
| | 1689 | | 172 |
| | 1690 | | 172 |
| | 1691 | | 172 |
| | 1692 | | 17 |
| π | 1693 | $12^3$ | $\sqrt[3]{\ }$ 17 |
| | 1694 | | 17 |
| | 1695 | | 17 |
| | 1696 | | 17 |
| π | 1697 | | 17 |
| | 1698 | | π 17 |
| π | 1699 | | 17 |
| | 1700 | | 17 |
| | 1701 | | 17 |
| | 1702 | | 17 |
| | 1703 | | 17 |
| | 1704 | | 17 |
| | 1705 | | 17 |
| | 1706 | | π 17 |
| | 1707 | | 17 |
| | 1708 | | 17 |
| π | 1709 | | 17 |

| | | |
|---|---|---|
| | 1745 | π 1777 |
| | 1746 | 1778 |
| | π 1747 | 1779 |
| | 1748 | 1780 |
| | 1749 | 1781 |
| | 1750 | 1782 |
| | 1751 | π 1783 |
| | 1752 | 1784 |
| | π 1753 | 1785 |
| | 1754 | 1786 |
| | 1755 | π 1787 |
| קדוש קדוש קדוש יהוה צבאור | | 1788 |
| ly, Holy, Holy, Lord GOD | | π 1789 |
| f Hosts ! | | 1790 |
| | 1756 | 1791 |
| | 1757 | 1792 |
| | 1758 | 1793 |
| | π 1759 | 1794 |
| | 1760 | 1795 |
| | 1761 | 1796 |
| | 1762 | 1797 |
| | 1763 | 1798 |
| $42^2$ | $\sqrt{\phantom{x}}$ 1764 | 1799 |
| | 1765 | 1800 |
| | 1766 | π 1801 |
| | 1767 | 1802 |
| | 1768 | 1803 |
| | 1769 | 1804 |
| $\Sigma$ (1—59) | 1770 | 1805 |
| | 1771 | 1806 |
| | 1772 | 1807 |
| | 1773 | 1808 |
| | 1774 | 1809 |
| | 1775 | 1810 |
| | 1776 | π 1811 |

| | | | |
|---|---|---|---|
| | 1812 | | π 18. |
| | 1813 | | 18. |
| | 1814 | 43² | √ 18. |
| | 1815 | | 18 |
| | 1816 | | 18 |
| | 1817 | | 18 |
| | 1818 | | 18 |
| | 1819 | ‖7 | 18 |
| | 1820 | | 18 |
| | 1821 | | 18 |
| | 1822 | | 18 |
| π | 1823 | | 18 |
| | 1824 | | 18 |
| | 1825 | | 18 |
| | 1826 | | π 18 |
| | 1827 | | 18 |
| | 1828 | | 18 |
| | 1829 | | 18 |
| Σ(1—60) | 1830 | | 18 |
| π | 1831 | | 18 |
| | 1832 | | π 18 |
| | 1833 | | 18 |
| | 1834 | | 18 |
| | 1835 | | 18 |
| | 1836 | | π 18 |
| | 1837 | | 18 |
| | 1838 | | π 1 |
| | 1839 | | 18 |
| | 1840 | | 18 |
| | 1841 | | 1 |
| | 1842 | | π 1 |
| | 1843 | | 1 |
| | 1844 | | π 1 |
| | 1845 | | 1 |
| | 1846 | | 1 |

|  | | | |
|---|---|---|---|
| | 1882 | | 1917 |
| | 1883 | | 1918 |
| | 1884 | | 1919 |
| | 1885 | | 1920 |
| | 1886 | | 1921 |
| | 1887 | | 1922 |
| | 1888 | | 1923 |
| | π 1889 | | 1924 |
| | 1890 | | 1925 |
| Σ(1—61) | 1891 | | 1926 |
| | 1892 | | 1927 |
| | 1893 | | 1928 |
| | 1894 | | 1929 |
| | 1895 | | 1930 |
| | 1896 | | π 1931 |
| | 1897 | | 1932 |
| | 1898 | | π 1933 |
| | 1899 | | 1934 |
| | 1900 | | 1935 |
| | π 1901 | $44^2$ | √ 1936 |
| | 1902 | | 1937 |
| | 1903 | | 1938 |
| | 1904 | | 1939 |
| | 1905 | | 1940 |
| | 1906 | | 1941 |
| | π 1907 | | 1942 |
| | 1908 | | 1943 |
| | 1909 | | 1944 |
| | 1910 | | 1945 |
| | 1911 | | 1946 |
| | 1912 | | 1947 |
| | π 1913 | | 1948 |
| | 1914 | | π 1949 |
| | 1915 | | 1950 |
| | 1916 | | π 1951 |

# SEPHER SEPHIROTH

| | | | |
|---|---|---|---|
| | 1952 | | π 198 |
| Σ(1—62) | 1953 | | 198 |
| | 1954 | | 198 |
| | 1955 | | 199 |
| | 1956 | | 199 |
| | 1957 | | 199 |
| | 1958 | | π 199 |
| | 1959 | | 199 |
| | 1960 | | 199 |
| | 1961 | | 199 |
| | 1962 | | π 199 |
| | 1963 | | 199 |
| | 1964 | | π 199 |
| | 1965 | | 200 |
| | 1966 | | 200 |
| | 1967 | | 200 |
| | 1968 | | π 200 |
| | 1969 | | 200 |
| | 1970 | | 200 |
| | 1971 | | 200 |
| | 1972 | | 200 |
| π 1973 | | | 200 |
| | 1974 | | 200 |
| | 1975 | | 20 |
| | 1976 | | π 20 |
| | 1977 | | 20 |
| | 1978 | | 20 |
| π 1979 | | | 20 |
| | 1980 | | 20 |
| | 1981 | Σ(1—63) | 20 |
| | 1982 | | π 20 |
| | 1983 | | 20 |
| | 1984 | | 20 |
| | 1985 | | 20 |
| | 1986 | | 20 |

L 2

|  | |  |
|---|---|---|
| 2022 | | 2057 |
| 2023 | | 2058 |
| 2024 | | 2059 |
45² | √ 2025 | | 2060 |
| 2026 | | 2061 |
| π 2027 | | 2062 |
| 2028 | | π 2063 |
| π 2029 | | 2064 |
| 2030 | | 2065 |
| 2031 | | 2066 |
| 2032 | | 2067 |
| 2033 | | 2068 |
| 2034 | | π 2069 |
| 2035 | | 2070 |
| 2036 | | 2071 |
| 2037 | | 2072 |
| 2038 | | 2073 |
| π 2039 | | 2074 |
| 2040 | | 2075 |
| 2041 | | 2076 |
| 2042 | | 2077 |
| 2043 | | 2078 |
| 2044 | | 2079 |
| 2045 | Σ (1—64). ☿ | 2080 |
| 2046 | Spirit of ☿ | תפתרתרת |
| 2047 | | π 2081 |
| 2048 | | 2082 |
| 2049 | | π 2083 |
| 2050 | | 2084 |
| 2051 | | 2085 |
| 2052 | | 2086 |
| π 2053 | | π 2087 |
| 2054 | | 2088 |
| 2055 | | π 2089 |
| 2056 | | 2090 |

83

| | | |
|---|---|---|
| | 2091 | 21 |
| | 2092 | 21 |
| | 2093 | 21 |
| | 2094 | π 21 |
| | 2095 | 21 |
| | 2096 | π 21 |
| | 2097 | 21 |
| | 2098 | 21 |
| π | 2099 | 21 |
| | 2100 | 21 |
| | 2101 | 21 |
| | 2102 | π 21 |
| | 2103 | 21 |
| | 2104 | 21 |
| | 2105 | 21 |
| | 2106 | π 21 |
| | 2107 | 21 |
| | 2108 | π 21 |
| | 2109 | 21 |
| | 2110 | 21 |
| π | 2111 | 21 |
| | 2112 | 21 |
| π | 2113 | 21 |
| | 2114 | 21 |
| | 2115 | 21 |
| $46^2$ | $\sqrt{\phantom{x}}$ 2116 | 21 |
| | 2117 | 21 |
| | 2118 | π 21 |
| | 2119 | 21 |
| | 2120 | 21 |
| | 2121 | 2 |
| | 2122 | 2 |
| | 2123 | 2 |
| | 2124 | 2 |
| | 2125 | 2 |

$\Sigma$ (1—65)

| | | | |
|---|---|---|---|
| | $\pi$ 2161 | | 2196 |
| | 2162 | $13^8$ | $\sqrt[3]{\ }$ 2197 |
| | 2163 | | 2198 |
| | 2164 | | 2199 |
| | 2165 | | 2200 |
| | 2166 | | 2201 |
| | 2167 | | 2202 |
| | 2168 | | $\pi$ 2203 |
| | 2169 | | 2204 |
| | 2170 | | 2205 |
| | 2171 | | 2206 |
| | 2172 | | $\pi$ 2207 |
| | 2173 | | 2208 |
| | 2174 | $47^2$ | $\sqrt{\ }$ 2209 |
| | 2175 | | 2210 |
| | 2176 | $\Sigma$ (1—66) | 2211 |
| | 2177 | | 2212 |
| | 2178 | | $\pi$ 2213 |
| | $\pi$ 2179 | | 2214 |
| | 2180 | | 2215 |
| | 2181 | | 2216 |
| | 2182 | | 2217 |
| | 2183 | | 2218 |
| | 2184 | | 2219 |
| | 2185 | | 2220 |
| | 2186 | | $\pi$ 2221 |
| $3^7$ | $\sqrt[7]{\ }$ 2187 | | 2222 |
| | 2188 | | 2223 |
| | 2189 | | 2224 |
| | 2190 | | 2225 |
| | 2191 | | 2226 |
| | 2192 | | 2227 |
| | 2193 | | 2228 |
| | 2194 | | 2229 |
| | 2195 | | 2230 |

| | |
|---|---|
| 2231 | 226 |
| 2232 | π 226 |
| 2233 | 226 |
| 2234 | π 226 |
| 2235 | 227 |
| 2236 | 227 |
| π 2237 | 227 |
| 2238 | π 227 |
| π 2239 | 227 |
| 2240 | 227 |
| 2241 | 22' |
| 2242 | 22' |
| π 2243 | 22' |
| 2244 | 22' |
| 2245 | 228 |
| 2246 | π 228 |
| 2247 | 228 |
| 2248 | 228 |
| 2249 | 228 |
| 2250 | 228 |
| π 2251 | 228 |
| 2252 | π 22 |
| 2253 | ε28 |
| 2254 | 228 |
| 2255 | 22 |
| 2256 | 22 |
| 2257 | 22 |
| 2258 | π 22 |
| 2259 | 22 |
| 2260 | 22 |
| 2261 | 22 |
| 2262 | π 22 |
| 2263 | 22 |
| 2264 | 22 |
| 2265 | 23 |

$\Sigma\,(1-67)$

| | | |
|---|---|---|
| | 2301 | 2336 |
| | 2302 | 2337 |
| | 2303 | 2338 |
| $48^2$ | $\sqrt{\phantom{-}}$ 2304 | π 2339 |
| | 2305 | 2340 |
| | 2306 | π 2341 |
| | 2307 | 2342 |
| | 2308 | 2343 |
| | π 2309 | 2344 |
| | 2310 | 2345 |
| | π 2311 | Σ (1—68) 2346 |
| | 2312 | π 2347 |
| | 2313 | 2348 |
| | 2314 | 2349 |
| | 2315 | 2350 |
| | 2316 | π 2351 |
| | 2317 | 2352 |
| | 2318 | 2353 |
| | 2319 | 2354 |
| | 2320 | 2355 |
| | 2321 | 2356 |
| | 2322 | π 2357 |
| | 2323 | 2358 |
| | 2324 | 2359 |
| | 2325 | 2360 |
| | 2326 | 2361 |
| | 2327 | 2362 |
| | 2328 | 2363 |
| | 2329 | 2364 |
| | 2330 | 2365 |
| | 2331 | 2366 |
| | 2332 | 2367 |
| | π 2333 | 2368 |
| | 2334 | 2369 |
| | 2335 | 2370 |

# SEPHER SEPHIROTH

|  |  |  |  |
|---|---|---|---|
| π 2371 | | | 24 |
| 2372 | | | 24 |
| 2373 | | | 24 |
| 2374 | | | 24 |
| 2375 | | | 24 |
| 2376 | | | π 24 |
| π 2377 | | | 24 |
| 2378 | | | 24 |
| 2379 | | | 24 |
| 2380 | | Σ(1—69) | 24 |
| π 2381 | | | 24 |
| 2382 | | | π 2. |
| π 2383 | | | 2. |
| 2384 | | | 24 |
| 2385 | | | 2. |
| 2386 | | | 24 |
| 2387 | | | 2 |
| 2388 | | | π 2. |
| π 2389 | | | 2. |
| 2390 | | | 2. |
| 2391 | | | 2. |
| 2392 | | | 2. |
| π 2393 | | | 2. |
| 2394 | | | 2. |
| 2395 | | | 2. |
| 2396 | | | 2. |
| 2397 | | | 2. |
| 2398 | | | 2. |
| π 2399 | | | 2. |
| 2400 | | | 2 |
| $49^2 = 7^4$ | $\sqrt{\ }\sqrt[4]{\ }$ 2401 | | 2 |
| 2402 | | | π 2. |
| 2403 | | | 2 |
| 2404 | | | 2 |
| 2405 | | | 2 |

| | | |
|---|---|---|
| π 2441 | | 2476 |
| 2442 | | π 2477 |
| 2443 | | 2478 |
| 2444 | | 2479 |
| 2445 | | 2480 |
| 2446 | | 2481 |
| π 2447 | | 2482 |
| 2448 | | 2483 |
| 2449 | | 2484 |
| 2450 | Σ (1—70) | 2485 |
| 2451 | | 2486 |
| 2452 | | 2487 |
| 2453 | | 2488 |
| 2454 | | 2489 |
| 2455 | | 2490 |
| 2456 | | 2491 |
| 2457 | | 2492 |
| 2458 | | 2493 |
| π 2459 | | 2494 |
| 2460 | | 2495 |
| 2461 | | 2496 |
| 2462 | | 2497 |
| 2463 | | 2498 |
| 2464 | | 2499 |
| 2465 | $50^2$ | $\sqrt{\ }$ 2500 |
| 2466 | | 2501 |
| π 2467 | | 2502 |
| 2468 | | π 2503 |
| 2469 | | 2504 |
| 2470 | | 2505 |
| 2471 | | 2506 |
| 2472 | | 2507 |
| π 2473 | | 2508 |
| 2474 | | 2509 |
| 2475 | | 2510 |

M

| | | | |
|---|---|---|---|
| 2511 | | | 25 |
| 2512 | | | 25 |
| 2513 | | | 25 |
| 2514 | | | π 25 |
| 2515 | | | 25 |
| 2516 | | | π 25 |
| 2517 | | | 25 |
| 2518 | | | 25 |
| 2519 | | | 25 |
| 2520 | | | 25 |
| π 2521 | Σ(1—71) | | 25 |
| 2522 | | | π 25 |
| 2523 | | | 25 |
| 2524 | | | 25 |
| 2525 | | | 25 |
| 2526 | | | 25 |
| 2527 | | | 25 |
| 2528 | | | 25 |
| 2529 | | | 25 |
| 2530 | | | 25 |
| π 2531 | | | 25 |
| 2532 | | | 25 |
| 2533 | | | 25 |
| 2534 | | | 25 |
| 2535 | | | 25 |
| 2536 | | | 25 |
| 2537 | | | 25 |
| 2538 | | | 25 |
| π 2539 | | | 25 |
| 2540 | | | 25 |
| 2541 | | | 25 |
| 2542 | | | 25 |
| π 2543 | | | 25 |
| 2544 | | | π 25 |
| 2545 | | | 25 |

M 2

| | | |
|---|---|---|
| 2581 | | 2616 |
| 2582 | | π 2617 |
| 2583 | | 2618 |
| 2584 | | 2619 |
| 2585 | | 2620 |
| 2586 | | π 2621 |
| 2587 | | 2622 |
| 2588 | | 2623 |
| 2589 | | 2624 |
| 2590 | | 2625 |
| π 2591 | | 2626 |
| 2592 | | 2627 |
| π 2593 | Σ (1—72) | 2628 |
| 2594 | | 2629 |
| 2595 | | 2630 |
| 2596 | | 2631 |
| 2597 | | 2632 |
| 2598 | | π 2633 |
| 2599 | | 2634 |
| 2600 | | 2635 |
| √ 2601 | | 2636 |
| 2602 | | 2637 |
| 2603 | | 2638 |
| 2604 | | 2639 |
| 2605 | | 2640 |
| 2606 | | 2641 |
| 2607 | | 2642 |
| 2608 | | 2643 |
| π 2609 | | 2644 |
| 2610 | | 2645 |
| 2611 | | 2646 |
| 2612 | | π 2647 |
| 2613 | | 2648 |
| 2614 | | 2649 |
| 2615 | | 2650 |

51*

| | | |
|---|---|---|
| 2651 | | 26 |
| 2652 | | π 26 |
| 2653 | | 26 |
| 2654 | | π 26 |
| 2655 | | 26 |
| 2656 | | 26 |
| π 2657 | | 26 |
| 2658 | | π 26 |
| π 2659 | | 26 |
| 2660 | | 26 |
| 2661 | | 26 |
| 2662 | | 26 |
| π 2663 | | 26 |
| 2664 | | π 26 |
| 2665 | | 27 |
| 2666 | $\Sigma(1-73)$ | 27 |
| 2667 | | 27 |
| 2668 | | 27 |
| 2669 | $52^2$ | $\sqrt{\ }$ 27 |
| 2670 | | 27 |
| π 2671 | | 27 |
| 2672 | | π 27 |
| 2673 | | 27 |
| 2674 | | 27 |
| 2675 | | 27 |
| 2676 | | π 27 |
| π 2677 | | 2 |
| 2678 | | π 27 |
| 2679 | | 2 |
| 2680 | | 2 |
| 2681 | | 2 |
| 2682 | | 2 |
| π 2683 | | 2 |
| 2684 | | π 2 |
| 2685 | | 2 |

| | | | | |
|---|---|---|---|---|
| | | 2721 | | 2756 |
| | | 2722 | | 2757 |
| | | 2723 | | 2758 |
| | | 2724 | | 2759 |
| | | 2725 | | 2760 |
| | | 2726 | | 2761 |
| | | 2727 | | 2762 |
| | | 2728 | | 2763 |
| | π | 2729 | | 2764 |
| | | 2730 | | 2765 |
| | π | 2731 | | 2766 |
| | | 2732 | π | 2767 |
| | | 2733 | | 2768 |
| | | 2734 | | 2769 |
| | | 2735 | | 2770 |
| | | 2736 | | 2771 |
| | | 2737 | | 2772 |
| | | 2738 | | 2773 |
| | | 2739 | | 2774 |
| | | 2740 | $\Sigma$(1—74) | 2775 |
| | π | 2741 | | 2776 |
| | | 2742 | π | 2777 |
| | | 2743 | | 2778 |
| $14^3$ | $\sqrt[3]{}$ | 2744 | | 2779 |
| | | 2745 | | 2780 |
| | | 2746 | | 2781 |
| | | 2747 | | 2782 |
| | | 2748 | | 2783 |
| | π | 2749 | | 2784 |
| | | 2750 | | 2785 |
| | | 2751 | | 2786 |
| | | 2752 | | 2787 |
| | π | 2753 | | 2788 |
| | | 2754 | π | 2789 |
| | | 2755 | | 2790 |

|  |  |  |  |
|---|---|---|---|
|  | π 2791 |  | 28 |
|  | 2792 |  | 28 |
|  | 2793 |  | 28 |
|  | 2794 |  | 28 |
|  | 2795 |  | 28 |
|  | 2796 |  | 28 |
|  | π 2797 |  | 28 |
|  | 2798 |  | π 28 |
|  | 2799 |  | 28 |
|  | 2800 |  | 28 |
|  | π 2801 |  | 28 |
|  | 2802 |  | π 28 |
|  | π 2803 |  | 28 |
|  | 2804 |  | 28 |
|  | 2805 |  | 28 |
|  | 2806 |  | 28 |
|  | 2807 |  | 28 |
|  | 2808 |  | π 28 |
| 53² | √ 2809 |  | 28 |
|  | 2810 |  | 28 |
|  | 2811 |  | 28 |
|  | 2812 |  | 28 |
|  | 2813 |  | 28 |
|  | 2814 |  | 28 |
|  | 2815 | Σ (1—75) | 28 |
|  | 2816 |  | π 28 |
|  | 2817 |  | 28 |
|  | 2818 |  | 28 |
|  | π 2819 |  | 28 |
|  | 2820 |  | 28 |
|  | 2821 |  | 28 |
|  | 2822 |  | π 28 |
|  | 2823 |  | 28 |
|  | 2824 |  | 28 |
|  | 2825 |  | 28 |

| | | | |
|---|---|---|---|
| π 2861 | | | 2896 |
| 2862 | | | π 2897 |
| 2863 | | | 2898 |
| 2864 | | | 2899 |
| 2865 | | | 2900 |
| 2866 | | | 2901 |
| 2867 | | | 2902 |
| 2868 | | | π 2903 |
| 2869 | | | 2904 |
| 2870 | | | 2905 |
| 2871 | | | 2906 |
| 2872 | | | 2907 |
| 2873 | | | 2908 |
| 2874 | | | π 2909 |
| 2875 | | | 2910 |
| 2876 | | | 2911 |
| 2877 | | | 2912 |
| 2878 | | | 2913 |
| π 2879 | | | 2914 |
| 2880 | | | 2915 |
| 2881 | | $54^2$ | $\sqrt{\ }$ 2916 |
| 2882 | | | π 2917 |
| 2883 | | | 2918 |
| 2884 | | | 2919 |
| 2885 | | | 2920 |
| 2886 | | | 2921 |
| π 2887 | | | 2922 |
| 2888 | | | 2923 |
| 2889 | | | 2924 |
| 2890 | | | 2925 |
| 2891 | | $\Sigma(1-76)$ | 2926 |
| 2892 | | | π 2927 |
| 2893 | | | 2928 |
| 2894 | | | 2929 |
| 2895 | | | 2930 |

| | | |
|---|---|---|
| | 2931 | 29 |
| | 2932 | 29 |
| | 2933 | 29 |
| | 2934 | π 29 |
| | 2935 | 29 |
| | 2936 | π 29 |
| | 2937 | 29 |
| | 2938 | 29 |
| π | 2939 | 29 |
| | 2940 | 29 |
| | 2941 | 29 |
| | 2942 | 29 |
| | 2943 | 29 |
| | 2944 | 29 |
| | 2945 | 29 |
| | 2946 | 29 |
| | 2947 | 29 |
| | 2948 | 29 |
| | 2949 | 29 |
| | 2950 | 29 |
| | 2951 | 29 |
| | 2952 | 29 |
| π | 2953 | 29 |
| | 2954 | 29 |
| | 2955 | 29 |
| | 2956 | 29 |
| π | 2957 | 29 |
| | 2958 | 29 |
| | 2959 | 29 |
| | 2960 | 29 |
| | 2961 | 29 |
| | 2962 | 29 |
| π | 2963 | 29 |
| | 2964 | π 29 |
| | 2965 | 30 |

|  |  |  |
|---|---|---|
| $\Sigma(1—77)$ | $\pi$ 3001 | 3036 |
|  | 3002 | $\pi$ 3037 |
|  | 3003 | 3038 |
|  | 3004 | 3039 |
|  | 3005 | 3040 |
|  | 3006 | $\pi$ 3041 |
|  | 3007 | 3042 |
|  | 3008 | 3043 |
|  | 3009 | 3044 |
|  | 3010 | 3045 |
|  | $\pi$ 3011 | 3046 |
|  | 3012 | 3047 |
|  | 3013 | 3048 |
|  | 3014 | $\pi$ 3049 |
|  | 3015 | 3050 |
|  | 3016 | 3051 |
|  | 3017 | 3052 |
|  | 3018 | 3053 |
|  | $\pi$ 3019 | 3054 |
|  | 3020 | 3055 |
|  | 3021 | 3056 |
|  | 3022 | 3057 |
|  | $\pi$ 3023 | 3058 |
|  | 3024 | 3059 |
| $55^2$ | $\sqrt{}$ 3025 | 3060 |
|  | 3026 | $\pi$ 3061 |
|  | 3027 | 3062 |
|  | 3028 | 3063 |
|  | 3029 | 3064 |
|  | 3030 | 3065 |
|  | 3031 | 3066 |
|  | 3032 | $\pi$ 3067 |
|  | 3033 | 3068 |
|  | 3034 | 3069 |
|  | 3035 | 3070 |

| | | | | |
|---|---|---|---|---|
| | 3071 | | | 31( |
| | 3072 | | | 31( |
| | 3073 | | | 31( |
| | 3074 | | | π 31( |
| | 3075 | | | 31) |
| | 3076 | | | 31) |
| | 3077 | | | 31) |
| | 3078 | | | 31) |
| | π 3079 | | | 31) |
| | 3080 | | | 31) |
| Σ(1—78) | 3081 | | | 31) |
| | 3082 | | | 31) |
| | π 3083 | | | 31) |
| | 3084 | | | π 31) |
| | 3085 | | | 31: |
| | 3086 | | | π 31: |
| | 3087 | | | 31: |
| | 3088 | | | 31: |
| | π 3089 | | | 31: |
| | 3090 | | $5^5$ | $\sqrt[5]{}$ 31: |
| | 3091 | | | 31: |
| | 3092 | | | 31: |
| | 3093 | | | 31 |
| | 3094 | | | 31 |
| | 3095 | | | 31 |
| | 3096 | | | 31 |
| | 3097 | | | 31 |
| | 3098 | | | 31 |
| | 3099 | | | 31 |
| | 3100 | | | 31 |
| | 3101 | | $56^2$ | $\sqrt{}$ 31 |
| | 3102 | | | π 31 |
| | 3103 | | | 31 |
| | 3104 | | | 31 |
| | 3105 | | | 31 |

98

| | | |
|---|---|---|
| | 3141 | 3176 |
| | 3142 | 3177 |
| | 3143 | 3178 |
| | 3144 | 3179 |
| | 3145 | 3180 |
| | 3146 | $\pi$ 3181 |
| | 3147 | 3182 |
| | 3148 | 3183 |
| | 3149 | 3184 |
| | 3150 | 3185 |
| | 3151 | 3186 |
| | 3152 | $\pi$ 3187 |
| | 3153 | 3188 |
| | 3154 | 3189 |
| | 3155 | 3190 |
| | 3156 | $\pi$ 3191 |
| | 3157 | 3192 |
| | 3158 | 3193 |
| | 3159 | 3194 |
| $\Sigma$(1—79) | 3160 | 3195 |
| | 3161 | 3196 |
| | 3162 | 3197 |
| | $\pi$ 3163 | 3198 |
| | 3164 | 3199 |

$32 \times 10^2$   The paths of the Whole   3200

| | | |
|---|---|---|
| | 3165 | Tree in excelsis |
| | 3166 | |
| | $\pi$ 3167 | בראשית ברא אלהים |
| | 3168 | 3201 |
| | $\pi$ 3169 | 3202 |
| | 3170 | $\pi$ 3203 |
| | 3171 | 3204 |
| | 3172 | 3205 |
| | 3173 | 3206 |
| | 3174 | 3207 |
| | 3175 | 3208 |

| | | | |
|---|---|---|---|
| $\pi$ 3209 | | | 3 |
| 3210 | | | 3 |
| 3211 | | | 3 |
| 3212 | | | 3 |
| 3213 | | | 3 |
| 3214 | $57^2$ | | $\sqrt{\ }$ 3 |
| 3215 | | | 3 |
| 3216 | | | $\pi$ 3 |
| $\pi$ 3217 | | | 3 |
| 3218 | | | $\pi$ 3 |
| 3219 | | | 3 |
| 3220 | | | 3 |
| $\pi$ 3221 | | | 3 |
| 3222 | | | $\pi$ 3 |
| 3223 | | | 3 |
| 3224 | | | $\pi$ 3 |
| 3225 | | | 3 |
| 3226 | | | 3 |
| 3227 | | | 3 |
| 3228 | | | 3 |
| $\pi$ 3229 | | | 3 |
| 3230 | | | 3 |
| 3231 | | | 3 |
| 3232 | | | 3 |
| 3233 | | | 3 |
| 3234 | | | 3 |
| 3235 | | | 3 |
| 3236 | | | $\pi$ 3 |
| 3237 | | | 3 |
| 3238 | | | 3 |
| 3239 | | | 3 |
| $\Sigma$(1—80) 3240 | | | 3 |
| 3241 | | | 3 |
| 3242 | | | 3 |
| 3243 | | | 3 |

| | | |
|---|---|---|
| 3279 | | 3300 |
| 3280 | | π 3301 |
| 3281 | | 3302 |
| 3282 | | 3303 |
| 3283 | | 3304 |
| 3284 | | 3305 |
| 3285 | | 3306 |
| 3286 | | π 3307 |
| 3287 | | 3308 |
| 3288 | | 3309 |
| 3289 | | 3310 |
| 3290 | | 3311 |
| 3291 | | 3312 |
| 3292 | | π 3313 |
| 3293 | | 3314 |
| 3294 | | 3315 |
| 3295 | | 3316 |
| 3296 | | 3317 |
| 3297 | | 3318 |
| 3298 | | π 3319 |
| π 3299 | | 3320 |
| Σ (1—81). ☽. | | 3321 |

| | |
|---|---|
| ...e Intelligence of the Intelligences of the Moon | מלכא בתרשישים ועד ברוה שהרים |
| ...e Spirit of the Spirits of the Moon | שדברשהמעת שרתתן |

[A pendant to this work, on the properties of pure number, is in preparation under ... supervision of Fratres P. and ψ. Also a companion volume on the Greek Qabalah ... them and Frater J. M.]

## STAY IN TOUCH

On the following pages you will find listed, with their current prices, some of the books and tapes now available on related subjects. Your book dealer stocks most of these, and will stock new titles in the Llewellyn series as they become available. We urge your patronage.

However, to obtain our full catalog, to keep informed of new titles as they are released and to benefit from informative articles and helpful news, you are invited to write for our bi-monthly news magazine/catalog. A sample copy is free, and it will continue coming to you at no cost as long as you are an active mail customer. Or you may keep it coming for a full year with a donation of just $2.00 in U.S.A. ($7.00 for Canada & Mexico, $20.00 overseas, first class mail). Many bookstores also have *The Llewellyn New Times* available to their customers. Ask for it.

Stay in touch! In *The Llewellyn New Times'* pages you will find news and reviews of new books, tapes and services, announcements of meetings and seminars, articles helpful to our readers, news of authors, advertising of products and services, special money-making opportunities, and much more.

### The Llewellyn New Times
### P.O. Box 64383-Dept. 296, St. Paul, MN 55164-0383, U.S.A.

• • •

### TO ORDER BOOKS AND TAPES

If your book dealer does not have the books and tapes described on the following pages readily available, you may order them direct from the publisher by sending full price in U.S. funds, plus $1.00 for handling and 50¢ each book or item for postage within the United States; outside USA surface mail add $1.50 per item postage and $1.00 per order for handling. Outside USA air mail add $7.00 per item postage and $1.00 per order for handling. MN residents add 6% sales tax.

### FOR GROUP STUDY AND PURCHASE

Because there is a great deal of interest in group discussion and study of the subject matter of this book, we feel that we should encourage the adoption and use of this particular book by such groups by offering a special "quantity" price to group leaders or "agents."

Our Special Quantity Price for a minimum order of five copies of *Godwin's Cabalistic Encyclopedia* is $45.00 Cash-With-Order. This price includes postage and handling within the United States. Minnesota residents must add 6% sales tax. For additional quantities, please order in multiples of five. For Canadian and foreign orders, add postage and handling charges as above. Credit Card (VISA, Master-Card, American Express, Diners' Club) Orders are accepted. Charge Card Orders only may be phoned free ($15.00 minimum order) within the U.S.A. by dialing 1-800-THE MOON (in Canada call: 1-800-FOR-SELF). Customer Service calls dial 1-612-291-1970. Mail Orders to:

### LLEWELLYN PUBLICATIONS
### P.O. Box 64383-Dept. 296 / St. Paul, MN 55164-0383, U.S.A.

## MYSTERIA MAGICA
(formerly Volume V of the Magical Philosophy Series)
**by Denning and Phillips**

The Inner Secrets revealed: The Secret Symbolism of the Aurum Solis is given to you for the first time! The Gates to Knowledge, Ecstasy, and Power are opened to give modern man powers undreamed of in past ages. No matter what your level of ability in Ceremonial Magick, this is one of the most important books you could ever own.

*Mysteria Magica* offers you essential and profound magical knowledge, authentic texts and formulae of the Western Mystery Tradition which have hitherto been hidden in inaccessible libraries, in enigmatic writings, or in rarely-imparted teachings passed on only by word of mouth; and, in addition, it contains ample sections showing you how to use all that is disclosed, how to give potent consecration to your own magical weapons, how to build rites on the physical and astral planes with word and action, sound, color and visualization, to implement your own magical will. Revised edition.

**0-87542-196-2, 450 pages, 6 x 9, illus., softcover** **$15.00**

## THE SWORD AND THE SERPENT
The Magical Philosophy, Vol. 2
**by Denning and Phillips**

Revising and expanding Books III and IV of the first edition, this is the comprehensive guide to the Magical Qabalah with extensive correspondences, as well as the techniques for activating the centers, use of images and the psychology of attainment.

Qabalah, magic and psychic skills are clearly explained in this book Topics include The Tree of Life, The Qlipoth, the Four Worlds, The Abyss, Qabalah, Names of Power and their Use, Invoking the Gods, Astral Projection, Designing and Performing Rituals, Using the Solor Scales and more. Also included are actual records of magical experiments.

**0-87542-197-0, 500 pgs., 6x9, illus., softcover** **$15.00**

## MODERN MAGICK
### by Donald Michael Kraig

Modern Magick is the most comprehensive step-by-step introduction to the art of ceremonial magic ever offered. It will guide you from the easiest of rituals and the construction of your magickal tools through the highest forms of magick: designing your own rituals and doing pathworking. Learn the secrets of the Kabalah in a clear and easy-to-understand manner, and discover the true secrets of invocation and evocation and channeling. It is not intended to supplant any other book; its purpose is to fully train and prepare anyone to use other books as he or she wills, with a full understanding of what the other writers are trying to present, along with what the other authors omit. *Modern Magick* is designed so anyone can use it, and is the perfect guidebook for students and classes. It will also help to round out the knowledge of long-time practitioners of the magickal arts.

**0-87542-324-8, 576 pgs., 6 x 9, illus., softcover**                  **$14.95**

## THE GOLDEN DAWN
### by Israel Regardie

The Original Account of the Teachings, Rites and Ceremonies of the Hermetic Order of the Golden Dawn as revealed by Israel Regardie, with further revision, expansion, and additional notes by Israel Regardie, Cris Monnastre, and others.

Originally published in four bulky volumes of some 1200 pages, this 5th Revised and Enlarged Edition has been entirely reset in modern, less space-consuming type, in half the pages (while retaining the original pagination in marginal notation for reference) for greater ease and use.

Corrections of typographical errors perpetuated in the original and subsequent editions have been made, with further revision and additional text and notes by actual practitioners of the Golden Dawn system of Magick, with an Introduction by the only student ever accepted for personal training by Regardie.

Also included are Initiation Ceremonies, important rituals for consecration and invocation, methods of meditation and magical working based on the Enochian Tablets, studies in the Tarot, and the system of Qabalistic Correspondences that unite the World's religions and magical traditions into a comprehensive and practical whole.

This volume is designed as a study and practice curriculum suited to both group and private practice. Meditation upon, and following with the Active Imagination, the Initiation Ceremonies is fully experiential without need of participation in group or lodge.

**0-87542-663-8, 744 pages, 6 x 9, illus.**                  **$19.95**

## THE MIDDLE PILLAR
### by Israel Regardie

Between the two outer pillars of the Qabalistic Tree of Life, the extremes of Mercy and Severity, stands THE MIDDLE PILLAR, signifying one who has achieved equilibrium in his or her own self.

Integration of the human personality is vital to the continuance of creative life. Without it, man lives as an outsider to his own true self. By combining Magic and Psychology in the Middle Pillar Ritual/Exercise (a magical meditation technique), we bring into balance the opposing elements of the psyche while yet holding within their essence and allowing full expression of man's entire being.

In this book, and with this practice, you will learn to: understand the psyche through its correspondences on the Tree of Life; expand self-awareness, thereby intensifying the inner growth process; activate creative and intuitive potentials; understand the individual thought patterns which control every facet of personal behavior; regain the sense of balance and peace of mind—the equilibrium that everyone needs for physical and psychic health.

**0-87542-658-1, 176 pages, softcover.** **$6.95**


## A GARDEN OF POMEGRANATES
### by Israel Regardie

What is the Tree of Life? It's the ground plan of the Qabalistic system—a set of symbols used since ancient times to study the Universe. The Tree of Life is a geometrical arrangement of ten sephiroth, or spheres, each of which is associated with a different archetypal idea, and 22 paths which connect the spheres.

This system of primal correspondences has been found the most efficient plan ever devised to classify and organize the characteristics of the self. Israel Regardie has written one of the best and most lucid introductions to the Qabalah.

*A Garden of Pomegranates* combines Regardie's own studies with his notes on the works of Aleister Crowley, A.E. Waite, Eliphas Levi and D.H. Lawrence. No longer is the wisdom of the Qabalah to be held *secret!* The needs of today place the burden of growth upon each and every person—each has to undertake the Path as his or her own responsibility, but every help is given in the most ancient and yet most modern teaching here known to humankind.

**0-87542-690-5, 176 pages, softcover.** **$6.95**

## A KABBALAH FOR THE MODERN WORLD
by Migene Gonzalez-Wippler

The Kabbalah is the basic form of Western mysticism, and this is an excellent manual of traditional Kabbalistic Magick! It contains one of the best introductions to the Kabbalah ever written.

If you have ever been intimidated by the Kabbalah in the past, and never studied its beauty, *this is the book for you*. It clearly and plainly explains the complexities of the Kabbalah. This is an ideal book for newcomers to the study of Kabbalah or mysticism and spirituality in general.

This book covers a variety of Kabbalistic topics including: Creation, the nature of God, the soul and soul mates, the astral and other planes, the four worlds, the history of the Kabbalah, Bible interpretation and more.

*A Kabbalah for the Modern World* is written so clearly that it makes complex kabbalistic ideas easy to understand. This book needs to be in the library of every occultist, Pagan, Kabbalist, mystic and person involved in the New Age.

In this book Wippler shows that the ancient Kabbalists predicted the New Physics. She goes on to discuss such topics as: Planck's Quantum Theory, God and Light, Archetypes, Synchronicity, The Collective Unconscious, the Lemaitre 'Big Bang' Theory, Einstein's Theory of Relativity and much more.

There have been many books over the past several years which have compared psychological theory and the New Age Physics with various Eastern philosophies such as Taoism and Zen. But there is only one which unites psychology, physics and *Western* mysticism: Migene Gonzalez-Wippler's *A Kabbalah for the Modern World*.

**0-87542-294-2, 240 pages, 5¼ x 8, illus., softcover.** **$9.95**

## THE COMPLETE BOOK OF SPELLS, CEREMONIES & MAGIC
by Migene Gonzalez-Wippler

This book is far more than a historical survey of magical techniques throughout the world. It is the most complete book of spells, ceremonies and magic ever assembled. It is the spiritual record of humanity.

Topics in this book include magical spells and rituals from virtually every continent and every people. The spells described are for love, wealth, success, protection, and health. Also examined are the theories and history of magic, including its evolution, the gods, the elements, the Kabbalah, the astral plane, ceremonial magic, famous books of magic and famous magicians. You will learn about talismanic magic, exorcisms and how to use the *I Ching*, how to interpret dreams, how to construct and interpret a horoscope, how to read Tarot cards, how to read palms, how to do numerology, and much more. Included are explicit instructions for love spells and talismans; spells for riches and money; weight-loss spells; magic for healing; psychic self-defense; spells for luck in gambling, and much more.

No magical library is complete without this classic text of magical history, theory and practical technique. The author, Migene Gonzalez-Wippler, is known for her excellent books on magic. Many consider this her best. Includes over 150 rare photos and illustrations.

**0-87542-286-1, 384 pages, 6 x 9, illus., softcover.** **$12.95**

## THE NEW MAGUS
**by Donald Tyson**

*The New Magus* is a practical framework on which a student can base his or her personal system of magic.

This book is filled with practical, usable magical techniques and rituals which anyone from any magical tradition can use. It includes instructions on how to design and perform rituals, create and use sigils, do invocations and evocations, do spiritual healings, learn rune magic, use god-forms, create telesmatic images, discover your personal guardian, create and use magical tools and much more. You will learn how *YOU* can be a *New Magus!*

The New Age is based on ancient concepts that have been put into terms, or *metaphors*, that are appropriate to life in our world today. That makes *The New Magus* the book on magic for today.

If you have found that magic seems illogical, overcomplicated and not appropriate to your lifestyle, *The New Magus* is the book for you. It will change your ideas of magic forever!

**0-87542-825-8, 6 x 9, illus., softcover.**                                    **$12.95**


## SIMPLIFIED MAGIC
**by Ted Andrews**

In every person, the qualities essential for accelerating his or her growth and spiritual evolution are innate, but even those who recognize such potentials need an effective means of releasing them. The ancient and mystical Qabala is that means.

A person does not need to become a dedicated Qabalist in order to acquire benefits from the Qabala. *Simplified Magic* offers a simple understanding of what the Qabala is and how it operates. It provides practical methods and techniques so that the energies and forces within the system and within ourselves can be experienced in a manner that enhances growth and releases our greater potential. *A reader knowing absolutely nothing about the Qabala could apply the methods in this book with noticeable success!*

The Qabala is more than just some theory for ceremonial magicians. It is a system for personal attainment and magic that anyone can learn and put to use in his or her life. The secret is that the main glyph of the Qabala, the Tree of Life, is *within* you. The Tree of Life is a map to the levels of consciousness, power and magic that are within. By learning the Qabala you will be able to tap into these levels and bring peace, healing, power, love, light and magic into your life.

**0-87542-015-X, 210 pgs., illus., softcover**                            **$3.95**

## THE INVISIBLE TEMPLE
by Peter Roche de Coppens

The Invisible Temple is not a building or location. It is not a particular congregation of people. It is wherever there is a focal point for spiritual energy. It is located where that energy is generated, amplified and transformed for whatever purpose is needed. In other words, The Invisible Temple exists for us when we become a spiritual light generator.

This book shows how you can generate, transform and amplify spiritual energy. Filled with illustrations and exercises, this book gives occult techniques for spiritual attainment. It can easily be used by Christians, Jews, Pagans and any others on a spiritual path. The structure of the book is also Qabalistic, and the symbols and rituals were actually drawn from a Qabalistic Tradition.

**0-87542-676-X, 300 pgs., illus, 5¼x8, softcover** **$9.95**


## TEMPLE MAGIC
William Gray

This important book on occultism deals specifically with problems and details you are likely to encounter in temple practice. Learn how a temple should look, how a temple should function, what a ceremonialist should wear, what physical postures best promote the ideal spiritual-mental attitude, and how magic is worked in a temple.

*Temple Magic* has been written specifically for the instruction and guidance of esoteric ceremonialists by someone who has spent a lifetime in spiritual service to his natural Inner Way. There are few comparable works in existence, and this book in particular deals with up-to-date techniques of constructing and using a workable temple dedicated to the furtherance of the Western Inner Tradition. In simple yet adequate language, it helps any individual understand and promote the spiritual structure of our esoteric inheritance. It is a book by a specialist for those who are intending to be specialists.

**0-87542-274-8, 240 pages, 5¼ x 8, illus., softcover** **$7.95**